RESEARCH PARADIGMS, TELEVISION, AND SOCIAL BEHAVIOR

Joy Keiko Asamen dedicates this book
to the memory of her father, *Keigi Asamen.*

———————∽◦⊖◦∾———————

Gordon LaVern Berry dedicates this book to his grandchildren:
Lyndsie Marie, Tenley Monet, Steven Wayne,
Christopher Johnathan, and Cierra Nicole.

RESEARCH
PARADIGMS,
TELEVISION,
AND SOCIAL
BEHAVIOR

JOY KEIKO ASAMEN
GORDON L. BERRY
EDITORS

SAGE Publications
International Educational and Professional Publisher
Thousand Oaks   London   New Delhi

For information:

SAGE Publications, Inc.
2455 Teller Road
Thousand Oaks, California 91320
E-mail: order@sagepub.com

SAGE Publications Ltd.
6 Bonhill Street
London EC2A 4PU
United Kingdom

SAGE Publications India Pvt. Ltd.
M-32 Market
Greater Kailash I
New Delhi 110 048 India

Printed in the United States of America

Library of Congress Cataloging-in-Publication Data

Research paradigms: television, and social behavior / edited by
  Joy Keiko Asamen and Gordon L. Berry.
   p. cm.
   Includes bibliographical references and index.
   ISBN 0-7619-0654-1 (cloth: alk. paper). — ISBN 0-7619-0655-X
   (pbk.: alk. paper)
   1. Television broadcasting—Social aspects. 2. Television
broadcasting—Psychological aspects. 3. Television and family—
Research. 4. Television and teenagers—Research. 5. Television
and children—Research. I. Asamen, Joy Keiko, 1953- .
  II. Berry, Gordon L.

PN1992.6.R465 1997
302.23′45—dc21   97-21129

98 99 00 01 02 03 10 9 8 7 6 5 4 3 2 1

Acquiring Editor:	Margaret H. Seawell
Editorial Assistant:	Renée Piernot
Production Editor:	Diana E. Axelsen
Production Assistant:	Denise Santoyo
Typesetter/Designer:	Janelle LeMaster
Indexer:	Janet Perlman
Cover Designer:	Ravi Balasuriya
Print Buyer:	Anna Chin

Contents

Epilogue

Preface

Researchers from many disciplines continue to study the medium of television and its impact on behavior because of its ubiquity in this country and many parts of the world. Television also is the object of much research because it is such an attractive medium that combines its ever-present formal features with powerful images and messages that help to set the agenda for the worldview held by many of its viewers. Social scientists, medical specialists, educators, child advocate groups, and politicians have especially been concerned about the social impact that the messages of television can have on developing children.

The early planning for this book grew out of a recognition that research efforts designed to study the effects of television needed to be bold enough to use a number of models or paradigms in a variety of settings and in a number of creative ways. This openness in the use of various models, coupled with firm scientific principles, was necessary for any investigator to ascertain the sociopsychological impact that the content, structure, and forms of television are having on viewers. Therefore, we wanted to explore methodologies that were broad enough to inform the thinking of developing researchers who are entering this field of study by showing how social science and related paradigms could be applied to understanding this medium. At the same time, we were committed to the view that experienced investigators might look again at the importance of reassessing their previous research models. Such a reassessment might ensure that their findings are grounded in firm theoretical and scientific principles that are consistent with the complexity of television usage in a dynamic and ever-changing multimedia environment.

This book, like so much of our previous work, is preoccupied with the role of television in the life of the child. Readers will note, therefore, that our efforts to provide a link between the theoretical and practical aspects of both quantitative and qualitative methodologies refer to research where children are the major participants or target group. We have, however, coupled the focus on children in selected chapters with some broader foci on older age groups and with methodologies that are employed to study television from diverse social science and communication studies perspectives.

Both editors would like to express our thanks to Margaret Seawell, our editor at Sage Publications, who supported us and provided us with guidance during the process of bringing this volume to fruition. We also thank Kim Cary, systems and instructional technologist, Graduate School of Education and Psychology, Pepperdine University, for providing us with technical consultation during the preparation of the book.

As the senior editor, Joy Keiko Asamen acknowledges the continued support of her mother, Kiyo Asamen, and Ron Kishiyama.

As the coeditor, Gordon LaVern Berry especially thanks Juanita Berry for her support during the development and completion of this project.

Introduction

Research Paradigms, Television, and Social Behavior: The Complexities of Studying a Complex Medium

Gordon L. Berry

Few persons, if any, could have predicted the social impact that this little-known device referred to as television would have on the United States and the world during its early development and first broadcast. An initial broadcast was reported as taking place in 1927, when Herbert Hoover (then secretary of the treasury) gave a speech in Washington, D.C., and it was picked up "live" in New York (Condry, 1989). We now live in a world where there are few places not touched by the sites and sounds of this medium, which can transform the social structure of a family and many of the sociocultural attributes of a nation. Indeed, it has been argued that in every society in which television has been introduced, there has been a subsequent decrease in the time devoted to socializing with friends, sleep, housework, and the use of other media such as going to the movies, listening to radio, and reading books, magazines, and newspapers (Condry, 1989; Murray & Kippax, 1978). Yet, the presence of television when its content is directed toward addressing some of the health, social welfare, and educational needs of children and adults really has no equal among its electronic and print cousins in terms of providing information in these areas and in molding public opinion toward them. It also is true that television has been effective in teaching values, social roles, and behaviors to children. Thus, television has taken its place, along with the family, school, and our religious institutions, as one of the agents of socialization in modern society.

The ever-present messages and images of television, especially among the young, consciously and unconsciously compete and challenge the teachings advanced in the home and the other traditional institutions concerned with their growth and development. It is this ubiquitous nature of television in American society, coupled with the attractiveness of its multidimensional audiovisual content features, that provides the medium with its power to influence various types of behaviors. No one can be surprised, therefore, that several thousand scholarly articles and research efforts in the past 40 years have been concerned with the role television plays in the lives of children in terms of its impact on their cognition, imagination, attention, values, aggression, comprehension, emotions, understanding of reality, and general social behavior.

John Murray observed that most of the early research on the topic of television and children focused on the effects rather than the uses of this medium (Murray, 1980). To Murray, this meant that the research question asked most often was, "What does television do to the viewer?" The question that also needed an answer was, "What does the viewer do to (or with) television?" Clearly, both the effects of television and its uses always have had to mentally intersect with the developmental stage and the sociocultural experiences of the receiver. The methodological processes we have used to ascertain what impact the content of television has on the behavior and social learning of children must now be seen as more complex than social researchers might have considered in the past. This complexity to understand television's impact as an electronic device grows more complicated every day as it begins to function as a computer. The multifaceted new role for the television set will not only open up to children the content of many entertainment channels and viewing options but also provide them the luxury of using it as an interactive tool from which they can design and control the very nature of the subject matter in their audiovisual environment.

■ The Emerging Transformation of Television and Information Processing

The transformation of the television set from a box that one watches to a device for receiving and transmitting interactive information now adds new types of cognitive and affective learning experiences that were not factored into some of the early research paradigms involving this medium. We now must consider that no longer is the television set just a box from which people speak to a viewer and to whom pictures are transmitted simultaneously. Television now has the potential to have viewers talk to it and to receive answers in one form or another. The new technology will provide an additional level of cognitive learning experiences that also can have a profound impact on the affective behaviors and beliefs of the viewers.

Cognitive learning theorists would argue that a complete understanding of many of the changes that are taking place with children as a result of being exposed to the emerging content of television would require some knowledge of how they process information. Information processing is a cognitive theory concept that examines the way in which knowledge enters and is stored and retrieved from memory. In addition, this concept stresses the important mental processes, such as reasoning, and focuses on what is happening in the learners. These also are the cognitive processes that allow learners to actively interpret and organize the information they receive from many audiovisual sources.

The cognitive processes (e.g., attention, perception, rehearsal, encoding, retrieval) that move and store information also must be involved in understanding the behavioral impact of the array of new content that will emerge from the television viewing of tomorrow. The implications from the technological capabilities of the television content of tomorrow must return researchers again to the basic questions of today, such as how children will respond (negatively or positively) to the acquisition of the ideas, values, and behaviors to which they are exposed in the future as well as the learning associated with the meta-cognitive processes that will drive much of the new learning. Meta-cognition is important to our discussion because it operates at the beginning of the learning process, gives the learner's attention a purpose by focusing it on the important features, plays a role in perception, and helps to regulate the flow of information through working memory (Eggen & Kauchak, 1997).

The magic of television as a vehicle for providing information and entertainment, as well as the degree to which young children engage in active cognitive transactions between this medium and their viewing environment, has important implications for how it functions as a teacher and how young children learn from it. Anderson and Collins (1988), in a major study on television's influence on cognitive development, pointed out that some understanding of the cause and effect of television might be achieved through field observations and laboratory experimental research directed at the behavioral and cognitive details of television viewing with an emphasis on the mechanisms of retention, transfer, and carryover from television viewing to other contexts, especially school. They further suggested that such a conceptual framework of proximal cause and effect should have four major areas, that is, that (a) television viewing should be carefully described in behavioral, cognitive, and developmental terms; (b) accounts of short- and long-term effects should be developed with explicit reference made to the processes identified in the description of children's television viewing; (c) conditions that modify the effects are altered by the viewers' experiences with other people and by activities both within and outside of the television viewing setting; and (d) understanding the effects on schooling will require an additional explicit account specifying the nature of interference with, or enhancement of, instructional methods and/or educational goals (p. 10).

■ National Research Efforts, Federal Legislation, and Content Rating Systems

There are a series of national events taking place that are worth mentioning as we begin to consider the direction of research models related to the study of television and its impact on behavior. These events relate to recent research findings in the area of violence, the continued exploration of cognitive and affective issues about the growth and development of children, the new initiatives supported by advocacy groups, the creation of systems to rate content, and legislation from the federal government. One of the present research efforts is the National Television Violence Study, a 3-year study of violence as portrayed on television in the United States. This project was funded by the National Cable Television Association. The 1st year of the study was under the administrative auspices of Mediascope, with various parts of the research conducted by researchers at the University of California, Santa Barbara; the University of Wisconsin–Madison, the University of Texas at Austin, and the University of North Carolina at Chapel Hill. Another multiyear study on violence among the broadcast networks of ABC, CBS, FOX, and NBC was conducted by the Center for Communication Policy at the University of California, Los Angeles. This project was funded by the major networks.

The Children's Television Act of 1990, which was implemented as of January 1, 1992, was a major piece of legislation instituted by the Federal Communications Commission (FCC), and it is just now having its real impact on the structure and content of programs for children. The act has four primary elements, but a major feature is that it established a ruling that each station must provide educational and informational programming for children to qualify for license renewal. In 1996, President Clinton signed into law the Telecommunications Act. Among other features, the law mandated that within 2 years of the signing of the bill, each new television set sold in the United States must contain a V-chip. The V-chip is basically a programmable chip that allows consumers to block shows, depending on their content rating.

Rating systems, which will provide a framework for assessing the viewing patterns of television content, also will begin to be developed in the future and are projected to provide a base from which research can be generated. A major effort in the area of rating television content was instituted by a committee under the leadership of Jack Valenti of the Motion Picture Association of America. This committee proposed an age-based rating system similar to that used by the movie industry. Since January 1, 1997, the networks have been labeling their shows with age-based type ratings (e.g., TV-PG, TV-14) created by the committee headed by Valenti. However, some members of Congress, social action groups, and child development specialists have been critical of the present system. Many of the critics of that rating system call for instituting one that uses labels that would rate television shows according to the sex, violence, and foul language content. This content-driven system would, according to its advocates, provide parents with greater information about programs and help them to gauge the age appropriateness and values being communicated to their children.

Ready or not, our society is one that is increasingly informed by the values, ideas, and information from our vast communication system. Indeed, Hiebert, Ungurait, and Bohn (1974) viewed communication, in one form or another, as the art of transmitting information. The use of the word *art* is worth noting when social scientists attempt to understand the complexities of the beauty and the beast of this medium, especially as it relates to its impact on children. That is, the social scientists bent on taking the research where the logic of the data leads must do so as scientists and as poets who understand that so much of the content viewed by children grows out of the imaginations of creative people. Thus, the paradigms used to understand the psychosocial effects that the medium has on human behavior must be designed within a framework that is able to tease out the types and purposes of the content and what they mean in terms of their ability to teach and to cause viewers to learn.

The social scientists who contributed to this book offer a number of innovative paradigms for studying the impact of television on behavior. At the same time, many of the traditional research paradigms are dissected by the contributors in such a way that the readers can identify both the strengths and weaknesses of the various methodological approaches used to better understand the complexities of studying a complex medium.

■ References

Anderson, R. A., & Collins, P. A. (1988). *The impact of children's education: Television's influence on cognitive development* (Office of Educational Research and Improvement, Working Paper No. 2, 1-94). Washington, DC: U.S. Department of Education.

Condry, J. (1989). *The psychology of television*. Hillsdale, NJ: Lawrence Erlbaum.

Eggen, P., & Kauchak, D. P. (1997). *Educational psychology: Windows to the classroom*. Columbus, OH: Merrill-Prentice Hall.

Hiebert, R. E., Ungurait, D. F., & Bohn, T. W. (1974). *Television and the child: An empirical study of the effects of television on the young*. London: Oxford University Press.

Murray, J. P. (1980). *Television and youth: Twenty-five years of research and controversy*. Boys Town, NE: Boys Town Center for the Study of Youth Development.

Murray, J. P., & Kippax, S. (1978). Children's social behavior in three towns with different television experiences. *Journal of Communications, 28,* 19-29.

Television Research:
Past Problems and Present Issues

George Comstock

The problems and issues that confront the application of the social and behavioral sciences to television present some interesting puzzles. They are in kind essentially the same as those that arise with any subject matter, but for those involved in the study of television they take on a rather depleting aspect.

What sets television apart is its social character, which affects and to a great degree undermines the effective use of popular research paradigms; the organization of the pertinent disciplines and fields (the sociological relief map of the community of inquiry) that renders problematic the choice of paradigms; and the economic, ideological, and political interests of the medium that often have placed the "industry" in an adversarial position in regard to research outcomes. Somewhat intractable subject matter, feuding and suspicious investigators, and a hostile business do not constitute a lazy breeze and a warm sun. It is a bit like combining a single-subject experiment with the antipathies of psychoanalysts and behaviorists and the welcome offered by the tobacco giants to evidence of the harmful effects of

■ 11

passive exposure to cigarette smoking. The same questions occur in other contexts, but not typically with the same severity or degree of threat to the conduct of science that will be recognized as successful and credible.

■ Social Character

Four attributes of television in modern Western societies make it problematic as a focus of the social and behavioral sciences. They are its ubiquity, popularity, cradle-to-grave presence, and innovative persons.

Ubiquity

More than 98% of American households have one or more television sets. About two thirds have multiple sets. These are mostly color sets; black-and-white sets, although still sold in miniature and portable versions, are a rarity. These households are served by about 1,200 commercial television stations (47% VHF and 53% UHF), about 360 public and educational stations (34% VHF and 66% UHF), and about 11,660 cable systems ("By the Numbers," 1996). The broadcasters reach about 96 million households; the cable systems reach about two thirds that number.

A quick historical comparison reveals the dramatic increase in the prevalence of television in American households (Comstock, 1991). Five decades ago, at the beginning of the introduction of television in the United States in 1946, two networks offered a total of 11 hours of programming *weekly* over a handful of outlets to about 10,000 households. Four years later, four networks—the familiar American Broadcasting Company (ABC), Columbia Broadcasting System (CBS), and National Broadcasting Company (NBC), as well as the short-lived DuMont Television Network (DTN)—were broadcasting 90 hours over about 100 stations to about 10.5 million households. Today, broadcast outlets typically exceed 18 hours of programming daily, cable networks offer 24-hour services, the three major networks have been joined by a fourth (FOX) and several neophytes, and independent stations are plentiful. The calculation of hours of weekly or daily programming has become whimsical.

Popularity

The public's acceptance of television is exemplified by a number of measures. They include rate of adoption, degree of diffusion, amount of viewing, public opinion, and response to deprivation.

In U.S. communities where adoption occurred in the late 1940s, it took about 4 years before 70% of households had acquired television sets. In communities where adoption was delayed for several years by an FCC freeze on the licensing of stations (ostensibly to sort out problems of spectrum allocation, but the argument of Winston, 1986, that the actual purpose was to give the existing radio industry time to move in on the new medium is both plausible and highly persuasive), familiarity with what the new medium would offer and greater assurance of broadcast service led to the same level being reached in only about 2 years (Cook & Campbell, 1979). When MacBeth (1996) and colleagues studied the introduction of television in an isolated British Columbia community in the mid-1970s, they found that many persons had purchased sets in anticipation of the first broadcasts. People expected to like television, and after having seen what it was, they were even more eager for it.

By 1960, only a decade and a half since the first broadcasts, almost 9 out of 10 households had one or more television sets. A decade later, the figure would surpass 95%.

Those in the late 1940s and early 1950s who advanced the "novelty hypothesis" that viewing would decline once television ceased to be a curiosity were proved wrong. Viewing by most categories of individuals and by households had increased steadily and continued to do so into the 1990s (Xiaoming, 1994). For example, time in television households devoted to viewing increased from about 4½ hours in 1950 to more than 7 hours in the 1980s (Andreasen, 1985).

Public opinion presents a complex but clear pattern. The average American has a favorable opinion of television (Bower, 1985; Comstock, Chaffee, Katzman, McCombs, & Roberts, 1978; Roper Organization, Inc., 1987). It ranks high among the half dozen or so appliances few would want to do without. Although there still are occasions when viewing takes on a festive garb, such as a Super Bowl, royal weddings, and the Olympics (Katz, 1988; Rothenbuhler, 1988), what has changed since its early days is that viewing progressively is less often thought of as something special or the centerpiece of a social event, and it is rated as less "exciting," "interesting," and "important." Viewing is a pleasurable experience that typically commands moderate, partial attention; it often is shared with some other activity such as eating, conversing, or reading; as much as half of the audience will be unable to recall the plot of a program the viewers are certain they have seen; and usually the pleasure expressed over the previous night's television experience is modest.

Preferred genres are very weak predictors of what people will view, favorite programs often are missed, and few (if any) see all the episodes of even the most popular series and miniseries (Barwise & Ehrenberg, 1988; Frank & Greenberg, 1980). Television takes a secondary place to competing activities such as escorting a car to the garage or a child to the dentist. The major predictor of viewing television is time available in the vicinity of an operable set (Comstock & Paik, 1991). However, people are very loyal to preferred programs when they do view, almost always making the same selection when viewing at a particular hour (Barwise, Ehrenberg, & Goodhardt, 1982).

Deprivation is quite unpleasant. Winick (1988) described families who lost their television sets to the repair shop:

> The first 3 or 4 days for most persons were the worst, even in many homes where viewing was minimal. . . . In over half of all households, during these first few days of loss, the regular routines were disrupted, family members had difficulties in dealing with the newly available time, anxiety and aggressions were expressed, and established expectations for the behavior of other household members were not met. (pp. 221-222)

Once having experienced television, people on the whole do not wish to do without it. Those who voluntarily or involuntarily are deprived generally welcome its return (Barwise & Ehrenberg, 1988; Kubey & Csikszentmihalyi, 1990).

The most plausible interpretation is that television's strength lies in its appeal as a medium. The decision to view often is a function of time available. The viewing options ordinarily do not attract people to the set. Rather, the choice among options represents the maximization of satisfaction by those who have decided to view.

Cradle-to-Grave Presence

Giving attentive interest to the screen begins as early as 6 months of age (Hollenbeck & Slaby, 1979). Regular viewing begins between 2½ and 3 years with average daily viewing of about 1½ hours (Huston et al., 1983). It increases to about 2¼ hours by 5 years, declines during high school and college (if attended), and then returns to the elementary levels, where it remains except for minor increases in the 40s and 50s until the early 60s (D. R. Anderson & Collins, 1988; D. R. Anderson, Field, Collins, Lorch, & Nathan, 1985; Comstock & Paik, 1991; Condry, 1989; MacBeth, 1996).

Condry (1989) charted the three most frequently engaged-in activities of sleep, school and/or work, and watching television at 5-year intervals from birth to 70+ years of age. Except for the very first few months, television viewing is omnipresent. Only among very young children does any other leisure activity, free play, outrank it (Timmer, Eccles, & O'Brien, 1985). Because it is a function of time available, it is greater for the elementary school years than for the high school and college years. Similarly, it is suppressed by transition points when other activities require attention: initial school entry and preparation for retirement. Because of the greater time available, it increases again for those in their 60s and is the sole mass medium for which use increases among the elderly (Comstock et al., 1978).

Television viewing is a part of American life from early childhood to old age. Throughout almost all of the life span, it ranks first among leisure activities and third in total time consumption behind sleep and school/work.

Innovative Persons

Day to day and season to season, television appears to be continually renewing itself by innovation and change: larger screens, color, remote controls, enhanced definition, additional stations, new networks, cable, in-home recording and playback (the videocassette recorder [VCR]). Each fall sees the introduction of new shows and the abandonment and replacement of those that fail to muster adequate ratings. There is the annual foray into quasi-taboo areas of character, language, subject matter, and visual display that arouses seasonal controversy.

The stability of television's years of maturity, from the early 1960s through the end of the 1970s, has given way to continual change in response to competition and technological developments. The pattern that endured for those two decades had three features: dominance by the three major networks, a minor role for independent stations with 90% affiliated with one or another of those networks, and an indifferent cable system as a disseminator of largely broadcast signals to a small proportion of households (Comstock, 1991).

Cable is now the principal disseminator, reaching two thirds of households with numerous original channels as well as broadcast signals. There are more than twice as many commercial stations as there were in 1960, enough for a fourth network (FOX). Three-network dominance is much reduced, with prime-time audience shares falling from above 90% to well below 60%. VCRs are in more households than is cable; the household that receives only those three networks and perhaps one or two independent stations, once the norm, has become the exception.

Television, nevertheless, also has displayed extraordinary continuity. Throughout its history, entertainment has ranked at the forefront. This is so whether the measure is the allocation of the overall schedule among program categories or documentaries, magazine, news, sports, and talk shows (Comstock, 1989). Cable is the principal disseminator, but broadcasting remains the principal source. This is a consequence of the popularity on cable of local and distant broadcast signals and the widespread reliance on syndicated shows originally presented on the broadcast networks as well as the viewing of the one third of households that do not subscribe to cable. The most popular genres among each year's top 10 or 20 shows remain much the same, with the major changes occurring long ago during television's earlier years—the abandonment of original, live drama in favor of taped series (mid-1950s); the disappearance of big-money, prime-time quiz shows such as *The $64,000 Question* in the scandal over fixing the outcomes to favor popular contestants (late 1950s); and the ending of the era of big-name variety shows (late 1950s). Early content analyses found that television entertainment was very violent (Head, 1954;

Smythe, 1954). And it has remained so. Gerbner and colleagues have tracked television violence for 20 years using the same paradigm (Gerbner, Morgan, & Signorielli, 1994). In the short run, marked differences among the networks and shifts from season to season occur. In the long run, it is a staple, merely oscillating except for a very slight but discernible decline over the past decade (as measured by the Gerbner violence index).

■ Effective Paradigm Use

These circumstances present several challenges for the social and behavioral sciences. The challenges can be framed in terms of three broad areas of inquiry and four particulars of the practice of science.

The three areas of inquiry are as follows:

1. *audience research:* the description and prediction of people entering and leaving the audiences for the mass media;

2. *informational research:* the examination of the role of the mass media in decision making about consumption, such as nutritional choices and product purchases, and civic behavior, including political support and voting; and

3. *behavioral research:* the investigation of the influence of exposure to media portrayals on subsequent modes of behaving, as exemplified by antisocial and prosocial behavior.

The four particulars are (a) application of the experimental paradigm, (b) measurement of television viewing, (c) identification of the independent variable, and (d) generalizability in regard to outcomes.

Experimentation

The ubiquity, popularity, and cradle-to-grave character of television make the application of the experimental paradigm problematic. There are few, if any, potential control groups in natural settings; the few instances in which investigators have been able to use the design recently stand as rarities (Murray & Kippax, 1977, in Australia and

Williams and colleagues [Williams, 1986] in British Columbia). The design was very useful when television was introduced, as exemplified by Schramm, Lyle, and Parker (1961) on the effects on children and by Parker (1963) on the effects on library use. Now, however, the medium has changed, the context of competing media and alternative leisure options is different, yet the most powerful tool for inferring television's role cannot be employed.

The problems are not limited to audience research, where the concern is with how people might behave in the absence of television. For example, Williams and colleagues (Williams, 1986), based on the findings of Schramm et al. (1961), hypothesized that the introduction of television would increase the vocabularies of schoolchildren. They found no such effect. One explanation is that they measured general vocabulary, whereas the contribution of television may be primarily in the jargon and terminology of news and entertainment (Comstock & Paik, 1991). An alternative explanation is that the influence of television is so widespread that it no longer is necessary to be exposed to the medium to be the recipient of its effects. Much the same can be argued in regard to informational research. The information disseminated by the medium may diffuse so widely that exposure ceases to be a prerequisite for influence. Television may go undetected as a source, particularly in the political realm where interpersonal exchange plays a larger role than in product purchases. This turns the concept of "two-step flow" (Katz & Lazarsfeld, 1955) topsy-turvy in recognition of the present media plenitude, with unmotivated agents of diffusion replacing gatekeeping opinion leaders.

Behavioral research is far from immune. Television violence and antisocial behavior is an example. Paik and Comstock (1994), in their meta-analysis, uncovered 217 empirical studies through 1990 with about two thirds of the 1,142 outcomes (a study can produce more than one) attributable to experimental designs. Any frailties, thus, undermine the bulk of the literature. The comparatively few field experiments were inference weak because (a) they typically employed intact groups that may have varied initially on important dimensions and (b) when television viewing regimens were imposed, reactions such as hostility or frustration may have been elicited and contaminated results; they do not readily deliver their promise of permitting credible causal inferences about real-life events (Comstock & Paik, 1991; Cook & Campbell, 1979; Cook, Kendzierski, & Thomas, 1983). Laboratory-type experiments, which accounted for four fifths of the designs, escape these problems but encounter a third problem that also affects field experiments. There is no true "no-TV" baseline. Both control and treatment subjects will have had extensive viewing histories. This makes the regularly and consistently demonstrated increases in antisocial behavior more impressive because they occur despite this contamination. However, it also raises the question of whether prior priming by violent portrayals (Berkowitz, 1990; Berkowitz & Rogers, 1986) is a necessary condition. The imitation of portrayals as early as 14 months of age (Meltzoff, 1988) indicates that it is unnecessary for like-aggression among young children but does not address the issue for those older and unlike-aggression.

Measuring Viewing

The measurement of viewing is fundamental to television research. It is not only the industry's basis for pricing commercials and discarding or retaining programs, it is the independent variable for a variety of important outcomes—opinion formation (as exemplified by agenda setting [McCombs, 1989] and cultivation [Gerbner, Gross, Morgan, & Signorielli, 1986]), scholastic achievement (MacBeth, 1996), the influence of commercials (Comstock & Paik, 1991), and cumulative effects of violence (Milavsky, Kessler, Stripp, & Rubens, 1982).

The way in which television is used precludes accurate measurement except as the function of arbitrary—but highly useful—operationalization. The stunning proof of this is that 50 years after the introduction of the medium, the Advertising Research Foundation's $10,000 Richard L. Lysaker Prize for outstanding research in 1994 was awarded for advancing a definition of viewing that would lead to more consistent, meaningful measurement (Clancey, 1994). The problem is the embeddedness of viewing in everyday life. Television sets are operating continually, and the attention of those in the vicinity varies from passing to partial to full. It becomes difficult to discern the boundaries between watching television and other activities.

There are three basic measurement paradigms:

1. questionnaires and interviews;
2. electronic set use recording coupled with the tabulation of those viewing; and
3. videotaping or otherwise recording the behavior of viewers.

When asked about their viewing, people readily give answers. The problem is that the answers vary considerably by the question asked. The more precise the focus of the question, the lower the amount of viewing. "Average day" produces higher figures than does "viewing yesterday," presumably because respondents do not factor in nonviewing days (Robinson, 1977). Probing by day part or program leads to still lower figures.

The A. C. Nielsen Company has been the foremost user of television set use recording with viewer tabulation. However, there have been two distinct Nielsen paradigms. In the first, television set use is recorded electronically while viewer composition is determined by diaries. In the second, viewer composition is registered electronically by people meters, remote control-like devices by which household members press personal buttons to indicate what they are viewing. The problem is that the two result in quite different figures for certain population segments (Comstock & Paik, 1991; Milavsky, 1992). In particular, people meters register lower viewing for children and for adult females—the former presumably because of fatigue, indifference, and/or ignorance, the latter because of involvement in distracting household tasks.

Those who have recorded viewers by time-lapse movie cameras (Allen, 1965) or videotape (D. R. Anderson et al., 1985; Bechtel, Achelpohl, & Akers, 1972) have reported congruent findings. About 40% of the time, there is no attention to the screen; attention is least for episodic elements (e.g., news, sports, commercials) and ritualistic storytelling (e.g., soap operas) and is greatest when a narrative has some novel elements (e.g., movies). Verbal reports (in this instance, by parents about children) correlate highly with videotape records in regard to time spent with television, but the amount of attention to the screen varies widely and correlates weakly, if at all. Among children, attention to the screen increases up to 10 years of age and then declines (D. R. Anderson, Lorch, Field, & Sanders, 1981); it rises as comprehension grows and then falls as attention becomes less necessary to understand what is taking place.

What is absent from these varied procedures is construct validity (Cook & Campbell, 1979). The referent—the experiencing of television—has been ignored in favor of measurement techniques. Clancey (1994) argued that the sole necessary requirement is presence in a room with a television set operating. The present author and colleagues (Comstock et al., 1978) essentially reached the same conclusion when defining viewing as "a discontinuous, often interrupted, and frequently nonexclusive activity for which a measure in hours and minutes serves only as the outer boundary of possible attention" (pp. 146-147).

The conventional wisdom of audience research has placed the burden of validity on (a) the representativeness of sampling and (b) reliability. This is inadequate. The two Nielsen paradigms would not rank individuals similarly. As a result, each would lead to different correlations with other variables, leading to the unavoidable conclusion that one or the other is decidedly less valid. Both have the merit of self-description so that whatever else is taking place, respondents consider themselves as "viewing" television, but the comparative lack of interaction with demographic attributes, such as age and sex, makes diaries clearly superior.

The greatest risk, however, is inaccurate social perception, an unrealistic discourse, and perhaps misplaced concern. The process of viewing is certainly better described most of the time by the concept of monitoring (Comstock & Paik, 1991) or paying only enough attention to follow the exposition or narrative. The overestimation of the attentional demands of television means that we continually misconstrue the world about us; for example, the Nielsen figures on children's viewing hide many other activities.

Independent Variable

Progressively, the precise identifying of the independent variable when television is involved has become more important. When misconstrued, findings will be misapplied or underused. Unfortunately, this occurs routinely as a consequence of the way in which the medium is embedded in everyday life and the paradox of innovation coupled with continuity.

Cultivation

Gerbner (1990), who developed the cultivation perspective, sees the technology of television as (a) unique among mass media in its reach and degree of use, with (b) a consistent and homogeneous set of messages dictated by its need to satisfy continually heterogeneous mass audiences (c) affecting (if only slightly) perceptions and outlook as (d) a function of quantity of exposure (see also Morgan & Signorielli, 1990). Hawkins and Pingree (1980, 1981, 1982), self-described as working within the same framework, see the effect on perceptions and outlook as a function of greater or lesser exposure to homogeneous content; thus, effects relating to violence are greater for those who view more violence. The first construes the independent variable as the content inexorably and inevitably disseminated by the technology, with the "cultivation effect" the difference in perceptions and outlook attributable to the technology. The second construes the effect as the outcome of greater exposure to a category of messages. If the first occurs (as a consequence of Items b and d earlier in this paragraph), then the second must do so as well (because Item b will be increased); the reverse is not the case (because Item b may be insufficient). The two are quite different formulations with differing independent variables mistakenly treated as the same. The findings lose focus, and interpretation becomes confused.

The Great American Values Test

Ball-Rokeach, Rokeach, and Grube (1984) tested the efficacy of a public affairs program designed in accord with Rokeach's (1960) theory to change values in a multicommunity field experiment in eastern Washington. Both program and research monograph have that same title. The data indicate considerable success. However, it is not helpful to think of the independent variable as a public affairs program. The appropriate terminology is "television that created discrepancies between desired and held values." This points away from the format, which is incidental, and toward the psychological dynamics employed, which is the crux.

Television: The Medium

Surveys document that viewers over past decades often have attended to programs they did not choose, frequently paid less than full attention to what they were viewing, were pleased but hardly enthusiastic over what they had seen on a typical evening, and, as often as not, could not remember the principal plot elements of programs they were sure they had seen (Barwise & Ehrenberg, 1988; Comstock et al., 1978). These data lead to the conclusion that viewing is an activity of low involvement (Comstock & Paik, 1991). More recent surveys indicate that VCR use is considered much more arousing and emotionally involving than "television" and not only is perceived as offering a wider choice of programming but also is placed in psychological space alongside theater movies and recorded music (Cohen, Levy, & Golden, 1988; Kubey & Larson, 1990), all media subject to extensive consumer discretion rather than television. In the first instance, the independent variable usually is labeled "television" (Comstock & Paik, 1991). The more recent data suggest that better labeling would be "scheduled broadcast television for the mass market" or "mass market television entertainment." The implication is that as the medium has come to offer increasingly diverse options with the multiplying of channels and new modes of dissemination, greater care must be taken in labeling the experience reflected by the measurement of exposure. This is not to dispute those who argue that in many ways what greater technological capacity will bring to the viewer will be more of the same. Gerbner and colleagues (1994) are an example:

> Given the convergence of communication technologies, the concentration of ownership, and the shrinking of independent creative alternatives, the notion that a new abundance of hundreds of channels will provide greater choice is a technocratic fantasy. The most profitable programs now being mass-produced for the vast majority of viewers will run on more channels more of the time, [whereas] infomercial hustle, direct marketing, and electronically-delivered magazines catering to small audiences will fill the rest. Cross-media synergy and the global consolidation of electronic marketing is more likely to reduce than increase the diversity of the total orchestration of cultural resources. (p. 20)

It is to argue whether increased options require newly vigilant care in identifying the independent variable when it is the viewing of television.

Generalizability

Potter, Cooper, and Dupagne (1993) recently reported that fewer than 5% of published communication research permits generalization to a known population and concluded that the field is "pre-scientific." If the standards are those of the social and behavioral sciences, then their concern is misplaced. Representative samples are the exception, not the rule; the refereed psychology journals spill over with examples. Protection against the inability to generalize instead comes from at least four sources.

1. *Samples that vary importantly in regard to the research question.* Examples include sex, ethnicity, socioeconomic status, and age. The crucial factor is that the samples not be biased for the question addressed. If not, outcomes will apply to a substantial, if not precisely specifiable, population. One high school does not represent the population of high school attendees, but it surely represents a population much larger than the enrollment of that school.

2. *Replication.* Replication guards against interpreting artifacts and permits exploration of the applicability of a finding to a distinctly different population. Replication is important for both experimental and survey outcomes, but it has a particularly important role for the former. Experiments are most sensitive (and, in the statistical sense, most powerful) when treatment and control groups are as much alike, or homogeneous, as possible; the attempt to be representative is counter to the logic of the design. Replication then becomes the means by which breadth of applicability across populations is examined.

3. *Elimination of alternative explanations.* Representativeness is only one means of meeting the challenge that an outcome is ascribable to peculiarities of those studied. The more important issue is whether alternative explanations can be dismissed with some confidence.

4. *Theory.* The testing of propositions derived from theory means that knowledge becomes cumulative. The fact that new findings fall into an established pattern gives them increased credibility. Kurt Lewin's dictum that there is nothing so useful as a good theory goes beyond managing the future to the process by which the means to do so is constructed.

These homilies obviously apply equally to television research. Two quite narrowly defined problems of generalizability remain to be addressed. The first is a special case of the independent variable problem. The second is a pervasive threat to the use of the experimental paradigm. As these comments imply, the fundamental issue, however characterized, is in fact generalizability.

Experimental research often focuses on some element of content or technique of production (often called a "form" element). The intended inference is that these vary in their effect on attention, cognition, or behavior. The generalizability problem arises because the power of the research design to examine these elements means that they occur only in isolation or in the specific context of the video used in the research. There is only limited surety that their effects do not depend on an interaction that may be missing in other contexts or that in other contexts an interaction may occur that will alter their effects.

Experimental research also employs a setting that in many respects will be artificial and different from the circumstances in which viewing normally occurs. Exposure is likely to be short term, set apart from other video stimuli, and in strange surroundings not of one's choosing. The measure of subsequent behavior may restrict options; constraints that ordinarily govern behavior, such as the possibility of retaliation if aggression or hostility is expressed, are likely to be absent. The registering of outcomes immediately after exposure, coupled with these factors, may exaggerate effects.

The assumption necessary for generalizability is that such findings are independent of stimulus contact or experimental setting. Unhappily for television research, this is a perilous assumption in the circumstances, yet it is necessary if findings are to have utility. As Brewer (1985) pointed out, the trick is not to imitate the real world within the research but rather to simulate conceptually within the design the elements that are influential in everyday life.

■ Paradigm Choice

Disciplines and fields represented in the application of the social and behavioral sciences to television are many and varied. Social psychology, sociology, child development, communication, political science, marketing, advertising, and education are among them. Each has made use of every available procedure, but typically there are predominant paradigms. Experimentation has been preeminent in social psychology, with the laboratory being more common, if less dramatic, than a naturalistic setting. In sociology, the survey and participant observation are more common. In child development, the laboratory experiment has had a major place.

This has had a singular benefit. It has made it possible to assemble evidence from complementary methods where the strengths of any one discipline or field would have been inferentially inferior. The prime example is that of television violence and antisocial behavior. About half of the empirical evidence has been collected within social psychology and about one third within communication (Hearold, 1986; Paik & Comstock, 1994).

The evidence from laboratory experimentation, largely from social psychology, has unequivocally answered what some have called the "can" question (MacBeth, 1996): Young people of all ages exposed to what the investigator considers a violent or antisocial television treatment subsequently behave more aggressively within the research setting, whether the outcome is measured by questionnaire, aggression machine (a device that ostensibly delivers noxious stimuli to a person in another room), or observed behavior. The evidence from survey research, collected largely within communication and sociology, has not unequivocally answered the more difficult "does" question—as to whether the experimental effect occurs regularly in the real world— but has provided information crucial to formulating an answer: Young people in the elementary school, teenage, and young adult years who view greater amounts of television violence are consistently more aggressive, and no attempt to ascribe this positive association entirely to the influence of some artifact or other variable has been successful (Comstock & Paik, 1991; Cook et al., 1983; Milavsky et al., 1982).

The inferential function of the surveys is to test the validity of the experiments as representing events likely to occur in everyday life.

They confirm that validity by documenting that the relationships it would require do in fact occur in the real world. The most plausible conclusion is that television violence facilitates antisocial and aggressive behavior. External validity (Cook & Campbell, 1979), or generalizability, in this instance of television research arises from the combining of findings from quite different venues.

The diversity of approaches also poses problems. On a minor note, investigators are likely to mistrust methods not central to their sphere. Psychologists will emphasize the inferential rigor of experiments, sociologists the descriptive authority of surveys. On a major note, several perspectives within communication offer paradigms that have taken on partisan coloring in regard to what "communication" as a subject ought to be.

Three will serve as examples:

1. *Ethnographic inquiry* (J. A. Anderson, 1987; J. A. Anderson & Meyer, 1988; Lull, 1995; MacBeth, 1996). The observation (meticulously recorded) of persons as they use media to determine the meaning assigned to content, individual responses to media, and the role of social interaction in assigning that meaning and making those responses.

2. *Cultural and critical studies* (Grossberg, Nelson, & Treichler, 1992; Hall, Hobson, Lowe, & Willis, 1980; Williams, 1968). The examination of the process of production, the content of messages, and the way in which those messages are received and interpreted, with emphasis on the complexity and cultural context of these processes and outcomes, to uncover the modes by which a predominant ideology is disseminated and sometimes resisted.

3. *Positivistic quantification* (Bandura, 1986; Comstock & Paik, 1991; Cook & Campbell, 1979; Kerlinger, 1986). The search for general, but not necessarily universal or permanent, laws or relationships through the collecting of empirical data by experiments and surveys that are statistically analyzed.

Each represents a set of values that lead to contention over what is worthy of study in, for example, the following: six families in Texas over the course of a year in regard to what they make of—as in "sense of" and "use of"—the television they view; the motion pictures of

Disney in regard to what they portray about class, ethnicity, and gender in regard to power; or a representative national sample of 2,000 in regard to the relationships between needs and interests and media use.

My view is cynical and conciliatory. It is cynical in its strong agreement with Campbell (1986) on the development of science that what you get is what you need and what you have produced. Philanthropic endeavors adopt new goals as old goals are met. Scientific specialties similarly adapt to maintain their viability. Science becomes what it must given the amounts and sources of funding, research opportunities, and available personnel. These could be phrased more sharply as economics; as norms, conventions, and laws; and as talent. In the case of television, dwindling funds for empirical, quantitative research accompanied by increased numbers of doctorate-holding faculty untrained to engage in it (a consequence of the increased popularity of communication in some guise as an undergraduate major, thereby increasing faculty career opportunities) has led to a polity in behalf of other strains of investigation. My view is conciliatory in that the present categorization of inquiry is artificial and should be abandoned for one longer on insight and shorter on political distinctions.

Three possible dimensions by which paradigms could be characterized (Comstock & Lindsey, 1975) are as follows:

1. *theory-policy* in regard to the intent of the research design and the immediate applicability of findings;
2. *micro-macro* in regard to the magnitude or breadth of the personal, social, or media element examined; and
3. *qualitative-quantitative* in regard to the degree to which statistical concepts are employed for description and analysis.

This three-dimensional schema in effect is a cube representing the spatial territory of the application of the social and behavioral sciences to television. Its chief merit is the abandonment of the jurisdictional use of paradigms to advance proprietary and parochial interests. By contrast, it highlights the properties of these paradigms. As a result, antipathies are minimized and the accurate perception of utility, strengths, and weaknesses is maximized.

The three dimensions are independent, but they interact. Theory can be applied to policy because it furthers accurate anticipation of future events. Nielsen data represent industry policy research but also may contribute to theories about audience behavior. The experimental research identifying elements of portrayals on which antisocial responses to television violence are contingent is theory-building research that could be, but generally has not been, applied to policy (Comstock & Paik, 1991). In this respect, the recent University of California, Santa Barbara content analyses of violence in cable and broadcast programming (Cole, 1996), sponsored by the cable industry, are exemplary. Under the leadership of Donnerstein, Kunkel, and Wilson, the use of an abitrary (if normative) definition, as exemplified by the work of Gerbner, is discarded and replaced by the specification of problematic violence in accord with the empirical scientific record —principally those experimental findings. If the concern is with the effects of violence on cognition and behavior, then this is a nec- essary step for research on violent content to be meaningful for policy, a point made earlier by a few researchers (e.g., Comstock, 1982).

Micro studies provide a good example of how seemingly disparate research may have much in common. The experiments that focus on one or a few aspects of violent portrayals and ethnographic examinations of families viewing television share the same difficulty of generalizing to a different context or larger population. In the case of the former, the problem was resolved by the evidence from surveys. Can the ethnographic research find comparable sources for validation?

Despite the profusion of research methods present in texts (Babbie 1986; Kerlinger, 1986; Wimmer & Dominick, 1987), there are in fact only two methods in the social and behavioral sciences. One is the experiment. The other is the survey. The first obtains knowledge by examining the aftermath of a treatment. Designs differ with the circumstances of the treatment—in the laboratory, in a naturalistic field setting, in society itself. The second obtains knowledge by describing the attributes of some population based on a sample or census. The nature of the population and the procedure leads to different terminology—content analysis when the population is media content, participant observation when it is the acts of coworkers. Fundamental to both is systematic observation (Weick, 1985), and, whatever their variants, both must address the same two questions:

1. What inference or meaning can be drawn from what has been done that has some relevance beyond the boundaries of the inquiry?

2. How well does the information collected permit the ruling out of alternative explanations for the interpretations offered of what has been observed?

The only acceptable answers are in the affirmative. The use of probability samples or modest disclaimers over the inapplicability of results from small or convenience samples neither solves nor evades these challenges. They are a case-by-case matter of reasonable judgment. To act otherwise is to demean the concept of empirical scholarly inquiry. The question of which paradigm is right should be deserted on behalf of another: Which serves the intended purpose better? Merton (1996) spoke to the essence:

> The cumulative point of this variety of intellectual and institutional cases is not—and it needs to be repeated with all possible emphasis—is not a proposal to replace the extreme Insider doctrine by an extreme and equally vulnerable Outsider doctrine. The intent is, rather, to transform the original question altogether. We no longer ask whether it is the Insider or the Outsider who has monopolistic or privileged access to social knowledge; instead, we begin to consider their distinctive and interactive roles in the process of seeking truth. (p. 261)

■ Industry

The television industry has a number of interests that lead it to take variously an antagonistic, adversarial, or evasive role in response to much research while at the same time ironically being the principal supporter of certain types of research. The former encompasses most, if not all, of the research on the social effects of television. The second consists of the audience research documenting the demographics of those attending to programming, which broadcasting has pioneered since the 1940s.

The political interests of the industry rest in getting along with the FCC and Congress. The primary strategy is defensive; the industry acquiesced in the mid-1970s to pressure from the FCC chairman to establish a "family viewing" policy that would reduce violence for two early evening hours, a policy that would later be overturned by the courts on First Amendment and due process grounds (Comstock et al., 1978). The underlying goal is to avoid constraints by licensing, regulation, or statute that would interfere with the ordinary conduct of business.

The economic interests of the industry similarly lead to hostility toward research that might be interpreted as justifying constraints such as (a) the curtailment or specification of what can be offered as entertainment, news, or sports in competition with other media; (b) the limitation of what can be disseminated from the vast archives of programming produced in earlier periods; and (c) the labeling of newly produced programming in any way that would delimit the size of potential audiences.

The ideological interests of the industry rest only in part in freedom of expression and support for the First Amendment. They also rest in adherence to and perpetuation of conventional concepts of entertainment and popular mass media. This is because these concepts are fundamental to the business practices of the television industry. Of the two, the latter typically takes precedence for that very reason; freedom of expression and the First Amendment are more peripheral to business practices.

The controversies over television violence and the V-chip provide a recent example. The threat of restrictive legislation led the cable industry, as a show of good faith, to sponsor the National Television Violence Study (Cole, 1996) at a 3-year cost of $3.5 million. The broadcast industry, displaying the usual paranoia, decided to finance its own similar 3-year study at a cost of $1.3 million (Cole, 1996). The V-chip, made mandatory in newly manufactured television sets by the telecommunications legislation of 1996, will automatically scramble signals on the basis of prior encoded ratings. Up to the last moment, the cable and broadcast industries promised a First Amendment fight, for the procedure involves all three of the economic threats cited earlier. But under pressure from the White House, Congress, and polls indicating that the public would like something done about violence in television entertainment, they acquiesced. Jack Valenti, the representative of the Motion Picture Association of America (which assigns the theater film ratings), stepped forward as point man for the development of a television ratings system (West & Stern, 1996).

However, the industry's action quickly assumed a wonderfully wily sociological cast (in the sense of how an institution motivated to avoid criticism and inconvenience would be expected to behave). What had begun as a concern over the harmfulness of violent portrayals, and especially in regard to the facilitation of antisocial behavior on the part of viewers, became an endeavor simply to inform parents so that they could better govern their children's viewing. Valenti openly scoffed at the social and behavioral sciences; violence and its effects were too complex for rigorous study.

This scenario contrasts with the analysis of the cable-sponsored National Television Violence Study. The investigators concluded, on the basis of the empirical literature, that there are three harmful effects of violent portrayals. They are the facilitation of aggression, fear, and desensitization. A fourth, distinct from fear, that the present author would add is pessimism or negative cognition (Comstock, 1982). The investigators then proceeded to calculate across the array of broadcast and cable channels the frequency with which the content elements that have been demonstrated empirically to have these outcomes actually occur.

Admittedly, the likelihood that we, the American public, will change the way in which we entertain ourselves on any grand scale is remote. This does not alter the circumstances. The social and behavioral sciences have empirically identified a problem and have offered a solution (however difficult): the reduction of harmful portrayals. If the problem is those three (or four) harmful effects, then labeling content for V-chip exorcism will succeed only if all households comply. And if they were to do so, then there would be no need for the V-chip because the incentives to produce such content would be absent. The industry has substituted appearance for substance.

■ References

Allen, C. (1965). Photographing the audience. *Journal of Advertising Research, 5*, 2-8.

Anderson, D. R., & Collins, P. A. (1988). *The impact on children's education: Television's influence on cognitive development.* Washington, DC: U.S. Department of Education.

Anderson, D. R., Field, D. E., Collins, P. A., Lorch, E. P., & Nathan, J. G. (1985). Estimates of young children's time with television: A methodological comparison of parent reports with time-lapse video home observation. *Child Development, 56,* 1345-1357.

Anderson, D. R., Lorch, E. P., Field, D. E., & Sanders, J. (1981). Television viewing at home: Age trends in visual attention and time with TV. *Child Development, 57,* 1024-1033.

Anderson, J. A. (1987). *Communication research: Issues and methods.* New York: McGraw-Hill.

Anderson, J. A., & Meyer, T. P. (1988). *Mediated Communication: A social action perspective.* Newbury Park, CA: Sage.

Andreasen, M. S. (1985). How people use media in home learning. In N. H. Miller (Ed.), *The home as a learning center: American Home Economics Association yearbook 5* (pp. 239-265). Peoria, IL: Bennett & McKnight.

Babbie, E. R. (1986). *The practice of social research* (4th ed.). Belmont, CA: Wadsworth.

Ball-Rokeach, S. J., Rokeach, M., & Grube, J. W. (1984). *The great American values test.* New York: Free Press.

Bandura, A. (1986). *Social foundations of thought and action: A social cognitive theory.* Englewood Cliffs, NJ: Prentice Hall.

Barwise, P., & Ehrenberg, A. (1988). *Television and its audiences.* Newbury Park, CA: Sage.

Barwise, T. P., Ehrenberg, A. S. C., & Goodhardt, G. J. (1982). Glued to the box? Patterns of TV-repeat viewing. *Journal of Communication, 32*(4), 22-29.

Bechtel, R. P., Achelpohl, C., & Akers, R. (1972). Correlates between observed behavior and questionnaire responses on television viewing. In E. A. Rubinstein, G. A. Comstock, & J. P. Murray (Eds.), *Television and social behavior,* Vol. 4: *Television in day-to-day life—Patterns of use* (pp. 274-344). Washington, DC: Government Printing Office.

Berkowitz, L. (1990). On the formation and regulation of anger and aggression: A cognitive-neoassociationistic analysis. *American Psychologist, 45,* 494-503.

Berkowitz, L., & Rogers, K. H. (1986). A priming effect analysis of media influences. In J. Bryant & D. Zillmann (Eds.), *Perspectives on media effects* (pp. 57-81). Hillsdale, NJ: Lawrence Erlbaum.

Bower, R. T. (1985). *The changing television audience in America.* New York: Holt, Rinehart & Winston.

Brewer, M. B. (1985, August). *Experimental research and social psychology: Must it be rigor less relevance?* Presidential address delivered at the annual meeting of the American Psychological Association, Los Angeles.

By the numbers. (1996, October 21). *Broadcasting & Cable,* p. 70.

Campbell, D. (1986). Science's social system of validity-enhancing collective belief change and the problems of the social sciences. In D. Fiske & R. Shweder (Eds.), *Metatheory in social science* (pp. 108-135). Chicago: University of Chicago Press.

Clancey, M. (1994). The television audience examined. *Journal of Advertising Research, 34*(4), 1-10.

Cohen, A. A., Levy, M. R., & Golden, K. (1988). Children's uses and gratifications of home VCRs: Evolution or revolution. *Communication Research, 15,* 772-780.

Cole, J. (1996). *National television violence study.* Thousand Oaks, CA: Sage.

Comstock, G. (1982). Violence in television content: An overview. In D. Pearl, L. Bouthilet, & J. Lazar (Eds.), *Television and behavior: Ten years of scientific inquiry and implications for the eighties,* Vol. 2: *Technical reviews* (pp. 108-125). Washington, DC: Government Printing Office.

Comstock, G. (1989). *The evolution of American television.* Newbury Park, CA: Sage.

Comstock, G. (1991). *Television in America* (2nd ed.). Newbury Park, CA: Sage.

Comstock, G., Chaffee, S., Katzman, N., McCombs, M., & Roberts, D. (1978). *Television and human behavior.* New York: Columbia University Press.

Comstock, G., & Lindsey, G. (1975). *Television and human behavior: The research horizon, future and present* (R-1748-CF). Santa Monica, CA: RAND.

Comstock, G., & Paik, H. (1991). *Television and the American child.* San Diego: Academic Press.

Condry, J. (1989). *The psychology of television.* Hillsdale, NJ: Lawrence Erlbaum.

Cook, T. D., & Campbell, D. T. (1979). *Quasi-experimentation: Design and analysis issues for field settings.* Boston: Houghton Mifflin.

Cook, T. D., Kendzierski, D. A., & Thomas, S. A. (1983). The implicit assumptions of television research: An analysis of the 1982 NIMH report on *Television and Behavior. Public Opinion Quarterly, 47,* 161-201.

Frank, R. E., & Greenberg, M. G. (1980). *The public's use of television.* Beverly Hills, CA: Sage.

Gerbner, G. (1990). Epilogue: Advancing on the path of righteousness (maybe). In N. Signorielli & M. Morgan (Eds.), *Cultivation analysis* (pp. 225-248). Newbury Park, CA: Sage.

Gerbner, G., Gross, L., Morgan, M., & Signorielli, N. (1986). Living with television: The dynamics of the cultivation process. In J. Bryant & D. Zillmann (Eds.), *Perspectives on media effects* (pp. 17-40). Hillsdale, NJ: Lawrence Erlbaum.

Gerbner, G., Morgan, M., & Signorielli, N. (1994). *Television violence profile No. 16.* Philadelphia: University of Pennsylvania, Annenberg School of Communication.

Grossberg, L., Nelson, C., & Treichler, P. (Eds.). (1992). *Cultural studies.* New York: Routledge.

Hall, S., Hobson, D., Lowe, A., & Willis, P. (Eds.). (1980). *Culture, media, and language.* London: Hutchinson.

Hawkins, R. P., & Pingree, S. (1980). Some processes in the cultivation effect. *Communication Research, 7,* 193-226.

Hawkins, R. P., & Pingree, S. (1981). Uniform messages and habitual viewing: Unnecessary assumptions in social reality effects. *Human Communication Research, 7,* 291-301.

Hawkins, R. P., & Pingree, S. (1982). Television's influence on construction of reality. In D. Pearl, L. Bouthilet, & J. Lazar (Eds.), *Television and behavior: Ten years of scientific inquiry and implications for the eighties,* Vol. 2: *Technical reviews* (pp. 224-247). Washington, DC: Government Printing Office.

Head, S. W. (1954). Content analysis of television drama programs. *Quarterly Journal of Film, Radio, and Television, 9,* 175-194.

Hearold, S. (1986). A synthesis of 1043 effects of television on social behavior. In G. Comstock (Ed.), *Public communication and behavior* (Vol. 1, pp. 65-133). New York: Academic Press.

Hollenbeck, A., & Slaby, R. (1979). Infant visual and vocal responses to television. *Child Development, 50,* 41-45.

Huston, A. C., Wright, J. C., Rice, M. L., Kerkman, D., Seigle, J., & Bremer, M. (1983). *Family environment and television use by preschool children.* Paper presented at the biennial meeting of the Society for Research in Development, Detroit, MI.

Katz, E. (1988). On conceptualizing media effects: Another look. In S. Oskamp (Ed.), *Applied social psychology annual,* Vol. 8: *Television as a social issue* (pp. 361-374). Newbury Park, CA: Sage.

Katz, E., & Lazarsfeld, P. (1955). *Personal influence.* Glencoe, IL: Free Press.

Kerlinger, F. (1986). *Foundations of behavioral research* (3rd ed.). New York: Holt, Rinehart & Winston.

Kubey, R. (Ed.). (1996). *Media literacy in the information age: Current perspectives,* Vol. 6: *Information and behavior.* New Brunswick, NJ: Transaction.

Kubey, R. W., & Csikszentmihalyi, M. (1990). *Television and the quality of life: How viewing shapes everyday experience.* Hillsdale, NJ: Lawrence Erlbaum.

Kubey, R. W., & Larson, R. (1990). The use and experience of the new video media among children and young adolescents. *Communication Research, 17,* 107-130.

Lull, J. (1995). *Media, communication, culture: A global approach.* New York: Columbia University Press.

MacBeth, T. (Ed.). (1996). *Tuning in to young viewers: Social science perspectives on television.* Thousand Oaks, CA: Sage.

McCombs, M. E. (1989). Agenda-setting. In E. Barnouw (Ed.), *International encyclopedia of communications* (Vol. 1, pp. 42-43). New York: Oxford University Press.

Meltzoff, A. N. (1988). Imitation of televised models by infants. *Child Development, 59,* 1221-1229.

Merton, R. (1996). *On social structure and science.* Chicago: University of Chicago Press.

Milavsky, J. R. (1992). How good is the A. C. Nielsen people-meter system? A review of the report by the committee on nationwide television audience measurement. *Public Opinion Quarterly, 56,* 102-115.

Milavsky, J. R., Kessler, R., Stripp, H. H., & Rubens, W. S. (1982). *Television and aggression: A panel study.* New York: Academic Press.

Morgan, M., & Signorielli, N. (1990). Cultivation analysis: Conceptualization and methodology. In N. Signorielli & M. Morgan (Eds.), *Cultivation analysis* (pp. 13-34). Newbury Park, CA: Sage.

Murray, J. P., & Kippax, S. (1977). Television diffusion and social behavior in three communities: A field experiment. *Australian Journal of Psychology, 29*(1), 31-43.

Paik, H., & Comstock, G. (1994). The effects of television violence on antisocial behavior: A meta-analysis. *Communication Research, 21,* 516-546.

Parker, E. B. (1963). The effects of television on library circulation. *Public Opinion Quarterly, 27,* 578-589.

Potter, W. J., Cooper, R., & Dupagne, M. (1993). The three paradigms of mass media research in mainstream communication journals. *Communication Theory, 3,* 317-335.

Robinson, J. P. (1977). *How Americans use time.* New York: Praeger.

Rokeach, M. (1960). *The open and closed mind.* New York: Basic Books.

Roper Organization, Inc. (1987). *America's watching: Public attitudes toward television.* New York: Television Information Office.

Rothenbuhler, E. W. (1988). The living room celebration of the Olympic games. *Journal of Communication, 38*(4), 61-81.

Schramm, W., Lyle, J., & Parker, E. B. (1961). *Television in the lives of our children.* Stanford, CA: Stanford University Press.

Smythe, D. W. (1954). Reality as presented by television. *Public Opinion Quarterly, 18,* 143-156.

Timmer, S. G., Eccles, J., & O'Brien, K. (1985). How children use time. In F. T. Juster & F. P. Stafford (Eds.), *Time, goods, and well-being* (pp. 353-382). Ann Arbor: University of Michigan, Institute for Social Research.

Weick, K. (1985). Systematic observational methods. In G. Lindzey & E. Aronson (Eds.), *The handbook of social psychology* (Vol. 1, pp. 567-634). Reading, MA: Addison-Wesley.

West, D., & Stern, C. (1996, March 18). Jack of all trades: The man in the middle of the V-chip. *Broadcasting & Cable*, pp. 26-30.

Williams, R. (1968). *Communications*. Baltimore: Penguin Books.

Williams, T. M. (Ed.). (1986). *The impact of television: A natural experiment in three communities*. New York: Academic Press.

Wimmer, R. D., & Dominick, J. R. (1987). *Mass media research: An introduction*. Belmont, CA: Wadsworth.

Winick, C. (1988). The functions of television: Life without the big box. In S. Oskamp (Ed.), *Television as a social issue* (pp. 217-237). Newbury Park, CA: Sage.

Winston, B. (1986). *Misunderstanding media*. Cambridge, MA: Harvard University Press.

Xiaoming, H. (1994). Television viewing among American adults in the 1990s. *Journal of Broadcasting & Electronic Media, 38*, 353-360.

PART I

Quantitative Research Paradigms in the Study of Television

The positivistic tradition that has been the mainstay of social science research continues to exercise a significant influence on what we choose to study, which, in turn, has relevance to the methodology that is selected to approach the problems for which we seek answers. The chapters in Part I provide a closer look at some of the major quantitative research paradigms that reflect the more positivistic theoretical framework for studying social science phenomena.

Edward L. Palmer begins this part of the volume by reviewing the diverse quantitative methods that have been applied to the study of television's influence on the viewing audience. He makes a case for maintaining an optimism in our search for answers while being realistic in conducting our search. Being realistic includes having an appreciation for the strengths and vulnerabilities of the methods we rely on for seeking the answers to our research questions and realizing that "A vulnerability of one design will be a strength of another, providing the net effect of counterbalance" (p. 58). Furthermore, he states, "As researchers, beginning from different methodological starting points, converge on synchronous research outcomes, the likelihood of a common Variable X becomes highly remote indeed" (p. 63).

As pointed out by L. Monique Ward and Patricia M. Greenfield in their chapter, "there is a richness in our interactions with television that much of traditional experimental research and traditional research methodology does not capture" (p. 68). On the other hand, a well-conceived experimental investigation provides an opportunity to test the cause we believe associated with a particular outcome. These researchers delineate seven methodological gaps that experimental investigators need to address in their studies to enhance the validity of their study outcomes, and they provide suggestions for minimizing the effect of these limitations.

Tannis M. MacBeth discusses how well-designed quasi-experimental research can enhance the ecological validity of the investigation while enabling investigators to make causal inferences about the effect of television on the viewing audience. She begins by reviewing the conditions required for making causal inferences and how well-designed quasi-experiments address these conditions. She also provides an overview of both natural and field experiments that have been conducted in diverse settings nationally and internationally.

The final chapter in this part of the volume is a model-building piece by Richard L. Allen. In his theory about the development of the black self-concept, majority and black media play salient roles in how African Americans learn to view themselves. In this chapter, he shows how to refine theoretical propositions through the use of structural equation modeling.

1

Major Paradigms and Issues in Television Research

Field of Dreams, World of Realities

Edward L. Palmer

Over the past four decades, television research tools have plowed a wide and varied acreage. The shape and angle of any given plow frequently has been tailored to the "lay of the land," the nature of a given set of questions, and the experience and resources of the specific research team. Because a single blade size never has fit all parts of the acreage, the panoramic view finds diversity in contours and furrow depth, each with its own identifiable strengths and weaknesses, each with its own set of issues and implications.

■ Research Background and Tool Designations

The earliest inquiries were *source related*. Entities such as the National Association of Educational Broadcasters (NAEB) in 1951 and the Senate Subcommittee (Kefauver Committee) investigating juvenile delinquency in 1954 focused their attention on the television programming day. Just how many entries on any given day's programming schedule were violent? As research questions go, it was a relatively easy question to answer. Programming schedules provided the data, and simple statistics provided the analysis. Only a working definition of violence lay between the researchers and their counting. Both the NAEB and the Kefauver Committee concluded there was an alarming degree of violent content within the television programming day, and they called on the industry to police itself and reduce violent content prevalence (U.S. Senate, Judiciary Committee, 1965).

The next set of inquiries were *child audience related,* spotlighting the individual child. How much television were children watching? And within that viewing time, how much violent programming were they seeing? The next breath voiced the question destined to define television research inquiry for some time to come: What effect was violent program viewing having on children's behavior? Was it making them more aggressive? Was it vicariously releasing their pent-up frustrations and aggressive tendencies? This new batch of questions was formidable, and the quest for answers would cover equally formidable new ground.

Two early plows set to this new ground were the *surveys* of Himmelweit, Oppenheim, and Vince (1958) and Schramm, Lyle, and Parker (1961). Himmelweit et al.'s (1958) survey of more than 1,800 British children concluded that crime and detective stories were not increasing children's aggressiveness, but children themselves were spending an enormous amount of their waking time tube gazing. The researchers registered concern that so much of a child's day was spent before the screen. Schramm et al. (1961) brought these child-based research concerns to U.S. soil and examined them extensively in *Television in the Lives of Our Children.* The 11 studies reviewed in this book spanned 3 years and five different sites ranging from San Francisco to the Rocky Mountains and two Canadian communities. With nearly 6,000 children and 2,000 parents participating, their work stands as a hallmark in the field, one to be viewed close-up later in this chapter.

Television research questions and concerns vividly reflect their times, and the decade of the 1960s was no ordinary set of times. Beginning in dreams and ending in nightmares, the 1960s felt like a

decade running violently out of bounds with no way to call "time out."
It was "a time of passion, a time to burn, and a time to grieve" (Morris,
1984, p. 70) as youthful idealism plunged headlong into troughs of
despair. There was war at home and war abroad. The war abroad was
Vietnam, whereas the war at home was the civil rights movement. Each
had its charismatic leader and an early idealism. Each had its stark
encounter with death, tragedy, and loss. In early 1963, Martin Luther
King, Jr. delivered his moving *I Have a Dream* speech by the Lincoln
Memorial in Washington, D.C., and late that same year Washington
and the nation mourned the assassination death of its president. John
F. Kennedy would be but the first of three tragic assassinations of our
nation's leaders. Martin Luther King, Jr. and Robert F. Kennedy soon
would follow, and a public reeling from violence and death at home
and abroad was groping for answers. What was happening to us? How
could we stem the tide and change our course? The questions ran as
deep as the passions, the grief, and the loss (Parker & Nelson, 1983,
pp. ix-xvi).

The decade's fabric and its threads of tragedy spawned two key
research initiatives. President Johnson established a commission on
the causes and prevention of violence. Led by Milton Eisenhower, part
of the Eisenhower Commission's mandate was to study the potential
link between television program violence and the incidence of violent
acts in our nation's streets and homes. Several of the nation's leading
research authorities contributed chapters to the commission's staff
report. Key among them was George Gerbner's meticulous review and
analysis of violence incidence in program content. Destined to become
longitudinal and comparative, Gerbner's content analysis stands as another hallmark in the research field to be viewed close-up later in this
chapter. The second key research initiative partially eclipsed the first.
Six months before the Eisenhower Commission reported its work,
Senator John Pastore, chair of the Senate Subcommittee on Communications, asked the surgeon general to appoint a distinguished scientific advisory committee to determine whether television violence
produced antisocial behavior in children. Events moved quickly, and
the surgeon general's Scientific Advisory Committee was convened
within 3 months of the request. With its funding for research, this
inquiry was destined to be the "high-water mark" in questions relating
to televised violence and children. A total of $1 million in research

funding supported key research initiatives by leading social scientists throughout the country. In addition to Gerbner's work, already cited for our later close-up view, the longitudinal study by Lefkowitz, Eron, Walder, and Huesmann (1972) and the laboratory work by Liebert and Baron (1972) broke new ground and notably demonstrated the diversity of approaches to these basic research questions. Each of these approaches is cited for close-up attention in our review of research methods and issues.

■ The Nature of the Research Tools

A variety of tools have tilled the children's television research area, and most of these tools have come from well-established use in other social science applications. Most tools in the inventory already have been introduced, among them the following:

Surveys: Gathering extensive data from large samples

Longitudinal (panel): Following identifiable individuals across time and taking intermittent measurements or noting significant behavioral differences between children in an experimental condition and children in a control condition

Cross-sectional: Examining different age group samples of the population simultaneously on a given specified set of dimensions or variables

Content analysis: Developing an operational definition of a concept such as aggression or violence and examining the concept's prevalence within a given body of content such as television programming schedules

Model building: Creating a model based on existing research evidence and testing each aspect of the model and refining its elements

Experiments: In the laboratory or in the field

Meta-analysis: Putting the entire body of research evidence under the microscope to analyze trends, outcomes, and literally "the weight of the evidence"

Less amenable to systematic research, and not covered within this discussion, is the case study. Although it has some resemblance to the longitudinal study of individuals, it moves in reverse direction. It says, in effect, "Here's Ronnie Zamora, the young teen who modeled a murder he had seen on television. How did he get to be that way, and what cumulative influence role did television viewing have on his criminality?" Fortunately, there are not many case studies as dramatic as Zamora's, although Gerbner and others suggest that the cumulative effect of viewing across time is widespread among our youth.

There have been notable occasions when a plow within a neighboring field has had significant impact on this acreage, the neighbor never envisioning that his or her work would take on television research dimensions and ramifications. Such was the case with the basic aggression modeling research of Albert Bandura (1965) and Leonard Berkowitz (e.g., Berkowitz & Alioto, 1973). Laboratory experimental in both instances, their work set the tone within this young television research area and has been the conceptual framework for much of the research that followed. Rare is the present-day investigation that does not cite the research findings from these two individuals.

■ Hallmark Research Tools at Close Range

Surveys

Himmelweit, Oppenheim, and Vince

The time was 1955-1956. The place was England. The goal was to determine the role and impact of television in the lives of children. Roughly one fifth of British homes had television, and the British Broadcasting Corporation's (BBC) audience research department had recommended that the Nuffield Foundation sponsor an inquiry examining the impact of television on children. Seeking scientific rigor, the foundation approached Hilde Himmelweit, social psychologist at the London School of Economics and Political Science. A psychologist colleague, A. N. Oppenheim, collaborated, and the two of them worked part-time with another psychologist, Pamela Vince (Himmelweit et al., 1958). The researchers keenly understood that "effect" was not a monolithic term. They identified several potential effects to be investigated: displacement (the time television viewing took away from other child activities); program content (television content effects on children's knowledge, school performance, outlook, and values); family life (the extent to which family interactive quality is affected either positively or negatively); and emotional reactions (children's emotional reactions as evidenced by their relationships with their friends, their general adjustment, and their level of anxiety). To address these questions, the researchers used group comparison, an experimental group comprising children exposed to television and a control group comprising children not exposed to television (pp. 3-5). To lend credibility and rigor to the comparison, each experimental group child was matched with a control group "twin," a child quite similar on a range of important dimensions such as sex, age, intelligence, social background, and, wherever possible, the same classroom setting. The researchers drew a sample total of 908 10- and 11-year-olds and 946 13- and 14-year-olds across four areas— London, Bristol, Portsmouth, and Sunderland. Before and after the introduction of television to their community, another 376 children from Norwich were interviewed. The Norwich study was designed to address the question of whether the television "haves" and "have nots" in the original sampling differed on some qualitative dimension beyond the presence of television in the home. The two specific age groups selected were based on the youngest age at which children could follow and respond to the survey questionnaire instructions and the oldest age at which all the children would be present and available in school. A total of 4,500 children were tested, including 1,854 matched pairs. Introduced simply as a study of their leisure activities, selected children were asked to keep diaries (filled in quietly and privately at school each day) in which they chronicled everything they did between leaving school and bedtime. They also were asked to rate the three daily activities they most enjoyed. Six weeks later, these children were given detailed questionnaires asking about their leisure activities and interests with corresponding questions for movies, radio, and reading activities. Personality ratings were taken along with teacher assessments of children's behaviors and personalities. As the researchers expressed it, they were seeking to gather the material normally found in a case study, tailoring that data gathering to the context of a large-scale survey involving thousands (pp. 5-9).

In their emerging picture profile, the researchers found television-viewing children spending 11 to 13 hours weekly in viewing (their most extensive leisure activity). Viewing time was inversely related to intelligence, active lifestyle, and active parental modeling. When viewers lacked channel choices, they grew to like programs they otherwise would not have watched. But when channel choice entered the equation, the educational and for-child programs became the notable casualties. Television's impact on children's outlooks and values was most marked within dramatic presentations, which met with children's emotional receptivity and inability to confer with parents or friends on these specific issues. Realistic violence frightened more than did stylized violence, aggression with knives and sharp instruments frightened more than did guns, and viewing while in the dark or alone heightened the fright potential. There was no evidence that viewing made children more aggressive, and there was no evidence of beneficial effects. Bright children fell behind their matched nonviewers in schoolwork, viewing time was being borrowed from moviegoing and radio listening, and, although families were staying home more, they were not bonding interactively. Chief correlates of addictive, heavy viewing were lower intelligence, insecurity, maladjustment, and inadequate social life and friendships (Himmelweit et al., 1958, pp. 11-34). The researchers realized that, even in their extensive inquiry, they left unanswered some critical questions about rural children, the very young, and disturbed children. They expressed hope that future inquiries would help fill these knowledge gaps and that researchers in other countries would undertake comparable inquiries. Such extensive inquiry planning already was underway in the United States and Canada.

Schramm, Lyle, and Parker

This trio of Stanford University researchers could have written the baseline textbook for all of television survey investigations. The size and comprehensiveness of their survey work seldom has been matched within or beyond the annals of television research. Their goals were unpretentious—"to understand better the conditions under which children go to television and the conditions under which television has an effect on them" (Schramm et al., 1961, p. 7)—and their quest for this understanding was thorough and meticulous. Their 11 studies sampled five different communities, varied in locale and character. Their first two studies focused on public school children and their families in San Francisco. Study 1 surveyed 2,688 children from the public school system in Grades 1 through 6, 8, 10, and 12. Data collection formats were tailored to the ages of the children, and research inquiries tapped information relating to the nature of the children's media behavior; how they used different media; how much they knew about public affairs, science, popular and fine art, and other parts of the world; the nature of their family life and relationships with their peers; and their personalities, mental abilities, and school performance. In addition to the data from the children themselves, information and insights were solicited from teachers, school administrators, and other knowledgeable individuals. Study 2 interviewed 188 entire families—meeting as a family unit for 2 hours or so, observing family process and interactions. Studies 3 through 7 interviewed virtually all the 6th and 10th graders in five Rocky Mountain communities and, in three communities, interviewed the 1st graders as well. The cumulative sample across these communities totaled 1,708 children and 284 parents. Questionnaires were designed to parallel the data gathered in San Francisco. Studies 8 and 9 examined two comparable Canadian communities, one with and one without television. In those two studies, 1st, 6th, and 10th graders were studied via the same materials used within the Rocky Mountain communities—913 children and 269 parents. Study 10 selected a metropolitan U.S. suburb and examined television, program choice, and time allocations of all 474 children in one elementary school. Study 11 tested hypotheses developed within the first 10 studies in a 10th-grade setting in Denver, Colorado. The study series encompassed 5,991 students, 1,958 parents, and hundreds of teachers, administrators, and knowledgeable individuals within each community setting (pp. 8-10). Throughout the survey series and its elements, the researchers intentionally shunned the question of what television *does to* children and, instead, asked what children *do with* television (p. 169). In the researchers' words, one may conjure one of two images to characterize the television-child context. In the first, children are "helpless victims to be attacked by television" (p. 1); in the second, television is a "great and shiny cafeteria from which children select what they want at the moment" (p. 2). The second image created the conceptual fabric from which this study emanated, and survey materials sought to discover how much television children watch, why they watch, what differentiates high users from low users as children mature, and the relationship between children's personal problems or insecurities and the amount and type of television programming watched (p. 119). This latter question built on the earlier work of Bailyn (1959) and Himmelweit et al. (1958). Moving one step beyond the Himmelweit et al. study, the researchers took on the challenges of data gathering with young elementary school children.

The television use profile closely matched its British predecessor in several areas. Displacement of other leisure activities was quite evident with deep cuts in time spent moviegoing, radio listening, and reading as well as significant reductions in play time. Like their British counterparts, television viewing among children in the American study far outdistanced and dominated all other leisure activities. One third of 3-year-olds were watching television, as were 9 of 10 first graders (Schramm et al., 1961, p. 168). The youngest were spending 14 hours per week viewing, and the sixth graders were watching 28 hours per week. Viewers preferred adult programming over children's programming and went to it for escape and entertainment, for information, and as a socializing tool. Although it reinforced the vocabularies of both bright and low-intelligence 1st graders, its effectiveness quickly declined in providing reality-based knowledge and information. Ambitious adolescents who had internalized the social norm of personal growth and delay of gratification turned more toward McLuhan's (1967) "hot" (content-intensive) media such as print and educational/public affairs programming. Children with more conflict in their family and peer relationships used television more heavily than did those experiencing little interactive conflict. Children seemed generally unaffected by television physically (e.g., sleep loss, eye strain), but the fright factor was prevalent emotionally, especially where violence involved cutting or stepping in a trap. Television attracts the naturally thrill-seeking bent of children. Whether this thrill heightening would result in a greater demand for excitement in daily life was yet to be answered (Schramm et al., 1961, p. 173).

The researchers found little or no evidence of harmful behavioral effects. In some cases increased passivity was found, and in some instances a child withdrawal into television viewing was found, but these seemed more prominently related to the child's feelings of love, security, and acceptance than to television itself. Correspondingly, the child who came to view television with an aggressive predisposition was more likely than his or her nonaggressive counterpart to find, remember, and carry away television's aggressive scenes and messages.

The outcome parallels to the work of Himmelweit et al. (1958) were indeed striking, And the size, extensiveness, and rigor of both surveys brought credibility to their outcomes as reliable and valid in their respective times and places. Each had been a tour de force inquiry, and researchers in each instance acknowledged that long-term effects were yet to be studied and determined.

Longitudinal Studies

Both literally and figuratively, longitudinal studies take time. Generally, they take lots of cross-calendar time and cannot be rushed. They involve identifying a variable the researchers believe to be central and, across time, following specific group samples scoring high or low on that variable. Invariably, the study is panel in design in that measurements will be taken intermittently rather than continuously. The scene is much like having little Jill or little Julio stand up straight against the door frame as we carefully make pencil marks on the frame along with their names and the date. Perhaps 1 or 2 years later, we will have not-as-little Jill and not-as-little Julio back up against the same door frame again as we make yet more pencil marks, named and dated. This interval and its markings will enable us to see how much each of them has grown within that time interval. We may repeat the procedure annually to see what the growth pattern is over a longer period of time. Because we are parenting both of these youngsters, we can assume they have equal nutritional access and opportunity. If we were unable to make that assumption, then yet another variable would come into play—a topic to be discussed more thoroughly in this chapter's "Research Tool Issues and Implications" section.

One of the most famous longitudinal studies was conducted by Lewis Terman. Beginning in 1922, he began following 1,300 gifted children (IQs of 140 or above) to see over time how they differed from a random sample of their age peers. As with our Jill and Julio, Terman would check in periodically and measure both his gifted children and the random sample of average children. As time progressed, he found some significant differences destined to explode long-held myths about the very bright. Instead of being stiff, sickly, maladjusted nerds, these gifted folks proved to be superior to the random sample in health, height, leadership, and social skills. Only the longitudinal approach had enabled these myths to be eradicated (cited in Corsini, 1987, p. 1112).

Lefkowitz, Eron, Walder, and Huesmann

Monroe Lefkowitz, Leonard Eron, Leopold Walder, and L. Rowell Huesmann planned their study and took their initial "child-against-door frame" markings in 1959-1960. The researchers themselves spanned three geographical locations—Lefkowitz from the New York State Department of Mental Hygiene in Albany, Eron and Huesmann from the University of Illinois at Chicago Circle, and Walder from Behavior Service Consultants in Greenbelt, Maryland. As their child sample, they selected the entire 3rd-grade population in Columbia County, New York. As their operational definition of aggression, they took the composite of four measures—peer ratings, parent ratings, a personality test, and a self-report questionnaire. For *peer ratings,* each child was to name all the other study-related children she or he knew who demonstrated specific aggressive behaviors such as "starting a fight over nothing." Ten of these specific questions were interspersed with other questionnaire items. Other peer rating items measured aggression anxiety, those classmates who avoided aggressive encounters and never responded aggressively when picked on. A child's aggression rating was determined by adding up the number of times she or he was peer named on the aggression items and dividing by the number of questions, a procedure used previously by several researchers (e.g., Feshbach & Singer,1971; Lefkowitz, Eron, Walder, & Huesmann, 1977, p. 40; Milavsky & Pekowsky, 1973).

The project took on its longitudinal dimension in 1970 when the research team began searching for their child sample, now in their late teens. The search itself was a challenging trip through yearbooks, telephone directories, voter lists, tax lists, and county directories. Every subject who participated was asked about any subjects who were yet to be located. By the end of the research "day," 735 of the original 875 subjects had been contacted, and 427 of them completed the follow-up procedures. Response from the aggression-rating quartiles was not evenly balanced. Whereas 57% of the lower quartile-scoring males were reinterviewed, only 27% of their upper quartile-scoring age mates were reinterviewed. Strikingly similar proportions—63%

lower quartile and 33% upper quartile—characterized the females who were reinterviewed. Researchers attributed this differential trend to family mobility. In their reinterview sample, they found a strong correlation between family mobility and child aggressiveness. It was concluded that the most aggressive also were the most mobile—very difficult, and in many instances impossible, to find and to reinterview (Lefkowitz et al., 1977, pp. 38-39).

The reinterviewed teens again provided peer-rated aggression measures, took the Minnesota Multiphasic Personality Inventory (MMPI), and completed self-report questionnaires. Scales 4 and 9 of the MMPI were added together to get an aggressiveness score, and Scales 6, 7, 8, and 9 were combined to get a psychopathology score. The self-report questionnaires provided two sets of scores, one for antisocial behavior propensity and one for aggressive habit intensity. Both sets were summed to obtain an "aggressive habit" score, which correlated highly with peer ratings of aggressive tendencies.

The research team cited four potential predictors of aggression—instigators, contingent responses, identification variables, and sociocultural variables. Frustration ranks among prominent *instigators*, behaviors that serve as stimuli that elicit aggression. *Contingent responses* related primarily to how parents responded to their children's aggression. From parental responses to 24 questions, a potential-for-punishment score was computed for each parent. The researchers defined *identification variables* as modeling an observed behavior or internalizing a set of values and behavioral standards. Using a Semantic Differential Scale format, the researchers calculated an Expressive Behavior Profile for both parents and children. A Games and Activities Preference List measured sex role identification among the 8-year-olds, and the violence level of their preferred television programs gauged violent model preference and identification at both ages. How frequently a child confessed wrongdoing to a parent and the child's level of guilt—each of these parent reported—provided the internalization measure. *Sociocultural variables* included parents' educational and occupational status, mobility orientation of parents and teen subjects, ethnic background, frequency of church attendance, and the subjects' educational/occupational aspirations (Lefkowitz et al., 1977, pp. 43-51). Using primarily correlational measures, the researchers found all four of their categories predictive of aggression. For the 8-year-olds, instigators, identification variables, and sociocultural variables were most predictive of immediate aggression, and the key predictive variables among the 19-year-olds were identification and sociocultural variables (Lefkowitz et al., 1977, p. 192). One could readily have guessed the predictors of low aggression, among them popularity, intelligence, and politeness as 8-year-olds borne of positive, warm, and enthusiastic parenting. High aggression was linked to psychopathology, and both, in turn, were related to violent models within television programming, hence, one of the television-based linkages on which the study had been premised (pp. 159-160). Huesmann took another longitudinal look at these subjects as 30-year-olds and reported that the earlier correlation between high television viewing at age 8 and high juvenile delinquency at age 19 had become a correlation with high criminality at age 30. Where the trend had been primarily male oriented at age 19, he now found similar correlational patterns among women subjects (Huesmann, 1996; Huesmann, Eron, Lefkowitz, & Walder, 1984).

Cross-Sectional Studies

It is February 1, and the research team wants to study a given variable and its effect on 6-, 9-, 12-, and 15-year-olds. Rather than waiting for the 6-year-olds to become all of those respective ages and testing them along the way, the researchers want to look at each age group simultaneously—on this very February 1. Their design is cross-sectional, and within it they have an opportunity to study a developmental range at a single point in time. As with many of the designs outlined here, cross-sectional design frequently is blended with other designs—in the instance that follows, with longitudinal design.

Huesmann and Eron

Huesmann and Eron (1986) wanted to broaden the cross-cultural horizons on questions of whether and how media violence influenced children's behavior. In their words, "One can hardly consider the boundary conditions under which media violence might influence a child's behavior without considering the child's culture, the child's age, and the child's gender" (p. 17). Their cross section included 1st and 3rd graders in the United States, Australia, Finland, Israel, and Poland. Country selection had been based not as much on diversity as on collaborative links with colleagues willing to give generously of their time and expertise to provide this cross-national perspective. Sample sizes ranged from 189 in Israel to 758 in the United States. The Finland, Poland, and Australia samples were 220, 237, and 289, respectively. To the extent practical, the same procedures were followed in each country. Huesmann and Eron acknowledged that each country's research collaborators had their own expertise, theoretical perspectives, and research approach, bringing some variation to procedures in any given country. In many respects, data collection resembled procedures followed within the Lefkowitz et al. (1977) study and Eron's (1963) early baseline work in this area. In most instances, data collection points included the children, their peers, their parents, and the school. When the study began, each country's children were half 1st graders and half 3rd graders. Measures were taken annually for 3 years, giving the study a longitudinal dimension and covering the age range from 6 to 10 years.

Aggression measures included peer nominations and self-ratings. Prosocial behavior measures (peer nominated) tapped popularity and avoidance of aggression, and child interviews provided data on television viewing frequency and program preferences. Children rated a list of programs on the basis of realism, or how true to life they judged the programs to be. Other measures included the extent to which children identified with given television characters (four aggressive and four unaggressive, gender balanced), gender-typed activity preferences, fantasy (aggressive and active-heroic), and intelligence. Parent interviews examined socioeconomic and demographic characteristics, nurturance, rejection, punitiveness, mobility orientation, and aggressiveness. Parent television viewing habits and fantasy behavior also were reviewed (Huesmann, & Eron, 1986, pp. 38-40).

In the U.S. sample, the researchers confirmed earlier findings that frequent television violence viewing promotes aggressive behavior among children ages 6 to 11. The aggression habits developed in this age range are highly resistant to extinction and generally continue into adulthood. A self-perpetuating cycle of violence viewing and behavior feeds aggression. In the words of the researchers, "More aggressive children watch more violence, and that viewing seems to engender more aggression" (Huesmann & Eron, 1986, p. 76). Profiling a child most likely to be aggressive, it is a boy or girl who frequently watches violent programs, thinks they portray real life, feels a strong identification with the shows' aggressive characters, engages frequently in aggressive fantasies, and, in the case of girls, prefers stereotypically boys' activities (p. 78).

Cross-culturally, Finnish children profiled very comparably with the profile just outlined for the United States. Aggression was positively correlated with frequency of television violence viewing, a correlation found among both boys and girls. Overall, the Finnish culture itself is notably lower than the U.S. culture in aggressiveness, most markedly evident in peer nominations, self-ratings, and very low levels of parental punishment (Huesmann & Eron, 1986, p. 114).

Poland and Israel mirrored the correlation outlined for the United States and Finland. For Poland, family context was given more significant weight. For Israel, the difference between city children and kibbutz children was striking, the latter finding aggressiveness in general less acceptable and viewing little, if any, television. Australian children also mirrored the television violence viewing correlation with aggressive behavior, but in their instance a much broader range of variables (e.g., age, sex, aggressive fantasy, realism) entered the "mix." Parent-child rearing practices emerged as the single most important variable predicting a child's aggressive behavior. In a recent presentation, Huesmann (1996) indicated that Australia "stands apart" from the other countries studied. The exact nature of that difference and its dynamics is not yet fully understood, but the children seem less affected by television violence viewing.

Content Analysis

Gerbner

Gerbner at the Annenberg School of Communication, University of Pennsylvania, stood alone among the leading researchers invited to contribute to the Eisenhower Commission report. He alone submitted new research data that marked the beginning of an annual violence analysis of program content on each of the major networks. By counting and cataloging the acts of violence within each program, he launched a massive data collection that provided unique and revealing longitudinal patterns. He tracked violence programming trends across years and networks, developing both a Violence Index (program rating) and a Violent-Victim Ratio (profiling the aggressor and the victim within violence portrayals).

His specific measures were prevalence, rate, and roles. The *prevalence* measure examines how much of the programming contains violence. If a child is randomly and indiscriminately viewing, then prevalence expresses the probability of his or her seeing violence. *Rate* measures the frequency of violent acts within the programming samples. It says, in effect, that if a child views the total programming sample, then she or he will see eight episodes of violence per hour. Simply put, it is an average number of violent acts per hour, spread across all the programming. *Role* examines the characteristics of those who are committing the violent acts and those who are the victims of those acts. It is here that Gerbner noted a pattern within which aggressors tend to be predominantly Caucasian, male, single, and middle class, whereas victims tend to be predominantly female, ethnic minority, elderly, and poor. Role tabulations provide the basis for Gerbner's (1972) Violent-Victim Ratio.

As the commercial networks unveil their new season's programming, Gerbner's content analysis examines every program entry within the first week's schedule. Using a violence definition of "overt expression of physical force intended to hurt or kill" (Gerbner, 1972, p. 39), the raters independently view and rate each program. Inter-rater reliability computations ensure accuracy and consistency among the ratings. The annual data, computer stored and compared across time, provide a unique longitudinal perspective on commercial television programming violence and violence patterns across time.

Gerbner's work has enabled advocacy groups and the public to target specific violent programs and, at times, to give national advertisers a violence rating based on the level of violence in the programs they sponsored. He finds the level of violence relatively constant across time. It generally runs in 4-year scallops, the overall level of program violence increasing in years following the Nielsen ratings success of a high-violence show (Gerbner, 1988).

Model Building

The model-building approach constructs a model on the basis of existing data and hypotheses. The hypotheses generally project beyond the bounds of the existing data, making assumptions about relationships among variables that are yet to be tested and refined. As specific aspects of the model are tested, a refinement process occurs. What no longer fits or proves relevant will be dropped, and the elements that demonstrate validity will be retained. In this sense, the process is one of model building, testing, and remodeling.

Dorr, Doubleday, Kovaric, and Muthen

Aimee Dorr and her colleagues at the University of California, Los Angeles, have used the model-building approach in testing theoretical explanations of how television affects 7-, 11-, and 15-year-old children. One of these theories, direct socialization, focuses on the amount of television a child views, the parental practices in relation to viewing, and what child behaviors get reinforced. Another theory, cognitive mediation, spotlights a child's understanding of parental practices, television content, and both the credibility and utility of content messages. Still a third theory blends the first two. Translating this approach to television's family-formatted programming, Dorr and her team integrate 20 variables (2 outcome based, 4 television based, 10 child based, and 4 family based) into their model.

In their four-phase research design, they first focus on content analysis within selected family-formatted programming with an eye toward identifying critical measures and assigning them appropriate weightings. Their second phase emphasizes assessment of hypotheses and constructs with a goal of eliminating measures showing no variance. The third phase establishes the final measures to be used in testing the hypotheses, and the fourth phase seeks to arrive at the most parsimonious model that best explains the data (Dorr, Doubleday, Kovaric, & Muthen, 1983).

A model-building approach is sweeping and comprehensive. It incorporates many of the methodologies—in this instance, content analysis and laboratory research—discussed elsewhere in this review. And, as was noted at the outset, testing along the way provides refinement and "remodeling."

Laboratory-Type Experiments

In a laboratory-type experiment, a researcher typically identifies a specific variable and sets up a research design to examine its relevance or impact. An experimental group is exposed to the variable, whereas a control group—matched in every other respect—is not exposed. The measured behavioral or performance difference between the two groups can then be attributed to the variable.

One of the earliest and most influential experiments in childhood aggression modeling was conducted by Bandura, Ross, and Ross (1963). It set the stage for observational learning research to follow. Liebert and Baron's (1972) study was inspired by Bandura et al.'s (1963) design and used many of its key elements.

Liebert and Baron

At Fels Research Institute in Yellow Springs, Ohio, Liebert and Baron (1972) set out to determine whether exposing a child to violent television scenes would increase the viewer's aggressive tendencies toward another child. They selected 136 children (68 boys, 68 girls; 65 5- and 6-year-olds, 71 8- and 9-year-olds). Within gender and age groups, children were randomly assigned to experimental and control groups. Each child individually was taken to a waiting room, where the experimenter asked the child to wait for a few minutes. A television monitor, already turned on in the waiting room, showed either a violent sequence (experimental group children) or a nonviolent active sports sequence (control group children). As the sequence concluded with a commercial buffer, the experimenter returned, indicating she was ready to begin. The child and the experimenter went into the next room and the child was seated before a response box containing a "hurt" button (red), a "help" button (green), and a white light. The child was told that the wires were connected to a game in the next room and that a child playing the game would turn a handle causing the white light to come on. When the white light was on, the "help" and "hurt" buttons were activated and this child must push one of them. Pushing the "help" button would make the handle easier to turn and would help the child in the next room to win the game. Pushing the "hurt" button would make the handle very hot, hurting the child and making it more difficult for him or her to complete and win the game. The child also was told that how long she or he kept the button pushed determined how much she or he helped or hurt the child. At the completion of 20 trials, the experimenter returned, indicating the game was over. Compared with the nonviolent-viewing children, the children who had seen the violent sequence were significantly more likely to "hurt" the "game-playing child" in the next room. (There actually had been no game-playing child in the next room.)

Meta-Analysis

When a variety of research methods and subject pools have been used within a given area of investigation, translating individual research findings into overall trends and central outcomes poses a significant challenge. The meta-analysis technique enables a researcher to gather the entire group of research studies into one statistical analysis designed to "weigh the evidence" and determine the overall significance of these research outcomes. G. Glass first introduced the term *meta-analysis* in 1976, and it has since become a highly accepted tool used in a variety of academic disciplines. The range of uses found within the social sciences includes vote counting, effect size, homogeneity, and psychometrics. Television research use focuses primarily on effect size. Based on the number of subjects within a given study and the range of significance found, an effect size is computed for each individual study. These effect sizes are then fed into the meta-analysis for an overall calculation of significance.

Comstock

George Comstock, an eminent television research authority from Syracuse University, cites meta-analysis as one of the field's most critical tools. In his words, it enables the researcher to go beyond the individual study, weighing the study outcomes as a whole (Comstock, 1980, p. 134). Two of the most comprehensive meta-analyses cited by Comstock have been those of Andison (1977) and Hearold (1979).

Andison

Andison's (1977) analysis covered a 20-year period. The 67 study outcomes were scored and equally weighted. Of the studies, 77%

supported the link between program exposure and aggressiveness, 40% of these either moderately or strongly. Negative or null outcomes were notably few in number (Comstock, 1980).

Hearold

Hearold's (1979) analysis covered an unprecedented 230 studies and more than 100,000 subject participants. She had broadened her scope to include and compare prosocial, neutral, and antisocial portrayals. Both prosocial and antisocial portrayals affect child viewers. The effect is greater for prosocial than for antisocial, and it reaches beyond the age range of young children, dropping off slightly with increasing age and the onset of adolescence. Once again, meta-analysis revealed an important overall trend, one that only the studies in aggregate could produce (Comstock, 1980).

■ Research Tool Issues and Implications

It is tempting to seek to design the ultimate research study—the one that will provide the "final word," the "be all and the end all" in a given field. But even before one puts the finishing strokes on the design, its final-word capabilities already have begun fading in the early morning mist. To its credit, the Surgeon General's Scientific Advisory Committee resisted this temptation and funded diverse study approaches and methodologies. It recognized the strength in diversity.

Diversity and its strength carry inevitable costs. Policymakers find results difficult to interpret, and individuals with a preexisting bias will find their own "results inconclusive" trapdoor in the far corner of the back room. In the best of social science investigations, as in the most rigorous studies on smoking and health, causal links are exceedingly difficult to draw. It is here that the value of meta-analysis truly comes to the fore, providing the literal "weight of the research evidence." Each design makes its own unique contribution to this weight, and, correspondingly, each carries its own set of vulnerabilities. A vulnerability of one design will be a strength of another, providing the net effect of counterbalance.

Surveys

The survey designs cited in this review were massive undertakings requiring major funding. In each instance, the magnitude of the project was enormous. Within that magnitude, the researchers needed to clearly delineate their goals at the outset and, with equal *clarity*, translate those goals into survey and questionnaire clarity. Field testing individual design elements was equally critical. Like a mammoth cannon or rocket, once this survey has been "fired" in its immensity, there is no going back. Whatever ambiguity lay undetected at the outset will come back to haunt the researchers in record response numbers.

Random sampling within the target population is critical. Both surveys cited here exercised great care in sampling. Schramm et al. (1961), for example, surveyed both urban and rural respondents in diverse geographical locations. Their exemplary approach erased the possibility that a midwestern result may differ from an East Coast or West Coast result or that an urban result may differ from a rural result.

Response rate provides a constant realm of concern for the survey researcher. In the cited studies, the response percentages were notably high. Where rates are lower, a researcher must face the possibility that those who responded are qualitatively different in a significant way from those who did not. It is the ghost of biased sampling potential—an unwelcome and troubling guest for survey researchers.

Method of data collection provides another important consideration and challenge. The mailed survey carries the advantage of privacy and confidentiality, but it leaves no room for clarification or following up in greater depth. The personal interview carries clarification and depth potentials, but with them it also carries a hefty price tag in both time and money. Within the interview itself, the verbal and nonverbal expressions also carry the potential for interviewer bias. Response speed, cost, confidentiality, clarification, and depth considerations are among those the survey researcher must consider in selecting a method of data collection. In many of the cited survey instances, data were collected within the classroom, ensuring both clarification potential and high response rate.

Survey *strength* resides in its unique ability to gather extensive data from a large sample of a population. It can be likened to "taking the population's temperature." Carefully crafted at the outset, it is without equal in providing this critical perspective.

Longitudinal Studies

Few methodologies prove more challenging than the longitudinal study. Because it is "slow brewed" across time with no assurance of any significant findings toward its end point, the methodology is reserved only for the professionally tenured and secure. Young researchers cannot afford the professional risk of the longitudinal study. They must look toward methodologies providing rapid outcomes and turnaround times. All too often, this rapid results path provides shallow outcomes and false leads when juxtaposed with the depth of a longitudinal study.

Initial design care becomes every bit as critical as in the survey. Here the weight of time will weigh exceedingly heavily on a researcher who wishes that she or he had included a measurement element at the outset when the researcher later discovers the gap left by that omission. There is no going back. For example, Lefkowitz et al. (1977) did not give an MMPI-type personality test to their 3rd graders. Later, as high school graduates, the subjects took the MMPI, but there was no comparative benchmark for these graduates as 3rd graders. Every researcher knows intimately the poignancy of 20/20 hindsight, and longitudinal studies rank among the least forgiving.

Follow-up proves exceedingly difficult in the longitudinal study. Children and their families do not "stay put" for 10 or 11 years, and the challenge of relocating them becomes major. Relocation successes and failures may contribute to the likelihood of bias. In Lefkowitz et al.'s (1977) valiant efforts through phone books, courthouse records, and such, they relocated twice as many low-aggressive subjects as they did high-aggressive subjects. The follow-up frustration was real, and the relocation difference was striking.

A notable *strength* of the design lies in the fact that each subject is his or her own control. There is assurance that the Jill or Joe tested 10 years ago is the same Jill or Joe now. This assurance lends power to the technique and approach. One is not faced with the possibility that two groups of subjects may not truly be matched or comparable.

Cross-Sectional Studies

What the cross-sectional study gains in time, it loses in assured comparability. By testing different-age children at the same point in time, one gains a panoramic, longitudinal-type perspective at a single point in time. Can we attribute differences found to the differences in age and developmental stage? Or, are there hidden variables and differences beyond our awareness? The questions do not lend themselves to easy answers.

When the cross-sectional study takes on massive cross-cultural proportions and several different research-colleague groupings, as it did in the case of Huesmann and Eron (1986), standardizing data collection procedures across the different cultures becomes a central consideration and challenge. Although Huesmann and Eron noted some procedural variability across research teams, in their instance it did not appear to have a notable effect on outcomes. Profiles across the large majority of countries were strikingly similar.

Cross-sectional *strengths* include time and practicality. The methodological opportunity to see various ages at a single point in time is no small or insignificant advantage.

Laboratory-Type Experiments

The laboratory affords maximum control. Temperature, light, furniture arrangement, procedures, and the experiment's independent and dependent variables all are within the province of the researcher. In all likelihood, there will be no freight trains, ambulances, power mowers, or beehives to factor into the experimental equation. The setting is contained, clean, neat, and tidy. This level of control maximizes the likelihood that any significant differences found within the experimental procedure can be attributed to the independent variable. For reasons of control, clarity, and efficiency, it is a very popular and frequently used research method. Researchers are far more likely to obtain significant results within a laboratory setting than in a field study. It is a case of "the generous lab and the stingy field."

Tidy indeed! But is it realistic? This question points to one of the laboratory's major vulnerabilities—the degree to which it simulates a real-life setting.

Field-Type Experiments

Field-type experiments ensure the reality that the laboratory setting lacks, but this reality carries a sizable loss of control. Bees, critters, and a world of "unexpecteds" await the field study researcher, and these unexpecteds carry with them the question of how much they—and not the variable of research interest—contributed to any research outcome. The "all-natural" carries with it a host of naturally occurring potential variables.

In the purest form of field-type experiment, the natural setting will remain virtually undisturbed. It is the person rushing to a class or the Good Samaritan as she or he passes a homeless person lying along the walkway. It is the dropped letter on the sidewalk that may or may not get mailed. It is the family members watching television in their den where a pre-installed camera intermittently comes on and videotapes family interaction. It is every bit as realistic as it is uncontrolled.

Model Building

There is a certain beauty in building and testing a conceptual model. The process enables a researcher to refine a model's conceptual elements. It is a bit like the skilled artisan—taking off the rough and splintered edges, smoothing and shaping the lines and the flow. Ironically, the point at which the smoothing process hits a major snag becomes as significant as the model itself. The research piece that irascibly protrudes carries an important message, and the "why" of its nonfit becomes as vital as the model itself.

Model building creates a pathway for theory building, and there has been a notable dearth of theories in the present rush-to-publish academic milieu. One must use care to ensure that the protruding or nonfitting pieces are not recklessly chopped or discarded in the name of consistency. They carry an important message.

Meta-Analysis

Meta-analysis comes into this varied array as "the great synthesizer." Critics might call it "the great artificiality," but the procedure itself has been generally accepted as a way in which to bring weighted clarity to the diverse array of methodologies and outcomes found within the television research field.

Irascible Variable X

All researchers, whatever their orientation and methodology, live in constant, uncomfortable awareness that a variable beyond the design may be accounting for differences found. Ronnie Zamora's criminality, for instance, may reach well beyond his television viewing history. The saving grace in this awareness lies in the diversity of methodologies. As researchers, beginning from different methodological starting points, converge on synchronous research outcomes, the likelihood of a common Variable X becomes highly remote indeed—yet another strength in diversity.

■ Field of Dreams, World of Realities

In a researcher's fondest dreams, the ultimate or penultimate study magically comes to center stage just before the final curtain. It is beautiful, spacious, and hallowed, much like a pedestaled deity. It answers every critic. It calms every misgiving. All effects and outcomes are clear and clearly labeled.

The dream carries a seductive beauty, but it cannot carry the reality of science and scientific inquiry, for in the latter one finds the sprawling acreage in which our predecessors began their research plowing. Its many slopes and angles tapped many tools and plow sizes. The acreage has needed them all and will continue to need all their flexibility and diversity well into the future.

Fresh eyes and voices note that mass communication researchers have generally overlooked or ignored computer-mediated communication and the Internet in favor of more traditional broadcast and print media (Morris & Ogan, 1996; Newhagen & Rafaeli, 1996). Whether existing tools will fit these upcoming slopes or new tools will be fashioned remains to be seen. A sprawling new acreage and challenge lies before us.

■ References

Andison, F. S. (1977). TV violence and viewer aggression: A cumulation of study results 1956-1976. *Public Opinion Quarterly, 41*, 314-331.

Bailyn, L. (1959). Mass media and children: A study of exposure habits and cognitive effects. *Psychological Monographs, 73*, 1-48.

Bandura, A. (1965). Influence of models' reinforcement contingencies on the acquisition of imitative responses. *Journal of Personality and Social Psychology, 1*, 589-595.

Bandura, A., Ross, D., & Ross, S. A. (1963). Imitation of film-mediated aggressive models. *Journal of Abnormal and Social Psychology, 66*, 3-11.

Berkowitz, L., & Alioto, J. T. (1973). The meaning of an observed event as a determinant of its aggressive consequences. *Journal of Personality and Social Psychology, 28*, 206-217.

Comstock, G. (1980). New emphases in research on the effects of television and film violence. In E. Palmer & A. Dorr, eds., *Children and the faces of television: Teaching, violence, selling* (pp. 129-148). New York: Academic Press.

Corsini, R. J. (Ed.). (1987). *Concise encyclopedia of psychology*. New York: John Wiley.

Dorr, A., Doubleday, C., Kovaric, P., & Muthen, B. (1983). *Project overview*. Unpublished manuscript, Graduate School of Education and Information Studies, University of California, Los Angeles.

Eron, L. D. (1963). The relationship of TV viewing habits and aggressive behavior in children. *Journal of Abnormal and Social Psychology, 67*, 193-196.

Feshbach, S., & Singer, R. D. (1971). *Television and aggression*. San Francisco: Jossey-Bass.

Gerbner, G. (1972). Violence and television drama: Trends and symbolic functions. In G. A. Comstock & E. A. Rubinstein (Eds.), *Television and social behavior*, Vol. 1: *Media content and control* (pp. 28-187). Rockville, MD: National Institute of Mental Health.

Gerbner, G. (1988). *The politics of media violence: Some reflections*. Unpublished manuscript, Annenberg School of Communication, University of Pennsylvania.

Hearold, S. L. (1979). *Meta-analysis of the effects of television on social behavior*. Unpublished dissertation, University of Colorado.

Himmelweit, H., Oppenheim, A. N., & Vince, P. (1958). *Television and the child*. London: Oxford University Press.

Huesmann, L. R. (1996, March). Invited address presented at annual meeting of Southeastern Psychological Association, Norfolk, VA.

Huesmann, L. R., & Eron, L. D. (Eds.). (1986). *Television and the aggressive child: A cross-national comparison*. Hillsdale, NJ: Lawrence Erlbaum.

Huesmann, L. R., Eron, L. D., Lefkowitz, M. M., & Walder, L. O. (1984). The stability of aggression over time and generations. *Developmental Psychology, 20*, 1120-1134.

Lefkowitz, M. M., Eron, L. D., Walder, L. O., & Huesmann, L. R. (1972). Television violence and child aggression: A follow-up study. In G. A. Comstock & E. A. Rubinstein (Eds.), *Television and social behavior*, Vol. 3: *Television and adolescent aggressiveness* (pp. 35-135). Rockville, MD: National Institute of Mental Health.

Lefkowitz, M. M., Eron, L. D., Walder, L. O., & Huesmann, L. R. (1977). *Growing up to be violent*. New York: Pergamon.

Liebert, R. M., & Baron, R. A. (1972). Short-term effects of televised aggression on children's aggressive behavior. In J. P. Murray, E. A. Rubinstein, & G. A. Comstock (Eds.), *Television and social behavior*, Vol. 2: *Television and social learning* (pp. 189-201). Rockville, MD: National Institute of Mental Health.

McLuhan, M. (1967). *The medium is the massage*. New York: Random House.

Milavsky, J. R., & Pekowsky, B. (1973). *Exposure to TV "violence" and aggressive behavior in boys, examined as process: A status report of a longitudinal study*. Unpublished manuscript, Department of Social Research, National Broadcasting Company.

Morris, C. R. (1984). *A time of passion*. New York: Harper & Row.

Morris, M., & Ogan, C. (1996). The Internet as mass medium. *Journal of Communication, 46*, 39-50.

Newhagen, J. E., & Rafaeli, S. (1996). Why communication researchers should study the Internet: A dialogue. *Journal of Communication, 46*, 4-13.

Parker, R., & Nelson, D. (1983). *Day-by-day: The sixties*. New York: Facts on File.

Schramm, W., Lyle, J., & Parker, E. B. (1961). *Television in the lives of our children*. Stanford, CA: Stanford University Press.

U.S. Senate, Judiciary Committee. (1965). *Hearings on juvenile delinquency*, Part 16: *Effects on young people of violence and crime portrayed on television* (88th Congress, 2nd session, July 30, 1964). Washington, DC: Government Printing Office.

2

Designing Experiments on Television and Social Behavior

Developmental Perspectives

L. Monique Ward ■ Patricia M. Greenfield

In pairs or small groups, the participants enter the laboratory and are presented with an intriguing cover story about what will follow. They are then randomly assigned to one of the following three television viewing conditions: (a) watching clips of Content X (e.g., antisocial behavior, stereotypical gender roles), (b) watching clips of Content Not X, or (c) watching no television at all. The stimuli have been carefully selected or created by the experimenter to represent the images or messages in question. Before and after viewing the clips, participants complete survey measures that include questions about their attitudes toward Content X. These data can then be compared across the three conditions to determine how people respond to different content and whether viewing the stimuli somehow affects their attitudes. Participants may not even realize that their responses had changed, thereby demonstrating that television's content has the power to influence on an unconscious level. Using this type of experimental design, an exciting and informative body of research has been produced concerning television's link to our social attitudes and behaviors.

However, television is more than just a stimulus to which people unconsciously respond. For many people, television is a rich and intricate part of the social fabric of their everyday lives. They retell jokes and stories seen on television. They incorporate television characters into their dreams and fantasies. They buy the mugs, T-shirts, and fan magazines associated with the programs. Viewers memorize dialogue from popular series, which then becomes a part of the lexicon of popular culture (e.g., "to the moon, Alice," "sit on it," "wild and crazy guys," "master of my domain"). They hum the theme songs, test each other with trivia, and debate controversial content presented. Young children act out scenes from programs and news events, pretending to be televised characters and people. To many, television serves as friend, teacher, and adviser. A recent survey by the Los Angeles district attorney's Gang Prevention Unit showed television to be the second most influential factor in adolescent decision making, ahead of parents, school, and church (Hanania, 1996). Thus, there is a richness in our interactions with television that much of traditional experimental research and traditional research methodology does not capture.

In this chapter, we review and discuss experimental designs used in research studying connections between television and viewers' social attitudes and behavior. We attempt to address both what is and what could be in the domain of experimental television research methodology. Our emphasis is on both developmental research and entertainment television, with little focus on older adults, television news, or information programming. We do not attempt to critique every experimental study ever published; instead, we focus on the general nature, strengths, and limitations of this type of research methodology. In our review of existing studies, we have chosen to focus on those that present televised stimuli of some type to participants, either in a social science laboratory or in their classrooms, and do not cover correlational or survey methods. However, in the discussion that follows, we point out the connections between different types of research designs and different theories concerning the mechanisms of television's influence. We also describe some particularly innovative lines of research and offer suggestions for new experimental methods and issues for future research.

■ General Issues

Several criticisms have been levied against the use of experimental design to examine the impact of television on social attitudes and behaviors (e.g., Cook, Kendziersky, & Thomas, 1983; Freedman, 1984; Gross & Jeffries-Fox, 1978; Stipp & Milavsky, 1988), mostly in the area of television violence and aggressiveness. A frequent concern with experimental design is the low external validity of both the stimuli used and the dependent variables tested. In many experiments, the stimuli are (a) created by the experimenters (potentially to maximize effects), (b) shown in isolation from other types of content (via the viewing of one selected clip), and (c) followed by an attitudinal or behavioral measure that is removed from real social cues, constraints, and concerns. Researchers have, therefore, questioned the ability of these techniques to assess long-term, real-world effects. A second concern raised is the potential bias resulting from the demand characteristics of the tasks. Laboratory experiments often involve an artificial setting in which viewers are instructed to attend to particular television content, thereby potentially enhancing its importance and validity. A final concern is that the laboratory viewing experience is too bare and excludes potentially influential aspects of viewing such as choosing the programs and discussing content with co-viewers. Thus, given the complexity of television content and of the viewing experience, it may seem as if the use of experimental designs in television research is inappropriate and inadequate.

However, experimental design has its own particular strengths. Indeed, because of its high internal validity, it often is a more precise way of answering effects questions than is field research. It is *because* laboratory experiments randomly assign subjects to treatments and deliberately manipulate independent variables that they permit researchers to make causal inferences and can ensure that the differences between groups are not a function of other unmeasured variables (Friedrich-Cofer & Huston, 1986). With this greater control and precision, experimental design may be especially well suited to address specific research questions, for example, those concerning the differential impact of specific television features or genres, the sex or race of the characters, or the priming effects of certain materials.

Indeed, a unique feature of experimental television research is that experimenters *can* make their own video stimuli, both animated and live action. With this option, experimenters can dictate the exact content of the dialogue as well as the presentation, look, and behaviors of all characters, allowing any variable to be manipulated. For example, it is only with this device that researchers could demonstrate that viewers evaluate identical content differently based on the sex of the actor (e.g., Durkin, 1985a; Ruble, Balaban, & Cooper, 1981). By making one's own video stimuli, the independent variables can be much more precise than would be possible with naturalistic television stimuli.

In addition, there are several new strategies that experimental researchers could employ to improve external validity. For example, stimuli could be selected from among the population's most preferred programs, thereby increasing the likelihood that the material would have been viewed outside the laboratory. To better approximate actual programming, a mixed selection of material could be presented that contains the stimuli in question as well as irrelevant materials and television commercials. These are but a couple of several possible approaches to improving external validity; more are presented later in this chapter.

Therefore, although experiments have some limitations, they can, if designed with care, offer a level of control and address specific questions and issues of causality better than can other methods. Consequently, our recommendation would be for the research enterprise as a whole to use experimental studies in conjunction with field and survey research, using each method to answer different but complementary questions. An experimental design can answer questions concerning the potential effects of a television stimulus in isolation. It can test some causal mechanisms suggested by field research or by other methodologies. A field study can report how often and in what contexts television stimuli similar to the experimental stimulus are actually viewed. Field methods can be used to assess the effects of a whole television diet or to examine behavioral reactions experienced during home viewing. Survey methods also can be used to identify the most commonly viewed programs, which can then be used as experimental stimuli in the laboratory. By using both experimental and nonexperimental formats as complements, the strength and validity of both formats can be improved.

▪ Existing Research: The Case of Research on Gender Roles

In this section, we move from theoretical issues concerning experimental methodology for television research to a consideration of what methods have actually been used. The range and depth of existing experimental research on television varies greatly by topic area. The television violence research has the greatest range and depth, with several meta-analyses and review pieces summarizing the hundreds of studies of all types (e.g., Andison, 1977; Comstock, 1991; Hearold, 1986; Paik & Comstock, 1994; Wood, Wong, & Chachere, 1991). In this topic domain, researchers have examined the differential impact of violent images based on variations in the viewer (e.g., prison inmates, preschoolers, adolescents, abused children, mentally retarded children, children in different countries), the stimuli (e.g., real vs. fictional violence, justified vs. unjustified aggression, harmful vs. harmless violence), and the dependent variables measured (e.g., physical aggression, rule breaking, verbal aggression, approval of aggression). By contrast, other content areas, such as race and sexuality, have been sparsely researched via experimental designs. Still other areas, such as television's impact on gender role norms, have received considerable experimental attention, albeit less than violence. Researchers interested in these social behaviors and topic domains can look to the violence literature and use the same techniques to study gender, race, sex, and other social topics.

To explore more closely the strengths and limitations of existing experimental paradigms, we offer an in-depth analysis of the methodology used to examine one particular issue: the impact of television's gender role portrayals on viewers. We have chosen to focus more closely on this area for three reasons. First, outside of experiments on violence, this probably is the topic domain with the largest core of experiments to discuss; thus, good models of experimental methodology already exist. Second, there remains much more to be done at the same time. Research in this area has petered out somewhat, with much of the work having been done from the late 1970s to the mid-1980s. This decline enables us to offer a broad range of suggestions for the use of experimental methods in future research. Third, a particularly innovative line of research has begun recently (e.g., Hansen & Hansen, 1988) that provides an excellent model for how future experiments can be conducted. Thus, we use research on television and gender roles both to illustrate certain types of experimental research methods and to point out methodological gaps and potential sites for further research.

A review of 26 experimental studies summarized in Table 2.1 revealed that research typically followed one of four experimental formats, with formats differing based on the theoretical questions and mechanisms of effects proposed. In the first and probably most obvious format, experimenters present different stimuli to the experimental groups, often with one group viewing stereotypical content and another group viewing counterstereotypical or neutral content (e.g., Carder, 1996; Davidson, Yasuna, & Tower, 1979; O'Bryant & Corder-Bolz, 1978; Pingree, 1978; Tan, 1979). These studies generally include either postviewing or pre- and postviewing measures of participants' attitudes or preferences concerning activities, occupations, and traits appropriate for males and females. Viewers' gender-related behavior is seldom the focus (but see McArthur & Eisen, 1976, for an exception). Generally, the question of interest here is whether watching stereotypical material on television will lead viewers to be more stereotyped in their attitudes or whether watching counterstereotypical material will lead them to be more open and accepting. The stimuli are commonly laboratory produced with a focus on who (what gender) is performing which job, role, or activity.

In a second experimental format, the focus is on whether gender will become linked with a neutral action or toy depending on the sex of the person modeling it (Cobb, Stevens-Long, & Goldstein, 1982; Ruble et al., 1981). Thus, the two groups of participants view similar content, but with different actors performing the activity. Postviewing measures of play with the toys modeled is then assessed. Here, the material must be laboratory produced to equate all factors except gender. At the same time, focusing on viewers' actual postviewing

(text continued on p. 76)

TABLE 2.1 Summary of Research Experiments Examining the Impact of Television's Gender Role Portrayals

Authors	Year	Ages or Grades	Conditions/ Design	Stimuli Form	Stimuli Origin	Dependent Variables
Type 1 Flerx et al.	1976	5 years	T vs. NT (books) vs. NT (films)	Short films	Professionally produced	Stereotyping of traits, activities, roles
McArthur & Eisen	1976	2 years 11 months to 5 years 6 months	Toy play: T vs. NT	9-minute clips	Laboratory produced	Play behavior, recall, preferences
Pingree	1978	3rd and 8th graders	T vs. NT (also three types of instructions)	Commercials	Network	Attitudes toward F, perceived reality
O'Bryant & Corder-Bolz	1978	5 to 10 years	F jobs: T vs. NT	Commercials	Network and laboratory	Job knowledge, preferences, stereotyping
Cordua et al.	1979	5 years 0 months to 6 years 8 months	M vs. F in job	Short films	Laboratory produced	Recall
Davidson et al.	1979	F 5 to 6 years	T vs. N vs. NT	Cartoons	Network	Trait stereotypes
Tan	1979	F 16 to 18 years	T (beauty) vs. N	Commercials	Network	Conceptions of social reality, liking, recall
Tan et al.	1980	3rd to 5th graders	M vs. F in job	Newscasts	Laboratory produced	Retention, believability

(continued)

■ 73

TABLE 2.1 Continued

Authors	Year	Ages or Grades	Conditions/Design	Stimuli Form	Stimuli Origin	Dependent Variables
Durkin & Hutchins	1984	12 to 13 years	NT vs. NT explicit vs. T vs. none	Clips of chats	Laboratory produced	Career aspirations and stereotyping
Waite	1987	5th and 9th graders, UG	Sexist vs. N vs. nonsexist	Music videos	Network	Gender role orientation, attitudes toward F
Jeffrey & Durkin	1989	1st, 4th, 6th, and 9th graders	NT_1 (high power) vs. NT_2 (low power)	9-minute clips	Laboratory produced	Interest, typicality, reasons
Carder	1996	F adults	N vs. stereotyped	Commercials	Network	Attitudes about stereotyping
Type 2 Ruble et al.	1981	3 years 8 months to 6 years 5 months	Modeling F vs. M	Commercial	Laboratory produced	Toy play, liking, recall
Cobb et al.	1982	4 to 6 years	Modeling F vs. M	Muppet clips	Laboratory produced	Toy play
Type 3 Cheles	1974	4th and 5th graders	Perceptions of roles	Commercials	Network	Stereotype acceptance, recall, television attitudes, others
Williams et al.	1981	4th to 6th graders	Perceptions of NT	30-minute dramas	Network	Liking, identification, job stereotypes, activity interests, others

List et al.	1983	3rd graders	Recall of T and NT	18-minute clips	Network	Sex Role Learning Index, content recognition
Eisenstock	1984	4th to 6th graders	Perceptions of NT	30-minute dramas	Network	Identification, activity and trait preferences
Dambrot et al.	1988	UG	Perceptions of characters	2-minute scene	Network	Personality Attributes Questionnaire (self, M character, F character)
Reep & Dambrot	1988	UG	Perceptions of characters	2-minute scene	Network	PAQ, character rating
Melville & Cornish	1993	UG	Perceptions of roles	Commercials	Network	Varied ratings, conservatism
Toney & Weaver	1994	UG	Perceptions of three types	Music videos	Network	Bem Sex Role Inventory, ratings for self and peers
Type 4						
Jennings et al.	1980	UG	Prime: T vs. NT	Commercials	Laboratory produced	Independence and confidence
Hansen & Hansen	1988	UG	Prime: T vs. NT	Music videos	Network	Views of M-F interaction
Hansen	1989	UG	Prime: T_1, T_2, N	Music videos	Network	Likability of M and F characters, recall, trait impressions
Hansen & Krygowski	1994	UG	Prime: T_1, T_2	Music videos, commercials	Network	Ratings of commercials

NOTE: T = traditional; NT = nontraditional; N = neutral (stimulus); F = female; M = male; UG = undergraduates.

behavior draws a stronger link between the laboratory and potential responses in the real world.

A third format focuses on factors that affect viewers' perceptions of the same televised content (e.g., Eisenstock, 1984; List, Collins, & Westby, 1983; Melville & Cornish, 1993; Reep & Dambrot, 1988). All participants typically view the same stimuli, whether they be commercials, music videos, or clips from television dramas, and then complete evaluations of the characters or the general material. Here, the material, which almost always is drawn from broadcast programming, is less of a focus than is the mind of the participant. The researchers typically are most interested in which aspects of the viewer (e.g., gender role orientation, level of stereotyping), or of the characters or scenarios depicted, will lead to variations in perceptions of the content.

The final experimental format focuses on the role that television content plays in priming viewers' subsequent impressions (Hansen, 1989; Hansen & Hansen, 1988; Hansen & Krygowski, 1994) and actions (Jennings, Geis, & Brown, 1980). This line of work differs from the others in the mechanism of effects proposed. It is not concerned with whether behavioral imitation or cultivation of gender role attitudes will result from viewing; instead, these studies test whether viewing stereotyped content primes viewers' existing gender schemas, which then color how they evaluate and conduct subsequent interactions. These experimental approaches are powerful because they emphasize a new mechanism for a direct link between what viewers see and what they do next, thereby attaining a high degree of external validity. We present two examples below.

In their 1988 experiment, Hansen and Hansen examined whether viewing stereotypical depictions of males and females would prime sex role stereotypical schemas, which, in turn, might color viewers' interpretations of subsequently observed male and female interactions. In the first portion of this experiment, participants viewed either neutral music videos or stereotypical music videos in which females were portrayed as pawns and sexual objects. All participants then viewed a videotaped interaction of a male and a female interviewing for positions as video jockeys. In the videotape, the male made sexual advances to the female, who either reciprocated or did not. After viewing this interaction, participants rated the characters on several dimensions. Results indicated that the music video was effective as a prime. When sex role stereotypical schemas were primed by the stereotypical music video, the female was judged according to whether she adhered to or did not adhere to the standard gender role script; this occurred significantly less in response to the neutral music video. The priming effect also extended to perceptions of the man's behavior; after viewing the stereotypical music video, stereotypical gender role behavior from the male was seen as more acceptable than it was after the neutral video.

In their 1980 experiment, Jennings et al. examined whether viewing traditional or nontraditional images of femininity might affect women's subsequent self-confidence and independence. In the first portion of the experiment, participants viewed either four commercials with males and females in traditional domestic roles or four commercials with the roles reversed (e.g., a man serving dinner to a woman). After completing ratings of the commercials (a procedure intended to increase the salience of their content), the women participated in two tasks individually. In one task, they were asked to rate the funniness of each of 16 cartoons on a scale of 1 to 7. A mean rating for each cartoon was posted on the board, and the women were told that their scores would be added in with the mean. Because the posted means for 6 of the cartoons were purposely misrepresented, experimenters could determine the extent to which participants' own ratings reflected the true mean (and therefore represented independent judgments) or reflected the false mean posted. For the second task, participants were asked to give a 4-minute extemporaneous speech before two judges, who subsequently rated the women's nonverbal behavior for signs of confidence and tentativeness. Results indicated that females who saw the four counterstereotypical commercials exhibited greater independence of judgment and more self-confidence than did women who viewed the stereotypical commercials. Thus, in both of these studies, the viewing of particular content affected viewers' subsequent impressions and/or behaviors in a conceptually related arena.

In these experiments, the intervening process of schema activation is not tested directly; instead, a relationship between the external schemas and subsequent behaviors is demonstrated. However, because the televised stimuli and the resultant behavior are similar on a conceptual rather than a concrete level, an abstract process such as schema activation more appropriately explains the results. Priming studies demonstrate a mechanism of television influence that assumes more sophisticated mechanisms of human learning and thinking than do studies based on the relatively simple mechanism of replication of a model. (Note that replication as a mechanism covers the replication of worldview as well as the imitation of behavior.) Even in cultivation theory (Gerbner, Gross, Morgan, & Signorielli, 1986), the subject simply replicates or "imitates" the worldview that is presented on television). Because these studies introduce more abstract and complex cognitive processes, the priming concept contributes a valuable addition to experimental methodology on television and social behavior.

The research questions and experimental designs discussed here offer critical information concerning television's role in shaping viewers' gender role attitudes and behaviors. These types of experimental design demonstrate well that even brief exposure to a particular content can have immediate short-term effects on viewers' attitudes, subsequent behaviors, and impressions. Particularly with the addition of the priming studies, the range of psychological mechanisms by which television exerts its social influence is expanded to include more complex and abstract human cognitive processes. Each of the four types of experimental designs can be used to research areas of social behavior beyond the topic of gender.

■ Methodological Gaps

Yet, within this research on television and gender roles, several dimensions and populations remain unstudied, thereby limiting the scope of the field. In many cases, new studies can address these limitations by making small alterations in the experimental designs currently in place. In others, more extensive thought and planning are required. In this section, we describe seven methodological gaps in the current field of experimental research on television and gender roles and discuss how these gaps can be filled. Although our critiques and suggestions are based on the gender role research reviewed earlier, they apply to other topics as well. Because the topic of televised violence has stimulated a more varied pool of methods, some of our suggestions already have been used in relation to television violence (for a review, see Hearold, 1986). (Note that the first two gaps are related in that both concern the ecological validity of the stimuli presented.)

Gap 1: Use of Popular Network Programs as Stimuli

First, apart from the commercials and music videos selected as stimuli, gender role research seldom uses popular television programming. Although situation comedies, dramas, and soap operas are among the most heavily watched formats, they seldom are used as stimuli (see Stipp & Milavsky, 1988, for a similar critique of the violence literature). Even the dramas selected in the few studies that used them (e.g., Eisenstock, 1984; Williams, LaRose, & Frost, 1981) were from a short-lived program aired on PBS. Therefore, more work is needed in which popular network programs are used as stimuli. In many cases, the stimuli were created in the laboratory, which, as stated earlier, is an excellent way in which to control and manipulate the content. However, for cases in which nontraditional images were needed, there is the additional concern of how well viewers will tolerate some of the counterstereotypical portrayals created (Durkin, 1985b). If the portrayals differ too much from an everyday viewing diet, will subjects assimilate them? In these cases, additional testing of specific stimuli may be needed.

Gap 2: Use of Programs Chosen by the Viewer as Stimuli

A second limitation is that, in all cases, participants viewed and responded to material that had been selected by the experimenter to represent a certain content area. However, it is not known whether viewers would actually be exposed to such content on their own or would choose to focus on the particular material presented. Although the experimenters' decision is understandable, it omits potential contributions that viewing familiar and likable characters may make on viewers' responses. In real life, research has shown that liked and admired people are more potent role models. Insofar as television characters and personalities are an extension of the real-life social environment (Meyrowitz, 1985), this principle might hold for television as well. Indeed, preliminary evidence suggests that liking and familiarity do influence viewers' perceptions (e.g., Brown & Schulze, 1993). For example, Miller and Reeves (1976) found that 3rd and 6th graders who were familiar with female television characters with nontraditional occupations were more accepting of girls' aspiring to them. Consequently, given that viewers of all ages have favorite characters and programs and often make deliberate viewing choices, how does character or even genre familiarity affect the richness of their interpretations and the social impact of the shows? For example, are viewers less likely to scrutinize and criticize actions in familiar programs and commercials, and are they perhaps more affected by them? Direct experimental testing of these questions would provide both substantive data and useful information about the ecological validity of many experimental formats.

How might these issues of choice, liking, and familiarity be addressed experimentally? One approach would be to use liking as an independent variable in a two-factor analysis of variance. Suppose, for example, that one were interested in exploring the effects on adolescent viewers of stereotypes about men's and women's ability to nurture. One might first select a set of eight clips from situation comedies of varying popularity among adolescents. In half of these clips, the female would be depicted as the nurturant one (the traditional image); in the other half, the male would be the nurturant one (a nontraditional image). During testing sessions, experimenters would first ask participants to rank the programs from which the stimuli had been selected to determine the most and least favored for each participant. These rankings would then be used to assign program stimuli to participants using a 2 × 2 design in which liking is crossed with traditionality. Thus, Group 1 would see four clips depicting traditional images of nurturers from their more favored shows. Group 2 would see four clips depicting traditional images of nurturers from their least favored shows. In the same way, Groups 3 and 4 would see clips depicting nontraditional images of nurturers from their more favored and least favored programs, respectively. Actual stimuli would vary from person to person in the same experimental group; what would be held constant would be the participants' evaluations of the stimuli. This is a version of the "individualized experiment" (Greenfield & Zukow, 1978). As possible dependent variables, participants could complete pre- and posttest measures assessing their attitudes on males and females as parents. Participants also could rate their willingness to hire male and female applicants as baby-sitters. With this design, the results would illustrate the effects of traditional images, the effects of liking, and any interaction between the two factors.

Gap 3: The Impact of Genre, Format, or Formal Features

A third methodological gap concerns the impact of the genre, format, or formal features of the televised material. For most television experiments concerning social behavior, the focus is on the content, with the stimuli selected all representing one particular program format (e.g., commercials, music videos). Yet, it also would be interesting to know whether the format, genre, or presentation style matters. Is stereotypical content more or less influential when it is part of a drama, situation comedy, cartoon, commercial, or music video? Is using a low camera angle to make a character appear more dominant equally effective for both males and females? Is a nontraditional female character selling auto parts in a commercial less likely to open viewers' minds than a nontraditional female doing the same in a drama? Studies involving material from two or more genres have been conducted in the violence literature (e.g., Atkin, 1983; Noble, 1973), often comparing fictional violence and realistic violence. We suggest that this type of research be extended to other areas and to all genres.

Gap 4: Developmental Research

A fourth gap in the field concerns developmental research. Few studies test a wide range of ages, with most studies focusing on a specific age group (but see Jeffrey & Durkin, 1989, and Waite, 1987, for exceptions). At the same time, the participants selected most often are grade schoolers (K-6) or undergraduates, with little attention given to adolescents (ages 12-17 years). Consequently, it is difficult to outline developmental trends or to know how specific stimuli affect viewers at different ages. Indeed, there may be particular developmental periods during which viewers are especially vulnerable to stereotypical or counterstereotypical portrayals (Durkin, 1985b). Individual critical periods that have been suggested include pre- and postgender constancy (Ruble et al., 1981) and adolescence (Tan, 1979). Thus, experiments testing children and adults of varied ages would provide valuable information on these issues.

Gap 5: The Impact of Misrepresentation Versus Underrepresentation

A fifth gap concerns knowledge about the contrasting impact of underrepresentation versus misrepresentation of people in various social categories. Many of the existing paradigms that study television's representation of particular groups focus on the influence of stereotypical versus nonstereotypical portrayals. However, content analyses across several decades (e.g., Comstock, 1991; Greenberg & Brand, 1994; Signorielli, 1989, 1993) indicate that certain groups (e.g., minority groups, the elderly, women in certain genres) not only are misrepresented (portrayed stereotypically) but also typically are underrepresented in relation to their numbers in the real world. For example, Huston and Wright (in press) summarize data indicating that from 1967 through 1985 the proportion of female characters increased from one fourth in the 1960s to about one third in the 1980s, with the proportion reaching only one fourth to one fifth for children's entertainment programming. Experiments would be an excellent tool for exploring the differential impacts of misrepresentation and underrepresentation on viewers' perceptions of the target group. Given the already demonstrated effects of positive versus negative or stereotypical portrayals, the main question here would be as follows: Are group members perceived as less important, competent, or powerful when they are minimally represented on television or when they are present yet depicted negatively or stereotypically?

A possible way in which to test this issue experimentally would involve a pretest-posttest design with four experimental groups and one control group. For example, if one were concerned about portrayals of the elderly as incompetent, one would have Experimental Group 1 view clips from television commercials (or situation comedies, soap operas, etc.) in which elderly characters are portrayed negatively—as feeble, indecisive, and/or senile. Experimental Group 2 would see clips of a similar format and content but in which elderly characters are presented positively—as capable, helpful, and/or intelligent. Experimental Group 3 would see clips of a similar format and content in which the elderly are presented in only one or two neutral roles. Experimental Group 4 would view clips of a similar format and content but with no elderly characters. The control group would view no television. This design would allow the comparison of positive (counterstereotypical) portrayals, negative (stereotypical) portrayals, peripheralized portrayals, omission, and baseline (no television).

The specific pre- and posttest dependent variables could vary considerably. Perhaps the focus could be on viewers' general attitudes toward the elderly, with both in-group (i.e., the elderly) and out-group members participating. Care would need to be taken here to reduce social desirability biases. This could possibly be done by including questions on different topics or by presenting an elaborate cover story concerning the purposes of viewing the clips (e.g., to rate the effectiveness of particular actors or products).

Another approach would be to assess priming effects. Participants could, for example, rate their willingness to hire job candidates of varying ages for a fictitious temporary position. The same applications and cover letters could be accompanied by pictures of different candidates. Another option would be for participants to interact directly with elderly confederates in a problem-solving task. How does watching negative clips of that group prime viewers' subsequent attitudes and behaviors? With each of these options, researchers could compare differences in viewers' attitudes toward or behavior with the elderly based on the type of television exposure they had received.

Gap 6: The Role of Individual Interpretations

A sixth methodological gap concerns the nature and impact of viewers' individual perceptions of the stimuli presented. As noted earlier, many of the experimental studies examined focused on cultivation and imitation as the mechanisms of effects, assuming that viewers would adopt the attitudes or imitate the behaviors in the content presented. However, because a segment's impact is likely to vary based on viewers' interpretations of it, research also needs to consider the role of viewers' individual perceptions. Indeed, a growing body of research indicates great variation in viewers' interpretations of even the most obvious actions or behaviors. For example, in their examination of undergraduates' interpretations of two music videos by Madonna, Brown and Schulze (1993) reported that perceptions varied greatly and that even this relatively homogeneous set of viewers "didn't all agree about even the most fundamental story elements" (p. 269). Further evidence comes from a study of undergraduates' perceptions of male–female interactions in four clips from situation comedies (Ward & Eschwege, 1996). Here, no more than 40% of the participants agreed that any one of the five themes presented was the dominant message of the scene viewed. Thus, given the complextity of actual network content, it should be expected that individual viewers often would see the same material differently and that the effects of this content would vary based on these interpretations (see Gunter, 1988, for a discussion on viewers' perceptions of television violence).

Even if viewers did interpret a given material in the same way, some might choose to accept the messages inferred whereas others might be offended by or even reject them. Content is likely to be interpreted in a way that reinforces one's existing views and perspectives. For example, Carder (1996) reported that adult females who viewed sex stereotyped (vs. neutral) commercials became *more* offended by sex role stereotyping after viewing them. Similarly, Ward and Wyatt (1994) reported that even when particular characters were seen to represent specific messages (e.g., Lucy as a smart, manipulative female), some chose to emulate and embrace such portrayals whereas others rejected them.

Consequently, more work is needed that takes a constructivist approach to television's role, one that focuses on individual interpretations as the dependent variables. Given that the construction of meaning is central to human culture and behavior, methods need to be developed that allow subjects to tell researchers what meanings particular television materials have for them. As reported earlier in Table 2.1, some studies have examined viewers' perceptions of specific content and have explored how these views relate to various demographic or developmental factors (e.g., level of gender constancy). To expand these paradigms further, new studies could explore additional factors affecting viewers' perceptions including their personal experiences in related areas, their motivations for watching particular programs, and their perceived realism of specific content.

Moreover, because differential interpretations are likely to mediate other effects, researchers can use subjects' interpretations as mediating variables to explore their impact on related social attitudes and behaviors. For example, will stereotyped material have a greater impact if viewers interpret the behavior of the characters as justifiable? To test this issue, one might develop or obtain a set of clips in which the male character is domineering and aggressive whereas the female is passive and meek but in which their motives for being this way are ambiguous. These clips could then be presented to viewers, who would be asked to evaluate the behavior of each male and female character and to rate how appropriate or justifiable their actions were. Participants could then be involved in a group task with a pushy or submissive confederate male and could offer reactions to this group member once the task is complete. Data could then be analyzed to determine whether the impresssions or subsequent behaviors of participants who saw the behavior of the television males as sexist *and* inappropriate differed from those who saw him as sexist yet appropriate or justified. Would viewers who accepted the behavior of a sexist male on television be more likely to put up with a pushy male in the real world? Could such a clip make viewers more tolerant of sexism in the real world? How would viewers respond if they read the behavior of the television male as nonsexist and inappropriate? In using the interpretive variables as independent variables, this type of design would make excellent contributions to all areas of research on television and social behavior.

From a different angle, another approach to investigating television's meaning to individuals would be to use television viewing itself as a dependent variable. What is watched, and why is it watched, under specific experimental circumstances? The class of research designs used to test this issue would be analagous to those used in experimental social psychology. Some type of social action or behavior would serve as the independent variable in this experiment, for example, witnessing a sexist or racist encounter, experiencing an assault to one's self-esteem, or being the recipient of an altruistic social move. Each participant would then be given the choice of several activities, of which at least one would be watching television. Whether the participant chooses television and, if so, what type of show is chosen under these circumstances would be the major dependent variables of interest. An alternative or complementary study would be to assign activities to participants after they had experienced particular social stimuli and then to assess how their reactions and feelings vary when different activities or types of television shows are used in these different socioemotional contexts. This type of experimental design investigates questions of interest in the uses and gratification framework—how and when people use television and what psychosocial functions it fulfills.

Gap 7: Multimedia Research

A final methodological gap is the testing of the effects of television content that is presented in multiple media. Although almost all research on television addresses the medium in isolation, television is part of an interlinked multimedia environment that includes supersystems built around the same characters and stories (Kinder, 1991). Not only can viewers see their favorite characters on television, they can buy the T-shirts, play the video games, read the comic books, and see the films in which the characters appear. What impact do these supersystems have on consumer behavior or on viewers' social interactions? Do viewers believe and identify more with characters they have encountered in several media? Do they see them as more realistic or like themselves? Whereas the only published study provides a model for examining the interactive effects of interlinked pairs of media such as toys and television (Greenfield et al., 1990), there is a total gap in methods for studying more complex systems consisting of more than two media. New methods for dealing with these social questions in the much more complex environment of the supersystem are needed.

■ Extending the Priming Paradigm: One Innovative Approach for Bridging Research Gaps

As noted earlier, some studies (e.g., Hansen & Hansen, 1988) have begun to focus on television's role in priming viewers' existing schemas that then color their subsequent behaviors and impressions. Because of the promise and uniqueness of this approach, it would benefit the field to attempt to expand it further. Several new questions can be addressed experimentally using the priming paradigms presented earlier.

It may be useful, initially, to test the parameters of the current findings. For example, how long will the priming effects last? Will male-female interactions witnessed hours later, or even the next day, still be colored by the content of the music videos viewed earlier? Different time windows could be tested experimentally. Are television genres that are longer and more complex than music videos and commercials equally effective primes? It may be the case that stereotyped content presented in a 30-minute situation comedy or in a 1-hour drama may be lost in the noise of the other content and may therefore be less salient to viewers and a less effective prime. Clips and programs of different lengths and different formats (e.g., documentary vs. comedy) could be tested for their effectiveness.

There also is considerable room to test and extend these paradigms using different dependent variables. In the area of gender role stereotypes, for example, researchers could examine priming effects on gender-related behaviors that focus on being submissive or being assertive. After they have watched stereotyped television content in which males are dominant and females play supporting roles, will female participants be less likely and males more likely to assert themselves? Here, situations and behaviors not depicted in the television content viewed would be used such as arguing an unfair outcome (e.g., a parking ticket, an altered price), asking someone to move his or her seat or to stop talking, or turning away an annoying person. Further questioning of their justifications for their postviewing behaviors also could be conducted. Are there differences in how viewers interpret their own behaviors based on the type of material that primed them? These testing situations could be incorporated into the laboratory either via written scenarios or via the use of confederates. It also would be useful to examine the priming effect of stereotyped material on viewers' gender esteem and affect. How does watching strong men and weak women (or the reverse) make females feel about being women and males feel about being men? The possible dependent variables that could be examined with this paradigm are virtually endless.

To explore the role of priming even further, an additional approach would be to reverse the paradigm and examine how priming stereotypes *before* viewers watch television affects their perceptions of the television content. Here, participants would be exposed to particular conditions or written materials that would prime their gender schemas. Participants in Experimental Group 1 would be exposed to material focusing on nontraditional gender roles. Participants in Experimental Group 2 would be exposed to material focusing on traditional gender roles. Participants in the control group would not be primed. All groups would then view the same complex television stimuli that would contain several messages with multiple interpretations. Participants' perceptions of the content and characters would then be assessed, perhaps with questions focusing on the salient themes or on their identification with the main characters.

■ Expanding Experimental Methodologies to Address These Gaps: Three Case Studies

In this section, we offer a more detailed analysis of the methodology in three specific studies we have conducted that have attempted to address some of the methodological gaps discussed in the preceding sections. Each study is by no means flawless and comes with its own set of limitations. Yet, each does provide a somewhat unique approach to television's link to viewers' social attitudes and behaviors. Moreover, because each study is in a different topic domain, we offer here a more thorough sense of how different issues can be handled via experimental means.

Perceptions of Television's Sexual Content: Bridging Gaps 1 and 6

Although television is a common source of input to teenagers about the world of romance (e.g., Buerkel-Rothfuss & Strouse, 1993; Fabes & Strouse, 1986), little is known about how this material is perceived. Indeed, much of the content of prime-time television programs is created with more mature adult viewers in mind. How, then, is this material perceived by younger viewers with less actual experience in this domain? More important, which factors—demographics, amount of television watched, or personal attitudes—best predict what is seen and believed? These questions can be answered only by the use of popular programming as stimuli (Gap 1) and by investigating viewers' individual interpretations of the programs (Gap 6); this strategy was used by Ward and Eschwege (1996) in the study described below.

These researchers explored adolescents' interpretations of television content dealing with dating and relationships. They also investigated the links from these perceptions and personal attitudes to both qualitative and quantitative aspects of television viewing. The general design of the study was simple. A multiethnic sample of 151 adolescent undergraduates ages 18-20 years was tested in groups during 1-hour testing sessions. For half the session, participants completed detailed survey measures assessing their television viewing amounts, motivations, and styles (i.e., active vs. passive) as well as their attitudes and expectations about gender roles, dating, and relationships. Demographic information on each participant's sex, age, socioeconomic status, and ethnic background also was elicited. For the other half of the testing session, participants watched four brief clips from actual prime-time television shows popular among adolescents and answered written questions about each clip. These questions focused on the main messages of the scenes, the realism and appropriateness of the characters' actions, and participants' identification with the main characters. Participants then ranked in importance five potential messages conveyed by each scene.

This design offered several benefits and opportunities. First, using a diverse set of clips from actual prime-time television shows enhanced the external validity. The clips had been selected from a previous analysis of sexual content on the television programs adolescents view most (Ward, 1995) and were chosen to represent different ethnic groups, stages of relationships, and ages of characters. Because the clips were popular among participants in the selected age group, the likelihood was increased that they would actually view that material on their own. In addition, having studied the programs first via content analyses provided greater assurance that the themes in the selected clips were representative of the types of sexual messages present on these programs. Second, via the detailed viewing surveys included, it was possible to determine both how familiar viewers were with each of the stimulus programs and whether this familiarity affected their interpretations of the clip. Third, using viewers' interpretations as the dependent variables, we were able to analyze which of several factors best predicted them. Ethnicity was the strongest demographic contributor, and both total television viewing amounts and viewer's attitudes toward relationships made large contributions. Finally, in future analyses planned, viewers' interpretations will serve as the independent variables to predict other aspects of adolescents' attitudes and expectations about sexuality. Whereas this study is limited in that it explored only one age group and one television genre, it does illustrate how popular material can be used as stimuli and how viewers' interpretations are informative as both dependent and independent variables.

Effects of Formal Features on Perceptions of Violence and Suffering: Bridging Gap 3

Research has indicated that the formal presentation features of television, such as editing cuts, fades, and the presence of music, will affect children's comprehension of the material and their understanding of its intent (for a review, see Huston & Wright, in press). Similarly, advertising research has demonstrated that the angle from which a product is photographed will affect viewers' perceptions of that product (Kraft, 1987; Meyer-Levy & Peracchio, 1992). Consequently, might differences in the presentation features of violent content influence viewers' perceptions of that content? For example, would violent confrontations viewed in slow motion be seen as more or less violent than attacks viewed at normal speed? These types of questions can be handled very well through experimental means.

Moving in this direction, we recently conducted a study examining the impact of presentation speed (slow vs. normal) on viewers' perceptions of real violent confrontations (Ward, Greenfield, & Colby, 1996). The general format required undergraduate participants to view a violent attack twice, each time in one of two speeds (slow or normal), and then to answer written questions about the specific content (recall test) and about the nature of the violence. In designing this study, we incorporated several methodological features that would address issues of individual differences in perceptions, external validity, and content effects.

First, to reduce variance caused by individual differences in ratings and perceptions, we used a within-subjects, repeated-measures design. Thus, all participants watched the same clip two times (approximately 30 minutes apart) in one of the following four viewing conditions: normal speed and then slow speed, slow speed and then normal speed, normal speed both times, or slow speed both times (the latter conditions controlled for mere repetition). With this design, we could compare differences in initial perceptions based on speed and could examine directly whether changes in speed changed viewers' perceptions of the attacks. We also were able to test the effects of mere repetition via the control conditions.

Second, to increase external validity, we selected videotaped footage from actual violent confrontations. By using short clips from documentary footage whose quality was not always superior, we hoped to better approximate the type of material that might appear as evidence in the courtroom. Finally, because viewers' perceptions are likely to vary based on the exact content of the attacks, we used three different confrontations as stimuli. These attacks varied in the number, race, and status (e.g., civilians vs. police) of the aggressors and the victims. In general, the results indicated that all three factors—speed (slow motion vs. real time), film content (lunch counter sit-in, attack of a black man by white men, riots at 1968 Democratic Convention), and time (first viewing vs. repeated viewing)—related in some way to viewers' perceptions of the violence depicted. Thus, with this design, we were able to both examine several possible factors affecting viewers' perceptions and reduce some of the noise at the same time.

Given the current use of video footage in the criminal justice system, concerns about the impact of television and televised violence have expanded to a new domain. Here, however, the focus is less on violence as entertainment and more on truth and on understanding events as they actually occurred. The experiment by Ward et al. (1996) was inspired by the trials of the police officers who beat Rodney King. In these trials, a videotape of the beating was at the center of the evidence. Moreover, the formal features of slow motion and repetition figured prominently in the way in which the tape was used during the trial. As video evidence and its manipulation become ever more important in the justice system, an understanding of how different formal manipulations affect interpretations of videotape takes on practical as well as theoretical importance.

Effects of Television Toy Tie-Ins on Interactive Storytelling: Bridging Gaps 4 and 7

Interest in television and social behavior also has focused on its relation to the development of young viewers' creative and imaginative play. Whereas many argue that television's audiovisual narratives may depress viewers' own imaginations and creative tendencies, some propose that television's images and characters may stimulate fantasizing and daydreaming (for a review, see Valkenburg & van der Voort, 1994). These hypotheses have been tested in several formats, often via correlational designs or via experimental media comparisons assessing viewers' imaginative storytelling or responses following material presented via video, audio, or print. Yet, in this age of multimedia supersystems, the same characters often are presented via film, television, video games, *and* consumer products (e.g., action figures, lunch boxes, T-shirts). How, then, can one tease out the effects of television's narratives and characters when those same characters are everywhere? Given this complexity, might watching a particular program and then playing with the action figures re-created from that program be doubly influential? Will any effects of multimedia combinations differ at different stages of development?

To begin to deal with the developmental effects of a multimedia environment in which television symbols can refer to toy characters and vice versa (Kinder, 1991), Greenfield et al. (1990) employed an experimental pretest–posttest design that focused on media combinations. Their design tested the effects of the *combination* of television-related toys and toy-based television on children's interactive storytelling at two different grades, first grade and second grade. These are ages during which such skills would be developing and advancing. This is an example of a study that addresses both Gap 4 (the gap in developmental research) and, more important, Gap 7 (the gap in research on multimedia).

In this study, the experimental treatment was divided into two elements, media experience and toy play, with a choice of stimuli for each element. For the media experience, some of the subjects saw a television program (*The Smurfs*) and the others played a table game. For the toy experience, some of the subjects had Smurf toys and the others had troll figures. By crossing the media experience with the toy experience, several combinations could be tested including the following three conditions examined in this study: experimental group (Smurf cartoon, Smurf toys), Contrast Group 1 (connect-the-dot game, Smurf toys), and Contrast Group 2 (Smurf cartoon, troll toys). Thus, with this design, the study moved beyond the usual television effects experiments that deal with single forms of stimuli. Its goal was to assess the effects of matching the characters in television programs and toys, as opposed to the effect of either element present alone.

Another notable aspect of the design was its use of interacting pairs of children as the unit of analysis for the dependent variables. The experimental task for both the pre- and posttest was to tell a story using the toy figures. The dependent variables assessed the freedom of the story content from the preceding stimulus, either the game or the television program. By using pairs of children constructing a story together, this experiment looked at the effect of television and the multimedia environment on a product of social interaction. (Ongoing social interaction is a process that has been understudied in research on the social impact of television. This study, therefore, provides a methodological model that could, in principle, be adapted to research on other effects of televised material on social interaction.)

Also notable was the study's use of a multivariate analysis of variance design to look at the impact of the independent variables on two groups of interrelated dependent variables (i.e., different aspects of interactive storytelling). In follow-up analyses, personal characteristics that correlated with the dependent variables were used as covariates in multivariate analysis of covariance analyses. This statistical methodology combined the analyses of factorial independent variables, interrelated dependent variables, and mediating individual differences. A similar statistical approach also was used in the study of the effects of slow motion and repetition on perceptions of violence and suffering described earlier. It should be applicable for other topics in which complex systems of dependent variables, multiple independent variable factors, and individual differences all come into play.

■ Into the Future, Part 1: Testing Old Theories With New Experimental Approaches

In addition to priming, there are other theoretical approaches to television effects that have as yet received minimal experimental testing. Whereas some theories lend themselves more easily to experimentation than do others, it would benefit our understanding of television's role to attempt to test each one experimentally. Assumptions of individual theories could be tested initially, followed by experiments in which competing theories are tested at the same time to begin to determine which hold stronger explanatory power. In the discussion that follows, we describe three sets of theoretical propositions that focus attention on overlooked aspects of television's influence and offer suggestions for how each might be tested via experimental means.

Greenberg's Drench Hypothesis

One set of propositions that has received minimal empirical testing is Greenberg's (1982, 1988) "drench hypothesis." In explaining the potential impact of television's often stereotypical portrayals, Greenberg proposed that "critical images may contribute more to impression-formation and image-building than does the sheer frequency of television characters and behaviors that are viewed" (Greenberg, 1988, p. 100). As a result, the strength of particularly salient or meaningful portrayals may override the messages of masses of others. Greenberg's notions differ from those of cultivation theory in his emphasis on the power of individual portrayals and performances. He asserted that not all portrayals have the same impact and that viewers probably "attend more closely to a limited set of portrayals, ones that become significant for us" (p. 99). This focus on specific portrayals may be especially relevant now because television networks appear to be developing more programming (and cable channels) aimed at particular viewing populations instead of general programming that appeals to everyone. Therefore, a thorough testing of Greenberg's drench hypothesis is needed.

Perhaps the most effective method for testing these propositions experimentally would involve a two-stage approach, first assessing what the critical portrayals are and then testing whether their themes and messages have a greater impact than those from noncritical portrayals. (Although this line of inquiry is similar to the one focusing on effects of liking and familiarity described earlier, here the emphasis is more on particular portrayals than on liked and disliked programs.) During the first stage, a population of viewers (e.g., African American adolescent females) would be surveyed concerning the television portrayals they most like and identify with—the characters who "speak to them." Participants could respond to open-ended questions or could be cued with lists of names of various television characters. Participants also would be asked to describe the particular aspects of those portrayals that heighten their impact. Once this information had been obtained and a list of critical portrayals and their attributes had been produced for that population, subgroups of students could be retested using experimental manipulations.

In this second stage, the emphasis would be on the effects of particularly salient portrayals versus the effects of messages culled from randomly selected stimuli. The specific design could take a number of forms, depending on the nature of the critical portrayals and on the research question at hand. Suppose, for example, one were interested in gender role portrayals and had first surveyed the population of African American adolescent females just mentioned. Three experimental conditions would then be needed to test the impact of the critical portrayals provided on viewers' expectations about gender roles. Participants in Group 1 would view five clips in which the chief female characters represented both noncritical portrayals and nontraditional gender roles. Participants in Group 2 would view five clips in which the chief female characters represented noncritical portrayals yet traditional gender roles. Participants in Group 3 would view five clips as well—four in which the chief female characters were noncritical and traditional and one in which the chief female character was a critical portrayal and nontraditional. Pre- and postviewing surveys would be administered to assess participants' gender role attitudes. Analyses would focus on the following question: Would the responses of participants in Group 3 be closer to those in Group 1, thereby demonstrating the strength of one nontraditional portrayal in a sea of traditional ones, or closer to those in Group 2, thereby demonstrating the strength of the predominant images? With this type of experimental design, researchers could assess whether the effects of viewing nontraditional behavior from one impactful portrayal equal the effects from several noncritical portrayals.

Meyrowitz's Theory

Meyrowitz (1985) opened up a whole new set of questions in his provocative book *No Sense of Place.* These are questions that current methods have been ill-suited to answer. Meyrowitz's theory begins with his experience of television as a child, growing up when the medium was in its infancy.

> I responded to television as if it was "a secret revelation machine" that exposed aspects of the adult world to me that would otherwise have remained hidden. My primary response to television was not imitation of the behavior I saw on it, nor was it to be persuaded that I needed to own the many products advertised. Rather, the information I received about social interaction on television affected my own willingness to accept other people's behaviors and claims at face value. Television educated me and my friends about certain aspects of adulthood that no longer allowed our parents "to get away" with some traditional parental behavior. It also affected our views of members of the other sex and of teachers, police, politicians and other "authorities." . . . Television changed the ways in which the walls of my home formed and limited my social experience. (p. x)

The major mechanism by which Meyrowitz (1985) posited these changes take place is through the access television provides to people's "backstage behavior." This is behavior that is not meant to be seen by the audience, behavior outside of a person's public role-playing behavior. For example, on television, children get to see parents' marital problems, which might be hidden from their view at home; students get to see teachers' personal lives, which would be hidden from their view at school; and voters get to see politicians' personal foibles, which could be hidden from their view in print and on radio. Access to backstage behavior, Meyrowitz posited, leads to a sense of closeness with these authority figures but also a loss of respect—both familiarity and contempt.

Meyrowitz's (1985) main criticism of research on the impact of television (and other electronic media) on social behavior was that it places too much emphasis on content and too little on "different patterns of information flow fostered by different media" (p. 14). The implication for experimental design is twofold. Studies are needed that demonstrate (a) the same effect on social behavior of different content in the same medium (i.e., television) and (b) different effects of the same content in different media (e.g., television, radio, print).

A general design might be to compare two programs or films providing opposite views on the same topic plus a print screenplay of one or both of the programs. Would divergent form matter more than divergent content? For example, segments of two films on teachers might be shown to two groups of subjects. One (e.g., *Stand and Deliver*) would present a positive view of the profession; the other (e.g., *The Nutty Professor*) would present a negative view. (Because films end up on television, we are not here making a distinction between the two media.) Based on a central idea in Meyrowitz's book that television lowers respect for authority figures by showing "backstage" (private) behaviors, the predictions would be that children's respect for their favorite teachers and for the teaching profession as a whole would go down after viewing either film, whereas empathy with one's own teacher (perceived similarity to self) would go up. The particular content of the stimuli (negative vs. positive portrayals) would not matter; both are predicted to have the same effect. Respect for one's own teacher might also diminish in the case of *Stand and Deliver* because one's own teacher's performance might pale in comparison with that of star teacher Jaime Escalante.

In this experiment, two other groups would read screenplays of the same film segments. The prediction, based on Meyrowitz's theory, is that, because of the relative lack of concrete detail and nonverbal behavior in the print medium relative to television, neither screenplay would affect viewers' evaluations of their own teachers or of the teaching profession as a whole. Once again, the particular content of the material read would not matter.

A similar design could be used to examine role perceptions of parents or doctors, perhaps using popular television series as stimulus sources. The innovations of this type of design would be twofold:

(a) demonstrating that the effects of medium form can override the effects of medium content and (b) using social attitudes as dependent variables in cross-media comparative studies. Indeed, so far most cross-media studies have used cognitive not social behaviors as their dependent variables. Insofar as perceptions of teachers, parents, and doctors affect one's ability to play the complementary roles of student, child, and patient, this research method could address what Meyrowitz (1985) saw as an important issue: "the ways in which new patterns of access to information about social behavior might be affecting people's ability to play old forms of roles" (pp. x-xi).

It also may be beneficial to directly test the effects of the presence of backstage behaviors. Is seeing them what lowers viewers' respect and increases their familiarity, or is it some other aspect of television? Testing this question would involve an intramedia design that uses different types of television stimuli. For example, continuing the research on television's portrayals of teachers, one might wish to compare responses to television stimuli in which the teacher's backstage behavior is shown with those in which it is not. Here, participants in Group 1 would watch clips from a situation comedy in which the teacher is the central character (e.g., *Welcome Back, Kotter*) and his or her flaws and personal problems are depicted. Participants in Group 2 would view clips in which teachers are included but are peripheral characters and are shown only in a formal authority role. Participants in Group 3 would view no clips. Pre- and postviewing attitudes on teachers and on the teaching profession could be compared across positions. Would viewers' respect for teachers' authority diminish for Groups 1 and 2, thereby demonstrating a general effect of teachers being depicted on television, or only for Group 1, which saw the backstage behavior? With this type of design, researchers could begin to tease out the specific effects of airing backstage behavior.

A second methodological issue raised by Meyrowitz's (1985) theory is that traditional experimental designs, with their distinctions between independent and dependent variables, have been ill-suited to deal with a model of the relationship between television and social behavior in which television settings, characters, actions, and events become an extension of the unmediated social environment. In the preface of his book, Meyrowitz states,

There were few models that dealt with both systems of communicating as part of a continuum rather than a dichotomy. Most of the concerns were about people imitating behavior they saw on television, or about the inaccurate reflection of reality as portrayed in television content—real life as opposed to the media. Few studies examined both media and interpersonal interaction as part of the same system of "behaving" or responding to the behavior of others. (p. x)

For example, Meyrowitz (1985) introduced the concept of media "friends," the illusion heightened by television of knowing and interacting with people one has never met. Horton and Wohl (1956) called this a parasocial relationship and noted that it has the greatest impact on the socially isolated. A needed type of research design would have as its goal to consider the television world and the real world as complementary sources of social relationships. This approach could, for example, lead to a study that would relate the strength and quantity of real-world social relationships to parasocial relationships based on television. The prediction would be an inverse relationship between the depth and quantity of real-world relationships and the depth and quantity of parasocial relationships. For example, people living alone would have more important parasocial relationships than would those not living alone. People relating to many real people every day would have fewer parasocial relationships than would those relating to fewer real people in an average day.

A cross-media design also could be used to test the very concept that parasocial relationships are stronger for television than for other media. For example, a book chapter and a television program from *Little House on the Prairie* could be compared. Based on Meyrowitz's theory, the prediction would be that subjects would feel they knew the characters better after viewing the television show than after reading the book chapter.

One distinctive feature of Meyrowitz's theory is that it includes real-life people and events as well as fictional ones. Any of these designs could be used in relation to actual people and events on television (e.g., news). For example, do subjects feel they know a news personality better after that person appears in documentary television (e.g., *60 Minutes*) or a magazine article? This idea also extends well to the political arena, where one of Meyrowitz's main applications concerns television's ability to lower respect for political figures. At the same time, his theory implies that television will make people feel that they know public figures better. A cross-media study could test these ideas by, for example, presenting the speech of an unknown political figure in three media—television, radio, and print. Dependent variables would include a sense of knowing the politician, level of respect and liking, and evaluations of his or her competence and similarity to self. The theory would predict that people would feel they know the politician better but would have less respect for him or her after the television contact compared with radio and print contact. A related literature concerning the ability of different media forms to persuade also supports such a finding (for a review, see Petty & Cacioppo, 1981). Thus, the designs and studies proposed here offer an exciting new approach to studying television's social impact.

Kinder's Supersystems

The work of Kinder (1991) discussed similar issues in a more extreme form and raised even more difficult methodological questions. She took up the issue of the effect of the primacy of image over thing. What is "the impact of seeing an imaginary world so full of rich visual signifiers before having encountered their referents or acquired verbal language?" (p. 35).

A central issue in Kinder's (1991) work was the postmodern prevalence of the sliding signifiers that "change meaning in different contexts and that derive their primary value precisely from that process of transformation" (p. 3). Kinder questioned whether the primacy of image over thing in the media-dominated world (particularly television) encourages "the sliding of the signifier, so that by the time one first encounters, say, an elephant in the zoo, the living animal is merely another signifier for the image already seen on TV in documentaries and animated cartoons—that is, merely part of the paradigm of elephant signifiers?" (p. 35). Research designs are needed that can assess the impact of prior media exposure on subsequent interaction with and evaluation of many types of people of various ages, occupations, genders, ethnicities, and nationalities. What is the impact of media priority on understanding of and relations with real people?

▪ Into the Future, Part 2: Using Experimental Approaches With New Television Genres and Technologies

Both television content and the viewing experience have changed greatly in the last decade. New satellite and cable technologies have increased viewing channels and options. The proliferation of videocassette recorders has made the renting, purchasing, and home viewing of theatrical film releases commonplace. New genres of reality-based programming have been introduced that provide more than enough information about the intimate lives of those around us. As a result of these changes, there are many new issues about the links between television and social behavior that can be explored with traditional and not-so-traditional experimental designs.

One genre of programming that has expanded in recent years is reality-based programs. Included in this group are programs such as *Cops, Rescue 911,* and *Unsolved Mysteries* that feature reenactments of real crimes or disasters; high-profile courtroom trials aired on Court TV and on other networks; and programs in which the lives of everyday people are followed, such as MTV's *Real World* and *Road Rules* and HBO's *Taxicab Confessions.* With this genre of programming comes a new set of questions concerning the use and impact of television content. For example, are the themes and events on these programs more influential because they are closer to reality? Are younger viewers more frightened by criminal acts viewed on *Unsolved Mysteries* than by similar acts viewed on fictional police dramas? Do viewers identify more with the everyday real-world characters than with characters from fictional dramas? These questions could easily be addressed experimentally using stimuli from different genres. In a related type of study, Pingree (1978) found that children were more influenced by commercials when told that the actors were real than when told that they were paid actors. These findings illustrate that a line of research examining the impact of this new reality-based programming would be of critical importance.

Yet, not only has the content of the programming changed, but the nature of the viewing experience has changed as well. With cable movie channels and home video systems readily available, viewers can now view their favorite movies, programs, and characters repeatedly. As a result, we no longer can assume that all viewing experiences consist of singular presentations of varied images, themes, and portrayals. Instead, viewers, especially young children and adolescents, can view the same programs ad nauseam. With repeated viewings, content often takes on a new level of importance. For example, in the Ward et al. (1996) study on slow motion and violence described earlier, just watching the same attack at the same speed two times was related to an increase in participants' perceptions of the level of violence involved. With repeated home viewings of particular films or miniseries, might already larger-than-life protagonists such as the Terminator, Simba in *The Lion King,* or fighter pilots in *Independence Day* assume even greater stature or familiarity?

Given this new dynamic of the television viewing experience, it would be beneficial to begin to examine the potential consequences of viewing the same material repeatedly. What additional meanings do viewers construct with repeated viewings? Are the characters in films and programs viewed repeatedly more influential because they have assumed a greater stature or less influential because they have become familiar friends (i.e., habituation)? Experimental research could examine links between single and repeated viewings of certain content as well as viewers' perceptions of the realism of the characters or programs, their acceptance of certain behaviors or attitudes depicted, their identification with specific characters, and their likelihood of behaving similarly. One level of experimentation could be correlational surveys, which would assess a general connection between number of viewings and these dependent variables. Field experiments could compare the responses of one population of viewers who rented a movie and viewed it only once with those of viewers who purchased that movie and viewed it repeatedly. Assessments could be conducted after the first viewing and then 1 and 3 months later. Laboratory experiments also could be conducted with shorter material, perhaps with music videos or 30-minute situation comedies. Responses of participants who viewed the stimuli three times in a row could be compared with those of participants who had only a single viewing and who had no viewing at all.

The nature of the viewing experience also has changed in that it has become somewhat more interactive. Many television programs have World Wide Web sites, allowing viewers to "chat" about the programs and content with each other and sometimes even with the actors and actresses. These interactions intensify television's role in our social world, highlighting the phenomenon described by Meyrowitz (1985). How are viewers' perceptions and acceptance of specific content affected by the extent of their postviewing behaviors and discussions? New experimental research exploring the consequences of active (vs. passive) viewing is needed here. Other television programs require direct viewer involvement to survive. A prominent example is *America's Funniest Home Videos,* where viewers send in their own video footage and potentially may appear on the show itself. Does experience in filming social behavior through home video affect interpretations of social behavior on television or the filmmaker's real-world social behavior?

In general, people are appearing on television more and more every day. It no longer is the province of actors—beautiful, well trained, and somewhat larger than life. Instead, with the proliferation of daytime talk shows, viewers see folks from every walk of life sharing their intimate problems and secrets on national television. How is this behavior perceived? Is their behavior seen as normative or representative of their group? What does people's willingness to reveal intimate information to a national audience say about the power and seductiveness of the medium and of fame in general? How does the experience of being on television affect viewers' perceptions of the medium and its content? Now that they have seen some of television's own backstage behavior, are they less likely to be influenced by it? New lines of experimental research could be designed to begin to address such questions.

■ Conclusion

Experimental design can be an excellent tool for investigating potential links between television and viewers' social attitudes and behavior. With its high internal validity and content control, experimental designs have served well for answering questions about the effects of particular content, genres, dialogue, and characters. Unfortunately, the scope of the existing literature has been somewhat constrained by concerns over potentially "harmful" content (e.g., violence, sexist portrayals) and by the use of a limited number of theoretical approaches. Moreover, the methods and research tracks have not kept up with the complexity of the media environment. As a result, other dimensions of television's potential influence, such as the impact of critical portrayals, backstage behaviors, and parasocial interactions, have received less attention. Creativity is therefore needed to continue to move this research forward and to expand its scope to address additional issues, technologies, and theoretical perspectives.

In the discussion presented in this chapter, we have attempted to offer several suggestions for future directions with experimental paradigms. What we propose is just the beginning. Although our focus has been on experimental methods, it also is possible to address some of the questions raised via field research or via survey and correlational measures. Indeed, for addressing the impact of more complex media supersystems, there may be a limitation to what experimental designs can offer. In addition, many of our suggestions involved using clips from popular television programs. However, finding broadcast content that represents a particular issue may be time-consuming, and matching content and behaviors across clips can be difficult. Consequently, more thought and work may be needed to make some of our proposals a practical reality.

Yet, the need and room for additional approaches is clear. More work is needed that incorporates the richness and complexity of television content, perhaps focusing on the consequences of multimedia portrayals, underrepresentation, or particular format features (e.g., slow motion). There also is a strong need for more theory-driven work, for experiments that test the assumptions of particular theorists and of specific causal mechanisms (e.g., priming). Including viewers' own perceptions and preferences will go a long way toward improving external validity in future experiments, as will selecting stimuli from popular television programming.

There still are many questions that experimental research can help answer regarding television's link to our social attitudes and behaviors. Future projects could examine traditional content areas (e.g., gender roles, violence) or could venture out to explore the impact of television on other social dimensions (e.g., helpfulness, cooperation, competition). We should not limit ourselves by what already has been done. Instead, we can use this existing literature and methodology to help address the provocative new questions that have surfaced in today's more technologically advanced society.

■ References

Andison, F. S. (1977). TV violence and viewer aggression: A cumulation of study results 1956-1976. *Public Opinion Quarterly, 41,* 314-331.

Atkin, C. (1983). Effects of realistic TV violence vs. fictional violence on aggression. *Journalism Quarterly, 60,* 615-621.

Brown, J. D., & Schulze, L. (1993). The effects of race, gender, and fandom on audience interpretation of Madonna's music videos. In B. S. Greenberg, J. D. Brown, & N. L. Buerkel-Rothfuss (Eds.), *Media, sex, and the adolescent* (pp. 263-276). Cresskill, NJ: Hampton.

Buerkel-Rothfuss, N. L., & Strouse, J. S. (1993). Media exposure and perceptions of sexual behaviors: The cultivation hypothesis moves to the bedroom. In B. S. Greenberg, J. D. Brown, & N. L. Buerkel-Rothfuss (Eds.), *Media, sex, and the adolescent* (pp. 225-247). Cresskill, NJ: Hampton.

Carder, S. T. (1996). Mediated women: The effects of sex role stereotyping in network television commercials using a quasi-experiment. *Dissertation Abstracts International, 56,* 2466A.

Cheles, P. J. (1974). *An investigation of whether the stereotypes of husbands and wives presented in television commercials can influence a child's perception of the role of husband and wife.* Unpublished doctoral dissertation, Ohio University.

Cobb, N. J., Stevens-Long, J., & Goldstein, S. (1982). The influence of televised models on toy preference in children. *Sex Roles, 8,* 773-784.

Comstock, G. (1991). *Television and the American child.* Orlando, FL: Academic Press.

Cook, T. D., Kendziersky, D. A., & Thomas, S. V. (1983). The implicit assumptions of television: An analysis of the 1982 NIMH Report on Television and Social Behavior. *Public Opinion Quarterly, 47,* 161-201.

Cordua, G. D., McGraw, K. O., & Drabman, R. S. (1979). Doctor or nurse: Children's perceptions of sex typed occupations. *Child Development, 50,* 590-593.

Dambrot, F. H., Reep, D. C., & Bell, D. (1988). Television sex roles in the 1980's: Do viewers' sex and sex role orientation change the picture? *Sex Roles, 19,* 387-401.

Davidson, E. S., Yasuna, A., & Tower, A. (1979). The effects of television cartoons on sex-role stereotyping in young girls. *Child Development, 50,* 597-600.

Durkin, K. (1985a). Sex roles and television roles: Can a woman be seen to tell the weather as well as a man? *International Review of Applied Psychology, 34,* 191-201.

Durkin, K. (1985b). Television and sex-role acquisition 3: Counter-stereotyping. *British Journal of Social Psychology, 24,* 211-222.

Durkin, K., & Hutchins, G. (1984). Challenging traditional sex role in career education broadcasts: The reactions of young secondary school pupils. *Journal of Educational Television, 10,* 25-33.

Eisenstock, B. (1984). Sex-role differences in children's identification with counter-stereotypical televised portrayals. *Sex Roles, 10,* 417-431.

Fabes, R., & Strouse, J. (1986). Perceptions of responsible and irresponsible models of sexuality: A correlational study. *Journal of Sex Research, 23,* 70-84.

Flerx, V. C., Fidler, D. S., & Rogers, R. W. (1976). Sex role stereotypes: Developmental aspects and early intervention. *Child Development, 47,* 998-1007.

Freedman, J. L. (1984). Effect of television violence on aggressiveness. *Psychological Bulletin, 96,* 227-246.

Friedrich-Cofer, L., & Huston, A. C. (1986). Television violence and aggression: The debate continues. *Psychological Bulletin, 100,* 364-371.

Gerbner, G., Gross, L., Morgan, M., & Signorielli, N. (1986). Living with television: The dynamics of the cultivation process. In J. Bryant & D. Zillman (Eds.), *Perspectives on media effects* (pp. 17-40). Hillsdale, NJ: Lawrence Erlbaum.

Greenberg, B. S. (1982). Television and role socialization: An overview. In D. Pearl, L. Bouthilet, & J. Lazar (Eds.), *Television and behavior: Ten years of scientific progress and implications for the eighties,* Vol. 2: *Technical reports* (pp. 179-190). Washington, DC: National Institute of Mental Health.

Greenberg, B. S. (1988). Some uncommon television images and the drench hypothesis. In S. Oskamp (Ed.), *Applied social psychology annual: Television as a social issue* (Vol. 8, pp. 88-102). Newbury Park, CA: Sage.

Greenberg, B. S., & Brand, J. E. (1994). Minorities and the mass media: 1970's to 1990's. In J. Bryant & D. Zillman (Eds.), *Media effects: Advances in theory and research* (pp. 273-314). Hillsdale, NJ: Lawrence Erlbaum.

Greenfield, P. M., Yut, E., Chung, M., Land, D., Kreider, H., Pantoja, M., & Horsley, K. (1990). The program-length commercial: A study of the effects of television/toy tie-ins on imaginative play. *Psychology & Marketing, 7,* 237-255.

Greenfield, P. M., & Zukow, P. G. (1978). Why do children say what they say when they say it? An experimental approach to the psychogenesis of presupposition. In K. Nelson (Ed.), *Children's language* (Vol. 1, pp. 287-336). New York: Gardner.

Gross, L., & Jeffries-Fox, S. (1978). What do you want to be when you grow up, little girl? In G. Tuchman, A. K. Daniels, & J. Benet (Eds.), *Hearth and home: Images of women in the mass media* (pp. 240-265). New York: Oxford University Press.

Gunter, B. (1988). The importance of studying viewers' perceptions of television violence. *Current Psychology: Research and Reviews, 7,* 26-42.

Hanania, J. (1996, August 18). Control panel. *Los Angeles Times,* p. E3.

Hansen, C. H. (1989). Priming sex role stereotypic event schemas with rock music videos: Effects on impression favorability, trait inferences, and recall of a subsequent male-female interaction. *Basic & Applied Social Psychology, 10,* 371-391.

Hansen, C. H., & Hansen, R. D. (1988). How rock music videos can change what is seen when boy meets girl: Priming stereotypic appraisal of social interactions. *Sex Roles, 19,* 287-316.

Hansen, C. H., & Krygowski, W. (1994). Arousal-augmented priming effects: Rock music videos and sex object schemas. *Communication Research, 21,* 24-37.

Hearold, S. (1986). A synthesis of 1043 effects of television on social behavior. In G. Comstock (Ed.), *Public communication and behavior* (Vol. 1, pp. 65-130). Orlando, FL: Academic Press.

Horton, D., & Wohl, R. R. (1956). Mass communication and parasocial interaction: Observations on intimacy at a distance. *Psychiatry, 19,* 215-229.

Huston, A. C., & Wright, J. C. (in press). Mass media and children's development. In W. Damon, I. E. Sigel, & K. A. Renninger (Eds.), *Handbook of child psychology,* Vol. 4: *Child psychology in practice* (5th ed.). New York: John Wiley.

Jeffrey, L., & Durkin, K. (1989). Children's reactions to televised counter-stereotyped male sex role behaviour as a function of age, sex, and perceived power. *Social Behaviour, 4,* 285-310.

Jennings, J., Geis, F. L., & Brown, V. (1980). Influence of television commercials on women's self-confidence and independent judgment. *Journal of Personality and Social Psychology, 38,* 203-210.

Kinder, M. (1991). *Playing with power in movies, television, and video games: From Muppet Babies to Teenage Mutant Ninja Turtles.* Berkeley: University of California Press.

Kraft, R. N. (1987). The influence of camera angle on comprehension and retention of pictorial events. *Memory and Cognition, 15,* 291-307.

List, J. A., Collins, W. A., & Westby, S. D. (1983). Comprehension and inferences from traditional and nontraditional sex-role portrayals on television. *Child Development, 54,* 1579-1587.

McArthur, L. Z., & Eisen, S. V. (1976). Television and sex-role stereotyping. *Journal of Applied Social Psychology, 6,* 329-351.

Melville, D. J., & Cornish, I. (1993). Conservatism and gender in the perception of sex-roles in television and advertisements. *Perceptual and Motor Skills, 77,* 642.

Meyer-Levy, J., & Peracchio, L. (1992). Getting an angle in advertising: The effect of camera angle on product evaluations. *Journal of Marketing Research, 29,* 454-461.

Meyrowitz, J. (1985). *No sense of place: The impact of electronic media on social behavior.* New York: Oxford University Press.

Miller, M. M., & Reeves, B. (1976). Dramatic TV content and children's sex-role stereotypes. *Journal of Broadcasting, 20,* 35-50.

Noble, G. (1973). Effects of different forms of filmed aggression on children's constructive and destructive play. *Journal of Personality and Social Psychology, 26,* 54-59.

O'Bryant, S. L., & Corder-Bolz, C. R. (1978). The effects of television on children's stereotyping of women's work roles. *Journal of Vocational Behavior, 12,* 233-244.

Paik, H., & Comstock, G. (1994). The effects of television violence on antisocial behavior: A meta-analysis. *Communication Research, 21,* 516-546.

Petty, R. E., & Cacioppo, J. T. (1981). *Attitudes and persuasion: Classic and contemporary approaches.* Dubuque, IA: William C. Brown.

Pingree, S. (1978). The effects of non-sexist television commercials and perceptions of reality on children's attitudes about women. *Psychology of Women Quarterly, 2,* 262-276.

Reep, D. C., & Dambrot, F. H. (1988). In the eye of the beholder: Viewer perceptions of TV's male-female working partners. *Communication Research, 15,* 51-69.

Ruble, D., Balaban, T., & Cooper, J. (1981). Gender constancy and the effects of sex-typed televised toy commercials. *Child Development, 52,* 667-673.

Signorielli, N. (1989). Television and conceptions about sex roles: Maintaining conventionality and the status quo. *Sex Roles, 21,* 341-360.

Signorielli, N. (1993). Television, the portrayal of women, and children's attitudes. In G. Berry & J. K. Asamen (Eds.), *Children and television: Images in a changing sociocultural world* (pp. 229-242). Newbury Park, CA: Sage.

Stipp, H., & Milavsky, J. R. (1988). U. S. television programming effects on aggressive behavior of children and adolescents. *Current Psychology: Research and Reviews, 7,* 76-92.

Tan, A. (1979). TV beauty ads and role expectations of adolescent female viewers. *Journalism Quarterly, 56,* 283-288.

Tan, A., Raudy, J., Huff, C., & Miles, J. (1980). Children's reactions to male and female newscasters: Effectiveness and believability. *Quarterly Journal of Speech, 66*, 201-205.

Toney, G. T., & Weaver, J. B. (1994). Effects of gender and gender role self-perceptions on affective reactions to rock music videos. *Sex Roles, 30*, 567-583.

Valkenburg, P. M., & van der Voort, T. H. (1994). Influence of TV on daydreaming and creative imagination: A review of research. *Psychological Bulletin, 116*, 316-339.

Waite, B. M. (1987). *Popular music videos: A content analysis and social-developmental investigation of their effects on gender orientation and attitudes.* Unpublished doctoral dissertation, Kent State University.

Ward, L. M. (1995). Talking about sex: Common themes about sexuality in the prime-time television programs children and adolescents view most. *Journal of Youth and Adolescence, 24*, 595-616.

Ward, L. M., & Eschwege, K. (1996). *Would that really happen? Adolescents' perceptions of television's tales of dating and romance.* Unpublished manuscript, University of California, Los Angeles.

Ward, L. M., Greenfield, P. G., & Colby, M. (1996). *Misuse of videotaped evidence in the courtroom: The effects of slow-motion on perceptions of violence and on memory for details.* Unpublished manuscript, University of California, Los Angeles.

Ward, L. M., & Wyatt, G. E. (1994). The effects of childhood sexual messages on African-American and white women's adolescent sexual behavior. *Psychology of Women Quarterly, 18*, 183-201.

Williams, F., LaRose, R., & Frost, F. (1981). *Children, television, and sex-role stereotyping.* New York: Praeger.

Wood, W., Wong, F. Y., & Chachere, J. G. (1991). Effects of media violence on viewers' aggression in unconstrained social interaction. *Psychological Bulletin, 109*, 371-383.

3

Quasi-Experimental Research on Television and Behavior

Natural and Field Experiments

Tannis M. MacBeth

Methodological discussions regarding research on the effects of television often contrast the advantages of laboratory experiments for making causal inferences with the advantages of more naturalistic or ecologically valid field studies. Laboratory experiments are designed to answer the question *"Can television affect viewers?"* whereas field studies are designed to answer the question *"Does television affect viewers as they use it over time in day-to-day life?"* Most field studies are correlational, however, and permit us only to determine whether television use is related to some other behavior, such as school achievement or aggression, not whether there is a causal relationship. This chapter focuses on two special and relatively unusual types of quasi-experimental field studies that have the potential to answer both the *can* and *does* questions. That is, if well designed, they enable us to make causal inferences about the effects of television as they occur naturally.

In *natural experiments*, researchers take advantage of a naturally occurring change in the availability of television reception to assess the impact of this change on viewers. For example, a preexisting group with access to television may be compared with another preexisting group that has less or no television reception. Or, a preexisting group may be studied before television reception first becomes available and then again after some period of use, usually a relatively longer term period of months or years. The group experiencing change in the availability of television may be contrasted with other similar groups whose exposure does not change over the same interval. In *field experiments*, researchers also often study preexisting groups, but in this case they assign different groups (e.g., preschool classes) to different television viewing "diets" (e.g., prosocial programs vs. cartoons vs. no television). The groups may be observed first during a baseline period, to establish their similarity, and then again after the exposure period. The many methodological problems, issues, and considerations confronting researchers interested in conducting natural and field quasi-experimental studies are the focus of this chapter.

In their now classic monograph, Campbell and Stanley (1966) explained the distinction between *true* and *quasi* experiments and described a series of quasi-experimental designs along with their strengths and weaknesses. That monograph formed the basis of both a chapter and a book by Cook and Campbell (1976, 1979) on methodological issues involving quasi-experiments conducted in field settings. Their work has since been revised and updated in a chapter by Cook, Campbell, and Peracchio (1990). That chapter provides the jumping-off point for this chapter on methodological issues involved in natural and field experiments on television and behavior.

According to Cook et al. (1990), experiments are "any experimenter-controlled or naturally occurring event with rapid onset (a "treatment") whose possible consequences are to be empirically assessed" (p. 492). Two major categories of experiments exist. In randomized experiments, participants are assigned to treatments at random, whereas "quasi-experiments primarily depend on self-selection or administrative decisions to determine who is to be exposed to a treatment" (p. 492). As Cook et al. pointed out, "It is generally easier to implement quasi-experiments than randomized experiments in many of the field settings where causal conclusions are needed" (p. 492). They defined a field setting as any one "that respondents do not perceive as having been set up for the primary purpose of conducting research" (p. 492).

When making causal inferences is the researchers' primary concern, random assignment to groups is the method of choice. Having stated that clearly, however, Cook et al. (1990) went on to point out that it rarely is possible in randomized experiments to manipulate more than a few independent variables, and so randomized experiments can test hypotheses about the independent and interactive effects of only a small number of manipulated variables. The complexities of real life typically involve many more relevant factors, most or all of which also operate in quasi-experiments.

■ Conditions Required for Causal Inferences

Cause Must Precede Effect

What conditions must be met before we can conclude that two variables are causally related in the direction that A causes B (Cook et al., 1990)? First, a cause must precede an effect in time. In the case of television and behavior, researchers know when television (or a certain type of televised content) first became available in their natural experiment or when they introduced it in their field experiment. Thus, for quasi-experiments, this first condition, which is at the core of the problem of being unable to draw causal inferences in correlational field studies, usually is easy to meet.

Covariation: Ruling Out Threats to Statistical Conclusion Validity

The second necessary condition for causal inference is that the treatment (exposure to television) and effect (behavior of viewers) must covary. In social science research on television, this usually is determined statistically. But, as Cook et al. (1990) explained, statistics sometimes fail to detect true patterns of covariation (this often is described as a Type II error) and sometimes indicate that covariation exists for the sample when it does not exist in the population (which often is described as a Type I error). Moreover, if the sample is very large and there is enough statistical power, then a trivial relationship can be statistically significant but may not be significant theoretically or for policy. Cook et al. discussed the factors that can lead to false conclusions about covariation as threats to *statistical conclusion validity*.

Statistical conclusion validity is concerned with sources of error (as opposed to bias, which is the domain of internal validity) and the appropriate use of statistical tests for dealing with such error. A special problem of statistical conclusion validity arises in designs with two or more experimental groups if the pretest-posttest difference within one or more groups is reliable but the difference between the groups is not (Cook et al., 1990). For example if there is overlap in the treatment components (which could well be the case for two different types of exposure to television, e.g., in terms of overlapping channels available or overlapping content), then the between-group comparison may underestimate a treatment's total potential impact. Cook et al. pointed out that, in effect, within-group and between-group analyses in such a design test different hypotheses. The within-group comparisons test whether change has taken place but do not specify the locus of change, which could be due to the treatment or to other factors that vary between the measurement waves. The between-group comparisons test whether there is more change in one experimental group than in another. Because irrelevant temporal change is controlled, the locus of change may be easier to identify, but this would not be true if, as already mentioned, there were overlap in treatment components. For these reasons, Cook et al. contended that it is not a genuine contradiction if the within-group and between-group tests suggest different conclusions about a treatment's effectiveness. They described the following six threats to statistical conclusion validity.

Statistical power. The probability of making a Type II error (e.g., concluding that there was no effect of television for the sample when there would be one for the population) increases when sample sizes are small, alpha is set low, one-sided hypotheses are incorrectly tested, major sources of extraneous variance are uncontrolled, variables are dichotomous, and distribution-free statistics are used. The obvious ways of dealing with the problem—increasing sample size, controlling extraneous variance, using continuous measures, and using the most powerful statistical tests appropriate for such measures—may, in some instances, not be possible. For example, some of the natural experiments I describe later in this chapter are based on relatively small samples. Given the paucity of opportunities to conduct such studies and their potential to answer the question of whether television does affect viewers as it is used in normal day-to-day life, they were, in my opinion, still worth pursuing. It is important, however, to keep their small samples and risk of Type II error in mind when evaluating the results.

Fishing and the error rate problem. As the number of statistical tests within a study increases, the experiment-wise error rate increases. That is, the probability of a Type I error (e.g., concluding that television has an effect when it does not) is cumulative. There are several ways of dealing with this problem including using multivariate tests, using conservative multiple comparison tests (e.g., Tukey), and dividing the usual alpha level by the number of tests conducted to set a new alpha level (Bonferroni, e.g., .05 / 6 tests = .0083). Avoiding fishing by testing specific hypotheses also is important. The difficulty, of course, is how to trade off the risks of Type I and Type II errors in any given study.

The reliability of measures. Measures with low stability or test-retest reliability will result in inflated error terms. Using longer tests with high inter-item correlations (but not restricting the conceptual domain) and decreasing the interval between waves or tests in longitudinal studies may help to control for such unreliability (Cook et al., 1990). Using group means rather than individual scores as the unit of analysis also will increase reliability, and the gain often will more than compensate for the loss of degrees of freedom. Standard corrections for unreliability also should be used. One of the major advantages of natural and quasi-experiments involving television is that they reduce the need to measure television use because exposure is specified as part of the design. In my opinion, measuring (and, for that matter, conceptualizing) use of television reliably is much more difficult than is usually acknowledged (MacBeth, 1996b; Williams,[1]

1986a; Williams & Boyes, 1986; see also Kubey & Csikszentmihalyi, 1990).

The reliability of treatment implementation. For a variety of reasons, the way the treatment is implemented may vary both across individuals and for the same individual on different occasions. This will inflate random error and decrease the chance of obtaining true differences. Cook et al. (1990) suggested trying to make the treatment as standard as possible or somehow measuring the variability in implementation and using it in data analyses. In both natural and quasi-experiments involving television, this threat to statistical conclusion validity is clearly evident. In natural experiments, there is considerable variation across individuals and occasions in exposure to television (e.g., number of channels, amount viewed, conditions of viewing including alertness and presence/absence of others, content viewed). In quasi-experiments, the content and conditions of viewing probably are controlled by the researchers, but there still are many relevant individual differences (e.g., comprehension, attention, prior desensitization to similar content).

Random irrelevancies in the setting. Settings vary and do not remain constant over time, and so some features of the setting other than the treatment will affect scores on the behavior of interest, thereby increasing error variance. This is the logic behind choosing a laboratory over a real-world setting. One approach to reduce this effect is to lower the saliency of environmental variables by focusing the participants' attention on the treatment (Cook et al., 1990). But doing so in a natural or field experiment might alter behavior. Instead, researchers may want to downplay or disguise their true interest in the effects of television so that participants will behave more naturally with regard to their attention to and use of television as well as other behaviors (e.g., aggression). Another approach is to measure some of the sources of extraneous setting variance and to use them in the analyses.

Random heterogeneity of respondents. Individual differences within treatment groups may be related to the dependent variables. For example, in the Steuer, Applefield, and Smith (1971) quasi-experiment described later in this chapter, some preschool children in each group differed in baseline levels of aggression, and it appeared that the mean group difference after exposure to the television content was due largely to an increase in aggression for just a few children (with some evidence of a later, perhaps retaliative, increase for others). Possible solutions to this threat to statistical conclusion validity are to select homogeneous participants (but this has external validity costs), to block respondents on characteristics most highly correlated with the dependent variable, and to choose within-participant error terms in pretest-posttest designs. Steuer et al. (1971) did use such a design. The reduction in error will be greater if the correlation between scores over time (the stability coefficient for the measured behavior) is higher.

Ruling Out Plausible Alternative Explanations: Threats to Internal Validity

The third necessary condition for causal inference is that there are no plausible alternative explanations of the behavior (B) other than the impact of television (A). For quasi-experiments, this is the most difficult of the three conditions to meet. Cook et al. (1990) presented a systematic list of these possible third-variable explanations, which they called *threats to internal validity*. All imply that the change observed in behavior is spurious because the same change would have occurred even if there had been no exposure to television or to certain types of content. In evaluating the results of the natural experiment we conducted using the communities with varying levels of television exposure—Notel, Unitel, and Multitel (described later in chapter)— we found it useful to consider each threat to internal validity very carefully in relation to the design and results of our study and to provide readers with a fairly detailed account of our reasoning (Williams, 1986a). Cook et al. (1990) described nine possible threats to internal validity.

History. The relationship between the presumed cause and effect might be due to some other event that took place between the pretest and the posttest. For example, some societal change other than a change in exposure to television might be the true cause of the behavior observed. Having more than two groups in the design reduces the likelihood that a general societal change affecting all groups would yield a pattern of findings that makes sense in relation to the differential availability of television, at least over a relatively short-term interval (in our natural experiment, 2 years). It also is important, however, to rule out any historical change specific to one or more of the groups. This is known as the internal validity threat of local history, or the interaction of history with selection. For example, if we had studied three isolated communities rather than three with normal road and rail service, and if accessibility had increased in Notel concurrently with the arrival of television (e.g., if a road had been built that also brought television reception), then it would have been more difficult to rule out history as a plausible threat to internal validity.

Maturation. A presumed causal relationship might be due instead to participants becoming older, becoming wiser, or changing in other ways between the pretest and the posttest. One approach is to include at least two age/grade levels in the pretest to see whether that cross-sectional comparison yields the same type of difference as the pretest-posttest longitudinal comparison. For example, we studied the aggressive behavior of children in Grades 1, 2, 4, and 5 in Notel, Unitel, and Multitel just before Notel obtained television reception (Joy, Kimball, & Zabrack, 1986). There were no differences in physical or verbal aggression among those four age/grade levels, and so 2 years later we studied children in Grades 1 and 2 (pretest-posttest cross-sectional comparison) and Grades 3 and 4 (longitudinal comparison). Finding no age/grade differences at both the pretest and the posttest enabled us to rule out maturation as an alternative explanation of change from the pretest to the posttest. We had even more confidence in ruling out maturation because we replicated the lack of age/grade differences; that is, it held true for all three towns and both genders at both the pretest and the posttest.

Testing. An effect might be due to taking a test more than once. For example, participants might look up correct answers and do better on the second test. Or, participants might become "testwise," that is, become better at taking those types of tests. We were concerned about this problem in some of the studies we conducted in Notel, Unitel, and Multitel. For example, individual adults were given difficult set-breaking creative thinking problems (Suedfeld, Little, Rank, Rank, & Ballard, 1986). Solving such problems requires thinking about the materials provided in a new and different way. Those who succeeded on the "Duncker candle problem" in the pretest probably would have remembered the solution (once a participant "breaks set," he or she tends not to forget), and those who did not succeed might well have worked at it further on their own or talked about it with neighbors. We therefore gave the "nine dot problem" at the posttest. This had the distinct disadvantage that we could not make direct pretest-posttest comparisons, but it did enable us to assess the similarities and differences in the pattern of results for the three towns in the pretest and posttest. In other studies we conducted (e.g., observation of aggressive behavior on the school playground), testing could be ruled out as an alternative explanation. Neither the students nor the teachers knew of our interest in aggressive behavior (or, for that matter, of our focus on television).

Instrumentation. A change might be found because the measuring instrument changed between the pretest and the posttest. This was true for our set-breaking creative problem-solving task, but we thought it more important in that case to rule out the internal validity threat of testing because it was not absolutely necessary to make individual pretest-posttest comparisons. Another type of change in measuring instrument mentioned by Cook et al. (1990) requiring caution is a physical instrument whose properties change, perhaps because of shifts in reliability or scaling artifacts such as ceiling (most scores are high) or basement effects (most scores are low). They also mentioned that having different persons recording observations could produce a change. The solution may be to have the same observers in the pretest and posttest and to be sure that interobserver reliability has been maintained over the interval. But it may be important in some instances to have different observers and for these observers to be "blind" to the hypotheses, insofar as possible, as well as blind to the results obtained at the pretest. This would be especially true if the correct hypotheses would be relatively easy for the observers to guess, which usually is the case for research on television.

Statistical regression to the mean. If respondents are grouped on the basis of pretest sources or their correlates and some error in measurement has occurred (which usually is the case), then high pretest scorers will score lower and low pretest scorers will score higher at the posttest. It is preferable not to use pretest scores or their correlates in assigning participants to groups in field experiments. In natural experiments involving preexisting groups, this particular form of the problem of regression to the mean is not relevant, although regression can still occur for other reasons.

Selection. It is essential to rule out the possibility that differences between the conditions in the study are due to different types of persons serving in each group rather than to the different treatments. This problem of potential preexisting group differences is the reason for using random assignment whenever possible. Selection has been a problem in a number of natural experiments involving television because media penetration varies systematically with socioeconomic status (SES). More affluent and better educated families tend to acquire new technologies sooner than do less affluent and less educated families, and such families also vary in a number of other ways (e.g., attitudes, interests, activities) that covary both with SES and with use of the newly acquired medium. Ruling out selection as a threat to internal validity is difficult because it is theoretically always possible that there are preexisting group differences on some variables that have not been considered. It is important to assess as many demographic variables as possible, as well as variables that may be correlated with the behavior of interest, and to show that the groups do not differ on these variables. If they do differ, then those variables can be used as controls (e.g., partialled out) in the analyses. The problem of selection lies at the core of the advantage of having a pretest for making causal inferences in quasi-experiments. The researchers can show not only that the groups do not differ on relevant demographic and related variables but also that they do not differ on the behaviors of special interest (e.g., creativity, reading skill, aggression). If they do differ at the pretest, then a variety of techniques can be used in the analyses to deal with the initial difference.

Mortality. The groups may differ at the posttest not because of the effect of interest (e.g., exposure to television) but rather because there has been differential mortality (e.g., attrition, dropout) from the groups. This is, in effect, the problem of selection operating at the posttest rather than at the pretest. One way in which to minimize this threat to internal validity is to minimize attrition. This can be done by choosing a pretest-posttest interval that is long enough to assess the effects of the treatment but not so long that many people will have moved (in a natural experiment) or left the group (in a quasi-experiment). For our natural experiment, we chose 2 years. Several other researchers have chosen 1 year. In addition, it is important to assess and report attrition rates and to show, whenever possible, that they are similar for the groups studied. For example, in Notel, Unitel, and Multitel, the proportions of all children in Grades 1 through 10 who still were in school in their same communities 2 years later were 72%, 71%, and 72%, respectively. This makes it unlikely that the arrival of television in Notel prompted an exodus of people who had previously chosen to live there because there was no television reception (Williams, 1986b). In this case, ruling out mortality also addresses the threat of selection. Another important way in which to rule out the threat of differential mortality as an explanation of posttest differences is to show that the individuals lost through attrition did not differ in the behavior of interest (e.g., aggression) at the pretest from those retained. This was a problem in the longitudinal correlational study of aggression and television conducted by the NBC research group (Milavsky, Stipp, Kessler, & Rubens, 1982). Attrition was highest for the most aggressive students, which reduced variability for the later comparisons.

Interactions with selection. Many of the foregoing threats to internal validity "can interact with selection to produce forces that can masquerade as treatment effects" (Cook et al., 1990, p. 500). The most common is selection-maturation; the groups may contain different types of persons (e.g., may vary in SES) who may mature at different rates for the behavior of interest (e.g., school achievement). Selection-history (or local history) as a threat is another interaction example (see my earlier comments in the "History" paragraph).

Ambiguity about the direction of causal influence. One could rule out all plausible alternative explanations of an A-B relationship and still not be sure whether A causes B or B causes A. This threat is most salient in correlational studies, for example, those in which television viewing and some behavior such as aggression are concurrently correlated. As Cook et al. (1990) pointed out, this threat is not a problem in most experiments, in most longitudinal research, or when one direction of causal influence is relatively implausible.

The preceding threats to internal validity apply in principle to all types of experiment but are more difficult to rule out for quasi-experiments than for randomized experiments. Selection (on its own or in interaction with maturation or history), history itself, maturation, and instrumentation are of particular concern in quasi-experiments. Mortality and selection-history can be of particular concern in randomized experiments. Cook et al. (1990) recommended that "researchers have to be their own most trenchant critics and systematically think through how each threat may have influenced the data" (p. 502). They went on to say, however, that it is difficult to be a harsh self-critic, and so it is desirable to obtain critical commentary from outsiders—the more tough-minded and more ideologically opposed to the findings, the better. When all plausible threats "can be ruled out—including those unique to the local setting studied and not in lists of validity threats—then the confident provisional conclusion can be made that the relationship is causal" (p. 502).

Threats to Construct Validity

Internal validity threats must be distinguished from threats to *construct validity,* which require ruling out alternative explanations of the *entities* claimed as A and B. What one researcher interprets as a causal relationship between A and B, another might consider to be a causal relationship between A and D, between C and B, or even between C and D. Construct validity is concerned with alternative interpretations of manipulations and measures, not of intervening causal processes. For research on television and behavior, this would involve examining carefully that the behavior studied (e.g., aggression) is not really something else (e.g., rough-and-tumble play) and that exposure to television is as it is purported to be.

Cook et al. (1990) recommended that researchers use "multiple operationalism" (i.e., multiple exemplars of each construct) and that these be chosen deliberately so as to share common variance attributable to the target construct as well as to differ in irrelevant components. In addition, independent measures of both the independent variable and the outcome measures are recommended. This facilitates judging how well the experimental manipulations and measures tap into the target content space of the constructs. In effect, such methods assess *convergent validity,* the extent to which different measures purported to assess the same construct actually do so. It also is important to establish *discriminant validity,* that is, that there is noticeably less correlation among measures of related but different substantive constructs than among different measures of the same construct (Campbell & Fiske, 1959).

Cook et al. (1990) pointed out that, especially in applied research, most social treatments are complex packages, making it difficult to identify the effective treatment components. Establishing high construct validity helps promote reproducibility, as well as efficiency, because information is obtained about ineffective components of the treatment that may be dropped in the future. In Cook et al.'s terms, the 11 possible threats to construct validity are as follows.

Inadequate preoperational explication of constructs. Researchers must be sure that the way in which they measure a construct is consistent with its conceptualization. Cook et al. (1990) provided the example that most definitions of aggression include both the intent to harm and the consequence of harm, but in some studies accidental physical harm is called aggression. In the realm of research on television, distinctions among physical, verbal, and other (e.g., psychological) aggression are not always specified clearly, and although most people distinguish conceptually between aggression and violence (as an extreme subcategory of aggression), that distinction is not always made in research.

Mono-operation bias. When only one example of a possible cause and/or one measure of the possible effect are used, construct validity will be lower. Cook et al. (1990) argued that there is no excuse for not using multiple outcome measures because this is not costly. Assessing two or more exemplars of a treatment does involve considerable extra effort but, in their view, should be attempted whenever possible. Our original plan for our before-and-after study in Notel included only one comparison group, Unitel, but the benefits of being able to assess patterns of findings across three towns far outweighed the additional time and expense involved in adding Multitel to the design (Williams, 1986b). Others who have included three or more groups in their natural (e.g., Kubey, White, Saphir, Chen, & Appiah, 1996; Murray & Kippax, 1977, 1978) and field (e.g, Friedrich & Stein, 1973) experiments likely would agree.

Interaction of procedure and treatment. Time might be conceptually interwoven with a construct that has no necessary temporal attribute. For example, measurement has to end at some point, but we may not know for how long the treatment will cause an effect. Research on the impact of changes in the availability of television provides a good example. At what point does "regular" viewing set in and any initial "novelty" effect of the change wear off? This is an important question for researchers studying natural experiments and involves weighing such questions against the internal threat to validity of attrition, especially selective attrition, from the pretest to the posttest.

Diffusion or imitation of the treatment. If there is a wide diffusion of the treatment (e.g., a health campaign via mass media), or if the experimental and control groups can communicate, then treatment crossover (Rubin, 1986) may occur. A version of this probably occurred in early natural experiments involving television in which children whose families did not own televisions were matched with children whose families did have them (e.g., Furu, 1962; see also the main study of Himmelweit, Oppenheim, & Vince, 1958). The former children may well have watched television at the homes of friends. This would reduce any differences, making the study a conservative test of effects.

Compensatory equalization of the treatment. This can occur because of ethical considerations concerning the availability of potentially positive benefits. Neither this threat nor the following one seems relevant to quasi-experimental studies involving television.

Compensatory rivalry. This can occur if control groups are aware of their situation and try to make up for being the underdogs.

Resentful demoralization of respondents receiving less desirable treatments. This situation might yield a difference between groups that would be wrongly attributed to the treatment rather than to one or more groups reacting in a resentful manner to not receiving the more desirable treatment. This particular alternative has been discussed (e.g., by Friedrich-Cofer & Huston, 1986; Huesmann, Eron, Berkowitz, & Chaffee, 1992; Joy et al., 1986; Liebert, Davidson, & Sobol, 1972; Liebert, Sobol, & Davidson, 1972; Stein & Friedrich, 1975) as an explanation of the anomalous findings obtained by Feshbach and Singer (1971) for their field experiment (described in greater detail later in this chapter). They found that the adolescent males residing in institutional homes who were initally high in aggressive behavior and low in fantasy aggression displayed more aggression over 6 weeks of watching a nonaggressive television diet than did their counterparts who watched programs with aggressive content. Huesmann et al.'s (1992) explanation for this aberrant finding was that "the frustration-induced instigation to aggression was stronger than the aggression-enhancing effects of the violent programs" (p. 195). Most of the youths preferred the aggressive shows to the nonaggressive programs, and their usual television diets included many aggressive programs. Thus, those assigned to watch nonaggressive programming they did not like as well may have been frustrated and resentful, particularly because they were aware that others were watching the more preferred shows. Indeed, the adolescent males in the nonaggressive condition objected so strongly to not being allowed to see *Batman* (a highly aggressive show) that it was made an exception and included in their list of allowable programs. Resentment may well be a problem in any study in which participants are not allowed to watch their favorite programs, especially if this is over a relatively long period. Both the Feshbach and Singer (1971) and Parke, Berkowitz, Leyens, West, and Sebastian (1977) studies were conducted with youths in institutional settings in the United States. Both teams of researchers used neutral movies/television programs that were not as exciting and interesting as the programs containing violence, although in Parke et al.'s case this was corrected in their second field experiment. As Leyens, Camino, Parke, and Berkowitz (1975) pointed out, "One could almost contend that subjects exposed to nonaggressive programs constitute the experimental group when they are compared with other subjects who are shown aggressive films, that is, what they usually see on their TV or movie theater screen" (p. 348).

Hypothesis guessing within experimental conditions. Some participants try to please the researcher(s) by responding as they think they are expected to respond. This problem can be reduced by making hypotheses hard to guess, decreasing the reactivity in the experiment, or deliberately providing different participants with different hypotheses. In some quasi-experiments involving television, the researchers' interest in the effects of television can be disguised; in others, that would be difficult or impossible. This threat to construct validity undoubtedly varies with development and is of less concern with younger children than with older children.

Evaluation apprehension. Participants may try to present themselves as psychologically healthy and competent so that they will be evaluated favorably by researchers they believe to be experts in personality adjustment and task performance. Again, this problem applies less to children than to adults.

Experimenter expectancies. Rosenthal (1966) showed that researchers tend to confirm their expectations and can bias their data. When those who conduct the study have no expectations or false expectations, this threat is reduced. In natural experiments involving television, it usually is not possible to keep raters and observers blind to the conditions of each group, but that often is possible in field experiments.

Confounding levels of constructs with constructs. When A and B (e.g., television exposure and another behavior, respectively) are not linearly related, then some but not all levels of A may affect B. In the case of television and school achievement, a threshold model has been suggested as more plausible than a linear model (Hornik, 1981; Williams, 1981). Up to some level of exposure, there may be no relationship or a positive impact of television viewing on school achievement, particularly for students at the lower SES levels. Over some middle range of viewing, there may be a linear negative relationship. Beyond some upper range of heavy viewing, there may be no additional impact. There is some evidence to support this model, although there also is some contradictory evidence (for a review, see MacBeth, 1996a). The best control for this threat to construct validity is to include a wide range for both variables.

Generalizing to Other Times, Places, and People: Threats to External Validity

In addition to being concerned with threats to statistical conclusion validity, internal validity, and construct validity, researchers conducting quasi-experiments on television and human behavior must consider *external validity*. To what extent can the findings obtained for the sample studied be generalized to other times, places, and people? For example, how representative of preschools in the same or other cities in the past, now, and in the future are the preschools studied in a particular field experiment? Another external validity question posed by Cook et al. (1990) that overlaps with, but is distinct from, this question is the question of extrapolation to unstudied universes and entities. To my mind, this would include variations in television across past and future decades, in its differing availability in various parts of the world and in its different forms (e.g., networks, specialty channels, interactive television).

In general, Cook et al. (1990) described threats to external validity as causal contingencies that yield a statistical interaction between the treatment (television exposure) and the threat. They described five such threats.

Interaction of treatments with treatments. When a group experiences more than one treatment, it is not clear whether a causal finding could be generalized to the situation in which only one is experienced. The solution is to give just one treatment or to vary the order so that the effect of the treatments received first and later can be compared. Parke et al. (1977) did this in their second field experiment (described later in this chapter). For most quasi-experiments on television, however, this problem and the next one do not seem to me to be particularly relevant. One could argue that certain designs (e.g., that being studied by Kubey et al., 1996) in which all groups have more than one television channel do not enable us to know about the impact of only one channel, but there have been other studies of just that situation.

Interaction of testing with treatment. Can the cause-effect relationship be generalized beyond the testing conditions in the study? Cook et al. (1990) said this is especially important if a pretest might somehow influence the way in which the treatment is experienced. A posttest-only control group is the solution.

Interaction of selection with treatment. To whom can the cause-effect relationship be generalized? This is an important issue when evaluating quasi-experiments involving television. Some natural experiments have been based on small samples. So far as I know, all involved samples that were relatively homogeneous with regard to racial/ethnic groups and thus different from the diverse, multicultural nature of urban North American and European society today. Nevertheless, several natural experiments have had the strength of including all or a high proportion of possible respondents in the samples studied, which reduces considerably the problems characteristic of volunteer samples. One of the techniques we used to address the issue of generalizability from our study of Notel, Unitel, and Multitel (Williams, 1986a) was to compare the performance of our participants with national norms, standardization samples (which are purposively structured to be representative of the U.S. or Canadian population), or urban samples when possible. To the extent that they were comparable (and in general they were), we felt more confident about the generalizability of the findings.

Interaction of setting with treatment. Do causal relationships obtained in a particular setting generalize to others? This threat to external validity, which is a common criticism of laboratory experiments on the effects of television, also must be considered when evaluating field and natural experiments. To the extent that similar findings are obtained across a variety of settings, including both more restricted (e.g., institutional) and more natural (e.g., elementary school) environments, as well as in different regions and countries, we can be more confident in drawing causal conclusions about the effects of television.

Interaction of history with treatment. To which other historical periods, both past and future, can a particular causal relationship be generalized? As much as possible, quasi-experiments should be replicated at different times. This seems especially important when the variable of interest, in this case television, changes dramatically over time on so many dimensions, including the number of channels available as well as the content, color, size, and location of television sets.

Ultimately, however, as Cook et al. (1990) pointed out, it is impossible to "extrapolate with any logical certainty from the persons, settings, and times of a study to all the different classes of person, setting, and time of interest to the various stakeholders in social research" (pp. 510-511). They did, however, suggest several techniques for increasing external validity in research involving causal hypotheses. A *random sampling model* may be used to obtain representative samples, but the financial costs are high and volunteer samples are more common. *Generalizing to modal instances* involves choosing a sample that reflects the mode. A third technique, which is a general version of the second, is to *impressionistically generalize on the basis of category membership alone.* The sample is selected in this case because it is typical of some target population of interest. A fourth approach is to purposively sample so as to have *heterogeneous samples* of persons, settings, and times. The goal is to sample many categories and to achieve robustness of results across them rather than formal representativeness. Meta-analysis does this by asking whether an effect is detectable despite heterogeneity in such external validity threats.

With regard to television, the causal generalization question might be stated as follows: Does the size or direction of a causal relationship depend on the type of television, amount viewed, developmental stage of the viewer, gender, country, or time period when the study was conducted? This requires evaluating the entire body of research rather than a single study or set of studies using a single methodology.

How Are the Four Types of Validity Related?

According to Cook et al. (1990), internal and statistical conclusion validity are similar in that both promote causal relationships, whereas construct and external validity are similar in dealing with generalization from such causal relationships. In designing any quasi-experiment (or other type of study), it is important to realize that trade-offs among the four types of validity are inevitable. For making causal inferences, Cook et al. (1990) argued that internal validity is the most important and that for quasi-experiments this is best accomplished through design rather than statistical adjustments.

■ Examples of Natural Experiments Involving Television

Natural experiments involve the study of intact or preexisting groups that vary naturally rather than through researcher assignment. What types of natural experiments assessing the effects of television on behavior have been conducted? Following the design terminology used by Cook et al. (1990), they fall mainly into four categories. Cook et al. wished to avoid rigid distinctions among the categories but stated that, generally speaking, the first three types of design do not usually permit causal inferences, whereas the last category of design involving nonequivalent control groups generally does produce interpretable causal results.

The One Group Posttest Design

In this design, participants are studied only once after the treatment of interest has occurred. Because there is no pretest or control group, the design is generally uninterpretable causally, but the findings may nevertheless be of interest in certain circumstances. Research conducted in New York City from 1976 to 1982 by Winick (1988) provides a good example. He interviewed families, each of which had only one television set, during the weeks following loss of the use of that set (because it broke down [81%] or was stolen [19%]). He obtained the names of such families from informal sources, repair services, stores, community groups, and law enforcement agencies. He conducted 1,614 interviews with individuals in 680 homes. When interviewed, the families had been living without television for an average of 6 weeks (range: 12 to 21) after having had their sets for at least 3 years. The sample was comparable in SES, ethnicity, and education to census data for the area. Winick noted, however, that television "superfans" probably were underrepresented, that is, families with more than one television set (which was not the norm at that time) or that obtained other sets while waiting for repairs. All available persons in each home were interviewed. The focus was on pre- and postloss use of media and the details, nature, and intensity of participants' responses to the loss of their television sets.

The One Group Pretest-Posttest Design

In television research of this type, observations would be made on individuals in a preexisting group prior to their exposure to television (pretest) and then again following exposure (posttest). The lack of any comparison group, either a no-treatment control or some other comparison, usually makes it impossible to rule out some alternative plausible explanations for any observed changes. In particular, the internal validity threats of history, maturation, and regression rarely are implausible, and so this type of design usually is not causally interpretable. For these reasons, when I became aware in 1973 of a town that had no television reception but would be obtaining it shortly, I decided that we could not study just that town (Notel) before and after it obtained television. We would have to study at least one comparison or control town on both occasions if we wanted to attempt to draw causal inferences about the effects of television. In the end, we studied Notel and two control towns (MacBeth, 1996a, 1996b; Williams, 1986b, 1995), as described subsequently under the heading "Untreated Control Group Designs With Pretests."

Posttest-Only Design With
Nonequivalent Groups

In some studies of the effects of television, comparisons have been made between individuals (or a community) who have acquired television reception and others who have not yet done so. There is no pretest against which to compare the posttest findings, and that is the main flaw of the design (Cook et al., 1990). It may not be possible to decide whether differences between the posttest groups are due to television exposure or simply to other differences between the groups that might have been apparent had there been a pretest. The main survey in the study of the introduction of television to the United Kingdom by Himmelweit et al. (1958) is a classic example of the posttest-only design with nonequivalent groups.

United Kingdom

In their main survey, Himmelweit et al. (1958) tested children in England attending state schools in London, Portsmouth, Sunderland, and Bristol. In their total sample of 4,500 children, there were 1,854 viewers (children with television at home). Himmelweit and her colleagues matched each viewer on gender, age (10-11 and 13-14 years), IQ (115 or above, 100-114, and below 100), and SES. They used the term *working class* for children with parents in blue-collar jobs and *middle class* for those with parents in white-collar jobs. As far as possible, matching was done within the same classrooms to hold constant the influence of teachers, school, other children, and geographic factors. The four factors on which children were matched were chosen because in previous research they had been found to account for many of the important differences in children's outlook and leisure activities.

Himmelweit et al. (1958) readily acknowledged that, with the design of their main study, any differences they observed could not,

> however, be automatically ascribed to viewing; our matching criteria were, of course, not exhaustive, and there remains the possibility that the differences might already have existed before the viewers acquired their television sets. We knew already that the two groups must have been to some extent different in that in one case their families decided to buy a television set, whilst the others—despite similar incomes—preferred to use their money in other ways. Such differences in home background might well find expression in the children's attitudes and behavior. If this were so, some of the differences found in the main survey would not be due to the effects of viewing but would be due to pre-existing differences between children from homes which bought televisions early and those which did not. (p. 5)

This is an excellent description of the internal validity threat of selection.

Having recognized the methodological limitations of their main survey because it lacked a pretest, Himmelweit et al. (1958) conducted an additional study that took advantage of a natural experiment in which a new transmitter was opened in Norwich. They gave survey questionnaires to all the 10- to 11- and 13- to 14-year olds (2,200 in total) in nearly every school in Norwich when very few families had television sets. A year later, they repeated their survey and at that point compared a group of 185 children whose families had since acquired television sets with a group of 185 whose families had not by matching them as they had done in their main survey. The design of the Norwich study falls into the category described by Cook et al. (1990) as the untreated control group design with pretests, which I discuss in more detail subsequently. The Norwich study had the methodological strengths associated with natural before-and-after studies, but the small sample size did not permit exploration of the roles of age, gender, IQ, and SES in relation to the use and effects of television, as was done in the main survey. Moreover, the Norwich study assessed only the more immediate effects of television following its recent introduction, whereas in the main survey all viewers who had had television for less than 3 months were excluded. By conducting their study in two parts with contrasting methodological strengths and weaknesses, Himmelweit et al. could then examine their results to see where the two methods yielded congruent and contrasting findings.

Since the Himmelweit et al. (1958) main survey, the posttest-only design with nonequivalent groups also has been used by several other researchers in other locales to study the effects of television.

North America

In North America, Schramm, Lyle, and Parker (1961) conducted 11 studies between 1958 and 1960. Most were conducted in the United States on children, parents, and families, with an emphasis on the use of television and other media in communities with television reception (San Francisco, Rocky Mountains, a metropolitan suburb, and Denver). Two of their studies were conducted in B.C., Canada, in two communities that were comparable except that one (Teletown) had television reception and one (Radiotown) did not. A total of 913 children in Grades 1, 6, and 10, as well as 269 parents, were studied.

Both Teletown and Radiotown had populations of about 5,000 and were similar in industrial support, social structure, government, and school system. But whereas Radiotown was 4,000 miles from a major metropolitan area and 200 miles from the nearest open-circuit television station, Teletown was within the television distance of a Canadian metropolitan area and also not far from the U.S. border. Almost all adults and most of the children in Radiotown had seen television elsewhere, but they could not watch it regularly at home. In Teletown, more than 75% of the children had television sets at home, and the others watched regularly at friends' homes. Information such as this about the penetration of the medium under study is important to document because of the problem mentioned earlier that speed of acquisition of new technologies varies according to a number of factors, including SES. In this case, most Radiotown residents were familiar with television and, as Schramm et al. (1961) stated, yearned for it. That, coupled with the fact that 25% of Teletown residents did not have television, made comparisons between the towns a conservative test of differences related to television.

As was the case for the Himmelweit et al. (1958) main study, the lack of a pretest in Teletown or a posttest in Radiotown makes it impossible to rule out the alternative possibility that any differences observed were due not to television but rather to preexisting differences between the two communities. At the end of this section, I describe some techniques suggested by Cook et al. (1990) for dealing with the absence of pretest assessments.

Australia

A third example of the posttest-only with nonequivalent groups design was conducted by Murray and Kippax (1977, 1978) in Australia. They studied three towns that were similar in size (populations of 2,000-3,000) and social structure but different in the duration, content, and magnitude of their experience with television. They were located in rural areas, and 1971 census information indicated that they did not differ significantly in total population, housing conditions, ethnic composition, or SES, although there were slight variations in educational level and family size. The "high-TV" town had had 5 years' experience with a commercial channel and 2 years' experience with the national public channel (Australian Broadcasting Corporation or ABC). Whereas ABC devoted 34% of its weekly broadcast time to specific educational/instructional programming for adults and children (including programs designed specifically for school use), only 3% of the commercial channel's programming was of this type. News and documentaries accounted for 20% of ABC's weekly output but only 13% of the commercial channel's weekly output. In addition, the weekly broadcast time was 66% greater for the public channel (98.8 hours) than for the commercial channel (59.5 hours). The "low-TV" town had had 1 year's experience with the public (ABC) channel, and the "no-TV" town did not receive a signal.

An effort was made to obtain a random 50% sample of families in each town with children under 12 years of age. Families were located using electoral rolls, town canvassing, school enrollments, and birth records. The towns were divided into geographic sectors, and interviewers contacted sequentially, without callback, all the families in each sector. There were no refusals by any family contacted, although there were some unsuccessful interviews because no one was home. The final sample sizes and their percentages of the estimated populations of families with children under 12 in each town were 82 (40%) for the high-TV town, 102 (40%) for the low-TV town, and 98 (52%) for the no-TV town.

The problem that when the penetration of a technology is less than near universal, it tends to vary with SES (which applied at least to some extent to the Himmelweit et al., 1958, English study and to the Schramm et al., 1961, Canadian study) did not apply to Murray and Kippax's (1977, 1978) Australian study. In addition, having three groups that vary on a continuum of exposure to television may make other preexisting differences among the towns easier to detect or rule out (Cook et al., 1990). With three towns, one is looking for a sensible pattern of findings in relation to the different levels of television exposure. Some preexisting differences that could account for differences between two towns that appear to be related to television probably would not map so well onto a three-town continuum. The caveat here, however, is that some preexisting differences might covary with the levels of television exposure and indeed map well onto the continuum.

Cook et al. (1990) described three ways in which researchers can, in some circumstances, attempt to deal with the main structural flaw limiting causal inferences in posttest-only designs with nonequivalent groups, namely the absence of a pretest. The first is to attempt to obtain a *retrospective pretest* measure. The problem, as they point out, is that there is a good deal of evidence that retrospective reports differ from prospective ones for a variety of reasons, including faulty memory, the influence of stereotypes, etc. This would apply to retrospective estimates of prior media use as well as to reports of other behaviors. The second technique for handling the lack of a pretest is to *form the treatment and control groups through matching* on correlates of the pretest (Cook et al., 1990). The potential hazard is undermatching, that is, not matching on enough or the most relevant variables. For example, Himmelweit et al. (1958) and Murray and Kippax (1977, 1978) provided evidence that the groups they compared were similar in terms of several demographic and social structure variables, but they may have differed in other ways that were not measured.

The third suggestion for overcoming the lack of pretest assessments is to measure proxies for them and then make statistical adjustments. Proxies are variables that correlate with the posttests but are not measured on the same scale. They include demographic measures such as SES, age, and gender, which, along with IQ, were used as a type of pretest proxy by Himmelweit et al. (1958) in their main survey. Proxies also include measures different from but conceptually closer to the posttest measures. For example, researchers using a posttest-only design with nonequivalent groups to assess the effects of television might have administered a vocabulary test to two or more groups varying in exposure, as Schramm et al. (1961) did to Grade 1 students in Radiotown and Teletown. Lacking a planned pretest assessment using the same vocabulary test, the researchers might find in the school records that another vocabulary test had been given prior to television exposure, and this could be used as a pretest proxy. Choosing to assess vocabulary in Grade 1 (a wise choice from a theoretical perspective) probably ruled out this possibility for Schramm et al. And it is important to note that although proxies may correlate with the posttest within each treatment group, they usually do so less well than pretests given with the same instrument as the posttest (Campbell & Reichardt,

1991). For that reason and others that they discuss, Cook et al. (1990) said they are "skeptical about proxy-based adjustment procedures, even though they are widely advertised in econometrics (e.g, Heckman & Holtz, 1989a, 1989b). Empirical work on these procedures has not been particularly promising (e.g., Lalonde, 1986; Murnane, Newstead, & Olsen, 1985), and many mathematical statisticians pronounce themselves skeptical (e.g., Holland, 1989)" (p. 522).

In the absence of a pretest, substantive theory may be good enough to generate a highly differentiated causal hypothesis that, if corroborated, would rule out most internal validity threats because they are not capable of generating the same pattern of empirical implications (Cook et al., 1990). That is, when a more complex data pattern is predicted from substantive theory, the outcome measures are quite reliable, and the sample sizes are large. Cook et al. stated that posttest-only designs with nonequivalent groups can be quite strong. This is what I had in mind when discussing the three-town design of Murray and Kippax's (1977, 1978) Australian study.

Untreated Control Group Designs With Pretests

According to Cook et al. (1990), this category of designs is generally more interpretable than the preceding two and facilitates causal inference but does not guarantee it. The natural experiments involving television that have been based on this category of designs all have been in the first subcategory discussed by Cook et al., the untreated control group design with dependent pretest and posttest samples.

Japan

The earliest study of a natural experiment involving television focused more on use than on effects and was conducted in Japan by Furu (1962, 1971). In 1957, he surveyed a group of children in Shizuoka whose families had televisions. At that time, it was rare in Japan to have a television set at home, although a "street-corner TV system" with sets in shrine compounds and plazas in front of railway stations had been popular since 1953. These children with television sets in their homes were compared with an individually matched group of children without television sets in their homes. Two years later, in

1959, a second survey in Shizuoka was conducted to provide a comparison with the first one.

Scotland

In Scotland, Brown, Cramond, and Wilde (1974) conducted a before-and-after study with three groups of children aged 5 to 11 years. The before-and-after television village was Arisaig, where 18 children were studied in May 1972 and May 1973, 4 months before and 8 months after the arrival of television reception. The neighboring district of Lochailort was the first control group, with 11 children who saw no television (except for daytime school broadcasts) in both 1972 and 1973. The second control group was the village of Furnace, where 18 children had television reception in both phases of the natural experiment. The research focused on functional similarities and differences in children's use of different media. Unfortunately, the very small sample sizes limit the conclusions that can be drawn from this otherwise strongly designed study.

Canada

A third example of a natural experiment involving television that used the untreated control group design with dependent pretest and posttest samples is the Canadian study I directed (MacBeth, 1996a, 1996b; Williams 1986b, 1995). We studied three towns twice, 2 years apart. During the first phase of data collection, in the fall of 1973, one of the towns (Notel) had no television reception but would begin to receive it when a repeating transmitter was installed about 2 months later. That transmitter brought one channel to Notel, the Canadian Broadcasting Corporation's (CBC)[2] national English-language channel. The first control town, Unitel, which is about an hour's drive away, had in 1973 been receiving that one channel, CBC, for about 7 years. The second control town, Multitel, had then been receiving three private national U.S. networks (ABC, CBS, and NBC), as well as CBC, for about 15 years. In the second wave or phase of data collection, Notel residents had received CBC for 2 years and reception had not changed in Unitel and Multitel.

Notel was not an isolated community but happened to be located in a valley in such a way that the transmitter meant to provide CBC reception prior to 1973, and that did successfully provide it to Unitel, did not succeed in doing so. As was the case in Radiotown in Schramm et al.'s (1961) study, Notel residents were very anxious to have television and had lobbied hard to obtain it. Almost all residents obtained reception as soon as it became available, and so the problem of penetration varying with SES did not apply. Notel, Unitel, and Multitel were similar in size (about 700 in the village, which served a population of about 3,000 via its shops, schools, medical facilities, etc.). The towns also were similar in their cultural diversity, SES mix, geographical and climate characteristics, types of industry in the area, and other dimensions, as reflected in Statistics Canada data (Williams, 1986a).

We studied a wide variety of behaviors including fluent reading skill, creativity, aggression, gender role attitudes, and participation in community activities. Some studies focused only on school-aged children, some on adults, and some on both. For most behaviors, we obtained both longitudinal and cross-sectional data for comparisons of Phase 1 with Phase 2. For example, in Phase 1 we assessed creativity for all students in Grades 4 and 7 in all three towns. In Phase 2, we reassessed these same students, now in Grades 6 and 9 (longitudinal comparison) as well as all students then in Grades 4 and 7 (cross-sectional comparison). The sample sizes for the studies were adequately large, ranging from 40 children in each town and phase for aggression, to 70 to 80 for creativity and reading skills, to more than 250 children and adults combined for participation in community activities.

United States

In a study that is still in progress, Kubey and his students (1996) are studying a natural experiment on the East Coast of the United States involving three small rural towns. Most residents of OldTVtown receive 2 to 4 channels, whereas residents of Cabletown receive a basic cable package of 20 to 25 channels. Dishtown residents used to receive the same channels as OldTVtown, and some still did when surveyed, but most Dishtown residents had gone from receiving 2 to 4 channels to receiving about 60 channels (plus some music, etc.). Dishtown was surveyed twice, 3 months and 20 months after start-up of the satellite dishes. OldTVtown and Cabletown were each surveyed once, at the same time as the second survey in Dishtown. In this natural experiment, like many others, the researchers only learned about the situation after the dishes had been installed and so could not obtain prospective before-dish data. They did, however, use some carefully worded retrospective measures, enabling them to make some longitudinal comparisons for some variables. Their data include hours of viewing; participation in various leisure, familial, and community activities; indicators of habitual or ingrained television habits; how parents deal with children's viewing; and so on. The data were obtained using surveys mailed to residents age 18 or over, with a 50% to 65% response rate for two mailings per wave of data collection. This study promises to provide some interesting findings about variations in television use as a function of the number of channels available.

In sum, a number of teams of researchers in different countries have taken advantage of natural experiments involving groups that differ in their access to television. Some have focused more on how television is used, whereas others have focused more on its effects. Survey methods, interviews, and behavioral observations have been included in the methodologies. Taken together, these natural experiments involving television provide an interesting set of models that could be used in studies of the inception and effects of other more recently available technologies as well as changes in the nature and availability of television itself (as Kubey et al., 1996, are doing). Let us turn now to some examples of field experiments involving television.

■ Examples of Field Experiments Involving Television

Like natural experiments, field experiments usually involve the study of intact or preexisting groups, but whereas in the former case the groups vary "naturally," in the latter case the researchers assign each group to some particular condition. What types of field experiments assessing the effects of television have been conducted? The examples discussed here all fall into what Cook et al. (1990) called the untreated control group design with dependent pretest and posttest samples.

In most field experiments involving television, two or more groups are assigned by the researchers to a particular television diet for some period, and their behavior is compared with that of an untreated control group that has no TV diet (other than, in some studies, regular home viewing) during the same period. Or, one group may be exposed to a particular type of television diet (e.g., aggressive content), whereas another group is exposed to a different type of television diet (e.g., television segments of equal length with no aggressive content or with prosocial content). Thus the word *untreated* does not necessarily mean no exposure; rather, it means no exposure to the content of special interest. Behavior assessed during a pretest period is used to demonstrate the equivalence of the groups on the behavior(s) of interest.

Preschool Studies

One of the early field experiments on the effects of televised aggression was conducted by Steuer et al. (1971). Previous randomized experiments conducted in a laboratory had shown that children's aggression toward inanimate objects when playing alone increased following exposure to filmed or televised aggression (e.g., Bandura, Ross, & Ross, 1963a, 1963b). That is, they showed that such exposure *can* lead to increased aggression. This raised the *does* question of whether children exposed to televised aggression would increase their aggressive behavior toward other children, that is, whether there would be evidence of increased interpersonal aggression among children playing in groups.

Steuer et al. (1971) studied five girls and five boys aged 41-60 months (mean: 51 months). They were ranked on the basis of a questionnaire about their amount of television viewing that their parents completed several weeks before the experiment, and for each successive pair of ranks (1 and 2, 3 and 4) one child was assigned to an experimental group (which saw aggressive videotapes) and one to a control group (which saw nonaggressive tapes). The groups played concurrently in different rooms for one 10-minute session per day, with the first 10 sessions/days providing a baseline comparison. For the next 11 sessions/days, each group viewed a videotaped Saturday morning children's television program for 10 minutes immediately prior to free play. The aggressive videotapes had been scored according to the same interpersonal aggression behaviors that were observed for the children and contained 15 to 32 (mean: 22) such behaviors.

The nonaggressive tapes were edited to contain no such aggression. During each session, each child was observed for 2 minutes, 1 minute in the first half of the session and 1 minute in the second half. Observers were systematically alternated between the groups. They were told (wrongly, so that they did not know which children had seen aggressive films on a given occasion) that children in both groups saw a random sequence of aggressive and nonaggressive programs. The analyses were conducted for each matched pair of experimental and control children. The focus was on the difference in mean interpersonal aggression scores between baseline and viewing sessions.

I have included this study as an example of a field experiment because it has many of the characteristics of such studies. It did not, however, involve comparison of strictly preexisting groups given that once the children in the five pairs were matched for reported home viewing behavior, each child was randomly assigned to the experimental or control group. With such small numbers, however, it would be difficult to achieve the goal of true randomization.

In another field experiment conducted in a summer nursery school program, Friedrich and Stein (1973) observed 52 boys' and 47 girls' free play over a 9-week period. They compared the children's behavior during an initial baseline period (3 weeks); a viewing period (4 weeks) in which the children watched either prosocial programs (*Mister Rogers' Neighborhood*), aggressive cartoons (*Batman* and *Superman*), or neutral children's films that had little or no prosocial or aggressive content; and a postviewing period (2 weeks). There were two morning and two afternoon classes of 25 children each that met for 2½ hours three times a week. In each classroom, the children were divided between one of the experimental conditions and the neutral condition, with experimental treatments assigned to classes by the toss of a coin. One morning and one afternoon class had 15 children in the aggressive condition and 10 in the neutral one, and one morning and one afternoon class had 15 in the prosocial condition and 10 in the neutral one. Gender, age, and SES were balanced in assigning individual children to classrooms; however, to include lower SES families (which were more difficult to recruit), it was necessary to give them their preferred (mostly morning) session. This provides a good illustration of the difficulties involved in establishing initially equivalent groups in quasi-experimental studies. And, as was the case with the Steuer et al. (1971)

study, the researchers were not faced with complete preexisting groups but had the chance to achieve some degree of balance with regard to some relevant variables (age, gender, and SES). In addition, other variables (e.g., short-form Stanford Binet IQ scores) could be used as controls and checks on group comparability in the analyses.

Procedurally, the television programs and films were shown in small, windowless rooms. Each classroom was divided into two shifts (A and B), each comprising children in both experimental and neutral conditions (7-10 children per shift). Children alternated between being in the first and second shifts, that is, whether they viewed earlier or later within their nursery school session on a particular day. In the aggressive condition, each cartoon consisted of two stories lasting slightly more than 20 minutes, with 6 *Batman* and 6 *Superman* cartoons shown on alternate days. The prosocial condition consisted of 12 *Mister Rogers* programs of about 28 minutes each. Two neutral films of 10 to 15 minutes each were shown per neutral session. There was almost no aggressive content in these films. Some prosocial content inevitably was included, but only if it was not emphasized and did not form the central theme. Observations of the children's aggressive and prosocial behavior, as well as of self-regulation in free play, were made throughout the entire nursery school session, with a total of 64 discrete categories of behavior observed.

Field Experiments in Institutions

Some quasi-experiments involving television have been conducted in institutional settings. Such settings have the advantage that the residents' media diet can be more precisely controlled over a longer period than is possible for participants living at home and attending a group setting on a part-time basis. The disadvantage, of course, is that external validity is limited to the types of individuals residing in those settings. The most well-known examples all have focused on adolescent males.

In the United States, Feshbach and Singer (1971) studied adolescent males residing in seven residential schools and institutions (five in California and two in the greater New York area). Three were private schools and four were residential homes for youths from lower SES families who were having difficulties at home. Both pretest and posttest assessments were obtained for 395 adolescents. In some cases, the individuals were randomly assigned to watch television with nonaggressive or aggressive content, whereas in other cases, they were randomly assigned by living group. In two residences, all were required to participate, whereas in the others, participation was voluntary. They were required to watch a minimum of 6 hours of television a week for 6 weeks but could watch as much as they wished provided that they watched only programs on the designated list (of nonaggressive or aggressive content). During the 6-week viewing period, and in most cases the week preceding as well as the week following the 6-week viewing period, a houseparent, supervisor, teacher, or proctor most familiar with each youth's daily activities completed a rating sheet 5 days a week covering aggressive acts toward peers and authority figures. Personality and other information (including television viewing habits) was obtained from each adolescent. The variations in the ways in which the treatment was implemented in each location provide a good illustration of the difficulties involved in doing research with intact groups. At first glance, the decision to include two different types of institutions, private schools and residential homes for youths with difficulties, might seem unusual. It did increase the range of SES and, thus, potentially increased the external validity. As it turned out, the differences between adolescent males who saw the aggressive versus nonaggressive content were greater for those in the youth homes, who also were rated higher in initial aggression. Differences for the private schools tended to be nonsignificant. Thus, the inclusion of both types of institutions enabled the researchers to address the potential threat to external validity of the interaction of selection with treatment.

In a minimum-security penal institution for juvenile offenders in the United States, Parke et al. (1977) conducted two field experiments. The adolescents males, ranging in age from 14 to 18 years (68% Euro-American, 26% African American, 6% other), were randomly assigned by the institution to cottages (30 each). During a 3-week baseline period, trained observers recorded the behavior of youths in two cottages about 2 hours per day for 3 consecutive days each week. Then, during the 5-day experimental period, the residents of one cottage saw an aggressive movie each evening, whereas the other cottage saw a neutral nonaggressive film. Behavior was observed before, during, and after the movies on Wednesday, Thursday, and Friday. The youths rated each movie on aggressiveness (e.g., brutal, cruel) and interest (e.g., interesting, funny) scales after seeing the movie and again at the week's end. Unfortunately, it turned out that the aggressive films were rated as more interesting and exciting, thus confounding interest and content (as occurred in the Feshbach & Singer, 1971, study). On the day after the final film, all youths participated in a laboratory test of aggression that involved shock to a confederate under either an angered or a nonangered condition. During the final 3-week follow-up phase, behavioral observations were made as in the baseline phase on 3 consecutive evenings. This study provides a good illustration of the importance of having a pretest because the youths in the cottage assigned to watch aggressive movies turned out to be more aggressive during the baseline phase than did those in the cottage who subsequently saw the nonaggressive films. This was dealt with by subclassifying them into high and low groups on the basis of their baseline aggression scores.

Having discovered some limitations in the design of their first field experiment, Parke et al. (1977) conducted a second one in the same institution. This study included two conditions. The first was a 7-week replication of the field experiment just described, with two changes. Behavioral observations were made on 5 days rather than just 3 days during the pre- and postmovie weeks, and more interesting neutral films were shown. The youths in this second field experiment rated them as being as interesting and exciting as the aggressive films, thus eliminating the confounding of interest and content that occurred in the first one. The second condition of this second experiment was a 2-week assessment of the impact of a single film shown on Friday at the end of the 1st week of observations. This provided a shortened version of the full-scale study to permit a direct comparison of single-exposure and repeated-exposure effects. All participants in this second field experiment took a verbal aggression laboratory test rather than the shock test used in the first field experiment.

In Belgium, Leyens et al. (1975) conducted a field experiment in a private secondary institution for delinquent secondary school youths. This was designed as a replication and extension of the Parke et al. (1977) U.S. studies, motivated in part by the problem, discussed earlier in this chapter, that resentful demoralization may have occurred in the

Parke et al. and Feshbach and Singer (1971) studies because the adolescents could not watch their preferred programming, which in the United States contained considerable violence. At the time the Leyens et al. (1975) study was conducted, this was not true of Belgian television, and many Belgian families and schools severely controlled their children's television and movie viewing. Youths in the Belgian institution resided in four cottages that differed with regard to number of residents (18, 16, 32, and 19) and space, but assignment of residents to the cottages "approximated a random procedure" (p. 348). Television viewing was very limited, strongly discouraged, and restricted to a list of permitted programs issued weekly (generally news, sports, and a few musical shows).

The study included three phases: a premovie baseline week, a movie treatment week, and a postmovie week. During the movie week, two cottages saw an aggressive film each evening and two saw a neutral film. During the noon period and at the end of the evening, an observer from each cottage recorded behavior using a time-sampling procedure, with each youth observed on several occasions. A total of 13 categories of behavior were noted, including both physical and verbal aggression. At the end of each movie, the adolescents rated it on 15 dimensions using 5-point scales. They rated the aggressive films as more aggressive, violent, brutal, and the like but not as more exciting, interesting, worthy of seeing again, and the like. Thus, the problem of differential preference for the aggressive and nonaggressive films characteristic of the Feshbach and Singer (1971) study and the first Parke et al. (1977) U.S. study did not apply in this field experiment. There were, however, preexisting differences in aggressive behavior among the groups. One of the cottages in the aggressive film condition and one in the neutral film condition had higher mean levels of aggression than did the other cottages in each condition. The data were therefore analyzed by cottage, noting which ones were initally high or low in aggression. The most likely explanation of the preexisting differences in aggression, according to the authors, was the strict control exerted by some counselors, especially in one of the cottages in the aggressive movie condition.

One potential design problem with this study, as well as with the Feshbach and Singer (1971) and Parke et al. (1977) studies in the

United States, is that the mean aggressive behavior data for each individual were used in the analyses, but interpersonal aggressive behaviors are not independent. Leyens et al. (1975) acknowledged this problem, but with only four groups (cottages) they could not surmount it. In the randomized field experiment by Josephson (1987) described subsequently, 66 groups, each comprising six boys, were included in the study, with the *group*'s behavior being the unit of analysis.

Randomized Experiments Conducted in Field Rather Than Laboratory Settings

In writing about research on the effects of television, I, along with other researchers, often have contrasted laboratory with field experiments (e.g., Freedman, 1984, 1986; Friedrich-Cofer & Huston, 1986; Huesmann et al., 1992; Joy et al., 1986; MacBeth, 1996b). To reiterate, laboratory experiments enable us to answer the *can* question of whether television exposure can cause a change in behavior but cannot tell us whether this *does* occur in day-to-day life, whereas some field and natural experiments do enable us to make causal inferences and answer the *does* question provided that certain conditions are met (e.g., threats to internal validity such as those discussed in this chapter can be ruled out). Random assignment of individuals to groups is a defining characteristic of laboratory experiments but usually is not true of studies discussed as field experiments. While writing this chapter, I have come to realize that distinctions among different types of research are fuzzy rather than clear-cut and that random assignment sometimes *is* true of studies conducted in field settings. They do not, therefore, all fall under the definition of quasi-experiments (Cook et al., 1990) and thus, technically speaking, the topic of this chapter. But they are potentially the strongest of all possible designs for studying the effects of television, enabling us to answer both the *can* and *does* questions and to make causal interpretations. So, I briefly outline one seminal example here.

The effect of television violence on boys' aggressive behavior was studied by Josephson (1987) in a complicated experiment conducted in a field setting. Groups of six boys were randomly selected from the eligible boys in Grades 2 and 3 at each of 13 schools. A total of 66 groups, each comprising six boys, was randomly assigned to one of the six different conditions of the experiment. All of the boys watched either a violent or a nonviolent 14-minute excerpt from a commercial television program. The nonviolent excerpt was about off-duty members of a state highway patrol coaching a boys' motocross bike-riding team. It contained no violence but was rated as being as exciting and as well liked as the violent excerpt by other boys the same age as those in the study. The violent excerpt was from a police action drama that included snipers and a SWAT team whose aggression was portrayed as justified revenge and was both successful and socially rewarded, features thought to make viewers more likely subsequently to behave aggressively (e.g., Bandura, 1983; Berkowitz, 1984). The violent excerpt also included a violence-related cue, which was the use of walkie-talkies by the snipers when the SWAT unit's attack began. Pilot testing revealed that 95% of boys who saw this excerpt remembered the walkie-talkie (Josephson, 1987).

The experiment also involved a frustration procedure. The boys were told that they would see some really neat cartoons, but when the videotape started it quickly became static and then "snow." Half of the boys were frustrated before they saw the television program (violent or nonviolent) and half after they saw it.

Procedurally, the boys were taken to a "TV room," were frustrated by the cartoon, and then saw the violent or nonviolent program (or vice versa). Then they were taken to the gymnasium for what they had been told was the second study. A male referee and two observers (one man and one woman) who did not know the boys' frustration order and television program type participated in this part of the experiment. The experimenter gave the referee a card with the six boys' team and number assignments (randomly determined) and left. The referee gave each boy his jersey and a hockey stick, explaining that the boys would play a short floor hockey game and take turns playing each position.[3] He also explained that observers would be doing a "play-by-play" of the game "like they do on the radio," and so he needed to know who the players were. The referee then did a pregame interview with each boy (name, class, and favorite position in hockey) and, following the instructions on the (randomly assigned) card, used either a tape recorder or a walkie-talkie for the interview. It was assumed that the tape recorder and microphone would be neutral to all boys and that the walkie-talkie would be neutral for those who saw the nonviolent television excerpt but would be a violence-related cue for those who saw the violent excerpt. The referee and observers were blind to the cueing hypothesis and had not seen the television excerpts.

The six boys then played floor hockey for three periods of 3 minutes each, rotating between periods so that each boy played center, wing, and goal. The observers watched the boys from the moment they put on their jerseys and dictated into a tape recorder every instance of aggressive action, identifying both the aggressor and target player by jersey color and number. Both physical and verbal aggressions were recorded, as were deliberate actions causing harm. If either rater was sure that an action was accidental, or if both thought that it might be, it was not included in the aggression score. Body checking was not included unless it involved pushing or elbowing.

This complicated randomized experiment conducted in a naturalistic field setting exemplifies the best principles of research design. Josephson's (1987) study, and some of the natural and quasi-experiments with strong designs I have described in this chapter, have been published since the mid-1980s. They were conducted subsequent to publication of some of the important reviews and debates about the effects of television (e.g., Freedman, 1984, 1986; Friedrich-Cofer & Huston, 1986). To my mind, they provide important new empirical evidence for such debates, and I find it perplexing that they have not been included in some more recently published reviews of that literature (e.g., Freedman, 1992; Huesmann et al., 1992).

■ Conclusion

The goal of this chapter has been to integrate up-to-date knowledge of the methodology of quasi-experiments (Cook et al., 1990) with the research designs of some natural and field experiments on television and human behavior. In the space and time available, it was only possible to provide examples of quasi-experiments involving television, not to provide an exhaustive overview. When well designed, natural and field experiments enable us to answer both the *can* and *does* questions about media effects, that is, to make causal inferences. Perhaps this integrative review can now serve as a starting point for new research that will further expand our knowledge regarding the effects of television and other media, including new technologies such as the Internet.

■ Notes

1. This and subsequent citations/references are to my former name, Tannis MacBeth Williams. I recently reverted to Tannis M. MacBeth.
2. CBC is a public service network, funded through a grant from the Canadian Parliament at arm's length from the government in power.
3. This study was conducted in Winnipeg, Manitoba, where boys are very familiar with both floor hockey and ice hockey.

■ References

Bandura, A. (1983). Psychological mechanisms of aggression. In R. G. Geen & C. I. Donnerstein (Eds.), *Aggression: Theoretical and empirical reviews*, Vol. 1: *Theoretical and methodological issues* (pp. 1-40). New York: Academic Press.

Bandura, A., Ross, D., & Ross, S. (1963a). Imitation of film-mediated aggressive models. *Journal of Abnormal and Social Psychology, 66*, 3-11.

Bandura, A., Ross, D., & Ross, S. (1963b). Vicarious reinforcement and imitative learning. *Journal of Abnormal and Social Psychology, 67*, 601-607.

Berkowitz, L. (1984). Some effects of thoughts on anti- and prosocial influences of media events: A cognitive-neoassociation analysis. *Psychological Bulletin, 95*, 419-427.

Brown, J., Cramond, D. J., & Wilde, R. (1974). Displacement effects of television and the child's functional orientation to media. In J. G. Blumler & E. Katz (Eds.), *The uses of mass communications* (pp. 93-112). Beverly Hills, CA: Sage.

Campbell, D. T., & Fiske, D. W. (1959). Convergent and discriminant validation by the multitrait-multimethod matrix. *Psychological Bulletin, 56*, 81-105.

Campbell, D. T., & Reichardt. C. S. (1991). Problems in assuming the comparability of pretest and posttest in autoregressive and growth models. In R. E. Snow & D. E. Wiley (Eds.), *Strategic thinking: A volume in honor of Lee J. Cronbach* (pp. 201-219). San Francisco: Jossey-Bass.

Campbell, D. T., & Stanley, J. C. (1966). *Experimental and quasi-experimental design for research*. Chicago: Rand McNally.

Cook, T. D., & Campbell, D. T. (1976). The design and conduct of quasi-experiments and true experiments in field settings. In M. D. Dunnette (Ed.), *Handbook of industrial and organizational psychology* (pp. 1-21). Chicago: Rand McNally.

Cook, T. D., & Campbell, D. T. (1979). *Quasi-experimentation: Design and analysis issues for field settings*. Boston: Houghton Mifflin.

Cook, T. D., Campbell, D. T., & Peracchio, L. (1990). Quasi-experimentation. In M. D. Dunnette & L. M. Hough (Eds.), *Handbook of industrial and organizational psychology* (2nd ed., Vol. 1, pp. 491-576). Chicago: Rand McNally.

Feshbach, S., & Singer, R. D. (1971). *Television and aggression.* San Francisco: Jossey-Bass.

Freedman, J. L. (1984). Effect of television violence on aggressiveness. *Psychological Bulletin, 96,* 227-246.

Freedman, J. L. (1986). Television violence and aggression: A rejoinder. *Psychological Bulletin, 100,* 372-378.

Freedman, J. L. (1992). Television violence and aggression: What psychologists should tell the public. In P. Suedfeld & P. Tetlock (Eds.), *Psychology and social policy* (pp. 179-189). New York: Hemisphere.

Friedrich, L. K., & Stein, A. H. (1973). Aggressive and prosocial television programs and the natural behavior of preschool children. *Monographs of the Society for Research in Child Development, 38,* No. 151.

Friedrich-Cofer, L., & Huston, A. C. (1986). Television violence and aggression: The debate continues. *Psychological Bulletin, 100,* 364-371.

Furu, T. (1962). *Television and children's life: A before-after study.* Tokyo: RTCRI (Radio and TV Culture Institute, Nippon Hogo Kyokai).

Furu, T. (1971). *The functions of television for children and adolescents.* Tokyo: Sophia University, Monumenta Nipponica.

Heckman, J. J., & Holtz, J. (1989a). Choosing among alternative nonexperimental methods for estimating the impact of social programs: The case of manpower training. *Journal of the American Statistical Association, 84,* 862-874.

Heckman, J. J., & Holtz, J. (1989b). Rejoinder. *Journal of the American Statistical Association, 84,* 878-880.

Himmelweit, H. T., Oppenheim, A. N., & Vince P. (1958). *Television and the child.* London: Oxford University Press.

Holland, P. W. (1989). Comment: It's very clear. *Journal of the American Statistical Association, 84,* 875-877.

Hornik, R. (1981). Out of school television and schooling: Hypotheses and methods. *Review of Educational Research, 51,* 193-214.

Huesmann, R. L., Eron, L. D., Berkowitz, L., & Chaffee, S. (1992). The effects of television violence on aggression: A reply to a skeptic. In P. Suedfeld & P. Tetlock (Eds.), *Psychology and social policy* (pp. 191-200). New York: Hemisphere.

Josephson, W. L. (1987). Television violence and children's aggression: Testing the priming, social script, and disinhibition predictions. *Journal of Personality and Social Psychology, 53,* 882-890.

Joy, L. A., Kimball, M. M., & Zabrack, M. L. (1986). Television and children's aggressive behavior. In T. M. Williams (Ed.), *The impact of television: A natural experiment in three communities* (pp. 303-360). Orlando, FL: Academic Press.

Kubey, R., & Csikszentmihalyi, M. (1990). *Television and the quality of life: How viewing shapes everyday experience.* Hillsdale, NJ: Lawrence Erlbaum.

Kubey, R., White, W., Saphir, M., Chen, H., & Appiah, O. (1996, November). *Social effects of direct broadcast satellite television: From 3 to 60 channels overnight.* Symposium presented at the meeting of the Speech Communication Association, San Diego.

Lalonde, R. J. (1986). Evaluating the econometric evaluations of training programs with experimental data. *American Economic Review, 76,* 604-620.

Leyens, J., Camino, L., Parke, R. D., & Berkowitz, L. (1975). Effects of movie violence on aggression in a field setting as a function of group dominance and cohesion. *Journal of Personality and Social Psychology, 32,* 346-360.

Liebert, R. M., Davidson, E. S., & Sobol, M. P. (1972). Catharsis of aggression among institutionalized boys: Further discussion. In G. A. Comstock, E. A. Rubinstein, & J. P. Murray (Eds.), *Television and social behavior*, Vol. 5: *Television effects: Further explorations* (pp. 366-373). Washington, DC: Government Printing Office.

Liebert, R. M., Sobol, M. P., & Davidson, E. S. (1972). Catharsis of aggression among institutionalized boys: Fact or artifact. In G. A. Comstock, E. A. Rubinstein, & J. P. Murray (Eds.), *Television and social behavior*, Vol. 5: *Television effects: Further explorations* (pp. 351-359). Washington, DC: Government Printing Office.

MacBeth, T. M. (1996a). Indirect effects of television: Creativity, persistence, school achievement, and participation in other activities. In T. M. MacBeth (Ed.), *Tuning in to young viewers: Social science perspectives on television* (pp. 149-219). Thousand Oaks, CA: Sage.

MacBeth, T. M. (1996b). Introduction. In T. M. MacBeth (Ed.), *Tuning in to young viewers: Social science perspectives on television* (pp. 1-35). Thousand Oaks, CA: Sage.

Milavsky, J. R., Stipp, H. H., Kessler, R. C., & Rubens, W. S. (1982). *Television and aggression: A panel study.* New York: Academic Press.

Murnane, R. J., Newstead, S., & Olsen, R. J. (1985). Comparing public and private schools: The puzzling role of selectivity bias. *Journal of Business & Economic Statistics, 3,* 23-25.

Murray, J. P., & Kippax, S. (1977). Television diffusion and social behaviour in three communities: A field experiment. *Australian Journal of Psychology, 29*(1), 31-43.

Murray, J. P., & Kippax, S. (1978). Children's social behavior in three towns with differing television experience. *Journal of Communication, 30*(4), 19-29.

Parke, R. D., Berkowitz, L., Leyens, J. P., West, S. G., & Sebastian, R. J. (1977). Some effects of violent and non-violent movies on the behavior of juvenile delinquents. In L. Berkowitz (Ed.), *Advances in experimental social psychology* (Vol. 10, pp. 135-172). New York: Academic Press.

Rosenthal, R. (1966). *Experimenter effects in behavioral research.* New York: Appleton-Century-Crofts. (enlarged edition published in 1976 by Irvington in New York)

Rubin, D. B. (1986). Which ifs have causal answers? *Journal of the American Statistical Association, 81,* 961-962.

Schramm, W., Lyle, J., & Parker, E. B. (1961). *Television in the lives of our children.* Stanford, CA: Stanford University Press.

Stein, A. H., & Friedrich, L. K. (1975). Impact of television on children and youth. In E. M. Hetherington (Ed.), *Review of Child Development Research* (Vol. 5, pp. 183-256). Chicago: University of Chicago Press.

Steuer, F. B., Applefield, J. M., & Smith, R. (1971). Televised aggression and the interpersonal aggression of preschool children. *Journal of Experimental Child Psychology, 11,* 442-447.

Suedfeld, P., Little, B. R., Rank, A. D., Rank, D. S., & Ballard, E. J. (1986). Television and adults: Thinking, personality, and attitudes. In T. M. Williams (Ed.), *The impact of television: A natural experiment in three communities* (pp. 361-393). Orlando, FL: Academic Press.

Williams, T. M. (1981). How and what do children learn from television? *Human Communication Research, 7,* 180-192.

Williams, T. M. (1986a). Background and overview. In T. M. Williams (Ed.), *The impact of television: A natural experiment in three communities* (pp. 1-37). Orlando, FL: Academic Press.

Williams, T. M. (1986b). *The impact of television: A natural experiment in three communities.* Orlando, FL: Academic Press.

Williams, T. M. (1995). The impact of television: A longitudinal Canadian study. In B. D. Singer (Ed.), *Communications in Canadian society* (4th ed., pp. 172-200). Scarborough, Ontario: Nelson Canada.

Williams, T. M., & Boyes, M. C. (1986). Television-viewing patterns and use of other media. In T. M. Williams (Ed.), *The impact of television: A natural experiment in three communities* (pp. 215-264). Orlando, FL: Academic Press.

Winick, C. (1988). The functions of television: Life without the big box. In S. Oskamp (Ed.), *Applied social psychology annual: Television as a social issue* (Vol. 8, pp. 217-237). Newbury Park, CA: Sage.

4

Class, Communication, and the Black Self

A Theory Outline

Richard L. Allen

To gain an understanding of Africans in the United States, it is fruitful to consider simultaneously both the African cultural and western hemispheric political realities. Highly sophisticated strategies of oppression and exploitation such as enslavement, colonization, segregation, and racism have had dramatic influences on the culture, socialization process, and consciousness of African people. The impact of slavery on Africans has been dramatic, and some of its manifestations may be observed today (Clarke, 1991; Hilliard, 1995).

The enslaved Africans were injected with the idea of their inferiority and taught to see things African as symbolic of subordination, to be enamored by the power of the enslaver, to merge their interest with that of the enslaver, thus minimizing their own needs. To facilitate this, several approaches were taken: the "discipline of hard labor, the breakup of the slave family, the lulling effects of religions . . . the creation of disunity among slaves by separating them into field slaves and house slaves, and finally the power of the overseer to invoke whipping, burning, mutilation, and death" (Zinn, 1995, p. 35).

After the Civil War was consummated in the Emancipation Proclamation, the Reconstruction initially was perceived as a means of healing the wounds of a divided country and ushering in equality across the races. Contrary to these expectations, the thrust of the Reconstruction was abandoned, and instead the Black Codes and other segregationist policies were introduced or strengthened. Second, at the onset of the industrial revolution, the free labor of Africans supplied the surplus for the capitalization of the industrial revolution, which needed a massive number of skilled and unskilled laborers; however, instead of seeking the services of its African citizens, there was a concerted effort to avoid use of black labor in favor of European immigrant labor. The missed moment could have changed favorably the economic lot of the African population. Third, World War II afforded the country an opportunity, after the defeat of fascism, to reconcile the inequities of the society as Africans had anticipated after their intensive and dedicated participation in the war effort. Finally, the great human rights moment that began in the 1960s again challenged the country to provide full citizenship to its African population, but again the will of the country was lacking (DuBois, 1985; Steinberg, 1995).

Consistent with the historical record of lost opportunities is a consistent policy of attempts at imposing a sense of inferiority among African Americans by elements big and small, institutionalized and noninstitutionalized, scientific and lay. If one just takes a cursory look at some of the utterances and policies of the aforementioned elements, one cannot help but be amazed at the rancor exhibited. Although the form in which the rancor has been expressed has varied a bit, its manifestation in prominent and nonprominent circles is evident even today (for a historical overview, see, e.g., Clarke, 1991; Gould, 1977, 1993, 1995; Harding, 1993; Hilliard, 1995; Karenga, 1993; Lewontin, 1992; Lewontin, Rose, & Kamin, 1984; Riggs, 1988, 1991).

Given the multitude of constraints, both physical and social, placed on Africans in the United States along with the continued attacks on their humanity and on the group to which they are members, many basic problems surface. A number of questions may be asked, foremost among them the following. What effect do these forces of inferiorization currently have on Africans in the United States, especially on their self-concept? Do these experiences result in Africans in the United States having a diminished sense of self? Do they have a diminished sense of the group? What are the class differences with respect to this sense of self? How important is the symbolic system of the mass media in fostering the sense of self and the group among African Americans?

Many conceptualizations and theories have been offered to understand the self-concept of Africans. Although the majority of past work has focused on children, there recently has been an increase in work directed at understanding the self-concept of African American adults. In this study, I briefly outline the major issues and recent thinking in this area with an emphasis on my own empirical work and with hypotheses derived from past and present theorizing. Last, I perform an exploratory test of my proposed theory.

■ The Self-Concept

The self-concept has a multidisciplinary origin. Scholars from many fields and disciplines with a variety of interests have sought to understand and penetrate the essence of the phenomenon of self-awareness. Although considerable overlap exists in the various fields and disciplines, there are a number of significant differences among them (Akbar, 1995; Oyserman & Markus, 1993; Rosenberg, 1989).

Many theories and theoretical orientations have been advanced to examine the self-concept, broadly defined. For example, Nobles (1973) outlined four primary theoretical approaches to the concept of self: phenomenological, behavioral, existential, and symbolic interaction. Rosenberg and associates (Rosenberg, 1986; Rosenberg, Schooler, & Schoenbach, 1989; Rosenberg & Simmons, 1972) and Crocker and Major (1989) focused primarily on just one self-concept —self-esteem—and presented the many theories that have been used to predict and explain its existence, including self-consistency, self-enhancement, social comparision, and exchange theory. With respect to social identity, Tafjel and Turner (1986) elaborated on Kurt Lewin's theory of social identity. Similarly, Phinney (1990) identified three broad, often overlapping theoretical frameworks for studying ethnic identity: social identity, acculturation, and ethnic identity formation.

Porter and Washington (1979, 1989, 1993) and Cross (1985, 1991) contributed mightily to the reviewing of theories used to explain the self-concept (self-esteem and group identity) and African Americans.

The selves and theories of the selves have been constructed within a European American cultural tradition or what sometimes is called the Western view of the individual (Akbar, 1984; Gaines & Reed, 1994, 1995; Kambon, 1992; Sampson, 1993; Triandis, 1994). According to Markus and Kitayama (1994), "The self is a pervasive, taken-for-granted assumption that is held in place by language, by the mundane rituals and social practices of daily life, by the law, the media, the foundational texts like the Declaration of Independence and the Bill of Rights, and by virtually all institutions" (p. 568).

Although the preceding view seems an apt description of European culture in general, it is important to point out differences in the United States. That is, within certain groups in the United States (e.g., Hispanics, African Americans), there is a strong sense of interdependence. Concerning Africans in the United States, many scholars have mentioned the differences in worldview between European Americans and African Americans. Nobles (1992) provided a graphic expression of the problem:

> The European worldview is tempered with the general guiding principle of (1) "survival of the fittest" and (2) "control over nature." These, in turn, naturally affect the nature of European values and customs. The emphasis on "competition," "individual rights," and the position of "independence" and "separateness" are clearly linked to the above guiding principles. Likewise, the overemphasis on "individuality," "uniqueness," and "difference" in European-based psycho-behavioral modalities is traceable to the values and customs characteristic of that community and the guiding principles reflected in it. (p. 298)

Thus, if one examines the African worldview and compares it to the view of the European, then one can readily note the differences and their implications for the understanding of the black self-concept. These differences should be taken into account with respect to theorizing and measurement. Of particular importance for this investigation is that much of the past work on African people and their self-conception was filtered through the European worldview. To the extent to which black people in the United States also are an African people, the nature of the processing of data regarding this group may have significantly distorted the validity of the work done on the black self-conception. For example, many of the scholars operating from a European-based conception of Africans find it difficult to fathom much of the recent literature suggesting that most Africans in the United States do not suffer from consuming self-hatred.

On the one hand, many powerful and enduring forces have worked systematically to place Africans in inferior positions and to present them as inferior beings to themselves and to the world at large. A frequent strategy employed to explain their lower status in American society is to argue that they are responsible for their own degradation and shortcomings, giving little weight to any major structural intrusions such as slavery and institutional racism and capitalism. On the other hand, Africans have developed a strong and comprehensive approach not only to resist the onslaught but also to fashion an alternative conception of the self and the group. This struggle to form a positive self-concept has taken many forms, and at various points in the history of Africans some forces have been credited with having a stronger influence than others. That is, many scholars have referred to these struggles in various conceptual terms. Probably the most insightful conceptualization was offered by DuBois (1961), who invoked the often-cited concept of double consciousness to express this phenomenon as

> this sense of always looking at one's self through the eyes of others, of measuring one's soul by the tape of a world that looks on in amused contempt and pity. One ever feels his two-ness—an American, a Negro— two souls, two thoughts, two unreconciled strivings, two warring ideals in one dark body, whose dogged strength alone keeps it from being torn asunder. The history of the American Negro is the history of this strife— this longing to attain self-conscious manhood, to merge his double self into a better truer self. (pp. 16-17)

Several other scholars have incorporated theoretical frameworks into their own thinking. For example, Nobles (1992) argued that although the African American community is under attack and makes adjustments based on these impositions, it retains its fundamentally

African base, which makes it different from the mainstream in basic ways.

> One cannot, however, talk about the African self-concept without talking about the effect of African people's being dominated, oppressed, and subjugated by European peoples. In noting that the juxtapositioning of Africans and Europeans affected the traditions of both Europeans and Africans, I do not believe that the negative contact with Europeans resulted in the total destruction of things African. I do believe, however, that each system was different and that even now, after a relatively long period of contact, the systems of consciousness (i.e., self-knowledge) are still different. (pp. 301-302)

Accordingly, Nobles maintained that one salient aspect of this enduring African culture is the strong concern for the collective, which allows it to withstand many horrendous experiences. He likened his position to Dubois's "double consciousness."

Past Empirical Literature

Based on recent empirical findings, and making some allowances for the quality of the studies, I can summarize the major tendencies as follows (for an extensive review of the literature, see Cross, 1991):

1. Going against most of the theoretical literature, African Americans tend not to have low self-esteem. The self-esteem of African Americans tends to be the same as, or in some instances higher than, the self-esteem of European Americans. The majority of the studies were conducted with children or adolescents.

2. Operating from a number of different theoretical paradigms, again, the empirical literature indicates that African Americans have high group identification and that this identification increases over time. Some literature suggests that the results are less certain when very young children are examined or when different income groups are considered.

3. There is some support for a positive relationship between black identity and self-esteem, but there are several studies that have found nonrelationships. Despite the popularity of this hypothesis (sometimes called the Lewinian hypothesis), there are few genuine tests of it.

One must be mindful of several shortcomings that reduce confidence in many of these findings. First, many of the measures of self-esteem or group identity did not have generally acceptable reliability when they were reported at all. This was particularly the case for the pre-1970s studies. Relatedly, many of the measures were nonvalidated. (This was especially the case for what Cross, 1991, called the "reference group measures.") Second, there is a wide variety of measures of self-esteem with substantially different theoretical and operational definitions. As Rosenberg, Schooler, Schoenbach, and Rosenberg (1995) showed, different operationalizations related to different conceptualizations of self-esteem often lead to demonstrably different outcomes. Third, because most of the studies were done with small samples (usually in experimental settings), the generalizability of the findings is unknown. Few researchers have investigated the relationship of the self-concept within different categories of the African American population, and even fewer have examined the influence of communication or the mass media (majority and black oriented) on the self-concept of African Americans, although there has been much speculation about either the negative effect or the positive effect of media content.

Using a large, more representative data set with data collected at several points in time over an extended period, I was able to add to the existing fund of knowledge on the black self-concept (Allen, 1996). Concerning self-worth, I provided evidence for the position that African Americans have a strong feeling of self-pride and that this sense of pride extends over time and is shared to different degrees by various class elements in the African American community, with those of a higher class showing a stronger sense of self-worth.

Likewise, African Americans demonstrate a strong attachment to the African American collective, and it too is manifested over time. Class position (education and income) influences this attachment to some degree. For example, those of lower income tend to feel closer to elites, but there are no appreciable differences between income groups in terms of closeness to the masses. Conversely, lower educated adults are more likely to feel a greater closeness to the masses, whereas those with the most education show less closeness to the elites as compared with the other education groups. In brief, all of these relationships must be interpreted in light of the fact that African

Americans of different class standings have a strong attachment to self and to the group. However, in a comparison of categories, there were differences. Contrary to the findings on self-esteem, those with a lower class standing showed a stronger attachment to the group.

Moreover, the longitudinal data revealed that the self-esteem constructs and the group identity constructs were stable over a 13-year period. They did not fluctuate dramatically, but there was change depending on the time period under investigation. Interestingly, an examination of the direction of the relationship of self-esteem and group identity yielded no discernible pattern. Self-esteem did not lead to group identity, and group identity did not lead to self-esteem.

■ Exploring a Synthesized Theory Outline

Given the many positive aspects of the previous theorizing and research, I would like to synthesize the thinking from many sources with an emphasis on transcending their shortcomings and incorporating their insights and revelations. This succeeding endeavor is an attempt to probe in a more profound and culturally relevant way the self-concept of African people, for what we think we know of the African self-concept is grounded in several faulty assumptions and inadequate methodological and epistemological conceptions.

To improve our understanding, I first present the major assumptions undergirding the literature on the self-concept. These are the assumptions that have been thought to be relevant across cultures. Second, I present the assumptions that are particularly pertinent to African Americans. I provide a rationale for treating Africans in the United States as being influenced by forces quite different from non-Africans. This entails an articulation of the thinking of many different scholars who have looked at the questions from many different ideological and philosophical perspectives. Third, from these different assumptions, I formulate different hypotheses and the rationale for each. This involves tapping into several theories of varying levels of formality to act as the theoretical linkages for the hypotheses. Finally, operating from an extended set of assumptions and with additional self-concepts drawn from these assumptions, I present an alternative representation of the African American self-concept and the forces that influence it. The approach leads to a new conceptualization of the self-concept.

Global Assumptions

Although I argue that an extensive set of assumptions is required to address the experiences of African Americans, I find that researchers have used several general assumptions to characterize the experiences of the self across cultures. Drawing from many sources (e.g., Baldwin, 1992; Kambon, 1992; Meyers, 1993; Nobles, 1986, 1992; Triandis, 1994), I conclude that the relevant general assumptions are as follows:

1. The self-concept is the cognitive component of the psychological process known as the self.
2. Individuals possess many self-concepts.
3. The self-concept is situation specific; that is, self-concepts tend to operate in specific situations, producing particular self-conceptions.
4. The self-concept is a highly complex, evolving entity, offering different components of its totality for investigation. Sometimes the structure of these components is studied, and sometimes the focus is on the broad dimensions of the self-concept such as self-esteem, identity, and self-confidence.

Throughout this analysis, as is often the case with any investigation of the self-concept of African Americans, there is a set of assumptions that are evident, if not always made explicit. Some recent theorizing has addressed the general issue of the self-concept as having two dimensions—Western and non-Western. The works of Markus and Kitayama (1991, 1994) are instructive in this regard. They noted that Western or European American theories of the self argue essentially that people are independent, bounded, autonomous entities that must strive to remain unshackled by their ties to various groups and entities. The individual is thought to be fundamentally removed from the group and to be an independent entity. This conception of the self is evident in almost all social institutions in the United States. Furthermore, social science embraces some aspect of this conception as reflected in the notion that the person is "a rational, self-interested actor, and it occasions a desire not to be defined by others, and a deep-seated wariness, in some instances even a fear, of the influence of the generalized other, of the social and of the collective" (Markus & Kitayama, 1994, p. 568).

In this view, the individual lives in opposition to the collective. Most contemporary thinking on the self characterizes the healthy self as one that is impervious to outside social intrusions (Gaines & Reed, 1995; Markus & Kitayama, 1991; Nobles, 1992). Moreover, social behavior often is fashioned as inimical to individual behavior and acts as a force that compromises individual behavior (Markus & Kitayama, 1994). That is, the enduring contemporary model of the self is asocial (Akbar, 1984; Kambon, 1992; Oyserman & Markus, 1993).

Criticism of this conception of self has been long, loud, and lavish. Shweder and Bourne (1982), for example, stated that people coming from different cultural backgrounds or societies exhibit distinct world-views and that these worldviews influence cognitive functioning. Although some aspects of the self may be universal, other aspects may be specific to certain cultures (Markus & Kitayama, 1991). The fundamental American conception of the self may be reflective of whites or Western Europeans. Markus and Kitayama contended that this conception is representative of white, middle-class men with Western European backgrounds but may be much less characteristic of other cultural groups and even less descriptive of white Western European women in general. Recent work exploring the self in other cultures, especially African Americans, has yielded relationships between the self and the collective quite different from those deemed representative of European Americans, male or female (Kambon, 1992).

Many scholars have distinguished the idea of conceptualizing the self-concept of African Americans from the standard conceptions of self most prominent in U.S. society. Nobles (1992) posited that the African conception of the self, unlike that exhibited for European Americans, emphasizes the survival of the group and the feeling of oneness with nature. From such guiding principles, he argued, a sense of cooperation and collective responsibility emerges. He went on to say that the modalities consistent with the African wordview are "commonality," "groupness," and "similarity." Akbar (1995) referred to the African self-conception as an unqualified collective phenomenon that acknowledges the uniqueness of the individual self as a component of the collectivity.

Elaborating on Africans in the diaspora, Nobles (1973) identified the African worldview as embodied in the following statement: *I am because we are, and because we are, therefore, I am.* He contended that there is no real distinction between one's self and one's people, that one's self-identity and the identity of one's people are not merely interdependent or interrelated but rather identical. He referred to this as the "extendend self." Unlike the Western concept of the self, the African worldview finds it difficult to make a distinction between the self, or the "I," and one's people, or the "we."

In support of his attributing an African worldview to peoples of African descent living in the United States, Nobles referred to the writings of scholars such as DuBois (1903) and Herskovits (1958). This list also could include several other prominent scholars who have done more recent work in this area such as Akbar (1995), Diop (1991), Hilliard (1995), Holloway (1990), and Thompson (1984). Although these scholars differed on emphasis, they argued for the existence of a substantial number of cultural retentions from Africa. This overall African worldview, an integral part of the life of Africans, is mostly unconscious, frequently disguised, and often disfigured (Kambon, 1992). Undoubtedly, Africans in the diaspora—and, to a lesser degree generally, Africans on the continent—have been informed by a basically European construction of reality, or what sometimes has been called the Westernization of human consciousness. This European conception overlooks the collective, social, and spiritual sense of the African conception of self (Kambon, 1992; Nobles, 1992).

As I suggested earlier, several scholars have questioned the usefulness of the European conception of self and have presented a recent alternative to the European conception of self, the essence of which is the following (Markus & Kitayama, 1994, pp. 569-570):

1. The self is an interdependent entity; the self is not separate from the collective.

2. The self is inherently social, with primacy given to the relationship between self and others.

3. The self becomes whole only through interaction with others. There is no self without the collective.

This alternative is compatible in several fundamental ways with the assumptions underlying the African worldview put forth by many African American scholars. Within this worldview, emphasis is placed on the survival of the group and the individuals as part of the natural rhythm of nature. The fundamental assumptions of the African worldview are as follows (Akbar, 1995; Kambon, 1992; Meyers, 1993; Nobles, 1992):

1. The self cannot be thoroughly analyzed into parts separated and isolated from the context of the whole.
2. The self is a collective and social phenomenon.
3. Like all human thought and practice, the self is socially rooted and, thus, most meaningfully understood within a given context.
4. The African self is exemplified not only in cognitive but also in emotional and spiritual components.
5. Humans are fundamentally spiritual entities whose physical forms are only reflections of a material expression of their true spiritual essence.
6. Africans hold a non-individualistic dualistic approach to the self (i.e., the incorporation within the self, the "I" and the "we"). The duality is more a consequence of divisions within the group and in an individual's notions about his or her relationship to others.
7. All aspects of nature, including consciousness, are interrelated and interdependent, resulting in a communal phenomenology (commonality, corporateness, groupness, cooperation, collective responsibility).

In gathering a more holistic view of Africans, it is crucial to also understand that aspects of their being transcend the external impositions over which they have little control and attempt to mold a healthy self. Here, I am referring to the culturally, philosophically, and spiritually distinct elements among Africans in the United States that make them distinct from other groups. It is from this basic understanding that I examine Africans in the United States. This examination takes into account the woeful experiences of chattel slavery but also keenly notes those aspects of African life that allow Africans in various locations to withstand onslaughts and to fashion a self that holds on to conceptions of the world grounded in African culture. This process is reflective of the double consciousness or duality, that is, being

> builders of an economic infrastructure, yet dispossessed of its fruit; creators of one of its truly original native cultures, in story and song, yet culturally demeaned and maligned; faithful adherents to the nation's basic ideals and values, yet shunned, abused, and stigmatized as if an alien people. (Holt, 1990, p. 303)

According to some researchers, this double consciousness also arises from Africans' attempts to achieve the American dream (National Research Council, 1989) or from tensions between pride and shame in the self (Gaines & Reed, 1994).

The concept has similarly been framed as a hypothesis about resilience in the face of major challenges, which led DuBois to speak of Africans in the United States as a proud people. A crucial aspect of the double consciousness concept, however, is that the African part of the equation has not been fully developed. I contend that the more an African American develops this element, the more he or she will get in tune with his or her self and the greater both individual and group health will be. This idea is reflected in the earlier quote from Malcolm X (1990), "In hating Africa and in hating the Africans, we ended up hating ourselves without realizing it. Show me a person who hates Africa, and I will show you a person who hates himself " (p. 85). Not only is one's sense of self connected to the collective, the collective is defined in broad, encompassing terms; that is, the extent to which the origin of most Africans' understanding of and attitude toward Africa is positive will determine the extent to which the individual will be positive toward himself or herself. Alternatively, as Malcolm X put it, "You can't hate your origin and not end up hating yourself. You can't hate Africa and not hate yourself " (p. 85).

The interesting question for many Africans in the United States is the following: What constitutes the "American Dream," or, at least, which aspects of the dream are they seeking? If the dream merely means having a fairly comfortable living with the associated accoutrements, then it may not require major psychic confrontations. Conversely, if following the dream means striving to acquire substantial wealth and perhaps influence, if not power, then within the context of contemporary America this usually will require that major choices be made. These choices often entail distancing oneself from the group and functioning for one's own separate advancement or, in short, embracing an approach more attuned to individualism as distinct from collectivism. This may involve an individual accepting a view of nature that may be at odds with his or her own and will likely produce identity tensions.

One might assume that these individuals will exhibit a greater acceptance of those aspects of mainstream American culture so as to reach their goal of the American Dream, meaning greater assimilation. One also might assume that this group would tend to be of a higher socioeconomic status (SES), either as a consequence of these individuals' compromises or as a strategy to maintain their status.

Tensions also exist for individuals who have a strong attachment to Africa and African Americans. If these persons are steeped in African culture or more generally have an African worldview, then they will be under pressure to modify or compromise their position. An African worldview that includes, for example, an emphasis on the collective and the spiritual would conflict with the individualistic and materialistic view that characterizes the European worldview and predominates among those in power in the United States. Given the unequal power relationship between the dominating European American group and the African American group, it would be difficult for members of the latter group to maintain an alternative African conception of reality.

Individuals who are attuned to an African worldview may strengthen this tendency to the extent that their actions or their conceptions challenge the dominant European worldview. Such persons would tend to be more collectivist in orientation and to foster a stronger sense of group identity, either as a consequence of their initial position or as a result of the response to their position by the dominant group. One might assume that these individuals would not be of high SES but yet might hold greater status in the community and perhaps be more highly educated.

Akbar's (1995) ideas concerning grafted knowledge and real knowledge illuminate the self-concept of African Americans. Just as DuBois's double consciousness may be used as an organizing scheme to explore the self-concept of oppressed people, so too can Akbar's idea of real and grafted knowledge be used to explore transformations among oppressed people. Akbar noted that his concept of human transformation was intended to have "direct and immediate relevance to the healing of the historically oppressed people of African descent specifically" but also may gain significance as a key to the "upliftment of spiritually oppressed humanity in general" (p. iv). He sees "grafted" knowledge (i.e., a form of knowledge that presents an incomplete and distorted picture of nature's processes but claims to be the entire picture) as interfering with this transformation. Grafted knowledge gives a retarded image of the human being and human capabilities, and it views human life in terms of its physical manifestation. Many Americans hold this view; they tend to be enamored by material life and to define themselves in those terms, often at the expense of other aspects of self—spiritual, moral, and mental (pp. 3-6).

Finding themselves encased in a deforming, alienating, and alienated context, African Americans often confuse actuality with potentiality and confuse established order with eternal order (Karenga, 1982). Nonetheless, African Americans have managed to fashion a favorable image of themselves and even their group—not individually, but with the support of the black community collectively. That is what has been referred to in the literature, in more restricted terms, as the "supportive black community thesis" or theory (Porter & Washington, 1979, 1993).

Hypotheses

I maintain that much past theorizing operated from inappropriate assumptions, or what Akbar (1995) called grafted knowledge. Nonetheless, earlier researchers have generated considerable data and subsequent theorizing that exposed their shortcomings. Making certain modifications in the theorizing and incorporating alternative assumptions, I was able to provide a consistent set of findings that were compatible with the findings reported by Cross (1985, 1991) and Porter and Washington (1993). For example, as noted previously, I found that African Americans had a strong sense of black identity and self-esteem. In addition, these two constructs were stable over a significant period. I was not able to confirm some of the assumptions that emerged from an African-centered perspective. The data requirements were not met because the African-centered assumption is that the self cannot be distinguished from the collective and that any measurement instrument that makes such a distinction violates the assumption of the "I" and "we" being inseparable.

Noting the need for a culturally specific instrument to assess the various areas of African American life, the creators of the Baldwin and Bell (1985) scale based it on an "Africentric" theory of black personality. The theory posits that the core component of the African American personality reflects the conscious-level expression of the "oneness of being"—a communal phenomenology that is thought to characterize the fundamental self-extension orientation of African people. The theory's fundamental operating principle is that "the American social reality comprises its own values, norms, and standards undergirding black behavior." This Africentric social reality therefore projects a normalcy referent for black behavior that is independent of Euro-American culture and Western racism (Baldwin & Bell, 1985, p. 62). Baldwin and Bell recognized, however, that there is an interplay between individual personality attributers and social and environmental elements that partly shape the individual self. They went on to say that this normalcy behavior has essentially positive outcomes, under natural conditions, and is proactive as opposed to merely reactive to negative and adverse environments. That is, this conception of the self has a normalcy referent for black behavior, namely, actions in the service of the "needs and social priority of the African American community (p. 62)."

The major dimension of Baldwin and Bell's (1985) self-consciousness construct is exemplified in (a) an awareness of collective consciousness (or black identity) and African heritage; (b) the recognition of a need for institutions to foster such things as values and practices that affirm African life; (c) involvement in activities that celebrate African dignity, worth, and integrity; and (d) participation in actions that resist onslaughts on the development and survival of African people.

Operating from a set of alternative assumptions presented in the preceding, I formulated the following hypotheses:

1. African Americans have a strong sense of the group.
2. African Americans have a strong sense of the self.
3. African Americans have a stronger sense of the group than of the individual self.
4. African Americans have a strong African self-consciousness.
5. The various self-conceptions are associated for African Americans.

The first three hypotheses have been examined with a national survey of African Americans, and so they are being replicated in the form of a new set of data. The first hypothesis refers to the group identity construct (ethnic identity and closeness to the masses and the elites). The second hypothesis makes the distinction between self and group, and it suggests that these two constructs are associated. The third hypothesis makes a comparison between the racial-specific group identity dimensions and the presumably nonracial self-esteem constructs. In short, it says that the attachment to the group is even more pronounced than individual self-worth. The fourth hypothesis grows out of the conception of self as represented by the African-centered conceptions of self. This normative construct of self reflects the collectivism and cooperation that, in contrast to European American culture, is hypothesized to have a notable existence in the African American community. The final hypothesis suggests that the different African-centered conceptions—one race oriented and one race neutral—are interrelated positively. This relationship, although not stated in the hypothesis, is assumed to be more strongly associated than the non-African-centered ideas of group identity.

Antecedents of the Self-Concept

The self-concept comes into being with a certain shape and form based on a certain social structure, institutional arrangements (e.g., economy, family), and a particular culture. Here, I attempt to provide some of the major social environments, socialization processes, and institutional processes most conducive to the particular self-concept. Different factors and processes often influence different reflections of the self. For example, as noted earlier, those processes that influence the nonracial conception of self may overlap less or have less influence than those factors that influence an individual's attachment to the group. These, in turn, may be quite different from those that influence a particular worldview as represented by the more philosophically based African self-concept. In short, the antecedent factors have varied tremendously depending on the self-concept under consideration. Given the range of constructs that I have been entertaining under the rubric of the self-concept, the most prominent and most consistent across the various self-concepts are religiosity, communication, age, and class. Several of these influences are actually categories of variables encompassing a number of specific variables.

The Race Perspective

Competing perspectives have identified class or race as dominating the lives of African Americans. Clearly, the perspective with a longer history of adherents is the race view. The essence of this perspective is that being African in the United States carries a certain burden beyond one's economic status, that because race continues to be a prominent social, economic, and political force in the United States, it is the major molder of African Americans' lives and determines what it means to be an African American.

On the social level, evidence has been provided that has shown that African Americans and European Americans still live in two distinct worlds. Massey and Denton (1993) described the persistent and deliberate racial segregation and related this to the ongoing poverty of African Americans. Furthermore, the analysis of racial incidents perpetrated against African Americans showed no differentiation for class background or breeding. Both those living very well and those barely living have been victims of these racist intrusions.

On the economic level, a view that cogently captures the significance of race was submitted by Oliver and Shapiro (1995). They stated,

> What is often not acknowledged is that the same social system that fosters the accumulation of private wealth for many whites denies it to blacks, thus forging an intimate connection between white wealth accumulation and black poverty. Just as blacks have had "cumulative disadvantages," many whites have had "cumulative advantages." Since wealth builds over a lifetime and is then passed along to kin, it is from our perspective an essential indicator of black economic well-being. By focusing on wealth,

we discover how blacks' socioeconomic status results from a socially layered accumulation of disadvantages passed on from generation. In this sense we uncover a racial wealth tax. (pp. 5-6)

In a similar vein, Boston (1988) presented evidence from historical and current investigations of the major stages of African American development that illustrates that racial hostility plays a definitive role in the formation of the social position of African Americans. That is, race then and now is responsible for placing African Americans disproportionately into the lower economic classes, thus disfiguring the class structure of Africans in the United States.

On the political level, those taking the position that African American political interest is dominated by a lack of competition for the black vote by both major political parties believe that this has led to the indiscriminate destruction of programs that were intended to help African Americans at different economic levels (Dawson, 1994).

In short, the gist of this race-first argument is that because African Americans' and European Americans' life experiences diverge so strikingly, race interest will take primacy over class interests and this understanding will manifest across economic strata.

The Class Perspective

The setting for my discussion of class surrounds recent dramatic changes in the economic conditions of the United States. Poverty and income inequality in the 1990s, even with highly divergent definitions, are high by historical standards (Danziger & Gottschalk, 1993, 1995). Although the economic contours are generally quite complex, they are magnified when exploring the economic standing of African Americans. For example, several social commentators have underscored the rising inequality of earnings between African Americans and European Americans, and they also have pointed out with great consistency the gaps among earnings of various groupings in the African American community. The most distressing aspect of this economic situation, many have said, is that there is a segment of the African American community that has been variously defined but often is labeled as an "underclass," a segment at the periphery of the economy. Conceptually, the underclass is universal, cutting across racial and regional lines; however, many scholars implicitly link the concept operationally to race and residence. This practice ignores the fact that poverty among blacks is greatest not in urban areas but rather in the rural South (Smith, 1995, p. 115). Furthermore, it has been noted that the present definition of *underclass* has moved from a general reference to poverty that included whites to an exclusive emphasis on the behavioral, cultural, and moral characteristics of the black urban poor (Lott, 1992).

Among the criticisms leveled at the concept of the underclass, one of the most fundamental is that the term is imprecise and vague in meaning (see, e.g., Boston, 1988; Jones, 1992; Lawson, 1992). With respect to the underclass being a new phenomenon, Jones (1992), taking a sorely neglected historical analysis, stated that if the underclass refers to African people who are uneducated, unskilled, unemployed (and often underemployed), living in unrelieved poverty, and engulfed in a culture conditioned by these abject conditions with little chance of upward mobility, then the term denotes nothing new. He argued that the creation of an underclass is a "logical, perhaps even necessary, outgrowth of American political economy conditioned by white racism" (p. 53) and that there still is an economic crisis that exists in the African American community that needs immediate attention.

What influence might these ostensibly new class configurations have for the group solidarity that has existed for some time and is a subject of much concern? Will changes in the class structure in the African American community result in a reduced sense of shared group interests across various class designations? Some shout a resounding *yes*, whereas others confidently cry *no*.

Clearly, wages of employed African Americans have risen, and a higher number of African Americans hold professional, managerial, and technical jobs than ever before. Just as the black middle class has increased, however, so too has the percentage of low-status and low-income blacks. Thus, the potential for class divisions, heightened by the racial climate of the larger society, also has risen (Dawson, 1994).

An issue of paramount concern when exploring the self-concept is the extent to which class status influences an individual's sense of self, whether it be self-esteem, group identity, or African self-consciousness as I have used these constructs. This issue possesses added meaning when one takes into account the much-discussed alleged cleavage in the African American community.

Up to this point, I have not defined the concept of class as I will use it. When one talks about class, one is talking about myriad different conceptualizations that often have conflicting theoretical implications. This impression in terminology is exacerbated for African Americans, whose class structure suffers from major distortions as a consequence of the historical legacy of racism and exploitation (Dawson, 1994; Wright, 1985; Wright, Hachen, Costello, & Sprague, 1982).

Two of the most widely explored and employed formulations are the Weberian and Marxian definitions. In the Marxian definition, classes are viewed in terms of their ownership relation to the means of production. This has been called the relational definition of class (Wright & Perrone, 1977). The Weberian definition of classes pertains to status groupings denoted by a common set of socioeconomic relations and life chances. This has been referred to as the gradational approach to class (Wright, 1985). Each has shortcomings related to setting boundaries (Boston, 1988).

Without question, the Weberian approach is the most commonly employed in the analysis of class in the African American community. However, it has several limitations, many of which were keenly observed by Boston (1988). He stated that the most serious problem was a misspecification of class boundary. He cited the unwarranted practice of merging the black capitalist class with the black middle class as if they were one. Although the smallness of the capitalist class was the reason usually given for the merger (the paucity of the black capitalist class being a reflection of decades of a legalized system of racial segregation), the practice leads to major conceptual oversights. Boston argued that the separate category for the black capitalist class is important for analysis because it is a fundamental part of contemporary racial inequality. Aside from these errors, he said that in the Weberian approach there also is a faulty tendency to classify the middle class arbitrarily by income boundaries. Finally, he noted that although the term *underclass* is bandied about, it is not defined in any precise terms. "We are generally led to believe this underclass consists primarily of black female-headed households and pathological misfits" (p. 7).

Because there are many different definitions of *class* and problems associated with each, I thought it most feasible to use a definition often employed to explore the self-concept. Although the definition and the rationale for it by Boston (1988) were inspiring, I decided to forgo it until I had more appropriate measures. Thus, I borrowed the definition of Wilson (1980), as did Dawson (1994) in his analysis of class and politics. Here, *class* is defined as individuals or a group of people who have comparable goods, services, or skills to offer for income in the labor market. As adequate indicators of the theoretical definition, two commonly employed measures were used—education and income.

A long and complicated debate marks the discussion of the relationship between class (sometimes referred to in terms of SES) and the self-concept. Some of the literature suggests that high-status African Americans have a high group identity. By contrast, a number of other observers have maintained that low-status African Americans have the highest levels of group identity. Concerning self-esteem, those of a higher status typically are thought to have more self-pride. Excluding self-esteem, a plethora of unreconciled and often contradictory findings is the rule for various measures of group identity. In the empirical analysis performed on a national survey sample, the picture that emerged was that the two most often employed indicators of class, income and education, influenced both the self-esteem and the group identity of African Americans. Those individuals with more education and, to an even greater degree, those with more income were found to have a greater sense of self-pride. However, those with the lowest income and with minimal education showed a high sense of group pride. Furthermore, those individuals with less income felt a greater closeness to the black elites. With respect to education, those with more education felt less closeness not only to the masses but also to the elites. These relationships need to be interpreted in light of the fact that the mean values of the two constructs are high. That is, most African Americans feel above-average closeness to African people, both to the masses and to the elites. Indeed, the African population generally shows a greater sense of closeness to the masses. The mean differences that were reported pertained to differences among income and education groups and to a high sense of closeness. The differences were real in a statistical sense, but they were of a small magnitude and, thus, of little substantive significance.

This relatively new, competing perspective maintains that race no longer is the most determining factor in the lives of Africans in the United States. Rather, because of the recent assumed economic polarization of Africans, class has become more germane. A fundamental aspect of the class perspective is that most humans are extraordinarily self-interested. This nonengaging assumption leads to two typical contentious claims. First, it emphasizes the dominance of self-interest over racial orientations; it posits that even when people have racist orientations, most will downplay them if doing so furthers their interest. Second, it stresses the dominance of self-interest over morality. It posits that most people will avoid the demands of justice or morality if such demands jeopardized their interest (Boxill, 1992). In summarizing this class perspective, Dawson (1994) remarked that the abject economic condition of a substantial segment of the African American population, especially when compared with the improved economic condition of large numbers of other African Americans, suggests that class will overwhelm race as a salient factor for African Americans.

Another Framework

I think that it is more useful to apply aspects of both the race and class perspectives, although I give the race perspective more weight. After all, it is the benighted concept of race that justifies the assignment of Africans into disproportionately lower socioeconomic groups. All too often, scholars and activists have overlooked the insidious working class racism and the involvement of organized labor in maintaining the "structure of occupational apartheid" (Steinberg, 1995).

The awareness of both race and class, it is argued, will allow for a greater sense of understanding, explanation, and prediction. Class is indeed a real consideration (i.e., class is responsible for real hardships and limitations), but with respect to African Americans' SES it is largely the outcome of past racism now reinforced by present racism. These limitations form the basis for continued racial division and inequalities.

From the class perspective, I accept the difficult-to-dispute notion that most humans are heavily self-interested. I also accept the notion that one's location in the social structure affects one's perspective, although this formulation loses much of its explanatory power in the case of African Americans because of other extenuating circumstances (i.e., shared life experiences regarding being African). From the race perspective, it is argued that the nature of racism in the United States makes it in the interest of most Africans to align themselves with the group, which suggests a group identity. That is, I am suggesting that their individual interest lies in collective action and that most African Americans share this assessment. Some suppose that an expanding new class of Africans will weaken collective identity and action. I am in agreement with the social observers who point to the very small number of "new class" Africans and, by and large, their tenuous economic position (Boston, 1988; Dawson, 1994: Franklin, 1991; Oliver & Shapiro, 1995). Such a small new black middle class, even if most identified outside of the group (which is highly doubtful), probably has little impact in dampening the nature of Africans' identification with the collective. It is important to note that many of the jobs that members of the new black middle class hold are those that, to a large degree, are earmarked for blacks and function within the framework of racial hierarchy and division. As a consequence of government policy decisions, the future of this class is susceptible to the uncertainty of politics. Because many African Americans have benefited from the growth of government jobs, they undoubtedly will be adversely influenced by the current reduction in the size and scope of the public sector (Jones, 1992; Steinberg, 1995).

Aside from those forces of exploitation and oppression that encourage greater closeness within the group, there also are certain indigenous cultural forces that encourage a closeness or sense of shared fate, a concern for the well-being of the group or collectivity. One such force is the ethos of Africans in the United States. It was presented earlier in the form of an assumption and an important part of an African-centered expression of African life. Finally, my past empirical findings revealed that there was a strong sense of self and group identity within various educational and income groups, with small differences across levels of education and income for certain measures of identity. Considering the preceding statements, I submit the following hypotheses:

1. Those who have less education feel closer to the masses and to the elites.
2. Those with more education and greater income have a greater sense of self-worth.

No hypotheses were offered for the relationship of class to African self-consciousness and to black autonomy. Because there is such a paucity of research and limited theorizing on this issue, I am left to weigh the existing evidence and rely heavily on my hunch. On the one hand, one may argue that because having an African consciousness (and, to a much smaller degree, black autonomy) entails, in part, having a greater knowledge of Africa, things African, and an individual's relationship to a higher aspect of self (i.e., sharing and collective responsibility), and because none of these things presently is the dominant perspective or societally encouraged, it is likely that the more educated, but not necessarily the more affluent, are more likely to exhibit this form of consciousness. Conversely, one also may argue that because the African consciousness reflects an African worldview, and because this view is thought to be fundamental to African Americans (whether they are conscious of its existence or not), one might assume that the African worldview would be equally distributed regardless of education or income. I assume that an African self-consciousness and ethnic identity will be related positively and that it, too, will not be influenced by class. That is, African Americans across educational and income groups also will have a strong ethnic identity and an African consciousness.

Age

Age situates African Americans in a specific sociohistorical context (Demo & Hughes, 1990); that is, it often is assumed that at one historical juncture, major psychological changes took place during what is commonly called the civil rights era. Thus, social observers will refer to African Americans' sense of self and of the group in terms of the pre- and post-civil rights movement. Depending on the self-concept under scrutiny, age tends to have either a profound effect, no effect at all, or a bimodal effect. For example, some theorists have argued that it is the young who are most likely to have a strong sense of self and the group. Others have argued just the opposite. For the self-concept associated with militancy or direct action, the young tend to have the stronger tendency. When the self-concept has more to do with an emotional tie to the group, the older tend to demonstrate a stronger feeling. Moreover, it is the older who are more likely to have a greater sense of pride. Trying to predict the influence of age in the African American community is very difficult and complex. This complexity is highlighted when one researches young to middle-age African Americans. It has been duly documented that African Americans in that group are disproportionately unemployed and in dire economic and social straits (Lusane, 1991; Tonry, 1995). The question is, how does that group maintain a strong self-concept? If that group's self-conception is extreme, presumably in the negative direction, then how does this influence this overall age category? Little theorizing or empirical work provides any convincing answers. However, weighing the quality of the theorizing and research, and taking into account my earlier empirical work, I hypothesize the following:

1. Those who are younger tend to have a greater closeness to the group (the elites and the masses).
2. Those who are older tend to have a greater sense of self-worth.
3. Those who are older are more likely to have an African self-consciousness.
4. Those who are older are more likely to have greater ethnic identity and a sense of black autonomy.

Religiosity

It is generally acknowledged that religion plays an essential role in the lives of Africans in the United States and elsewhere. Aside from the most obvious physical manifestations of an abundance of places of worship in the African American community, the pervasiveness of religiosity has been duly noted and consistently documented (see Cone, 1986; West, 1982). In the spirit of clarity, I would like to indicate what I consider religion to be. Borrowing from Karenga (1982),

I view religion as the thought, belief, and practice concerned with the transcendent and ultimate question of existence.

Although the church in the African American community has been at various times lagging in the struggle against oppression, it has a history of social involvement and upliftment that continues today. Karenga (1993, pp. 233-234) identified five factors that relate to its past and present relevance in the African American community. First, the church has served as a spiritual protector against the violent and destructive transgressions of slavery. Thereafter, it buttressed the racist attacks on the "dignity, relevance and self-worth" of African Americans. Second, the church acted as an agency of "social reorientation and reconstruction." It reinforced the traditional "values of marriage, family, morality, and spirituality" that had been undermined during enslavement. Third, it was the place where African American economic cooperation was intensely encouraged and initiated, providing "social services for free blacks, purchasing and helping resettle enslaved Africans, and setting up business for economic development." Fourth, the church created its own educational projects, training its own ministers and teachers alike. Fifth, as an invisible spiritual community, it supported social change and struggle, providing leaders and leadership at various points in the struggle for black liberation and a higher level of human development.

In previous studies, my colleagues and I (Allen, Dawson, & Brown, 1989; Dawson, Brown, & Allen, 1990) and other researchers (e.g., Ellison, 1991) hypothesized that those with a firm sense of religious commitment also would have a strong sense of racial identification and consciousness. Accordingly, we found that religiosity was a potent force in shaping African American group identity and consciousness. With the same logic used to predict a positive relationship between identity and consciousness, I assume now that religiosity will have a strong impact on one's sense of self-worth given that it is one of the major activities of the church.

From the preceding considerations, I hypothesize the following:

1. Those with a greater sense of religious commitment or religiosity are more likely to have a strong group identity.

2. Those with a greater sense of religiosity are more likely to have a strong sense of African self-worth.

3. Those with a greater sense of religiosity are more likely to have a strong sense of African self-consciousness.

4. Those with a greater sense of religiosity are more likely to have a strong ethnic identity.

Symbolic Social Reality: Black Media and Nonmedia Communication

Under the rubric of symbolic social reality, I include any form of symbolic expression of objective reality such as art, literature, or media content (see Adoni & Mane, 1984), all of which have been used to fashion the image of the African. In the current context, the mass media (television, newspapers, radio, and magazines) are clearly the most influential purveyors of information. They create and foster the objectivity of the autonomous, independent self (Markus & Kitayama, 1994) that is realized by the acquisition of things. The majority mass media crystallize and reinforce certain racist conceptions by changing history to accommodate the preferred image of the dominating group and by presenting pejorative images of dominated groups. They perpetuate the idea that in the United States only the reality of certain people is valid or worthy of consideration (Meyers, 1993).

Several theoretical frameworks illuminate the influence of the mass media. One of the better known is the cultivation analysis. Its proponents assert that the mass media, and especially television, make specific and measurable contributions to the audience's conceptions of reality. The basic premise is that television images cultivate the dominant tendencies of a culture's beliefs, ideologies, and worldviews. The observable independent contributions of television sometimes can be relatively small. Indeed, the size of an effect is far less critical than the direction of its steady contribution. For many people, television viewing overshadows other sources of information, ideas, and consciousness. Thus, the cultivation theory suggests that the more time one spends "living" in the world of television, the more likely one is to report perceptions of social reality that can be traced to (or are congruent with) television's most persistent representations of life and society.

The influence of television on African Americans has been conceptualized as having debilitating or dysfunctional "trace contaminants."

Using an analogy from medicine, these contaminants were described as elements that are plentiful in microscopic quantity and typically are without obvious influence on the organism (Pierce, 1980). Over an extended period of time, these elements are thought to inflict serious cumulative harm to the organism. Furthermore, Pierce (1980) stated that despite superficial improvements in many portrayals of African Americans, the images still carry subtle levels of social trace contaminants. While noting the increased frequency of African American portrayals, many social observers have pointed out that the roles often convey stereotypical messages. Television has been reluctant to present African Americans in a wide range of settings and personalities or in a variety of social roles. Rarely have lower working class or dispossessed African Americans been presented in their own cultural milieu or terms. Typically, these groups are most evident in crime and conflict stories appearing on local and national newscasts. Specifically, Gray (1995) contended that television's depiction of Africans relies substantially on the programs about family, the genre of black situation comedies, entertainment and variety programming, and the social issues tradition of Norman Lear. Two insightful documentaries, *Color Adjustment* (Riggs, 1991) and *Ethnic Notions* (Riggs, 1988), further buttress these observations.

Electronic. Black media are viewed as a filter of African Americans' information sources pertaining to the general status of African Americans as an autonomous group and its relations with the dominating society. Thus, black media should play a significant role in determining the content of the African American self.

The increase in shows about Africans written by Africans and often directed toward Africans, albeit small, may require a reassessment of the direction of the impact on African Americans. African American-controlled alternatives have long existed for the print media, but only recently have there been any serious African alternatives on television. It may be, as many have argued, that these new shows and new stations (one on cable, Black Entertainment Television) would have a more salutary effect on African Americans' self-concept because the creators of such programs would have greater sensitivity to and understanding of African American culture and aspirations. On the other hand, others have suggested that it does not matter whether an African or a non-African American was responsible for the programming; the crucial issue is whether the fare presented represents, accurately and with sensitivity, the lives of African Americans. Thus, there are those who argue that a distinction should be made between black-oriented (content pertaining to blacks but presented through an outsider's perspective, usually nonblack) and black television fare (written in an attempt to capture black experiences and history and usually written by an African American), whereas others maintain that this is a superfluous distinction because the difference in content is imperceptible.

In fact, many factors impinge on the creation of black television fare beyond the group to which the individual belongs, for example, whether the individual has sufficient independence to produce a product that resonates with the audience or whether restrictions are placed on this endeavor. That is, is the fare directed essentially at African Americans, or is it essentially an attempt to explain African life and culture to a non-African American audience? If it is the latter, then the conceptual distinction may not be pertinent. If it is the former, then, all things being equal, I would think that, on average, an African would be better able to represent the African image to the African audience, particularly given the constraints placed on non-Africans to know Africans and African culture. Whether the media product is black or merely black oriented, I assume that it has a demonstrably different effect on African Americans' self-concept than does majority television fare.

Black television has a substantially different relationship with the African American community than does the black press. Unlike the black press, the black electronic media, especially television stations, are more likely to be controlled but rarely owned by African Americans. This means that relatively little of the television fare is written by and directed to African Americans.

Although television often is considered to have a more pronounced effect on various attitudes and behavior of African Americans than it does on those of non-African Americans, the black print media also have commanded a considerable amount of attention from African Americans.

In regard to electronic media, both majority and black, I generated several hypotheses:

1. Those who attend more to black-oriented or black television are more likely to have a greater sense of pride.
2. Those who attend more to black-oriented or black television are more likely to have a positive attachment to the group (elites and masses).
3. Those who attend more to black television are more likely to have a strong African-centered belief system.
4. The greater the amount of time spent with nonblack electronic media (i.e., majority television), the less the self-esteem, group identity, African self-consciousness, and ethnic identity.

Print. The black press consists of a number of weekly newspapers, periodicals, and magazines directed at African American readers. What little theorizing that exists concerning the black press suggests that it is generally a positive and progressive force in the African American community. Historically, this press has received an honored place in the African American community. At particular historical periods (e.g., the antislavery period), the black print media answered the cry for independent newspapers to portray positive aspects of the group and uplifting images. It relayed the messages of self-help organizations that could instill a sense of pride, identity, and black racial consciousness (Allen et al., 1989). Significantly, black print media outlets still are vehicles for galvanizing group solidarity and support. Some critics maintain, however, that the press has not fulfilled its mandate to the people. Nonetheless, the print media still influence political activists because they are in a communication network with people who are more likely to have information about how the political system can be used to foster the group's interest (Dawson et al., 1990). The black press, particularly magazines, also continues to offer viable alternatives for expressing African American views and perspectives.

Empirical evidence shows that the black print media have a positive influence on various measures of the self and group identity. There is considerable ideological variance in the black press, especially with

184 ■ QUANTITATIVE RESEARCH PARADIGMS

respect to magazines, many of which have local circulations. For example, some print media might be classified as traditional and nontraditional or as assimilationist and nationalist. But the classifica- tion that seems to capture the essence of these media was provided by Gray (1995). When referring to the images presented of Africans in the electronic media, he identified three conceptual categories: assimi- lation or discourse of invisibility (the marginalization of social and cultural differences), pluralist or separate-but-equal discourse (com- mitment to universal acceptance into the transparent "normative" middle class), and multiculturalism or diversity (an exploration into the interiors of black lives and subjectivities from the angle of, or in terms of, African Americans). These categories were not conceived as being mutually exclusive or independent; rather, they were assumed to have considerable overlap. The labels and their descriptions, how- ever, capture their essence. These categories provide a basis for exam- ining the relationship of different print media on the self-concept.

From these considerations of black and nonblack print media, I hypothesize the following:

1. Those who attend more to black print media are more likely to have a greater sense of pride.
2. Those who attend more to black print media are more likely to have a positive attachment to the group.
3. Those who attend more to black print media are more likely to have a strong African self-consciousness.
4. Those who attend more to black print media are more likely to have a strong ethnic identity.
5. Those who attend more to black print media are more likely to have a greater sense of black autonomy.
6. The greater the exposure to nonblack newspapers, the less the self- esteem, closeness to the group, black autonomy, African self-conscious- ness, and ethnic identity.

Many of the aforementioned concepts are assumed to relate to the attention given to the media, especially the black media. I have not specified these relationships because they are of lesser importance to my theorizing. Based on previous work, for example, more religious people are more inclined to attend to black media, both print and electronic. Furthermore, the more educated and higher income groups are more likely to relate to the black media, especially print.

Nonmedia communication. The focus of this section has been on electronic and print media. It should be noted, however, that there is what I refer to as "nonmedia communication," which involves the degree to which a person participates in black cultural activities and rituals. The level of participation of an individual in nonmedia communication activities calls for us to consider a hypothesis to cover this area. I hypothesize the following:

> Those who are more likely to participate in black cultural activities and rituals are more likely to have a greater sense of self-esteem, closeness to the group, black autonomy, African self-consciousness, and ethnic identity.

The essence of this conceptualization is embodied in Figure 4.1, and the many arguments presented in the preceding paragraphs may be summarized as follows. The broad assumption is that African Americans—despite the major internal tensions and struggles and despite enduring, consistent, real, and symbolic denigrations—have a strong sense of self and the group. The level of this positive self-worth and group identity is influenced by several categories of variables: class and background characteristics and responses to the symbolic social reality. The direction and strength of influence of these variables vary depending on the conceptualization and measurement of the self.

I argue that those better placed in the social system tend to have a greater sense of self-worth but that these differences are less obvious in regard to identity and African self-consciousness constructs. When examining the self as a combination of self-worth and group identity (typically associated with an African-centered conceptualization), the relationship of class disappears.

Age, another background variable and an indicator of life experiences as well as a reflection of an era, has a positive effect on self-esteem and group identity, but younger individuals will feel a greater closeness with a wider range of African people, that is, people from various stations in life.

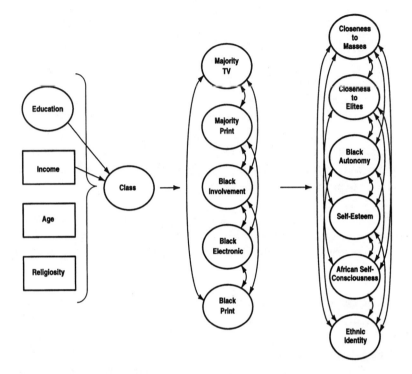

Figure 4.1. Schematic Representation of a Model of the Black Self-Concept

Religiosity is conceived as a positive force on all forms of identity. That is, the more religious individuals are more likely to have a greater sense of self-worth, group identity, and African-centered self-conception.

With respect to symbolic social reality, the assumption is that those who are more involved in black life (e.g., the music, the literature, the rituals) are better able to ward off the impositions on their self-conception. Thus, those who read more black literature, attend to black-oriented materials on television, and actively engage in or even attend African American-initiated activities are more likely to have a greater sense of self-worth. On the other hand, those who attend more to the majority media, especially television with its latent and manifest negative portrayals of Africans, are less likely to have a strong sense of self.

■ Method

Research Procedures

The data were collected in Detroit, Michigan, among African American adults. The sample was selected to reflect a wide range of views on social issues. This purposive sample contained respondents from identifiable social and religious groups and was selected to reflect different ages, income groups, and a similar composition of males and females. The sample was stratified in the following manner: a total of 200 respondents from two different religious institutions (one Baptist and one Methodist), 100 respondents from a community college, and 70 respondents from social and professional groups. Of these respondents, 311 were included in the analysis.

The questionnaire was self-administered and took approximately 40 minutes to complete. Each individual received $10 for participating. The questionnaire covered topics such as self-esteem (two different scale versions), several versions of scales tapping the identity construct (general and race specific), and a number of social beliefs and opinions on individualism and collectivism, individual well-being, and a host of media attitudes and behaviors.

Measures

To cover the topics under consideration in the development of the theory outline, the following measures were administered:

1. An abbreviated version of the Rosenberg Self-Esteem Scale that required respondents to use a 5-point scale to assess the degree to which they agreed with items such as "I feel that I'm a person of worth, at least on an equal plane with others"

2. A six-item instrument that measured the construct of closeness to the masses that required respondents to use a 4-point scale (1 = *not at all close*, 4 = *very close*) to indicate their closeness on items such as "I feel close to black people who are young"

3. A measure of the construct, closeness to the elites, that asked respondents to use the same scale as they used in assessing closeness to the masses to indicate their closeness on items such as "I feel close to elected officials"

4. A measure of black autonomy that required respondents to use a 5-point scale (1 = *strongly disagree*, 5 = *strongly agree*) to indicate the degree to which they agreed or disagreed with items such as "Black parents should give their children African names"

5. An abbreviated version of the Baldwin and Bell (1985) African Self-Consciousness Scale that asked respondents to use a 5-point scale to indicate the degree to which they agreed or disagreed with items such as "I don't necessarily feel mistreated in a situation where I see another black person being mistreated"

6. An abbreviated version of the Phinney Ethnic Identity Scale, selecting the non-race-specific identity items, that asked respondents to express how well each item (e.g., "I have spent time trying to find out more about my own ethnic group, such as its history, traditions, and customs") described themselves using a 5-point scale (1 = *does not describe me at all*, 5 = *totally describes me*)

On all six of these measures, the constructs were coded to reflect a higher degree or greater amount of the attribute in question. Thus, for example, the higher the score, the higher the African self-consciousness.

Furthermore, a basic background measure and a religious background measure were administered to collect information on respondents' educational level, income, age, and religious practices. Finally, a measure of symbolic social reality was administered that asked respondents to indicate on a 5-point scale (1 = *never*, 5 = *all the time*) how often they engage in the use of various media. This measure was operationalized by a number of indicators: (a) majority television viewing and reading majority print and (b) black communication behaviors such as black television viewing and the use of other black electronic media, reading black print, and the degree of involvement in black cultural activities and rituals.

■ Results

Structural equation modeling was used to analyze the data. A general program for estimating the unknown coefficients in a set of linear structural equations (LISREL) was used (Jöreskog & Sörbom,

TABLE 4.1   Means for the Self-Concept Scales

Construct	Mean
Closeness to masses (6 items, 4-point scale)	19.53 (3.25)
Closeness to elites (2 items, 4-point scale)	5.44 (2.72)
Black autonomy (6 items, 5-point scale)	21.08 (3.51)
Self-esteem (6 items, 5-point scale)	26.53 (4.42)
African self-consciousness (18 items, 5-point scale)	64.11 (3.56)
Ethnic identity (12 items, 5-point scale)	45.69 (3.81)

NOTE: The initial value is the sum of the item means. The value in parentheses is the average value of the scale (the sum of the items divided by the number of items).

1988). The first step in the analysis was to test for the overall model fit to see whether the general theorizing was sound. This involved the examination of the measurement aspect of the model. The second step was to estimate the many hypotheses to see whether they were confirmed. Before investigating the many relationships, it is useful to examine the descriptive statistics, for some of the hypotheses are examined with these summary measures.

The means for all the constructs indicate that African Americans have a particularly high sense of self-esteem, ethnic identity, African self-consciousness, and closeness to the masses (in order of importance) (see Table 4.1). Although closeness to the elites shows the smallest mean, it still is above the midpoint of the scale. Thus, the hypotheses that predicted that African Americans have a high sense of the individual self and the group, variously defined, received support.

As an important initial step in the examination of the full model, an assessment of the scale reliability is in order. Using a measure of internal consistency, the Cronbach alpha, Table 4.2 indicates that the reliability of the scales ranges from fair to good, with a couple of exceptions (majority print exposure, .57, and black involvement, .68). This outcome increases our confidence that the obtained relationships are less influenced by the inadequacy of measurement.

It was hypothesized that the different self-concepts are related positively. Table 4.3 provides information on these associations. As can be seen, there are several moderate to large correlations, most are positive, and most are statistically significant. The negative relation-

TABLE 4.2   Reliability Estimates for All the Self-Concept Scales

Construct	Alpha
Self-esteem	.90
Closeness to masses	.82
Closeness to elites	.74
Black autonomy	.83
African self-consciousness	.88
Ethnic identity	.86
Majority print	.57
Black involvement	.68
Black electronic	.74
Black print	.72
Religiosity	.82

ships also are predictable. We can see that those who embrace the notion of black autonomy have a high African self-consciousness and that those with high ethnic identity are associated with feeling less close to the elites. The picture that emerges is that the self-concepts have positive relationships, both African self-consciousness and ethnic identity are strongly related to the other self-concepts, and there is a substantial association between African self-consciousness and ethnic identity. Moreover, the strongest relationship exists between African self-consciousness and black autonomy. The only two relationships that were not statistically significant were the relationships between closeness to the masses and black autonomy and between closeness to the elites and self-esteem.

Turning to the full model, there is a variety of relevant overall measures of model fit. Each explores different aspects of model adequacy. Although opinions differ as to what constitutes the best measure, I present several generally agreed on fit measures. First, the chi-square is 3.92 with 8 degrees of freedom. The p value is a statistically nonsignificant .864, indicating that the model provides an adequate fit. Moreover, the Goodness of Fit measure was 1.00, the Adjusted Goodness of Fit measure was .98, the Comparative Fit Index was 1.00, and the Nonnormed Fit Index was .99. All of these suggest

TABLE 4.3   Zero-Order Correlations for the Self-Concept Scales

	(1)	(2)	(3)	(4)	(5)	(6)
(1) Closeness to masses	—					
(2) Closeness to elites	.46*	—				
(3) Black autonomy	.04	−.13*	—			
(4) Self-esteem	.22*	.00	.14*	—		
(5) African self-consciousness	.14*	−.25*	.64*	.15*	—	
(6) Ethnic identity	.11*	−.13*	.50*	.38*	.44*	—

*$p < .05$.

that the model fit the data well. Hence, it is possible to examine the component fit measures and the hypotheses.

Figure 4.2 presents the relationships found to be statistically significant and, thus, sheds light on the hypotheses. Looking at the relationship between the constructs of symbolic social reality and the various self-concepts, many interesting patterns emerge. The majority media measures, majority television exposure and print media exposure, have observable effects. Although they do not have an influence on the extent to which African Americans feel close to the masses and the elites, greater exposure to majority television had a negative influence on black autonomy, African self-consciousness, and self-esteem. Majority print media also had an influence on several forms of self-concept; they had a negative effect on self-esteem but had a positive effect on African self-consciousness. With the exception of the positive relationship between the self-consciousness construct and majority print media, all support the proffered hypotheses. Black involvement was positively related to four of the six self-concepts. The greater the black involvement, the greater the black autonomy, African self-consciousness, ethnic identity, and self-esteem. These relationships support the hypotheses; however, it was hypothesized that black involvement also would have a positive impact on closeness to the masses. This relationship was positive, but the critical value was only borderline ($p < .10$). These obtained statistically significant relationships were moderate to strong in magnitude. Similarly, greater exposure to black print media led to greater self-esteem, greater closeness to the elites, greater black autonomy, greater ethnic identity, and, to a

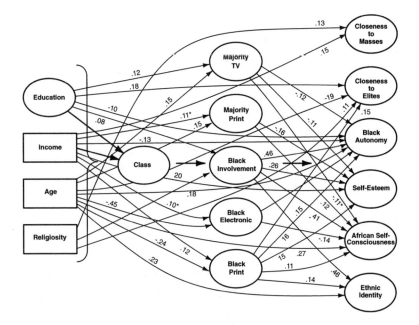

Figure 4.2. Statistically Significant Estimates of the Black Self-Concept Model

lesser degree, greater African self-consciousness. All these relationships were supportive of the hypotheses. One hypothesized relationship did not reach statistical significance, namely, the relationship between black print media and closeness to the masses. The exposure to black or black-oriented electronic media (television and movies) showed surprising relationships. It had a relationship with only two of the six self-concepts, each in a negative direction. The greater the black or black-oriented electronic exposure, the less the sense of black autonomy and African self-consciousness.

Focusing on the relationships of the antecedent class and background constructs with the other constructs in the model, we can see that there are many statistically significant relationships. The two indicators representing the gradational conception of class had several statistical relationships but often on different variables or in a different direction. Education had a positive influence on two measures of symbolic social reality: majority television exposure and, to a lesser degree, black involvement. Income had a positive influence on majority and black print media exposure. Whereas education had positive influence on closeness to the elites, it had a negative relationship on black autonomy. On the other hand, income had a positive influence on closeness to the masses and self-esteem, as predicted, but, as in the case of education, it had a negative influence on black autonomy.

Turning to the complex age variable, the findings reveal that older individuals tend to watch more majority television and to read more majority print media, whereas younger individuals tend to watch more black or black-oriented visual fare and to read more black print media. Concerning the self-concepts, younger individuals feel closer to both the masses and the elites, whereas older individuals tend to have a greater sense of black autonomy, ethnic identity, and African self-consciousness. These results gave substantial support to the hypotheses.

More religious individuals tended to have greater black involvement but were not demonstrably different on any of the other symbolic social reality variables. Moreover, religiosity had a positive influence on the closeness to the masses and closeness to the elites constructs but did not have relationships with any of the other self-concepts. I had hypothesized that religiosity would have a much more extensive effect across the self-concepts.

A relatively small amount of the variance was explained in the symbolic social reality measures, that is, 6% of majority television exposure, 3% of majority print exposure, 4% of black involvment, 20% of black-oriented electronic exposure, and 7% of black print media. A larger amount of variance was explained for the self-concepts, that is, 9% of closeness to the masses, 11% of closeness to the elites, 31% of black autonomy, 17% of self-esteem, 31% of African self-consciousness, and 33% of ethnic identity.

■ Conclusion

I have sought to determine the extent to which African Americans withstood the brunt of denigrating images and the onslaught of a racist society, how they managed to maintain their sense of the self and the group. Conceptualized as a dynamic process, the theory I outlined emphasized that Africans' sense of self and their sense of the group are engaged in an ongoing battle. The original formulation of this battle was presented by DuBois as double consciousness. One of the major thrusts of double consciousness is that despite the many challenges, African Americans, because of the power of their culture and the fortitude derived from it, will in struggle have a healthy sense of self and an attachment to the group.

I developed the outline of a theory, consistent with the notion of double consciousness and its many contemporary modifications, and I identified the forces that influence the African self, variously defined. I posited that there is a set of assumptions that inform the African self-concept. Some of these assumptions are shared by and manifested in all groups, others apply to other oppressed groups, and still others are unique to the experiences and historical context of African American life. From these assumptions, I was able to formulate an interrelated set of hypotheses that took into account the different conceptions of self. I fashioned hypotheses for the variables conceived to influence the self. I maintained that religion, age, and class influenced how the individual feels toward the internal self and the external self, or the individual's self-esteem and group identity. Furthermore, I argued that the symbolic social reality also has a major bearing on the self, where those who attended more to black-oriented information and activities were substantially different in self-conception.

In broad terms, I hypothesized that those who aspire to a higher order of morality or who attach themselves to a supreme being (i.e., those who are more religious) will feel a strong relationship to African people no matter what station in life those persons might hold. Age also was thought to have an inverse relationship with the self. That is, those who were older were more likely to have a stronger sense of self and a stronger sense of African self-consciousness, but younger individuals were more attached to the various elements within the African American community. Class, a complex variable both operationally and theoretically, reflected a complex picture. The people who had a greater income were more likely to feel closer to the masses but not to the elites, and they tended to not have an appreciably different African self-consciousness from those with less income. They did, however, have a greater sense of self-worth. The income/closeness to the masses connection is put in stark relief when you consider the other element of class: education. Those who had more formal training tended to feel closer to the elites but not to the masses. Moreover, those with more education did not have a greater sense of self-worth, nor did they have a relationship with any of the other self-concepts, save black autonomy or independence (and that relationship was negative).

Many analysts have speculated about how the media, both majority and black oriented, militates against or facilitates the self-concept. I found that those who attend to the black print media are more likely not only to think more highly of themselves but also to hold the group in higher esteem. Relatedly, those who participate actively in black affairs also are more likely to relate positively to themselves and to the group and to have an African self-consciousness.

The major aspect of my theorizing, as reflected in the proposed model, was supported. Of special interest is the contention that the black media would have a positive effect on the black self-concept and that the majority media would have a negative effect. Generally, this assumption was supported. That is, the black print media exposure was compatible with having a strong self-concept, and the majority media exposure, especially television, militated against a strong black self-concept. This outcome provides added strength to the charge that the majority media presented less than inspiring images; at the very least, it says that these images are interpreted that way. No matter the interpretation, however, the effect is the same. Another symbolic social reality category, black involvement, produces striking effects. Those who engaged in activities and rituals initiated by blacks tend to have a greater sense of the self and the group.

A few other points are worth mentioning. First, although the majority media tend to have a negative influence on the black self-concept when they had any influence at all, there was an exception. Those who read more majority print media were more likely to have a greater African self-consciousness. Second, watching more black-oriented electronic media led to less of a sense of black autonomy and African self-consciousness. Perhaps because these two self-concepts present a more normative conception of what constitutes desirable African behavior, this would conflict with the more mainstream, more super-

vised content of the electronic media. An intriguing alternative interpretation is that the electronic media, whether black oriented or
majority, follow a format (and pursue certain content themes) that
operates in opposition to the fostering of a strong black self-concept,
albeit the effect is stronger for majority television. All of these interpretations need to be explored. The preceding outcomes have profound theoretical and practical implications.

A point that was stressed throughout this study was that the different aspects of the self that are under investigation should be clarified.
Within my theoretical framework, three different orientations are
evident. One important distinction of concern is that between self-
esteem or self-worth and group identity. Although this distinction has
not always been made, the concepts of self-esteem and group identity
have been popular areas of research. A number of researchers (e.g.,
Cross, 1991) have pointed out the significance of this conceptual
distinction. Others (e.g., Kambon, 1992; Nobles, 1992) have argued
that self-esteem and group identity are best conceptualized as different
aspects of what they call an African self-consciousness. These scholars,
often identifying themselves as operating from an African-centered
perspective, maintain that the individual conception of self and the
individual concept of the group are intertwined. That is, Africans'
self-conception is strongly connected with the group conception and
vice versa.

A second distinction addressed in this study was between the
theoretical and operational definitions of personal self-identity and
group identity. Although I used the self-esteem concept in terms of
self-worth in a global sense, it would be possible to use self-esteem in
the sense of performance in concrete settings. Similarly, under the
heading of group identity, many aspects might have been examined,
for example, black militancy, black consciousness, and black alienation. Extending this line of reasoning, how one defines the self-
concept dictates the concept names one will use, the operationalization, and, ultimately, the direction of the hypotheses. In my theorizing
and model development, I remained acutely aware of this fact.

The revelation that African Americans have a strong sense of self,
variously defined, is attuned to some of the more recent research;
however, the mechanisms that account for this rarely have been
investigated. There has been relatively little attempt at explicating the

antecedents of the self-concept, especially in its many manifestations. It is instructive to point out that my conceptualization differs in fundamental ways from some of the major theorizing done in this area of research, especially by mainstream researchers. Much of the literature speaks of in-group/out-group bias as a universal. This conception maintains that there is a proclivity for individuals to regard in-group members as possessing more desirable qualities than do members of out-groups. Contemporary psychological theorizing tends to treat the presumed in-group/out-group bias as "psychological realities and the sociohistorical realities of racism as merely footnotes" (Gaines & Reed, 1994, pp. 14-15). I argue, along with several other scholars, that Africans' sense of self is influenced heavily by their African heritage and is not merely a response to the hostility demonstrated toward them by European Americans. This sense of self, as I have noted, is essentially collectivist, as distinct from individualist, and is informed by a sense of "we-ness" as elaborated by Nobles (1973, 1992). In short, this conceptualization has a keen awareness of culture and acknowledges individual differences among ethnic groups within the United States and undoubtedly across the world. It is decidely historically and culturally specific, however, as argued for one conceptualization of the black self, namely, that African self-consciousness is similar throughout the African diaspora specifically because of the similarity in history and culture.

In summary, across self-constructs, age has powerful effects. Younger people feel closer to African Americans, but older people have a stronger sense of ethnic identity and black autonomy as well as a more African-centered consciousness. Furthermore, the black print media tend to have a positive effect across the self-constructs. The majority media, on the other hand, tend to have a negative effect when they have any effect at all. Class, as represented by the two indicators of education and income, has quite different effects on the different self-constructs, with its influence being entirely absent from the African self-consciousness. With direct reference to the race/class influence on the self-concept, I argued that although race was the overriding factor, class modified this connection in most instances, and that the impact of class depended on the conception of self being explored. This interpretation received clear support. In the case of the self-concept that explores self-esteem and group identity, class has a certain importance. When the self-construct is linked to black autonomy or a sense of black independence, class garners substantial importance. Conversely, class has little significance in producing an African self-consciousness or ethnic identity. Furthermore, it is worth considering that education and income often had quite different relationships with media behavior and self-conception. Significantly, the only self-concept that both education and class predicted (and in the same direction) was black autonomy. This negative relationship suggested that those of a higher class tend to be in opposition to the notion of independence and separateness as embodied in the black autonomy construct. Taken together, the findings reveal how important the symbolic social reality (media and nonmedia, black and nonblack) and class are in fashioning the black self-concept. The area is a need of great theoretical and empirical attention.

Double consciousness was the overarching theoretical framework that informed the formulation of the hypotheses, their rationales, and the construction of a testable model. In essence, it alerts us to the challenges and impediments that confront African Americans daily. Furthermore, it specifies, in general terms, the dynamics that exist and suggests that, although a struggle persists, the likelihood is that African Americans will have the fortitude to maintain a strong sense of self and the group by creating institutions or other mechanisms to sustain themselves. In one sense, this framework is a prescription for psycho-logical survival (develop alternative institutions and conceptions) and an assessment of the success of such an endeavor at any one point in time. It describes African Americans as active participants in their own mental liberation rather than as merely passive receptacles or reactive entities. Clearly, the double consciousness framework needs to be further explicated and refined, and social observers and activists are beginning to see its usefulness as a conceptual tool. The contribution that this study has made is to tie together this framework with others into a larger system that weights the importance of symbol systems in society, especially the mass media. We have yet to find out whether double consciousness, or the hypotheses partly derived from it, applies to the same degree to other oppressed groups, especially those expe-riencing major cultural impositions.

As was acknowledged in this study, the sample was relatively small and nonprobabilistic. Thus, it may not generalize to the larger African

American population. It is worthy of note, however, that the pattern of the findings for the self-esteem and group identity constructs were quite similar to those found using a national probability sample. To my knowledge, no other study has used as elaborate a model to examine the several conceptualizations of the self, so I cannot comment in any detail on the extent to which this study supports past findings. This study must be considered an exercise in theory construction rather than in theory testing. A test of theory must await a larger and richer data set.

■ References

Adoni, H., & Mane, S. (1984). Media and the social construction of reality: Toward an integration of theory and research. *Communication Research, 11,* 323-340.

Akbar, N. (1984). *Chains and images of psychological slavery.* Jersey City, NJ: New Mind Productions.

Akbar, N. (1995). *Natural psychology and human transformation.* Tallahassee, FL: Mind Productions and Associates, Inc.

Allen, R. L. (1996). *The concept of self: A study in black.* Unpublished manuscript, Department of Communication Studies, University of Michigan.

Allen, R. L., Dawson, M. C., & Brown, R. E. (1989). A schema-based approach to modeling an African-American racial belief system. *American Political Science Review, 83,* 421-441.

Baldwin, J. A. (1992). African (black) psychology: Issues and synthesis. In R. L. Jones (Ed.), *Black psychology* (3rd ed., pp. 125-140). Berkeley, CA: Cobb & Henry.

Baldwin, J. A., & Bell, Y. (1985). Psychology of black Americans. *Western Journal of Black Studies, 9,* 61-68.

Boston, T. D. (1988). *Race, class and conservatism.* Boston: Unwin Hyman.

Boxill, B. R. (1992). The underclass and the race/class issue. In B. E. Lawson (Ed.), *The underclass question* (pp. 19-32). Philadelphia: Temple University Press.

Clarke, J. H. (1991). *Notes for an African world revolution: Africans at the crossroads.* Trenton, NJ: African World Press.

Cone, J. H. (1986). *Speaking the truth: Ecumenism, liberation and black theology.* Grand Rapids, MI: Eerdmans.

Crocker, J., & Major, B. (1989). Social stigma and self-esteem: The self-protective properties of stigma. *Psychological Review, 94,* 608-630.

Cross, W. E. (1985). Black identity: Rediscovering the distinction between personal identity and reference group orientation. In M. Spencer, G. Brookins, & W. Allen (Eds.), *Beginning: The social and effective development of black children* (pp. 155-171). Hillsdale, NJ: Lawrence Erlbaum.

Cross, W. E. (1991). *Shades of black: Diversity in African-American identity.* Philadelphia: Temple University Press.

Danziger, S., & Gottschalk, P. (1993). *Uneven tides: Rising inequality in America.* Cambridge, MA: Harvard University Press.

Danziger, S., & Gottschalk, P. (1995). *American unequal.* Cambridge, MA: Harvard University Press.

Dawson, M. C. (1994). *Behind the mule: Race and class in African-American politics.* Princeton, NJ: Princeton University Press.

Dawson, M. C., Brown, R. E., & Allen, R. L. (1990). Racial belief systems, religious guidance, and African American political participation. *National Review of Political Science, 2,* 22-44.

Demo, D. H., & Hughes, M. (1990). Socialization and racial identity among black Americans. *Social Psychology Quarterly, 53,* 364-374.

Diop, C. A. (1991). *Civilization or barbarism.* New York: Lawrence Hill.

DuBois, W. E. B. (1903). *The souls of black folk.* Chicago: McClurg.

DuBois, W. E. B. (1961). *The souls of black folk.* New York: Fawcett.

DuBois, W. E. B. (1985). *Black reconstruction in America.* New York: Atheneum.

Ellison, C. G. (1991). Identification and separatism: Religious involvement and racial orientations among black Americans. *Sociological Quarterly, 32,* 477-494.

Franklin, R. S. (1991). *Shadows of race and class.* Minneapolis: University of Minnesota Press.

Gaines, S. O., & Reed, E. S. (1994). Two social psychologies of prejudices: Gordon W. Allport, W. E. B. DuBois, and the legacy of Booker T. Washington. *Journal of Black Psychology, 20,* 8-28.

Gaines, S. O., & Reed, E. S. (1995). Prejudice: From Allport to DuBois. *American Psychologist, 50,* 96-103.

Gould, S. J. (1977). *Ever since Darwin.* New York: Norton.

Gould, S. J. (1993). American polgeny and craniometry before Darwin: Blacks and Indians as separate, inferior species. In S. Harding (Ed.), *The racial economy of science: Toward a democratic future* (pp. 84-115). Bloomington: Indiana University Press.

Gould, S. J. (1995). Mismeasure by any measure. In R. Jacoby & N. Glauberman (Eds.), *The bell curve debate: History, documents, opinion* (pp. 3-13). New York: Times Books.

Gray, H. (1995). *Watching race: Television and the struggle for blackness.* Minneapolis: University of Minnesota Press.

Harding, S. (1993). Introduction: Eurocentric scientific illiteracy: A challenge for the world community. In S. Harding (Ed.), *The racial economy of science: Toward a democratic future* (pp. 1-22). Bloomington: Indiana University Press.

Herskovits, M. J. (1958). *The myth of the Negro past.* Boston: Beacon.

Hilliard, A. G. (1995). *The maroon within us: Selected essays on African American community socialization.* Baltimore: Black Classic Press.

Holloway, J. E. (1990). The origins of African-American culture. In J. E. Holloway (Ed.), *Africanisms in American culture* (pp. 1-18). Bloomington: Indiana University Press.

Holt, T. C. (1990). The political use of alienation: W. E. B. DuBois on politics, race, and culture, 1903-1940. *American Quarterly, 42,* 301-323.

Jones, M. (1992). The black underclass as systemic phenomenon. In J. Jennings (Ed.), *Race politics and economic development* (pp. 53-65). London: Verso.

Jöreskog, K. G., & Sörbom, D. (1988). *LISREL 7: A guide to the program and applications* (2nd ed.). Chicago: SPSS, Inc.

Kambon, K. K. (1992). *The African personality in America: An African-centered framework.* Tallahassee, FL: Nubian Nation.

Karenga, M. (1982). Society, culture and the problem of self-consciousness: A Kawaida analysis. In L. Harris (Ed.), *Philosophy born of struggle: Anthology of Afro-American philosophy from 1917* (pp. 212-228). Dubuque, IA: Kendall/Hunt.

Karenga, M. (1993). *Introduction to black studies*. Los Angeles: University of Sankore Press.

Lawson, B. E. (1992). Uplifting the race: Middle class blacks and the truly disadvantaged. In B. E. Lawson (Ed.), *The underclass question* (pp. 90-113). Philadelphia: Temple University Press.

Lewontin, R. C. (1992). *Biology as ideology*. New York: Harper Perennial.

Lewontin, R. C., Rose, S., & Kamin, L. J. (1984). *Not in our genes*. New York: Pantheon.

Lott, T. L. (1992). Marooned in America: Black urban youth culture and social pathology. In B. E. Lawson (Ed.), *The underclass question* (pp. 70-89). Philadelphia: Temple University Press.

Lusane, C. (1991). *Pipe dream blues: Racism and the war on drugs*. Boston: South End Press.

Markus, H. R., & Kitayama, S. (1991). Culture and the self: Implications for cognition, emotion, and motivation. *Psychological Review, 98*, 224-253.

Markus, H. R., & Kitayama, S. (1994). A collective fear of the collective: Implications for selves and theories of selves. *Personality and Social Psychology Bulletin, 20*, 568-579.

Massey, D. S., & Denton, N. A. (1993). *American apartheid: Segregation and the making of the underclass*. Cambridge, MA: Harvard University Press.

Meyers, L. J. (1993). *Understanding an Afrocentric worldview: Introduction to an optimal psychology*. Dubuque, IA: Kendall/Hunt.

National Research Council. (1989). *A common destiny: Blacks and American society*. Washington, DC: National Academy Press.

Nobles, W. W. (1973). Psychological research and the black self-concept: A critical review. *Journal of Social Issues, 29*, 11-31.

Nobles, W. W. (1986). *African psychology: Toward its reclamation, reascension and revitalization*. Oakland, CA: Black Family Institute.

Nobles, W. W. (1992). Extended self: Rethinking the so-called Negro self-concept. In R. L. Jones (Ed.), *Black psychology* (3rd ed., pp. 295-304). Berkeley, CA: Cobb & Henry.

Oliver, M. L., & Shapiro, T. M. (1995). *Black wealth/white wealth: New perspective on racial inequality*. New York: Routledge.

Oyserman, D., & Markus, H. R. (1993). The sociocultural self. In J. Suls (Ed.), *Perspectives on the self*, Vol. 4: *The self in social perspective* (pp. 187-220). Hillsdale, NJ: Lawrence Erlbaum.

Phinney, J. (1990). Ethnic identity in adolescents and adults: Review of research. *Psychological Bulletin, 108*, 499-514.

Pierce, C. M. (1980). Social trace contaminants: Subtle indicators of racism in TV. In B. Withey & R. P. Abeles (Eds.), *Television and social behavior: Beyond violence and children* (pp. 249-257). Hillsdale, NJ: Lawrence Erlbaum.

Porter, J. R., & Washington, R. E. (1979). Black identity and self-esteem. A review of the research literature. *Annual Review of Sociology, 5*, 53-74.

Porter, J. R., & Washington, R. E. (1989). Developments in research on black identity and self-esteem: 1979-88. *Revue Internationale de Psychologie Sociale, 2*, 341-353.

Porter, J. R., & Washington, R. E. (1993). Minority identity and self-esteem. *Annual Review of Sociology, 19*, 139-161.

Riggs, M. (1988). *Ethnic notions* (video). San Francisco: California Newsreel.

Riggs, M. (1991). *Color adjustment* (video). San Francisco: California Newsreel.

Rosenberg, M. (1986). *Conceiving the self* (rev. ed.). Melbourne, FL: Krieger.

Rosenberg, M. (1989). Self-concept research: A historical overview. *Social Forces, 68,* 34-44.

Rosenberg, M., Schooler, C., & Schoenbach, C. (1989). Self-esteem and adolescent problems: Modeling reciprocal effects. *American Sociological Review, 54,* 1004-1018.

Rosenberg, M., Schooler, C., Schoenbach, C., & Rosenberg, F. (1995). Global self-esteem and specific self-esteem: Different concepts, different outcomes. *American Sociological Review, 60,* 141-156.

Rosenberg, M., & Simmons, R. G. (1972). *Black and white self-esteem: The urban school child.* Washington, DC: American Sociological Association.

Sampson, E. E. (1993). Identity politics: Challenges to psychology's understanding. *American Psychologist, 48,* 1219-1230.

Shweder, R. A., & Bourne, E. J. (1982). Does the concept of the person vary cross-culturally? In R. A. Shweder & R. A. LeVine (Eds.), *Culture theory: Essays on mind, self, and emotion* (pp. 158-199). Cambridge, UK: Cambridge University Press.

Smith, R. C. (1995). *Racism in the post-civil rights era.* Albany: State University of New York Press.

Steinberg, S. (1995). *Turning back: The retreat from racial justice in American thought and policy.* Boston: Beacon.

Tajfel, H., & Turner, J. (1986). The social identity theory of intergroup relations. In S. Worchel & W. Austin (Eds.), *Psychology of intergroup relations* (2nd ed., pp. 7-24). Chicago: Nelson-Hall.

Thompson, R. F. (1984). *Flash of the spirit: African and Afro-American art and philosophy.* New York: Vintage.

Tonry, M. (1995). *Malign neglect: Race, crime, and punishment in America.* New York: Oxford University Press.

Triandis, H. C. (1994). *Culture and social behavior.* New York: McGraw-Hill.

West, C. (1982). *Prophecy deliverance: An Afro-American revolutionary Christianity.* Philadelphia: Westminister.

Wilson, W. J. (1980). *The declining significance of race* (2nd ed.). Chicago: University of Chicago Press.

Wright, E. O. (1985). *Classes.* London: Verso.

Wright, E. O., Hachen, D., Costello, C., & Sprague, J. (1982). The American class structure. *American Sociological Review, 47,* 709-726.

Wright, E. O., & Perrone, L. (1977). Marxist class categories and income inequality. *American Sociological Review, 42,* 32-55.

X, Malcolm. (1990). *Malcolm X on Afro-American history* (3rd ed.). New York: Pathfinder.

Zinn, H. (1995). *A people's history of the United States: 1492-present.* New York: Harper.

PART II

Qualitative Research Paradigms in the Study of Television

Part II of the volume focuses on how studies from a phenomenological theoretical perspective can provide us with an understanding of how television influences our attitudes and behaviors. Unlike experimental investigators who are concerned with studies in controlled settings so that Variable A can be causally linked to Variable B, qualitative investigators emphasize the value of the social context in furthering our understanding of social phenomena. The meaningfulness of the observations made by qualitative investigators is inextricably tied to the context, thereby enhancing the ecological validity of the findings.

James A. Anderson contrasts the theory and methods of hermeneutic empiricism with those of objective empiricism and makes the point that these methods are different "not because they call for ostensibly different procedures but rather because they have a different meaning in the claims we make about the world" (p. 206). By engaging in this interpretive model of study, a "standpoint" emerges that goes beyond "describing what is there"; rather, "Science is an active agent in the construction of the significance from which we act" (p. 231).

Thomas R. Lindlof and Timothy P. Meyer state in their chapter that "the qualitative paradigm assumes that human beings organize their social behavior on the basis of shared meanings that are understood and negotiated through the reflexive use of language and other symbolic resources" (pp. 242-243). A feature of this piece is how a qualitative method, specifically ethnographic research, can be used to study how the videocassette recorder, video game player, and personal computer with CD-ROM and Internet connections have influenced the use of television in the lives of six families.

5

Qualitative Approaches to the Study of the Media

Theory and Methods of Hermeneutic Empiricism

James A. Anderson

When the so-called qualitative approaches began to reemerge in the 1970s from the shadow of the various metrics of the 1950s and 1960s, they initially were understood by perhaps the majority as methods that would clean up the leftovers. These leftovers were transitory states, individual differences, ephemeral judgments, prescientific description, and complexities yet to be unraveled by objective measurement techniques. Qualitative methods were necessary and even important because there certainly were leftovers—difficulties, anomalies, cracks, and fissures—that had to be handled, but as methods they were hardly the main event.

We have come to realize in the 25 years since that the reemergence of qualitative methods was at least one visible expression of a cosmological shift in our formulation of the human sciences. That shift has been called "the interpretive turn" (Bohman, Hiley, & Shusterman, 1991) or, as I prefer, "hermeneutic empiricism" (Anderson, 1992). The methods of hermeneutic empiricism are different from those marginalized in traditional objectivist empiricism, not because they call for ostensibly different procedures but rather because they have a different meaning in the claims we make about the world.

■ Foundational Beliefs: The Meaning of Methods

One of the gifts of feminist scholarship (Harding, 1986; Hekman, 1990; Nelson, 1990) has been the recognition of the political and ideological character of methods. Methods immerse the user in the system of beliefs by which those methods become the sensible and trustworthy means of evidence production. When there is general agreement on that prior system of beliefs, methods disappear as an object of scrutiny, although disagreements about particular techniques remain. Our current state involves a disagreement about *methods* that indicates that foundational beliefs are in contention. The next two subsections provide an overview of the characteristic beliefs of objectivist empiricism and hermeneutic empiricism.[1]

Objectivist Foundations

Objective empiricism typically assumes phenomena that are naturally configured, are perceptually accessible but autonomous of the perception, and reside in a stable network of relationships on which their characteristics and actions are dependent. Such phenomena are independent objects of analysis that become the subject of our claims. Our claims themselves are reported acts of discovery, which is to say that they accurately describe objects and relationships that are independent of both the discovering observations and the reported claims.

In sum, it is a material, independent, determined, and unified world of phenomena that is the axiomatic support for the methods of research in objectivist empiricism.

Research in this venue often begins with questions about the characteristics of things, their causes, or their consequences. It begins with the premise that there is *something* there—beyond the obvious—to investigate and that *something* is affected by other things and affects still others as well.

That something (or somethings) is made available for study in the research protocol, which will include the methods of assessing and engaging the phenomenon. These methods produce the presence of the phenomenon, often through operational definitions, and present it to some method of measurement.

The method of measurement nearly always provides for the quantification of the phenomenon as, at least, a unique existence and likely an ordered one as well. Quantification both allows and invokes the language of mathematics and the methods of statistical analysis as well as the assumptions of both.

If the research question involves cause or consequence, then the deductive logic of hypothesis testing and the experimental method may be brought in as the analytic frame of the argument.

Because many of the phenomena we study are definitionally and often actually infinite in number, most studies use some sort of selection procedure to produce the analytic samples. Sampling introduces aggregation, surrogacy, and a requirement for the logic of statistical decision rules.

All of these methods show a great deal of conventionalization. Researchers can appeal to these conventions as justification for the choices that are made and the conclusions that are drawn.

Hermeneutic Foundations

Hermeneutic empiricism assumes a world of multiple domains of phenomena with no common foundation. A typical formulation would recognize us to be first of all material entities in a physical world but also living organisms giving expression to the principles of animation and sentience and, finally, the creators and inhabitants of the domain of the sign.

The assumption of multiple domains, however formulated, strikes at the idea of the common foundation of a material, independent, determined, and unified world of phenomena that underpins objectivist empiricism. It situates the realm of human studies as well as all explanations in the domain of the sign. It is in the domain of the sign where hermeneutic empiricism finds its targeted phenomena. These phenomena are, at least in part, a human construction, ontologically dependent on the perspective of their engagement, and they reside in ad hoc relationships whose effectiveness is defined in terms of human achievement.

Hermeneutic empiricism places an interpretive accomplishment between the object of analysis and the subject of the claim. Claim itself does a variety of political works, including the political work that sets the conditions by which the claim can achieve acceptance as true.

The phenomenal world of hermeneutic empiricism incorporates the material, independent, determined, and unified products of the "big bang" with the significant, complicitous, improvisational, and localized products of collective human accomplishment. It is a world of material facts and interpretive achievements made meaningful in human action. Claim is a truth-making performance, and science is part of the action.

Studies within hermeneutic empiricism often begin with interests in how something is done, the social value of an activity or symbolic resource, the meaning of action or text, or the requirements of some consequential accomplishment. It is assumed that these interests are best explored in the everyday contexts of the actions, texts, and accomplishments or other targets of analysis. There is a resistance to, if not an outright rejection of, formal, decontextualized, or recontextualized approaches to study. The place of analysis is the lifeworld, and the first task of hermeneutic methods is to enter the analyst into the meaning production sites.

Once the scene has been entered, the researcher works back and forth between reading and writing the scene. There are different types of reading and different types of writing. Participation is a method of reading; participation as a member is a privileged form of reading. Conversations (often called long-form interviews) and walking one through (sometimes called protocol analysis) are types of interactive reading. Collecting artifacts—member-made photographs, maps, and written materials—is a form of noninteractive reading. Taking photographs and making maps, recordings, transcriptions, site notes, and field notes are forms of writing *down* the scene.

This reading and writing produce the research text archived in experience, in collection, and in discursive products of various sorts.

This text is read, in some method of intimacy, and written up^2 in the interpretations of representational description, referential analysis, meaning attribution, and critique. Far from being conventionalized (Coffey & Atkinson, 1996), this reading and writing are provocative and contentious; they are at risk and risky.

Implicative Differences

The axiomatic differences between objectivist and hermeneutic empiricism are implicative in that each forces its own definition on the elements that, from all appearances, are the common objects of their study. These differences appear in conceptualization of the media, the nature of content, the character of audiences, and the consequences of their engagement. I turn to these issues next.

■ Theorizing Media, Content, Audiences, and Consequences

The different epistemic priors of objectivist and hermeneutic empiricism establish different affinities for ways of thinking about mediated communication. Objectivism, with its material-determinism coloration, has been message centered. Media have been defined by the types of messages they produce, content by its intentional characteristics, audiences by the effects messages elicit from them, and consequences by attribution to the messages that produce them.

In this intellectual tradition, to offer some oversimplified examples, television is an entertainment medium (except when it presents the news). Commercials are compliance messages because they intend to persuade. People attend because they are hedonists or information-seeking individuals and may be manipulated into all sorts of results. Those results are understood as the consequences of the characteristics of the content attended.

Hermeneutics, on the other hand, is marked by interpretive constructionism and is practice centered. Media are defined by industry codes and praxis, content by its means of production, audiences by their practices of engagement, and consequences by the performances in which they are invoked.

To continue the oversimplifications, television is understood as a set of interrelated industries, each of which can itself be composed of quite separate elements. Commercials are the result of certain industry practices, but whether they are compliance gaining is entirely in the practices of the audience. Media attendance is a culturally situated routine—part of a life to be lived. And consequences are the resources of media accommodated within that life.

With this overview in place, I turn to the specific issues in media, content, audiences, and consequences that appear to be the boundaries between these two groups.

Media Issues

The message centeredness of objectivism positions media almost universally in a communication relationship in which media, content, audiences, and consequences are inextricably linked in a semiotic process. Indeed, media develop, it is commonly argued, as an institutional means by which the power of speech can be extended.

The practice centeredness of hermeneutics shows that, at least, there are other relationships that define media and often are more important than communication—particularly an economic relationship. Hermeneutic analysis tends to separate media and audiences into two domains: the domain of production and the domain of reception. That separation allows us to consider the other relationships that may be operating.

For example, consider media as industries that produce popular culture products that have their own market value. In a capitalist system, the push is to maximize that value, not communication effectiveness. The best news program is the one that attracts the largest audience, not the one that best informs.

As another example, the practice of the remote control device produces in the hands of many an entirely new product, devoid of initial intent, structurally fractured into fragments, and exquisitely under local control. In this practice, the message disappears.

Neither of our examples needs communication as an explanation for what is going on. That is, I can better understand much of print and broadcast journalism by applying an economic model to the industry than I can by applying a communication model to the media and their audiences. Furthermore, the claim that an audience is entertained, informed, or persuaded by a popular culture product is demonstrated not in the characteristics of the product but rather in the methods of engagement used by the members of the audience (auditors).

Just as production need not be directed by ordinary communication criteria (e.g., effectiveness), so too reception need not account for intentions or encoded meanings. Neither producers nor auditors need enter a communication relationship to do their work. The fact that they need not means that the analyst cannot simply proceed on the assumption of communication. The presence of a communication relationship in which the members mutually discipline their sign usage to produce a joint effort has to be empirically demonstrated for it to rightly appear in our explanations.

Popular culture commodities are an industrial product that are a rich resource of signification as well as multilayered messages. As an auditor, I can participate in that signifying resource through the process of interpretation, perhaps without attending to any of the messages. I can spend time with the paradigmatic and syntagmatic elements of a culturally formatted narrative without attendance to the story. In the same manner, I, as an author, can assemble the paradigmatic (here the analytic voice) and syntagmatic (here the logocentric argument) elements of the culturally formatted narrative of a textbook chapter without attending to the audience.

The phenomenology of hermeneutics requires that production and interpretation (as well as communication) each be considered an intentional act, which means that each is work to be done rather than a cognitive spasm to be effected. Because production, interpretation, and communication are achievements (and different achievements at that) rather than responses, the manner of their accomplishment becomes a focal point of analysis.

Content Issues

The primary boundary issue in content is the relationship between content and meaning. Objectivist theory typically conflates the two.

Content has a literal meaning that is delivered to the audience. Hermeneutic theory, on the other hand, inserts an interpretive step between content and meaning. Hermeneutics, therefore, first separates signification from meaning. The words I now write formally *signify,* in part through the act of writing; what these words will *mean* will depend, in part, on the actions of readers. It then separates content from activated text. The words as formatted in this chapter create the factual content that encodes their signification; the manner in which that content is engaged will create the activated text from which meaning will be achieved.

There are a number of implications of this hermeneutic separation that need to be extracted. First, the hermeneutic analyst no longer can declare what some content means to another. The analyst can declare the facts of the case—this word and not that word, this structure and not that structure. One may even argue for the potential that the signifying resource of content provides. But to declare that some content is, say, sexual or not sexual is to impose an interpretive response before it has occurred. That declaration, in turn, promotes some political end.

For hermeneutics, the common effects study does just that— promotes some political end. In such studies, the analyst declares some content (say, Internet files) to be something (say, pornographic) and then attributes whatever appears on the measures—or speculations— to exposure to pornography without verifying the interpretive response that makes both the declaration and the attribution legitimate.

Second, the presence of content with its assumption of exposure to content is no measure of consequence. For example, much is made about survey results that show the average household television set is on 7+ hours per day. The only factual prediction that can reasonably be made from that measurement is on the electric bill. A social analyst may not like the fact of the hours the television set is on and may even be affronted by what is shown (Denby, 1996), but in the absence of a careful analysis of the methods of engagement, no authentic conclusion of consequence can be drawn.[3]

Third, the more technical issues of referentiality, representation, and the trustworthiness of observation are brought to the table. These issues are so damaging to the objectivist project that theorists such as

Ellis (1991) could do no more than reject them summarily. (They bedevil hermeneutics as well.)

Referentiality speaks to the relationship between the signifier and the signified (a word/symbol/icon/image and what it stands for). Signs are referential when the signifier is firmly and consistently connected to the signified, which itself is reliably stable. Signs lose referentiality and become contingent when the signifier can migrate or the signified is reconstituted or simply disintegrates. Personal relationships (and communities of scholarship) depend on a mutually supervised referentiality, but the industrial products of popular (and even scholarly) culture deliberately promote a semiotic float (as in the meaning of the word *new* in any commercial). It is up to the interpretive community (Lindlof, 1988) to manage this float and up to the individual auditor to execute the community instructions. The result is that meaning is described more by when, where, how, and by whom than by what (Jensen, 1991). Or, in the poetics of social action, meaning is the local, partial, and improvisational expression of significance by a socially situated agent.

If signs are contingent on the time and place of their usage, then representation is equally historicized and necessarily ideological (Atkinson, 1990; Van Maanen, 1995). Just as contingent referentiality is the threat from hell to objective measurement, so too the collapse of representation is the demon of hermeneutics. Because I have developed the argument elsewhere (Anderson, 1992), I will cut to the conclusion: The fact that a representation also is a construction places the ethical burden of the consequences of our claims squarely on our shoulders.

Last, empiricists of any stripe are challenged by the provocations of observational trustworthiness. The arguments of empiricists are built on the bedrock foundation that reality will independently correct our claims about it through experience (van Fraassen, 1980). That foundation has held up well in the material domain (at least at a Newtonian level) but has turned to sand in the socially constructed reality of the semiotic domain. When the processes that participate in the construction of our lived reality also participate in the observations of that reality, we lose the independent validation of claim. When we build the case for the character of friendship, the physiological correlates of lying, and the effectiveness of certain organizational structures, we provide the instructions for how to prove us correct. Human science, therefore, helps to create what it claims to be true.[4]

Audience Issues

Recasting the vision of the mediated communication contract to one in which the social action determining the production of texts is mostly independent of the social action of their interpretation shifts the governance of interpretation from content to audiences and auditor practice. It firmly declares that should we wish to make claims about the social roles of media, then those claims need to be grounded in a sustained audience study. It also means that we need to take stock of the theoretical presumptions by which we enter into such a study. We do so in the following subsections, starting with the auditor and moving to various formulations of the audience.

The Auditor

Our constructions of audience are, quite naturally, inextricably bound up with our constructions of the individual. For our purposes here, these latter constructions break nicely on the views of the individual auditor as site and the auditor as agent.

In the Enlightenment's invention, the individual is the autonomous agent—the good person thinking well. By the late 19th century, the twin forces of psychological science and material philosophies such as Marxism had mounted a concerted attack on Enlightenment rationality and had converted the individual to a site for the expression of internal and external forces. There presently are at least three strains of this "site *geist*" (pardon the pun).

First, consider the cognitivists. Cognitivists emphasize internal mental structures and can be seen as viewing the individual as an archive site—a repository of the processes of socialization in which cognitive structures such as values, beliefs, attitudes, scripts, schemata, and the like are stored. The analyst need not know the person because it is the value structure or the schema or whatever that is being played out. The individual is simply the particular place of its expression.

Second, the sociologists and culturalists, who emphasize external societal and cultural forces, see the individual as the site of the acts of society in which individual power is submerged, often overwhelmed, and in radical formulations rendered useless in the face of cultural forces. The individual represents a particular point of intersection of these forces.

The third view is the structuralist perspective. Structuralists see the individual as an address where the outcomes of organism, community, and language are materialized in the fundamental structures of human action. It is these structures that are the object of scholarly interest. Radical structuralists have proclaimed the disappearance of the individual—"the death of man," as Foucault has put it.

In our current phase of poststructuralism, the view of the agent has reappeared. Actional theorists, for one, are recouping the idea of agency, but the agency is now socially directed rather than autonomous. Social action theorists (of whom I am one) see the individual as a socially bounded, knowledgeable agent who is a local and partial representative of societal memberships and whose actions are improvisations on cultural themes. The notion of agent used here recognizes the two senses of the term: the acting entity and the representative. As the acting agent, the individual recovers choice or "the ability to do otherwise." The local outcome of any improvisational performance, therefore, depends on the individual actor. As representative agent, however, the individual is immutably referenced to some "other" and loses the autonomy and independence characteristic of free agency. Actors and actions both are understood as situated in meaningful systems of memberships and behavior. The result is that the individual can be neither proclaimed dead nor decontextualized in global explanations. Explanation itself always will be local and partial.

In any extended discussion of audiences, we will, of course, find a wondrous multitude of variations of conceptualizations of the individual auditor. The particular presumptions concerning the nature of auditors move the analyses of audiences in particular directions. So too do different forms of analysis. The next several subsections look at the audiences that arise in different sorts of formal and empirical analyses.

Formal Audiences

Formal audiences are those constructed in the discourse and practices of practitioners in the arts and industries of content production, criticism, and scientific analysis. Formal audiences are the creation of these practitioners as both a requirement for and an achievement of their occupational accomplishments. Of these, I would point out two. The first is the audience written to or encoded in the mediated product. The second is the foundation for or the prior assumption of any critical analysis.

The encoded audience. Eagleton (1983) noted, "A writer may not have in mind a particular type of reader at all, he may be superbly indifferent who reads his work, but a certain type of reader is already included within the very act of writing itself, as an internal structure of the text" (p. 84). I would call this formal audience the "encoded audience." It is the audience that the community "knows in its bones," according to Gitlin (1985, p. 218).

One finds this audience in the discourse of industry and organizational stories. The repertoire of stories is diverse and sufficiently contradictory that it serves as an explanatory resource (Brown, 1990) for multiple positions on the same issue. Data from ratings, circulation studies, letters, personal contacts, close relatives, and the like are made sense of within these stories and within the standard practices of the industry and organizations for processing such information (Anderson & Meyer, 1988; Burgoon, Burgoon, Buller, & Atkin, 1987; Turow, 1984). Representations of the audience are constituted from these explanatory resources for the internal and external political ends of the media organization.

In the industrial products of popular culture, multiple conceptions of the audience come into play (Tunstall, 1991). Individual decisions affecting content are grounded in different visions of the audience to be. Writers, directors, actors, and editors each participate in the final product with these different visions.

Unless we are privy to hall and office talk, the encoded audiences of popular culture products appear to us primarily in promotional work as well as in the politicized statements about the audience media people make to the press, watchdog committees, regulatory agencies, and/or buyers. There is, at least, some amusement in the clear contrast between the "intelligent audience," which appears in the discourse before legislative and social activist committees, and the "seducible audience," which appears in the sales pitch to advertisers and affiliates. In fact, the industry believes in both—as might most of us.

The analytic audience. The second formal audience I would identify is the "analytic audience." The characteristics of a particular analytic audience are established in the requirements of a critical or scientific claim. When C. Anderson (1987) wrote, "In a medium that changes perpetually—even when the television set is switched off—nothing on television is precisely as we [the audience] imagine, remember, or hope" (p. 114), he invoked an audience that behaves as it ought for his claim. Who are the members of this addled "we" who feel their dislocation at each power surge to the set? They are the clones of Anderson's argument.

The audience symposium headed by Allor (1988) in the journal *Critical Studies in Mass Communication* demonstrates the different sets of terms for audiences that are expected by the separate critical perspectives of political economy, poststructuralist film theory, feminist criticism, cultural studies, and postmodernism. Each of these critical approaches requires a somewhat different audience to propel its arguments. For example, feminist criticism requires an audience living the terms of a patriarchal society, cultural studies requires an audience that represents the semes of narrative, and postmodernism requires a fractured and disconnected audience. The practitioners of all forms of criticism present their analytic audience to an encoded audience, a circumstance that complicates Hartley's (1988) claim that the critic is writing to improve audience behavior. It usually is not the encoded audience one wishes to improve (for those members typically are our own) but rather the analytic audience—an audience safely removed from the writing.

It is not only critics who produce analytic audiences. Everett and Everett (1989) created an archetypal audience of newspaper readers when these authors considered "the benefits of competition" for such readers. If one is to argue benefits, then one must presume readers all seeking certain ends. And, analytic audiences are created in survey and experimental studies where the requirements of a data collection protocol are founded on some set of assumptions of audience behavior. For example, the evidence in Helregel and Weaver (1989) that pregnant women select situation comedies in the first trimester and action dramas in the final stages of pregnancy is based on the assumption that program choices in the home can be modeled by selections from a list on a questionnaire. This belief is an analytic creation of argument that must occur prior to any empirical evidence.

Empirical Audiences

The remaining audiences fall into what I call the empirical set.[5] The discourse on empirical audiences breaks on the issue of transcendence (which also can be read as generalizability or ahistoricity). Audiences constituted in the discourse of the objectivist empiricism are characteristically transcendent or somehow independent of the particular circumstances by which they become audiences. As a result, the constituting discourse does not locate the audience in time and place. As we have seen, this discourse talks about cognitive or structural predispositions that are applicable to all humanity.

Transcendent audiences (generally conceptualizing auditors as independent actors or sites) are contrasted with situated audiences (auditors as social agents). The discourse constituting situated audiences takes direct account of the circumstances of being an auditor and accepts the responsibility (more or less) not to promote claims that transcend those circumstances. Audiences, therefore, appear in time, place, and situation and are uniquely marked by those conditions. Such is not to say that there are no common requirements for being an auditor (e.g., the necessity of interpretation); rather, it is to say that the performance of those requirements will be locally controlled.

In the subsections that follow, I consider more closely the discursive terms of transcendent and situated audiences and a few variations of each.

Transcendent empirical audiences. Objectivist empiricism works to support categorical rather than situational claims. Categorical claims are presumed to be true for all elements that fall within the scope of the claim. Consequently, talk about an "adult audience" is assumed to be effectively true whenever an adult audience arises, with noted exceptions excluded.

The concept of the transcendent audience, then, depends on the principle of equivalent units. Within the scope of the claim, any adult, child, 18- to 49-year-old working woman, or whatever, is as good as any other and is functionally equivalent to any other. Adding one more increases the audience by just that much. In most theories and industry practices that depend on transcendence, each equivalent unit is complete, autonomous, and similar in its influences and determinants (e.g., Brabrow, 1988; Webster & Newton, 1988). Other than their common categorical identification, there is no necessary connection among audience members—no "working" of the program material among members.

The transcendent audience nearly always is defined by discrete episodes of exposure (with the episodic characteristics of place, who is there, frequency, and duration) to content that has specifiable boundaries (generally industry defined such as this newspaper article or that compact disc) whose meaning is fixed in that content, the decoding of which is dependent on the skills of literacy and an objective reading. The model in place in its simplest form is the exposure of an autonomous, more or less skillful, more or less objective auditor to a meaning delivery system of content. Some form of this model, of course, is necessary if the analyst is going to make claims based on content characteristics about why people are there and about predictable outcomes from exposure.

There are many variations on this model that emphasize the different components. Content emphases are found in so-called forms and conventions analyses, skills emphases are found in literacy programs, and the character of the auditor is found in uses and gratifications as well as in lifestyle approaches.

Each of these variations, however, makes use of one of two approaches in which audiences are made visible. One is the method of aggregation by which audiences are "collected" by post hoc identification; the other is surrogation, a metonymic method by which selected individuals stand for all. The following few paragraphs explore these audiences.

First is the *aggregate audience.* In practice, most displays of an aggregate audience occur in the definitions and procedures of some sampling protocol. A. C. Nielsen's category "working women 18-49" is one such audience. As an audience, it exists in Nielsen's definitions of working women, ages 18-49 years. It is an audience created by the set definitions and not necessarily by any theoretical understanding of what it means to be an audience or by any self-identification of the individuals selected.

Some enlargement of these two points is instructive. The categories used in the most common audience studies have nothing to do with differentiated practices of audience members. They are in place because of the buying and selling practices of the industry. An 18- to 49-year-old woman watching the news is equally a "member of that audience" if she is there because someone else insisted on having the news on, if she watches intently, if she is more intent on reading the newspaper, or even if she does not consider herself an audience member.

In our description of the audience, however, she is there because she is an 18- to 49-year-old working woman, thereby producing a cause out of a difference in distribution rates. This move makes a congregation—people mutually engaged—out of a post hoc aggregation.

Second is the *surrogate audience.* Surrogate audiences arise primarily in the discourse surrounding experimental studies when the focus of such studies is some purported universal human trait. Universality has been implicitly or explicitly claimed for physiological (Lang, 1990), sexual (physiology rather than gender: Meadowcroft & Zillmann, 1987; as analog to gender: Krendl, Broihier, & Fleetwood, 1989), cognitive (Abelman, 1989), psychoanalytic (Tamborini & Stiff, 1987), and even interpretive (Hoffner, Cantor, & Thorson, 1989) characteristics or practices, among many others. Because the trait under study is assumed to be held by all humans, it does not matter which humans get examined so long as "proper" experimental controls are put in place. The respondents in the study are the surrogates for all of us.

The situated audience. The appearance of ethnographic methods in the study of media has given rise to descriptions of historic individuals performing the actions of media attendance (Alexander, Ryan, & Munoz, 1984; Anderson & Meyer, 1988; Lindlof, 1987; Lull, 1988;

Morley, 1980, 1986; Traudt, Anderson, & Meyer, 1987; Wolf, Meyer, & White, 1982) situated in the social action of everyday life.

Situated audience members are identified as embedded in an ongoing social action that must be accounted for, thereby eroding the autonomy of the act of attendance and the functional equivalence of audience members. The behavior of any audience member becomes particularized by the actual circumstances of attendance.

It is in this latter issue, the assumption of interpretive practices, that arguments from the situated audience differ most clearly from those using transcendent audience concepts. The concept of interpretive practices, as we have seen, argues that content potentiates but does not activate meaning. The activation of meaning occurs in practices of interpretation in response to the demands of the ongoing social action. Content no longer is a delivery system that evokes meaning as a cognitive reflex; rather, content is a resource for the production of texts in the audience (Anderson & Meyer, 1988; de Certeau, 1984; Fiske, 1987).

Content, nonetheless, is not an unmarked resource, equally open to any interpretive action. Sense making is a struggle among competing interests. Theorists recognize the struggle between content and audience by posing activated texts that are (a) "overdetermined" by content, (b) the result of collective strategies of interpretation, and/or (c) tactically produced in social action.

Overdetermined texts are interpretations that are ideologically "naturalized," the default or representational interpretation. Texts that affirm the dominant ideology are considered overdetermined. (The production of texts that repulse the overdetermined impulse are considered acts of resistance, a type of semiotic guerrilla warfare.) The level of analysis engaged here is the most conventional and the least dependent on evidence of actual interpretive practice (Evans, 1990).

The concept of collective strategies of interpretation recognizes the multi-ideological nature of the postmodern world. Individuals typically have access to and must enter multiple domains of discourse (e.g., the classroom of a media literacy course, the family watching television). Such domains or "ways of speaking" are organized around strategic interpretations. Strategic interpretations produce the overdetermined texts of different memberships.

Tactical texts are those put into action to accomplish some work. The evidence for tactical interpretations arises from the actual practices of situated individuals and is the least conventional. Tactical texts are those needed to buy this product now, to make a comment in an ongoing conversation, and the like. Tactical texts invoke, represent, and play with overdetermined and strategic interpretations as an accomplishment in the current social action.

Interpretation, then, is improvisational sense making by a knowledgeable agent using communal tools of understanding. It is a socially embedded performance responsive to the demands of the social action in progress to be achieved with the resources at hand. It achieves a text "made meaningful" according to the terms of that action as supported by the available resources. Its accomplishment is the local application of content resources in the service of some social action routine.

This perspective of interpretation clearly changes the traditional equation. The facts of content no longer are secure. They can be poached by auditors in interpretations that accomplish different work (e.g., Livingstone, 1990). Consequently, we no longer can solve the equation by the careful study of content characteristics or by the detailing of audience composition.

Situated audience models require a dependent self emerged in some collective engaging the materialization of cultural semes within practices of interpretation themselves located in domains of discourse and everyday social action in which those interpretations are made visible. Splitting that sentence into its elements, we have the concepts of the dependent self, the collective, the semiotic resources of cultural meanings in the repository of content, the practices of interpretation, and the performances of social action that form the core of the discourse constituting situated, interpreting audiences.

The manner in which these elements come together in the action in progress implicates the character of the audience in different ways. I offer three examples.

First is the *strategic audience*. The strategic audience is one defined by a common set of interpretive strategies. I belong to an academic audience *if and when* I practice the interpretive strategies of that community. The strategic audience concept shifts the emphasis from the autonomous individual to a collective, most often called an interpretive community (Lindlof, 1988; Radway, 1984). It is the community that develops the strategies, provides the means for dissemination and instruction, and supervises particular performances of them. The individual in any strategic situation is a local and partial representation of the interpretive community. Clearly, the members are not equivalent units as the normal political processes of membership are presumed. Some members will be more important than others, directing the others as to both what to "read" and how to read it.

The strategic audience concept obviously lessens the emphasis on exposure to any particular content. It is not so much exposure but the practice of interpretation as governed by the community that is the agency of import. Meaning becomes a community production. Furthermore, the community itself will rematerialize in many different ways (in collective publications, public speech, conversations, etc.) the "active semiotic ingredients," if you will, of the industrially produced content. Consequently, the connection to *an* exposure is not all that clear or necessary. Understanding the strategic audience, then, also initiates both an extended study of content and an extended study of the collectives to which the interpretation of content refers.

The theory of strategic audiences is far better developed than the evidence for them (Carragee, 1990). Although there seems to be little doubt of their existence, the workings of interpretive communities remain to be revealed despite Radway's (1984) celebrated analysis of the romance reader. More work needs to be done.

Second is the *engaged audience*. The engaged audience is a genuine membership whose attendance to a text is directed as a sign of that membership. (Membership here refers to a recognizable relationship between an individual who seeks it and a collective that grants it.) The engaged audience is a "declared" strategic audience openly practicing its strategies of interpretation in part to be recognized as a member. It is obvious, for example, that the political elite use both media and content, particularly that of news, in radically different ways from the nonelite. For most of us, the news approaches something like the soap opera of life (Anderson, Chase, & Larson, 1990). For the political elite, news and its manipulation are stock in trade.

There are a number of useful distinctions that can be drawn between the strategic and engaged audience concepts. Strategic audiences tend to be loosely coupled. The interpretive community is less well developed, and community supervision is less effective. Engaged audiences as memberships are tightly coupled in contracts of mutual dependencies. There are solid interpersonal networks and personal histories. Both audiences promote texts about their texts, but those of the interpretive community are less sophisticated—the fan magazine type. Engaged audiences often support costly, deeply insider newsletters that interpret the major texts of the membership.

Engaged audiences appear much more likely to participate in the production process itself, supplying material or even content (e.g., press releases, planted stories). The symbiotic relationship extends well beyond the quid pro quo of purchase or subscription. In fact, the more the engaged audience constitutes the total audience for the text and its production enterprise, and the more homogeneous the audience itself, the more this audience approaches the classical form. In short, there is a substantially greater number of layers of connection (hence the term) with the engaged audience.

Third is the *emergent audience*. If the engaged audience is the most deeply dependent on content, then the emergent audience is simply opportunistic. Its connection to content is to take advantage of the common understandings that widely distributed content can make available. The emergent audience appears in the practice of some social action not related to audience membership. For example, if in the practice of gifting I determine that my gift qualifies as a gift by virtue of its *appearance in the media as a gift,* then I emerge as an audience member of the commercial or other content that does that work even though I may never have been exposed to the particular material. As another example, most of us have not been to a "Rambo" film, unless I am seriously and sadly mistaken; nonetheless, most of us know the essence of the character (it is not much) and can both recognize and use a reference to it. So, in days past, when President Reagan was presented as Ronbo, it was a generally recognizable characterization.

The notion of the emergent audience extends the influence of media well beyond exposure. But it is an influence that is modified and perhaps entirely made over by social practices. This is not our predecessors' two-step flow, where the media delivered their content to opinion leaders, who passed it on untrammeled. Here we are talking of knowledgeable agents who reconstruct content for the political ends of the social action collectives in which they participate. The emergent audience lets us understand the ordinary practices of opposition, resistance, and inversion that populate the interpretations of any audience.

The emergent audience is clearly the most distant from our classical heritage, but it may be much more informative of the way in which most media are accommodated in our lives. I have not seen the *Power Rangers* (narratives widely available in live-action video and animated television) as of this writing, although I have read reviews, know several folks who have seen the content, and have listened to their recountings and judgments. I could carry on a lengthy, if not intelligent, discussion concerning the film (much like American journalists on Marxism). Without having the heart of the experience, the film still is present in my life, and that presence has been accommodated. Given the small proportion of our populace who participate directly in the programs of national and international news, this dispersed contact with what might be considered by journalism scholars as the significant affairs of the day must be the experience of most people. Most of the articles on the recent Balkan fractures probably have not been read by any of us, but that does not prevent us from knowing about and acting on them.

Does this gauzy contact qualify as an audience? Probably as much as the generalized action of watching television or reading the newspaper, where the act of attendance is the end itself. How often have we stepped away from the television set with little memory trace save a recognition of the reproduction of industry forms and conventions? Exposure may or may not be significant.

Implications

The effort of this analysis has been to show that our conceptualization of audiences has consequences for the methods we use to study them. Audiences appear in the creation and analysis of content. They justify that work. If one believes that content delivers meaning that is engaged by generalizable mental states, then methods of aggregation and surrogation are appropriate. But if one believes that meaning arises locally in the progress of some culturally understood action, then one must go where the action is and use methods that will encompass it.

Consequences

The work that we have done to this point has (a) disconnected the media from a necessary communication relationship with their audiences, thereby releasing us from the necessity of always considering content as messages; (b) inserted an interpretive step between content and its auditors, thereby establishing the importance of local methods of engagement in the production of the on-site activated text; and (c) grounded actual audiences in a nexus of relationships and practices, thereby shifting the agency of effects to the ongoing social action.

The consequences of engaging the products of media, then, are contained in the field of social action[6] that has provided for the engagement. Objectivist empiricism traditionally has asked us to consider only disembodied moments as effects; hermeneutic empiricism asks us to look for effects in the naturalized provenance of action.

Let me work an example. The other day, I was reading in the newspaper about 30-second attack commercials in political campaigns ("Election Debate," 1996). The reporter claimed they were very effective. I wondered how the reporter knew. The obvious answer is that people who use such commericals get elected. The obvious reply is that people who use them also lose elections.

Focusing on the commercial will not give us the answer. To understand effectiveness, we must look to the action that will accommodate the commercials as change agents. If I never vote or always vote the same party, then attack ads of any sort have no effectiveness. Why? Because the action known as voting is performed in such a way that choice is not at issue and, therefore, a change agent cannot be accommodated. If, however, I am an authentic undecided voter (a person who will vote and for whom more than one candidate is a genuine choice), then change agents will be actively accommodated. I may well choose not to pay attention to attack ads, but I will have to change if I am to complete the performance of the undecided voter.

To understand effectiveness, then, the analyst must investigate the repertoire of performance in which the unfinished resource of content becomes activated as an agent. This is not a case-by-case analysis, by the way. Remembering that social action is a language of human behavior—the jointly held signs of what is being done—the performance of the undecided voter (or of any other action seme) is open to general analysis, although it will be performed locally and contingently. The consequences of one type of performance cannot, however, be exported as the consequences of another type. Laboratory simulations are their own explanation, not the explanation of something else.

The Requirements for Methods
From Hermeneutic Theory

Hermeneutic empiricism considers the field of action as performed in everyday life to be the proper object of analysis. Action has to be understood as a language of behavior whose expression is sensible in the actual historic conditions of its performance. Just as this part of this sentence will be understood "as an example" by its presentation in this paragraph, so too is a performance understood by its presentation in the ongoing action.

The basic requirements for methods, then, are to somehow provide for the study of meaningful performances in the action of everyday life.

1. Let me take that sentence apart. Life is not the blank slate on which we write our experience. Life is both performance and position. I live the life of a white, middle-class, middle-aged, American male not by any choice of my own but because of happenstance and because our society is organized in such a way that color of skin, income, age, and gender make a difference. I struggle against reproducing the racism, sexism, and materialism associated with this life, but I know I have both benefited and been penalized by the differences. I also know that those differences are of the set of marks by which I am constituted as a person. The first requirement of methods, then, is a deep understanding of the cultural elements by which lives are constituted and given.

2. "Everydayness" privileges the ordinary. It holds that ordinary performances are systematically and intentionally organized to be

ordinary performances of something. During the 1996 Summer Olympics, I watched a young woman gymnast complete a routine despite the pain of a badly sprained ankle. It was an ordinary act of heroism. We understand it as heroic because it is reproduced as such in thousands of sporting events from Little League to professional. The ordinary is what we already know to be true. The second requirement of methods, then, is that we make explicit and accessible what we already know.

3. Action is the sign of what is being done. At the moment, I am involved in a performance of writing. The broad scope of what I do is understood from the action of writing. Even when I go downstairs for a cup of coffee, I am in the "taking a break" phase of writing. Without a finger to the keys, I am still under the governance of that action. A writer will understand why that cup of coffee is different from the cup taken in friendship. The behavior may look exactly the same, but the action is different. It is up to the analyst to understand and document the difference. The third requirement of methods, then, is to know what the action is from a performer's perspective.

4. A performance is a local and contingent expression within some action provided by a life to be lived. Performances reveal the actions of our lives. They are, therefore, the object of our study because they are the route by which we come to know human action and human life. The fourth requirement of methods, then, is to be at the site and in the presence of performance.

5. The meaningfulness of performances is constituted on several levels. I understand what I am doing as I strike these keys. If I were to describe the action in a protocol analysis, I would be talking about fashioning sentences to meet the requirements of the implied outline in the topic sentence of this section, itself part of a larger outline submitted to my editors, in an effort to produce the daily requirement of pages needed to finish on time. The listening analyst would want me to speak to the larger organization of the publishing enterprise—my feelings of necessity imposed by my own devices, codes of writing, and the scholarly life I lead. The analyst might want to explore the nuances of missing a deadline (or, worse, finishing early, which calls

the enterprise into question) and so on. This action of my writing has other players who participate in and bring their own perspectives to the performance. My editors may understand the performance as the production of the necessary resource for the book they wish to produce. Student readers may see it as one more episode of the hegemony of an academic elite in the service of capitalism. My colleagues may understand this writing from the larger purview of professionalism and from our local agreements of merit evaluations. All of these are invoked in every sentence. The performance is owned in part by all players and is made meaningful by each. The fifth requirement of methods, then, is to locate (find the time, place, and conditions of) the meaningfulnesses of the performance.

■ Strategies and Tactics

The professional practice of research, be it objectivist or hermeneutic, is a full-time job. A colleague of mine, already an accomplished experimentalist, took an ethnography course I offered. At the end, she wrote, "One of the most striking things is how much more work qualitative research requires of the careful researcher. Demands of time and rigor are unimaginable" (J. Meadowcroft, personal communication, December 1982). Rose (1990) called this work "living the ethnographic life." The practice of this life requires us to advance five strategies drawn from our five requirements of methods. They are (a) to have a ready knowledge of the characters, allusions, motives, themes, and narratives that constitute our cultural understanding of "how it works out there"; (b) to systematically catalog the ordinary practices of acting as *someone* doing *something*; (c) to approach a member's understanding of the action by (d) being in the action; and (e) to deliberately manipulate the perspective of one's analysis to begin again. In the following, I offer a ruminative list of tactics—some good, some gratuitous.

Cultural Knowledge

Tactics would include traveling; studying a language (including one's own); critically engaging popular culture (e.g., going to a Disney movie and relating characters to body type, to sources of power, to motive, to action, etc.); reading folktales, popular biographies, and/or successful fiction; watching television (particularly cartoons) for character, quality, the valued and its attainment; and evaluating print and broadcast news not for facts but rather for structure, identity, voice, authority, and significance (see Altheide & Snow, 1988). Talk to people, listening for allusions, themes, incentives, and forms of reasoning. Write it down. Build a resource.

Ordinary Practices

The strategy of ordinary practices is moved forward through the tactics of iconic, discursive, and performative analyses. Iconic analysis documents the encoded instructions of the practice site. People organize environments to provide for the ordinary practice of what goes on. Discursive analysis explores the communicative forms that mark the ordinary. Who says what to whom in what manner is a start; who is silenced and what is suppressed moves toward the more sophisticated. Performative analysis considers the structural character of a practice—what is the beginning, middle, and end as well as what relationships, forms of power, motives, and outcomes are involved.[7]

Member's Understanding

Participant observation usually is considered the preeminent tactic of this strategy. But any method that systematically approaches performance and allows some form of rehearsal is tactically appropriate. Protocol analysis is one of those. Protocol analysis involves being with a competent performer (assuming that an understanding of competent performance is the analytic goal) during the action and getting the performers to "talk the analyst through" what is being done. Observation and interview when interviewer and respondent have a common experiential reference also might be appropriate.

Being There

There is no heavier burden in hermeneutic research than being there. It is what clearly separates hermeneutic empiricism from objectivist empiricism, criticism, critical theory, cultural studies, and continental poststructuralism. One may not speak where one has not been.

The tactics of gaining access, learning the ropes, building an identity, gaining confidences, sustaining a presence, completing an exit, and gaining reentry are more than a paragraph can handle. I would direct the reader to J. A. Anderson (1987), B. Jackson (1987), Lofland (1976), Lindlof (1995), Morris (1977), and Strauss and Corbin (1991).

Managing Standpoints

The collapse of representation has forced us to recognize that any claim to "what is" is accomplished from some point of view. The result is a restlessness of analysis that withdraws at the moment of certainty. Tactical questions include the following. Who else makes sense of this performance? Who is the other? What is the hidden stance of the analysis? What do I have to believe to be true to make this claim? Each time the questions are asked, the analysis begins anew in a reaffirmation of the hermeneutic spiral in which both object and analyst are informed and revealed. Returning to my colleague, she asked, "If it weren't for deadlines, would qualitative analysis ever be considered complete by the researcher?" (J. Meadowcroft, personal communication, December 1982). My answer would be "No—finished, yes, but always partial, incomplete, in progress."

■ Arguments and Claims

In general, hermeneutic empiricism has replaced the naive representation of objectivist empiricism with the notion of standpoint argument. A *standpoint,* as we have seen, is the assembled set of priors—assumptions, beliefs, paradigmatic axioms—that permit the argument. Change the priors, and the argument also must change or fail. Standpoint argument radically changes the enterprise of science (M. Jackson, 1989). Instead of simply describing what is there, science is an active agent in the construction of the significances from which we act. An example often used is that gender is a set of social practices by which we understand the feminine and masculine. As science "describes" those practices, they come under critical scrutiny and forces for change. The results are a feminine and masculine no longer as they were. The claims made about them, however, remain as a standpoint.

As another example, if I choose to find the causes of street crime in the products of television rather than in the practices of racial injustice, economic inequality, and educational opportunity, then I serve to preserve those latter inequities. The choice to nominate television as important through my interest and allocation of resources is a standpoint and, therefore, an ethical (not a veridical) decision.

As a final example, the use of statistical decision rules, tests of significance by which one acts toward a claim as if it were or were not true, is an epistemological method to reduce the inherent uncertainty of the meaning of an empirical event. The test is a social practice of sense making. It tells us how to act toward an event without telling us anything about the event itself. The decision to use tests of significance is a standpoint.

Writing as Method

The social constructedness of the reality we study, as well as the necessity of some standpoint from which to address it, historicizes and politicizes the claims we make about it. By *historicize,* it is meant that a claim is valid in time and place. The families I studied 10 years ago are not the families of today. By *politicize,* it is meant that a claim is valid by means of its rhetorical rather than its (now lost) representational quality. A claim must resonate; it must serve some interests to be maintained in the social practices of knowledge production.

The consequence of these circumstances is that the production of the final argument (preeminently a written argument) is the ultimate method. In the end, it is the writing that counts. Good writing will not correct the strategic and tactical failures of engagement, but bad writing and inopportune conditions of publication and distribution will cripple the strongest of engagement efforts.

Good writing is not a durable commodity; no 12-step program will follow here (but see Van Maanen, 1988; Wolcott, 1990). It is a continuing effort of both the field and the individual author to find ways in which to achieve presence.

The Modern and the Postmodern

Tied up in all these epistemological and methodological positions is the clash between the modern and the postmodern. The modern, with its ideal of progressive attainment and its goal of increasing control, is contrasted with what Mumby (1997) called the postmodern's "discourse of vulnerability." The modern argument, secure in its foundationalism and independent of its consequences, presumably is bulletproof in its self-contained archive. It is the coin of the academy that passes through the body politic without change to either. The postmodern argument in the face of deconstructionism and the conflation of the true and the good—a claim of "what is" is a claim of "what ought to be"—appears to be without protection of any sort.

The postmodern argument finds its protection—and its value—in its instrumentality: what it promotes, maintains, and advances. The postmodern responsibility is both to find an answer to the insolent "So what?" and to create the conditions by which its "That's what" reply will be accepted. The postmodern returns us to the streets.

Justified Claim and Knowledge Production

The effort that we all share—modern or postmodern, objectivist or hermeneutic—is that of justified claim. We seek to construct those platforms of action from which others may justifiably risk acting. We attempt this construction through careful and committed study and are responsible when we fail.

It is what others can do with our claims (not our self-satisfactions or disciplinary successes) that produces knowledge in society.

■ Notes

1. Two caveats are in order. First, the descriptions of ideological centers are inherently contentious given that there is no Archimedean point from which to address them. Second, the space between and beyond these centers is populated as well. These descriptions, drawn as they are to emphasize internal coherence and external difference, do not exhaust the possibilities. I offer a larger description of these possibilities in Anderson (1996), from which the present descriptions come.

2. The difference between "writing down" and "writing up" is useful for understanding the different writing tasks. Writing down privileges experience; writing up privileges interpretation. My thanks to Tom Lindlof for pointing out these terms.

3. We, of course, draw such conclusions regularly. They generally entail "bad results" and people who are not us. Correcting television, film, and rap music has become the substitute for economic and racial justice.

4. For example, intelligence tests nominate certain human traits as more important than others (German physicists have been claimed as the model). Because people categorized as having greater intelligence get privileged treatment within an education system built on the same model, they are more intelligent.

5. This nomination is not to claim that such audiences are necessarily "actual audiences" or even populated by actual people. Empirical audiences are no less a discursive subject than formal ones and always require some prior definitional work before they will appear.

6. "Social action" recognizes that, as humans, our "behavior" is organized semiotically as meaningful expressions of what is being done. Recognizable action is "social" not because we are together with others but rather because, as with language, social mechanisms create the conditions that govern meaningful performances and by which we know what we are doing.

7. Riding along the bicycle path in Klagenfurt, Austria, I pass two 12-year-old boys riding side by side. They look at me with some surprise. Moments later, one of them is beside me and gives me a nod. Instantly, we are in a race. He wins, of course. "Sehr gut," I call out, hoping it is somehow appropriate. A performative analysis would examine how the action was fitting, initiated, executed, and completed (e.g., passing the boys was a challenge because they were traveling faster than ordinary traffic).

■ References

Abelman, R. (1989). From here to eternity: Children's acquisition of understanding of projective size on television. *Human Communication Research, 15,* 463-481.

Allor, M. (1988). Relocating the site of the audience. *Critical Studies in Mass Communication, 5,* 217-233.

Alexander, A., Ryan, M. S., & Munoz, P. (1984). Creating a learning context: Investigations on the interaction of siblings during television viewing. *Critical Studies in Mass Communication, 1,* 345-364.

Altheide, D., & Snow, R. (1988). Toward a theory of mediation. In J. A. Anderson (Ed.), *Communication yearbook 11* (pp. 194-223). Newbury Park, CA: Sage.

Anderson, C. (1987). Reflections on *Magnum, P.I.* In H. Newcomb (Ed.), *Television: The critical view* (4th ed., pp. 112-125). New York: Oxford University Press.

Anderson, J. A. (1987). *Communication research: Issues and methods.* New York: McGraw-Hill.

Anderson, J. A. (1992). On the ethics of research in a socially constructed reality. *Journal of Broadcasting and Electronic Media, 36,* 353-357.

Anderson, J. A. (1996). *Communication theory: Epistemological foundations.* New York: Guilford.

Anderson, J. A., Chase, R. S., & Larson, T. (1990). *Patterns of viewing and descriptions of use for broadcast television news.* Dublin, Ireland: International Communication Association.

Anderson, J. A., & Meyer, T. P. (1988). *Mediated communication: A social action perspective.* Newbury Park, CA: Sage.

Atkinson, P. (1990). *The ethnographic imagination: Textual constructions of reality*. London: Routledge.

Bohman, J. F., Hiley, D. R., & Shusterman, R. (1991). Introduction: The interpretive turn. In D. R. Hiley, J. F. Bohman, & R. Shusterman (Eds.), *The interpretive turn: Philosophy, science, culture* (pp. 1-14). Ithaca, NY: Cornell University Press.

Brabrow, A. S. (1988). Theory and method in research on audience motives. *Journal of Broadcasting and Electronic Media, 32,* 471-487.

Brown, M. H. (1990). Defining stories in organizations: Characteristics and functions. In J. A. Anderson (Ed.), *Communication yearbook 13* (pp. 162-190). Newbury Park, CA: Sage.

Burgoon, J. K., Burgoon, M., Buller, D. B., & Atkin, C. K. (1987). Communication practices of journalists: Interaction with public, other journalists. *Journalism Quarterly, 64,* 125-132, 275.

Carragee, K. M. (1990). Interpretive media study and interpretive social science. *Critical Studies in Mass Communication, 7,* 81-96.

Coffey, A., & Atkinson, P. (1996). *Making sense of qualitative data*. Thousand Oaks, CA: Sage.

de Certeau, M. (1984). *The practice of everyday life*. Berkeley: University of California Press.

Denby, D. (1996, July 15). Buried alive: Our children and the avalanche of crud. *The New Yorker,* pp. 48-59.

Eagleton, T. (1983). *Literary theory*. Minneapolis: University of Minnesota Press.

Election debate centers around ads. (1996, July 22). *Salt Lake Tribune,* p. A12.

Ellis, D. (1991). Poststructuralism and language: Non-sense. *Communication Monographs, 58,* 213-224.

Evans, W. A. (1990). The interpretive turn in media research: Innovation, iteration, or illusion? *Critical Studies in Mass Communication, 7,* 147-168.

Everett, S. C., & Everett, S. E. (1989). How readers and advertisers benefit from local newspaper competition. *Journalism Quarterly, 66,* 76-79, 147.

Fiske, J. (1987). *Television culture*. London: Metheun.

Gitlin, T. (1985). *Inside prime time*. New York: Pantheon.

Harding, S. (1986). *The science question in feminism*. Ithaca, NY: Cornell University Press.

Hartley, J. (1988). The real world of audiences. *Critical Studies in Mass Communication, 5,* 234-238.

Hekman, S. J. (1990). *Gender and knowledge: Elements of a postmodern feminism*. Boston: Northeastern University Press.

Helregel, B. K., & Weaver, J. B. (1989). Mood management during pregnancy through selective exposure to television. *Journal of Broadcasting and Electronic Media, 33,* 15-33.

Hoffner, C., Cantor, J., & Thorson, E. (1989). Children's responses to conflicting auditory and visual features of a televised narrative. *Human Communication Research, 16,* 256-278.

Jackson, B. (1987). *Fieldwork*. Urbana: University of Illinois Press.

Jackson, M. (1989). *Paths toward a clearing*. Bloomington: Indiana University Press.

Jensen, K. B. (1991). When is meaning? Communication theory, pragmatism, and mass media reception. In J. A. Anderson (Ed.), *Communication yearbook 14* (pp. 3-32). Newbury Park, CA: Sage.

Krendl, K. A., Broihier, M. C., & Fleetwood, C. (1989). Children and computers: Do sex-related differences persist? *Journal of Communication, 39,* 85-93.

Lang, A. (1990). Involuntary attention and physiological arousal evoked by structural features and emotional content in TV commercials. *Communication Research, 17,* 275-299.

Lindlof, T. (Ed.). (1987). *Natural audiences.* Norwood, NJ: Ablex.

Lindlof, T. (1988). Media audiences as interpretive communities. In J. A. Anderson (Ed.), *Communication yearbook 11* (pp. 81-107). Newbury Park, CA: Sage.

Lindlof, T. (1995). *Qualitative communication research methods.* Thousand Oaks, CA: Sage.

Livingstone, S. M. (1990). Interpreting a television narrative: How different viewers see a story. *Journal of Communication, 40,* 72-85.

Lofland, J. (1976). *Doing social life.* New York: John Wiley.

Lull, J. (Ed.). (1988). *World families watch television.* Newbury Park, CA: Sage.

Meadowcroft, J., & Zillmann, D. (1987). Women's comedy preferences during the menstrual cycle. *Communication Research, 14,* 204-218.

Morley, D. (1980). *The "nationwide" audience.* London: British Film Institute.

Morley, D. (1986). *Family television: Cultural power and domestic leisure.* London: Comedia.

Morris, M. B. (1977). *An excursion into creative sociology.* New York: Columbia University Press.

Mumby, D. K. (1997). Modernism, postmodernism, and communication studies: A rereading of an ongoing debate. *Communication Theory 7,* 1-28.

Nelson, L. H. (1990). *Who knows: From Quine to a feminist empiricism.* Philadelphia: Temple University Press.

Radway, J. (1984). *Reading the romance: Feminism and the representation of women in popular culture.* Chapel Hill: University of North Carolina Press.

Rose, D. (1990). *Living the ethnographic life.* Newbury Park, CA: Sage.

Strauss, A. L., & Corbin, J. (1991). *Basics of qualitative research: Grounded theory, procedures and techniques.* Newbury Park, CA: Sage.

Tamborini, R., & Stiff, J. (1987). Predictors of horror film attendance and appeal: An analysis of the audience for frightening films. *Communication Research, 14,* 414-436.

Traudt, P. J., Anderson, J. A., & Meyer, T. P. (1987). Phenomenology, empiricism, and media experience. *Critical Studies in Mass Communication, 4,* 302-310.

Tunstall, J. (1991). A media industry perspective. In J. A. Anderson (Ed.), *Communication yearbook 14* (pp. 163-186). Newbury Park, CA: Sage.

Turow, J. (1984). *Media industries.* New York: Longman.

van Fraassen, B. C. (1980). *The scientific image.* Oxford, UK: Clarendon.

Van Maanen, J. (1988). *Tales of the field: On writing ethnography.* Chicago: University of Chicago Press.

Van Maanen, J. (Ed.). (1995). *Representation in ethnography.* Thousand Oaks, CA: Sage.

Weaver, J. G., & Newton, G. D. (1988). Structural determinants of the television news audience. *Journal of Broadcasting and Electronic Media, 32,* 381-389.

Wolcott, H. F. (1990). *Writing up qualitative research.* Newbury Park, CA: Sage.

Wolf, M. A., Meyer, T. P., & White, C. (1982). A rules-based study of television's role in the construction of social reality. *Journal of Broadcasting, 26,* 813-829.

6

Taking the Interpretive Turn

Qualitative Research of Television and Other Electronic Media

Thomas R. Lindlof ■ Timothy P. Meyer

One of the more engrossing works of television research, *Tuned in: Television in American Life* (DeGrane, 1991), offers no literature review, no hypotheses, and no findings or arguments—at least in the sense we are used to thinking of them. Allowing only a brief preface and no captions, Lloyd DeGrane assembled 36 black-and-white photographs of people watching and living with television in their own habitats. DeGrane took these pictures of viewing rituals in 1980s Chicago by simply entering the places in which they lived— apartments, homes, dormitories, a prison—"with a certain reverence or respect, as a traveler might come upon a holy place." One turns the pages to encounter scenes that are by turns mundane and exotic, remote and close to one's own experience. We see the different styles of television sets these people have acquired and the places chosen for them: kitchen counters, bedroom dresser tops, a sidewalk, the foot of the bed, and, of course, living rooms. Some of the television sets are adorned, shrine-like, with personal artifacts and plants; others seem strangely blank in their surroundings. Some of the photos frame both the viewers and the screen, showing us something of this relationship by the distance the viewers keep and what it is they find amusing, intriguing, or boring; in others, we see only their expressions as they gaze off-frame at the unseen source. Every reader surely will have his or her own favorites. One of ours is a floor-level shot from behind two young children who seem completely involved in a game of their own devising, their legs up in the air, a Barbie doll headset prominently in the foreground between them. The television is on in the background, but the children are not watching.

Although voiceless and frozen in time, the photos nevertheless give readers a means of access to a part of other people's symbolically constructed world. It is a part of their world that "makes sense" for us at an elemental level and elicits our immediate interest because the common thread through all of the pictures—television—also is the referent of greatest commonality for all Americans regardless of region, ethnicity, class position, or any other cultural distinction one could name. But what of our assertion, in the opening sentence, that the DeGrane photos are an example of television research, to say nothing of research of high quality? Despite not having been run through a gauntlet of three anonymous journal reviewers, this set of photos can be considered seriously in light of the aims of ethnographic research: "to find out what people who belong to a system of significance do, to determine how what they do is meaningful inside that system, and ultimately to explain the system itself" (Anderson & Goodall, 1994, p. 88). Certainly, the latter two goals are achieved only partially, if at all, given that the terms of argumentation that would permit such an explanation from evidence cannot be provided through visual representation alone.

Yet, these finely crafted exemplars do provide (again, partial) responses to the question, How do people practice the use of television? *Tuned In* does something characteristic of nearly all good ethnographies: It offers close-up description of how a social act is performed. These photos are evidence of how *some* people included television in *some* of their cultural and interpersonal relationships at a certain historical moment in the United States. Through this analytic frame, the entire collection of these relationships is far more meaningful than any individual photos (even our favorites) can be. Aided by the deeply intuitive knowledge of television that we share with DeGrane and the actors captured on film, we can look across the series and reflect on the unities and particularities of the medium's role in American life.

This chapter presents some of the key issues, problems, and considerations that confront those who would conduct a qualitative social analysis of electronic media audiences. Among the other social science paradigms, qualitative inquiry occupies a unique place; it is interested in audience activity as *a cultural performance of everyday life.* Mass media, as Lull (1980) wrote years ago, are "handy expediants which can be exploited by individuals, coalitions, and family units to serve their personal needs, create practical relationships, and engage the social world" (p. 198). These "expediants" are constructed anew in each instance of use as a communicative resource, whether as a source of programming, as a part of conversations or other speech situations, or as a symbolic figure in public life. At the same time, as the *Tuned In* photos were meant to show, television viewing is a well-practiced ritual. It meshes so thoroughly into the routines of domestic living, and increasingly the public domain as well, that it hardly makes sense anymore to speak of a nonmediated social reality except, perhaps, as a foil for arguing the "effects" of media. Television may or may not be the dominant standard by which cultural assumptions are built in modernity, however, it undoubtedly is true that these assumptions, as they now exist, could not be built without television.

Of course, television is not just any household appliance, and the choices involved in using television cannot always be considered innocently personal ones. Rather, television serves up a flow of material relentlessly in pursuit of both specific persuasive ends and more broadly hegemonic interests. In a variety of formats, images, and voices, television attempts to convince viewers not only of the rightness of its portrayals (ranging from American military interventions in news to sexual relations in soap operas) but also of the very taken-for-granted nature of their televised appearance. However, this ideological work often is contradictory or conflicted, as we notice when a news story critical of the tobacco industry airs soon after coverage of a women's tennis match sponsored by a cigarette brand. What is seen on television may conflict crucially with the values and beliefs that circulate in other areas of life. Depending on one's social affiliations, television could be either more conservative or more progressive than what one would wish it to be, causing even more complicated means of negotiating usage.

Qualitative media analysts are interested, therefore, in how people apply media resources within the circumstances of their lives and how cultural meanings arise out of the changing uses of these texts and technologies. Such an arena of action demands descriptions of the local contexts, social rules, lived experiences, and interpretations in which television and associated media, such as the videocassette recorder (VCR) and microcomputer, participate. Researchers should be willing to move tactfully into the customary spaces of others, understand how they engage a technology or text, and be open to comprehending alternative notions of mediated reality.

An exhaustive review of this thriving body of research is beyond the scope of this chapter.[1] Instead, we present what we consider to be basic to an understanding of qualitative television research: some definitions and axiomatic concepts of the paradigm, applications in electronic media studies over the past two decades, and exemplars drawn from an ongoing study of several families and the evolution of their practices with television, VCRs, and computers.

■ The Qualitative Paradigm in Television Research

Definitional Work

Like any term that gains rapidly in popularity, *qualitative* has acquired a variety of meanings for the many communities that have proclaimed their interest. The first distinction to make also is the most obvious: its contrast to quantitative forms of inquiry. As Anderson and Meyer (1988) put it, "Qualitative research methods are distinguished from quantitative methods in that they do not rest their evidence on the logic of mathematics, the principle of numbers, or the methods of statistical analysis" (p. 247). Although interpretive studies sometimes use tools such as surveys and engage in statistical analysis of numbers, the evidence they characteristically deal with is discursive: transcripts, field notes, and written documents. Nondiscursive materials such as photographs, videos, music, maps, and artifacts also may enter into an analysis, at which point their significant elements usually will be converted into narrative description. For most qualitative researchers, the reductionist and objectifying rationales for quantifying behavior run counter to their interest in capturing the uniqueness of a communicative act.

Qualitative methodology also encompasses a distinction between the methods and subjects belonging to *empirical science,* which concerns the analysis of experience, and the subjects and methods of *humanistic criticism* (e.g., rhetoric, hermeneutics, literary criticism), which studies the forms, meanings, and values of already produced texts and speech. On the face of it, this distinction has mostly to do with whether or not there is some unfolding human action involved, and to a great extent this does distinguish the field-worker from an armchair critic. However, some theorists of interpretive social science (e.g., Geertz, 1973; Ricoeur, 1977) argue that the cultural analyst "reads" a segment of social action by retracing its multiple historical and contextual frameworks, that is, by analogy to a hermeneutic breakdown and reassembly of a written work. In other words, their working procedures are not so different despite the difficulty some field researchers have with the static and print-biased connotations of "text."

There also has been a blurring recently in the epistemological assignments of the empirical and humanistic disciplines that subscribe to a qualitative orientation. There is increasing recognition that all empirical descriptions are, in a sense, fictions because they require a careful reconstruction of actors, actions, events, and points of view. Some field researchers have turned to concepts and methods in rhetorical and literary analysis to advance their experimentation with nonrealist ways of writing research narratives. Humanists, for their part, now recognize that different social positions can produce differently read versions of a single work, even leading some of them beyond theoretical speculation about unstable, semiotically "excessive" texts to study the reading activities of actual readers (e.g., Radway, 1984).

Finally, the term *qualitative* has come to stand for a broad group of strategies and traditions that, individually, differ in key ways. Some members of this set include the case study, naturalistic inquiry, emancipatory action research, phenomenological research, and the life history study (Tesch, 1990). *Ethnography* probably is the chief competitor as a covering term. From long usage in anthropology and interpretive sociology, ethnography typically refers to a long-term involvement within a cultural scene (e.g., a tribe, an organization, a family) in which the researcher undergoes the experience of learning a membership role as a way of pursuing the strategy of participant observation (Ellen, 1984). A multiple method approach, in which a variety of data sources are used as complements and validity checks to each other, is a hallmark of thick ethnographic description. Learning a culture's language is one of the most essential, and often arduous, tasks of the ethnographic enterprise. Whether it is truly a distinct language, a dialect, or phrases of jargon, a practical knowledge of the way a group codes its experiences opens up the content of its culture in the most direct, vivid way possible.

Very few studies have been published in the media literature that qualify as ethnography under all of the criteria mentioned in the preceding. Some of the reasons for this scarcity of ethnography may include too little time spent in the field (which reduces the chances for achieving rapport with the participants), the frequent focus on audience response to a single text or genre (which constricts the overall scope of inquiry as well as time spent with any one informant), a perceived thinness in the media culture itself (in which no participant role seems possible), and perhaps even a misunderstanding of what ethnography is and what it takes to fully undertake it. Media scholars do in fact discuss ethnography in a variety of ways (Jankowski & Wester, 1991, pp. 54-56; Moores, 1994, pp. 3-5). For many of them (e.g., Fiske, 1988), ethnography has come to mean the act of listening in as people who are identified in terms of social-structural categories (e.g., gender, economic class) describe what they think and feel about a television text. Some argue for ethnographic strategies in virtually the same breath that they pronounce the "audience" unknowable except as discursive subjects (e.g., Allor, 1988). Others counter this view by promoting ethnography as a proven means for documenting "patterns of audience activity [that] are socially constructed, culturally located, and politically potent" (Lull, 1988, p. 242).

In summary, qualitative research is concerned with interpretive processes in social contexts. We can put it just a little more formally as follows. The qualitative paradigm assumes that human beings organize their social behavior on the basis of shared meanings that are understood and negotiated through the reflexive use of language and other symbolic resources. Methods of qualitative research seek to comprehend these processes of sense making by participating in their production in ways that are both systematic and flexible.

Interpretive Axioms and Qualitative Tool Kits

The interpretive turn in studying television and social behavior began in the United States in the late 1970s and stemmed from a recognition of limitations in the then dominant approaches.[2] Studies of television's behavioral and cognitive effects, for example, typically rely on experimental designs to isolate medium-specific causal influences. However, the artificial conditions that are required to carry them out undercut the ecological validity that would permit one to generalize the findings to natural televiewing situations, where an array of richly textured social influences are in play. Moreover, the positivist belief in material determinism severely curtails the roles of personal agency and the cultural collective for deciding on lines of action in the media environment.

Another major approach, uses and gratifications, raised high the flag of the "active" audience and, as such, seems compatible with the interpretive stance. However, the sort of active television viewer portrayed by gratifications research is one whose sole interest is in satisfying an unvarying set of social-psychological needs. As many critics have pointed out, there is no need that cannot be fulfilled in some manner in this functionalist circle. Only by viewers creating a meaning *about* the value and sufficiency of alternatives to media use (which would admit both context and political consciousness into the picture) can they get past the tautology.

By locating inquiry within social action in the everyday world, a process view, and reflexivity, we gain a surer empirical access to how media choices are made and how these choices generate meaning.[3] In what follows, we describe three axioms of the interpretive paradigm and mention some of the tools from the qualitative "tool kit" that enable us to put these axioms into action.

Social Action in the Everyday World

That we will go back to work on Monday as usual, that a presidential election will be held exactly 4 years after the last one, that the next regularly scheduled program listed in our television guide will in fact be there in 12 minutes—each of these expectations (and so many others that we would never have time in our lifetimes to name them all) constitute the bedrock of our everyday world. The everyday world, as social phenomenologists explain it (Berger & Luckmann, 1967; Drotner, 1995), is a vast field of assumptions about the "realities" of social life. Each of us has an embodied perspective within these collectively created worlds that we learn and relearn over the course of our lives. It is through the repetitive practice of a social *routine* (i.e., an assembly of purposeful behavior) and a strong faith in the "facts" that make up these routines that human beings are able to reduce the risks of knowing what they should be doing at any moment. My routine (e.g., handing over 60 cents to buy gum) will not make sense unless it meshes with yours (e.g., accepting my 60 cents and ringing it up on the register), and in the practice of these mundane behaviors the two of us reaffirm (without having to directly comment on it) the logic of the exchange. Informing the performance of gum buying are many levels of tacit knowing, including the monetary system of exchange, a commodity pricing structure, the types of places where one can buy gum, who can sell gum, the appropriate interpersonal conduct for handling the "transaction," and so on. Even in the physical absence of others, we continue to acknowledge the force of social convention by the ways in which we organize a "grammar" of behavior (e.g., pressing my used gum under a theater seat) and by the use of a language to make an accounting of our actions to ourselves (e.g., "I wouldn't want the next person to sit down on my gum").

Purely subjective action, then, is not "action." As Kirschner (1987) observed, "In promoting a vision of the human being as a meaning-maker and symbol-user, the interpretive stance highlights the primacy of language in shaping experience" (p. 216). In this view, human behavior acquires coherence when a community finds meaning and value in its performance. The survival of any community depends on introducing into its historical routines new persons (whether they are children arriving at preschool or an adult logging onto the Internet for the first time) who may learn enough from the consequences of their actions to become capable social actors. That is, we learn to interpret "what is being done" as we learn the methods and materials for doing it. Through the doing of a routine, and through our ability to distinguish *this* routine from other available routines and to integrate it with other ones, the "objects" encountered in the phenomenal world acquire meaning for us. Such understandings result from becoming well versed in the cultural predispositions that favor the emergence of some routines over others. Our dialogical relationships with others allow us to improvise on old themes and thus invent new means of expression and new ways of doing things.

Qualitative researchers are fundamentally interested in studying television viewing routines, for example, the ways in which television content and the use of the medium become appropriated in different types of discourse. This social action approach to media research, as Schoening and Anderson (1995) explained it,

> emphasize[s] that the organization and performance (i.e., coding) of action—that collective understanding of what is being done—sets the terms by which media content is selectively attended to and interpreted (or decoded). Here, social actors are said to give meaning to their behaviors and to use their everyday routines as reference points by which to produce those meanings. (p. 94)

How do researchers identify the mass-mediated features of a person's everyday world? Perhaps the surest way is through the strategy of *participant observation,* "by which [an] analyst seeks to make explicit the commonly held meanings of the social action in which he or she participates" (Anderson, 1987, p. 383; see also Becker, 1958). By participating in a meaningful act with another person, we try on a role and perform it in the way it is "supposed to be done." Usually, a substantial amount of time needs to be spent with a family or group, in their own space and on their own schedules, to accomplish this (see, e.g., Bryce, 1987). Even in the brave, new but ambiguous world of cyberspace, learning the sense and style of on-line interactions requires a rather lengthy period of participation (Correll, 1995).

If researchers stay with it long enough, they probably will learn not only about the environment of media use but also about the social exigencies and assumptions that shape the routines found there. For example, until we know how it is used in social interaction, the television guide qua "object" means little. However, as we spend more time in a household, we might see it being used in small but integral parts of many routines, from the husband trying to decide with his wife whether to rent a video for the evening to one of them discussing with their daughter why a show would not be good for her to watch. When it is employed in discourse for accomplishing a social end, the television guide becomes a significant media object. Our artful use of these resources will tell us a great deal about "commonly held meanings."

In some cases, researchers might act incompetently, as judged (kindly, it is hoped) by the actors themselves. Even then, careful attention to our own violations can teach us much about the norms of social action and interpretation.

Process

It is commonplace to read or hear communication described as a process. Probably many of us do reflect on our communicative performances as an unfolding, even seamless type of action. One sense of process is its *durational* quality. As a segment of action extends over time, the self experiences some change in perspective during the course of this extension. That is, we never are exactly the same at the end of some action as we were at the beginning—our knowledge increased, our anxiety deepened, our emotions calmed, and so on. Another sense of process is its *indeterminacy*. There always is uncertainty about the direction a process will take, even if it is seen as a series of stochastic events. Finally, process is conceived as a process only after it has somehow ended. That is, we realize the *meaning of an action* only after the fact, when it can be grasped as an act or a stretch of experience (Schutz, 1967).

Despite the communication field's allegiance to a process view, Smith's (1972) question from 25 years ago still may be relevant for much of the research being done today: "Why have we talked about process in this 20th century sense but have done so little about it? Because we have been unwilling to accept the methodological correlates of that idea. Our view of research and our view of communication have been contradictory" (p. 178). Interpretive researchers attempt to build a process dimension into all aspects of *project design.* Researchers generally begin with a conceptual interest as well as a social setting or group to be studied. They then attempt to gear research activities into the temporal and social processes in which the participants themselves are involved. By so doing, researchers learn what it is like for other people to live processually. The ongoing cycles of participating and then stepping aside to analyze or interpret data before participating again enable researchers to reflect critically on the social scene while still being a part of it (Lindlof, 1995).

The methods of qualitative inquiry also are well suited for studying process. The loose, nondirective style of most forms of qualitative *interviewing* encourages a sense of emergent conversation. Focus group interviewing, for example, is designed to stimulate discussion over a wide range of issues in a way resembling other types of group talks (Lunt & Livingstone, 1996). Delli Carpini and Williams (1994) found the focus group to be a most effective method for exploring their "conversational metaphor" of public opinion formation. The focus group process was able to generate a surprisingly large number of comments about environmental issues participants had seen on television without the moderators' direct prompting. However, it remains unclear how the dialogue produced in focus groups, or in other contexts, can or should be represented in a study's final form. The issue of how to textualize fieldwork is one area of process that remains underdeveloped in qualitative media studies.

Reflexivity

We all have had the experience of walking into a room of people and having our mere appearance change the whole tenor of the scene; we are greeted with jubilation, stony silence, or good-natured taunts. On many other occasions, such as going into a darkened theater after a movie has started, we enter a place without anyone seeming to notice. Invariably, however, someone *does* notice, even if it is only by moving a few inches so that we can reach our seat.

Similarly, a qualitative researcher attracts notice wherever he or she goes. Because a researcher's work depends on observing symbolic practices, often at the sites where they occur, his or her encounters with people must be highly proximal, even intimate. On many levels, those being studied must decide how they are going to respond to the researcher who has entered their field of action—as someone who is not "qualified" to be one of them; as someone who is not fluent in their customs, language, and schemes of valuation; as someone who is doing a "job" that has only slight bearing on their own jobs; or as someone who will write about them to future audiences. These judgments affect what they will reveal in the researcher's presence in addition to (but in more attenuated ways) how the group conducts its internal business.

It is not surprising, then, that qualitative findings frequently are questioned on grounds of human subject *reactivity,* or the production of nonnatural behaviors induced by the research instrument itself (the presence and actions of the researcher). Even those who concede that all social science is susceptible to this problem still criticize ethnographers for their use of techniques that seem to encourage obtrusiveness and for lacking the means of detecting the level and forms of reactivity.

Qualitative researchers respond to these criticisms by recasting the issue of reactivity as one of *reflexivity.* Self-conscious participation lies at the heart of reflexive analysis. Rather than finding ways of eliminating traces of their presence from the field, researchers use their active involvement as a method for making inferences about patterns of social action and nuances of meaning. The interplay between researchers' own assumptions, personal and social attributes, and cultural competencies and those of the people under study forms a continually revised set of questions that advances the research process toward valid understanding. Some of these questions, as they could arise sub rosa in an interview, might be as follows. Did I understand that phrase correctly? If I asked about it in a different way, how would he answer? We are having a more open talk today, but is it because his girlfriend isn't here? Later, as one starts data analysis and interpretation, reflexivity again becomes important. Data texts are coded, categorized, and recoded in a recursive manner according to the usefulness, innovativeness, synthesis, resonance, and adequacy of the inferences they produce (Spiggle, 1994). In effect, what is considered by some as a methodological problem is seen instead by qualitative practitioners as the theoretical problem of the dialectic of identity and difference.

This view of reflexive researchers has several consequences for field practice, only a few of which can be mentioned briefly here. First, if a relationship or cultural scene is to be comprehended from the inside, then researchers must be willing to subject their own self-identities to many of the same situational risks as do the participants (Lindlof & Grubb-Swetnam, 1996). The trick here, at which not every researcher can become adept, is to negotiate each relationship on its own terms and yet to also weave all of the individual relationships into a whole that makes sense for the social unit. Such fashioning of a successful field "role" often must undergo a long period of adjustment (see Wellman, 1994). Second, there are in fact culturally coded aspects of anyone's appearance, demeanor, and capabilities that may not work well for gaining research access in a setting. Ascriptions of appropriate gender behavior, for example, vary widely across cultures and can affect the freedom, efficacy, and safety of either male or female researchers in particular contexts (Warren, 1988). A third issue with special meaning for television concerns the overwhelming sense of familiarity that can be felt for the object of inquiry. When studying an artifact or practice that is seemingly omnipresent in society and, therefore, culturally banal, one faces the prospect of not being able to even discern its significant features. Acting reflexively in that case calls for making banality itself (or matter-of-factness) the "strange" phenomenon. In Western cultures, however, there is hardly any object or sentiment that does not receive at least some dissenting, satirical, or otherwise novel treatment from some quarter—often a cue to that which is widely cherished or accepted.

■ Faces of the Television Audience

One of the hallmarks of qualitative inquiry is its capacity to see the audience in nonessentialist terms. "Audience," for such studies, has come to mean many things: a situated practice, an interpretive strategy, a social formation, a context of usage, an occasion for attendance, and so on. This section reviews five ways of conceptualizing television audiences, the first three of which have been a significant focus of qualitative or ethnographic research to date; the latter two have gained greater prominence in recent years.

The Family Audience

The family has long been a favorite in ethnographic research on the impact of television. The family's popularity as a locus of study no doubt stems from the central role played by television in its first 20 or so years. Most families were fortunate to be able to afford one television set; even with growing affluence and cheaper sets, the typical family spent a great deal of its available leisure time gathered around the "main" television set. Although traditional social science research on television has focused on how various forms of television content have had antisocial (or, later, prosocial) effects on individuals, a continuing interest was established in identifying how the family unit was affected by the presence of television and what activities television viewing displaced (e.g., reading, conversation, activities outside the household).

Ethnographers studying families have been chiefly concerned with how television is integrated into the infrastructure of daily family life. Some researchers have limited their focus to television-specific behaviors such as rules for using television, negotiating the meaning of televised content, or how to "watch" television (see Lull, 1982, for a good example). With such a limited focus, ethnographers spent a limited amount of time with volunteer families (per visit and number of visits); little effort was made to get to know family members outside of the viewing context. Other researchers (Meyer & Meyer, 1994; Traudt & Lont, 1987) have spent extended periods of time with just one or several families, getting to know the family members to the point where the researchers were accepted almost like other members of the families. The purpose in this case is to treat television as a multidimensional force that is only one part of an overall context in which families participate in the creation of a dynamic process of "doing" daily life.

The value of intensively studying a small number of families over a long period of time has been articulated by several scholars (e.g., Anderson, 1987; Meyer, 1995; Traudt, Anderson, & Meyer, 1987). Family ethnographies reveal some of the underlying complexities of human behavior that ordinarily escape researchers who rely only on traditional research protocols such as survey questionnaires, interviews, or diaries. Moreover, ethnographies also provide useful, interesting, and often provocative insights into "process." As mentioned earlier in the chapter, communication researchers speak honorifically of process but generally do everything they can to avoid actually studying it. Process, notably in contexts such as the family, requires an extended commitment of resources from researchers—money, effort, and time (usually 6 months to a year or longer). Family ethnographies produce insights into how the meanings of television change over time for various family members. They also enable researchers to study how television and other technologies are actually used by family members, often invalidating self-reports of media use obtained through questionnaires, interviews, or diaries.

The Receptive Audience

At roughly the same time as some U.S. media researchers turned to the qualitative paradigm, British cultural studies scholars and others began studying the audience "reception" of media discourses. This interest grew out of several theoretical and methodological issues (see Jensen & Rosengren, 1990; Moores, 1994; Morley, 1992). For one thing, neo-Marxist assumptions about the role of the media industries in extending political dominance or cultivating a false consciousness could not account for how this process occurs at a micro level or why the process sometimes does not occur as predicted. As a result, among critical social theorists, explanations of economic determinism generally have been displaced by theories of discursive power in the cultural sphere.

There also was the question of how to study meaning. Structuralist semiology, for example, could produce insightful studies of how signifying elements are ordered *within* a text but not what aspects of the text are relevant for its users. Similarly, the psychoanalytic-based notion that a television or film narrative creates a unified subjectivity for hypothetical viewers was clearly useful for analyzing texts, but it ignored the personal agency of viewers. With elite criticism of art under attack, if not discredited, by the 1970s, the path was clear for considering audiences as the major site of cultural reproduction.

Reception analysis studies "viewers' interpretations, decodings, readings, meaning productions, perceptions or comprehension of programmes" (Hoijer, 1990, p. 29). It is the text-audience point of contact, not the context of viewing, that is of greatest interest. The sociological basis of reception studies lies in their focus on where viewers are located in the societal structure, especially the categorical identities of gender, race, economic class, educational attainment, and sexual preference. Such categories are treated as analytically salient because they represent significant divisions in society's allocation of opportunities, resources, and political power. Different configurations of these identities will tend to shape media choices and interpretations differently. Viewers who are, for example, female, white, middle class, college educated, and heterosexual should interpret television in ways that vary from those of viewers whose categorical identities constitute their life experiences differently.

Many reception studies consider the ways in which viewers articulate the ideological dimensions in television programs. Press (1991), for example, found that working-class women spoke more critically about abortion than did middle-class women after viewing a television program featuring the issue. Reception analysis, therefore, retains a remnant of belief in the idea that politically charged meanings are already situated in texts. It is the readers who accept, negotiate, or oppose these meanings (Hall, 1980), depending on how the encoded "message" becomes actionable within the world of discourse in which they live.

Reception studies rely heavily on semistructured interviewing to elicit these audience readings, especially focus group interviews (e.g., Liebes, 1988). In some studies (e.g., Morley, 1986), interviews provide testimony of viewing activity, although it is best regarded as evidence of what viewers think and say about how they view. For all of its insights into how viewers evaluate programs, reception analysis reveals less about the cultural environments of viewing, the social practices of viewing, or how people learn to be viewers.

The Community Audience

Television, film, and other popular forms often are considered to be *polysemic,* or open to a wide range of interpretations and "pleasures" (Fiske, 1988). Any text is polysemic because its meanings can proliferate as widely as there are contexts and individuals available for using it. Absolute polysemy, a type of "big bang" of ever-expanding and indeterminate meanings, exists only in a particle physics of semiosis (i.e., as a field of possible significations). Communication analysts need the concept, however, as a device for explaining how "the text becomes a site of contested interpretations with different audience communities producing different sense-making achievements" (Anderson & Meyer, 1988, p. 314).

Whereas polysemy opens up the possible meanings of a text, the concept of *interpretive communities* tries to locate its actual meanings in the lived experiences of audiences. From its origins in literary theory (Fish, 1980), the concept has been adapted widely to mass communication theory and research for more than a decade (Jensen, 1991; Lindlof, 1988; Radway, 1984; Schroder, 1994). An interpretive community characterizes readers, or viewers, who share certain strategies for interpreting and using a media genre or text. These strategies arise within a commonly socialized collectivity of people who interact on a regular basis, although this "community" need not be geographically based and may, in fact, be quite diffuse. Gradually, this community evolves a set of core strategies by which its members can reliably generate meanings that make pragmatic sense among each other. To a strong degree, then, any interpretation is the property of the community as a historical social body.

Most researchers turn to familiar audience groupings—the *Star Trek* subculture (Jenkins, 1988), genre readers (Radway, 1984), the fans of a television show (Schaefer & Avery, 1993), and the like—for access to the strategies of viewing and reading. To some extent, this is an approach of methodological convenience; it seems easier to find the community by first finding the text it likes to use. An audience, however, is not a self-evident identity. The coherent readings that signify the presence of an interpretive community do not always occur within a social unit alone, such as a family or fan club, or even in a simple association with a category of content. For example, how could jokes about O. J. Simpson circulate so widely among socially disparate individuals without the operation of a semiotic community—or multiple communities—that shares the same competencies and interests in popular culture as well as the act of telling irreverent jokes? Some theorists believe that most such communities span or crisscross many different sectors of the social structure (Jensen, 1991; Lindlof, 1988). In this sense, interpretive communities can be "multiple, overlapping, and contradictory" (Jensen, 1991, p. 13). Moreover, a community may not be a stable entity at all but rather an improvised, dynamic series of interpersonal encounters that create meanings in its wake (Machin & Carrithers, 1996).

Although multiple readings of a text usually surface in interpretive community studies, most of their claims center on some degree of convergence in the strategies the readers or viewers use. Schaefer and Avery's (1993) study of *Late Night With David Letterman*'s audience is a good example of this line of research. The authors first examined some of the more innovative features of the *Late Night* program via the concept of meta-television aesthetics. Then, discourse from focus group interviews was used to show how *Late Night* viewers recognize the ironic, bad boy attitude of the host and the show as well as the playful, "spontaneous" program devices that seem to mock the classical talk show. Through the respondents' knowledge of the way in which the show works self-reflexively and other evidence of a socially interacting *Late Night* community, we can see how involvement in a single text can span a wide spectrum of people who do not know each other and who might have few other reasons to enter into a relationship, real or imagined.

The Public Audience

The faces of the social audience previously reviewed all hold certain assumptions in common about the user-medium relationship: The television/VCR or computer is located at home, the users studied usually are in an enduring or even intimate relationship, and the operation of the television can be carried out under the local control of the users. Given the prevalence of television use in private living quarters, all of these assumptions may seem quite reasonable.

However, with the proliferation of portable media (e.g., Walkmans, Watchmans), place-based advertising vehicles such as Whittle Communication's Channel One in public schools, and the growth of video in places such as airlines, stadiums, fast food restaurants, and sports bars, we now have an ecology of media use zones that extends far beyond the household and involves shifting routines of reception by "nomadic" viewers (Lindlof, 1996). In many of these zones, institutions do more than simply make media resources available; they often design the viewing situation so as to promote a specific type of group experience, one example being the noon-hour "Rush Rooms" set up by many restaurants in the United States in the early 1990s for the enjoyment of Rush Limbaugh devotees (Bernstein, 1993).

Naturalistic studies of persons consuming television in places such as university and shopping locations, hospitals, and bars have been conducted (Eastman & Land, 1995; Lemish, 1982) and yield evidence of the rule-governed nature of viewing attention, social etiquette, and the conversational rituals that occur in those contexts. Some researchers focus on the appropriation of televised material (e.g., characters, story lines, dialogue, slogans) in the conversations of persons in their work lives (Hobson, 1990; Pacanowsky & Anderson, 1982) to show how it serves functions such as enhancing the members' moral solidarity, defining interpretive competence, and labeling out-groups. Other public scenes such as churches, schools, and prisons often take an interventionist approach to media. Lepter (1996), for example, studied the discourse about media attendance among both lay members and clergy of the Church of the Nazarene, a conservative Christian denomination that has long held a restrictive policy against the consumption of movies in theaters and on television. Seiter (in press) studied the different ways in which child care centers articulate the role of television and create opportunities for its use in the lives of children.

Increasingly, out-of-home media use seems to be commingling with, and perhaps even altering, many of the rituals of community life. Qualitative researchers face the challenge of documenting media practices under varying conditions of institutional control, public norms of behavior, and the multiple definitions of usage that apply across diverse settings.

The Historical Audience

An objective motivating much of the anthropological fieldwork conducted since early in this century has been *preservationist*—to travel to societies that have long been isolated from "history" and to carry out a cultural inventory before regular intercultural contacts start to contaminate their ways of life. The same impulse to preserve vanishing cultures may not appear to be as critical for media researchers given that contamination is a fact of life in an information-surfeited world. Only by the most strenuous efforts can any group of people sequester itself from the ebbs, flows, and surges of popular fashion and technological innovation. In addition, the field of communication has expanded its global activities and revises its research agendas on a more rapid basis than ever, to the point that few events of any significance escape the attention of at least some of its scholars. Yet, many contemporary audience phenomena do seem to slip away before attempts are made to record and understand them. Jensen (1993) stated the problem this way:

> Compared to other aspects of the communication process, which may be examined through traditional historical sources such as legislative documents, the records of media organizations, and some (admittedly imperfect) archives of media contents, *reception does not exist in the historical record*; it can only be reconstructed through the intervention of research. Whereas ratings and readership figures presumably will survive, the social and cultural aspects of mass media reception are literally disappearing before our eyes and ears. (pp. 20-21, emphasis in original)

Accordingly, Jensen (1993) called for the use of resourceful methods to recover the activities and sensibilities of audiences of the past and for the implementation of new data-capture systems—especially multimedia, multimethod databases—for preserving the audiences of the future. The former task sometimes is frustrated by the inability of documentary materials to answer some questions very adequately. A couple of examples will show why. Advertisements for the new medium of television in American women's magazines of the early 1950s provided Spigel (1992) with a useful perspective on the public discourse about television's role in domestic gender relations. But they do not tell us how the advertisements, or television itself, were actually interpreted by people of the day. Ganas (1995) interviewed former contestants and production staff members from the *Queen for a Day* radio and television programs to study how women used their understandings of early television to craft confessional true stories about themselves. Gaining entry to a club of former "queens" made her project feasible, but the problem of subject attrition after more than 30 years kept Ganas from widening her sample.

The study of historical audiences is difficult but not insurmountable (see McCarthy, 1995, for a sensitive analysis of archival material). Certainly, there needs to be more discussion of the types of questions that should be asked of the historical record as well as of techniques for reconstructing aspects of reception and use. The payoff lies in a greater understanding of the popular response to the products and strategies of the media industries.

■ Ethnographic Research and Electronic Media: Some Exemplars

For the past 13 years, six families have been part of an ongoing study of how television use has been affected by the introduction of the VCR and other home technology products such as video game players and the personal computer with CD-ROM and Internet connections. Some aspects of this ongoing study have been reported previously (see Meyer, 1995; Meyer & Meyer, 1994). The findings have been valuable in the sense that they have been able to track the dynamics of electronic media use over time and point to patterns of use and meaning that elude traditional social science procedures—actually studying processes as process. The following subsections provide concrete examples of the values of qualitative, ethnographic research in this area.

The Family Gets a Videocassette Recorder: Prepurchase and Postpurchase Comparisons

When VCRs were first mass-marketed to consumers in the early 1980s, the presumed advantages emphasized time shifting, creation of home video libraries, and family viewing opportunities. For the first time in television history, consumers could tape programs to watch at their convenience that they could replay again and again, and they could experience these events as a family. Actual uses of the VCR turned out to be dramatically different.

VCRs were (and still are, to some extent) sold much like microwave ovens. With a microwave, one can prepare an entire meal for the family without using the range plates or oven. However, most people quickly discovered that the main value of the microwave was its ability to heat food items very quickly. Despite the fact that prepurchase expectations were not met in actual consumer uses of the microwave, this appliance remains an invaluable addition to most households. The VCR has traveled a similar road. Far and away, the predominant use of the VCR is to play prerecorded tapes—a product that did not exist when the consumer VCR was first developed and marketed for home use. Again, despite the failure for prepurchase expectations to be realized, the VCR, like the microwave oven, remains a valuable consumer possession that is part of nearly 90% of all U.S. households, many of them having two or more VCRs. Ethnographic research has shown how actual postpurchase VCR uses differed from anticipated use and how consumers have come to terms with the disparity between the two. Moreover, this research has shown how VCR use has changed over time and why the VCR has been so widely embraced as an essential household appliance.

One heavily anticipated use of the VCR was for time-shifting purposes—taping a show that aired when those wishing to view the program were not available. In two households, for example, the VCR was used to tape soap operas that were broadcast when people were at work. For a period of several months, the VCR was programmed daily to record the proper channel at the correct time, the tape was rewound and viewed in the evening, and the VCR was set up to repeat the process on the following day. The process began to degenerate over time. It was not always possible to watch the program that evening, or an error in programming the VCR occurred. As one exasperated consumer summed it up,

> It seemed that it just wasn't worth the hassle. I mean, after a while, the whole business of getting the VCR set and having to do it every day became a real drag. Sometimes I'd have it all set and ready to go and Bob or one of the kids would have taken out my tape and watched a movie or something of theirs, and of course they forgot to put my tape back in and make sure it was all set to tape my soap the next day. Some days I just didn't get around to watching it. For a while I would tape the whole week's worth and watch them all over the weekend. But then it seemed like something I *had* to do rather than something I wanted to do. I mean, that's just ridiculous. Hell, it got to the point where half the time I couldn't

even find the damn remote for the VCR so I could set up the thing. I figured, "Screw it." It just wasn't worth it.

Another area related to programming the VCR for time shifting centered on who in the household, if anyone, actually knew how to operate the VCR. Claims of expertise usually were overstated, as the ethnographic researchers discovered. When each family member was asked who knew how to operate the VCR, including programming it for time-shift purposes, he or she had a public declaration of the claimed level of operating expertise. In the course of observing and monitoring the household as the study progressed, the researchers made it a point to ask each household member who was an "expert" to tell them about the household VCR so that the particulars of the device could be understood. (Different VCRs have different features and capabilities beyond the simple playback function.) When the researchers would "innocently" ask, "What are these buttons for?" or "How do you get this machine to tape a program when you're not here?" the usual response was "I'm not sure what those are for, but they're not important anyway" or "I forgot. It's been a while since I even used this thing." Children and adolescents also were eager to expose exaggerated claims of VCR use. As one 16-year-old female said, "Dad'll tell you that he knows everything about [the VCR], but he really has a hard time just getting a movie to play back through the TV. Please don't say that I told you, okay? I don't want him to feel bad, but it's the truth. . . . Us kids know how to make it work, not him."

Regarding operation of the VCR, some households had rules on who was authorized to use the VCR and who was not. One parent described his family rules just prior to the VCR purchase: "Now, if we get a VCR, you kids aren't going to be wrecking it. These things cost a buttload of money, and your mother and I work too damn hard to have you guys break the thing." In those households where kids could not operate the VCR without parental supervision or permission, the kids went ahead and used the VCR when their dad was not at home. Their mom usually knew about it but often said nothing to the kids or, of course, to the dad. In one particular instance, the dad announced to the family over the evening meal that the VCR was broken and would need to be repaired: "I just noticed the VCR is shot. I put a tape in and it's moving too fast and the sound is missing. I'm gonna have to take it to the store and get them to take a look at it." Without missing a beat, his 8-year-old son blurted out, "It's not broke. You just have to change the speed. I can fix it in 2 seconds." Luckily, he was right in his diagnosis. The VCR was quickly "fixed." Curiously, however, nothing was said of dissolving the rule of "no kids touch the VCR," but from that time on the kids used the VCR in the presence of their dad without asking permission or inquiring whether the rule no longer was in effect. Over time, the dad came to realize that the kids were skilled VCR operators.

Another major expectation of having a VCR was the opportunity for families to watch movies together. With the rapid availability of prerecorded movies, the family presumably could now find a convenient time and a suitable movie or program to watch together. This expectation, like all the others, quickly went unrealized. As one 47-year-old mom expressed it,

> Just before we got the VCR, I thought to myself how nice it would be for the whole family to get together and watch TV together. When everybody was home, it seemed like there was never anything we all wanted to watch. Then we got the VCR, and Tom and I decided to let the kids pick out a movie for all of us to watch together. After we did this a couple of times, it seemed like there wasn't anything we could agree on, so we went from all five of us to four to three and got to the point where even Tom "had something more important to do." You know, we just quit it and nobody even mentioned it out loud. I guess we all realized that it wasn't going to work . . . but I still think it's a good idea. But I guess I'm the only one.

The final area of dashed expectations was the VCR library. Here, a household could create a video resource that would provide the optimal solution to all those frequently occurring times when there was "nothing on TV" worth watching. Researchers found that videotape libraries went through distinct phases, beginning with a flurry of taping just following the VCR purchase. After the initial burst of taping all types of programs for future viewing, the families began to realize that buying blank tapes became expensive and that most households did not have the space to accommodate the ever-expanding libraries. The result was significantly less recording of programs and the rapid disintegration of tape cataloging or labeling activities. Family members were generally surprised when researchers reported on how infrequently archived tapes were viewed even one time, to say nothing of repeated viewings. No one was surprised at the finding that tapes in the library were mislabeled, not labeled at all, or not arranged in any usable scheme that would facilitate access and use within a reasonable period of time. (Perhaps given 24 hours notice, a specific tape might be located.) The library became a difficult-to-use and, therefore, seldom-used resource. The most accessible tapes were purchased tapes with jackets that had the movie titles clearly visible. Exceptions to this included tapes, usually numbering no more than three, that an individual family member would keep in a special place for frequent viewing or tapes that were brought out for a specific holiday (e.g., *A Christmas Story, National Lampoon's Christmas Vacation, Yankee Doodle Dandy*).

Yet, having tapes in the library reflected a certain sense of value and security. As one 54-year-old male mused,

> I might not watch any of these tapes too much, but at least I know they're there in case I want to watch something I know is good. Sometimes I watch something really good and I'm really glad I taped it. I put it on the shelf and then later on, maybe 6 months later, I haul it out and play it. I sometimes forget some part. It's not the same as the first time I watched it, but it's still real good.

Another 63-year-old male reflected on the fact that he had more than 30 "fishing" tapes but had never watched any of them once they were taped:

> Boy, let me tell you, when I retire in a couple of years, I'll be wearing those out I'll be watching 'em so much. I hardly have enough time to even go fishing now. . . . I don't even have near enough time to watch somebody else doin' it. But fishing is what I love the most. I wish I could do it every day. But those tapes are great; some of them got that Babe Winkleman on, and he's funny too. He knows a lot about fishing, and he's not afraid to tell you. Some other guys are good at it, but they don't want to give away any of their secrets. . . . I told my oldest boy [age 24 years] that if he uses any of my fishing tapes, I'll take out after him in 2 seconds flat. But, hell, I'm not worried. . . . He knows better than to fool with my fishing tapes.

Household members also made unstated judgments of the relative value of keeping films versus television programs. Films were far more likely to be considered worthy of keeping and of repeated viewings, the content apparently having enduring value that transcends the immediate moment. Television programs, on the other hand, apparently held only a transient value. It was as if people were saying, "It's only a TV show. There are plenty more just like it." If television was designed to be a disposable medium, it has succeeded. One 27-year-old female expressed it this way:

> Films, you know, you like to see over again. Sometimes I enjoy a movie the more often I see it. . . . I see things that I missed the first or even the second and third time around. It's not the same with TV. TV seems so easy to get, I mean, you know right away what's going on. Besides, with TV, if you see it today, you'll get the chance to see it again in a couple of weeks, and then they keep showing the same stuff over and over. I always feel that you can always see something you missed or see it again on TV if you just look around and wait for it to come out again. TV shows are, you know, so much alike. . . . They're all the same, it seems.

New Technology Replaces Old Technology

Another example of the value of ethnographic research of electronic media usage comes from a household that dealt with the introduction of a newer, more powerful microcomputer with a CD-ROM player and Internet access. This computer, which replaced a much older computer that was used mostly for word processing and financial recordkeeping, meant new opportunities for the household. Changes occurred, some more rapidly than others. These changes were monitored and noted in the course of the ethnographic study.

Game playing was a major venue of change. The 20-year-old son, home from college during the summer when school was not in session, had been spending a great deal of time when at home using the video game player downstairs in the family room. He would enjoy all the latest game cartridges and monopolize the television set for his own personal use. He discovered that the new computer had a CD-ROM player with a sound card and was capable of new, more interesting games with attractive features. As his familiarity with the CD-ROM grew, so did his desire to spend more and more time with the new computer and, correspondingly, less and less time with the video game player. Enter the 22-year-old son, who learns that the computer has an Internet connection. He quickly discovers the many intriguing sites to "hit" and becomes formidable competition for use of the computer for games and certain "adult-oriented" content available on the Internet. This sibling rivalry was punctuated by the dad, the one who bought the new computer to be able to do some work at home without enduring the time-consuming trip to the office. The dad convincingly argues that his needs come first and that the boys would have to work it out between themselves as to who gets to use the computer and for how long.

Surprisingly, the 20-year-old shows little interest in returning to the video game player. This is fortunate because the mom has discovered the Tetris game and now can be found downstairs in the family room using the recently abandoned video game player. Throughout all of this, the VCR goes from being used regularly once or twice a week to virtually no use at all. The boys go back to college, the dad continues to use the computer as needed, and the mom continues to play Tetris, even using the portable version on Game Boy, a welcomed birthday gift from her loving sons. When the boys return home from college, one brings along his own laptop computer and does not have to compete with dad for time on his home computer; the other son seems content to be away from interactive video and to just watch television, including movies on the VCR.

All of these changes become apparent only when monitored by the qualitative research protocols engaged in by ethnographers. A telephone survey regarding media usage would have only very limited value in that it would pertain to only a fixed point in time and would assume that the questions being asked were appropriate and commonly understood by all household members and that family members in fact knew the answers to the questions being asked of them. A process that unfolds in a context like a household, in which the members negotiate their goals and interests according to certain tacit understandings, requires research procedures that are capable of monitoring that process. Qualitative research, like the family ethnographies described in this chapter, is the best, and arguably the only, means available to document the complex processes of human behavior when people interface with technology. Although some observations may be unique to those being observed, many others suggest similarities of practice and interpretation from one setting to another; they resonate with common human experience. This research also shows that although many externally observable outcomes can be easily documented, how these outcomes are produced and what they mean depend on a dialogical relationship with others as gained through participant observation, interviewing, analysis, and interpretation.

■ Conclusion

This chapter has provided an overview of the aims and value of the qualitative research approach in developing an understanding of television and social behavior. In closing, we note the challenges that lie ahead in the dual emergence of global communication and multicultural communities. As cultural groups worldwide become more mobile, styles of media use have grown more profuse and creative, not less so (Lull, 1995). At the same time, new forms of "intelligent" media are complicating the distinctions between work and leisure, private and public, and local and global. The ability of qualitative researchers to study process in natural contexts should enable them to help society understand what these rapid changes mean. However, this probably can happen only if they are open to new ways of generating and sharing data (perhaps using the very media they study) and if they learn multiple ways of communicating their work to general audiences as well as academic ones.

■ Notes

1. For some historical and critical reviews of qualitative media research, readers should consult Jensen and Jankowski (1991), Lindlof (1991), Lull (1990), Moores (1994), Morley (1992), and Potter (1996).

2. Occasional examples of qualitatively oriented research surfaced decades before then. These included the Payne Fund investigation of emotional and fantasy engagements with motion pictures under the direction of Herbert Blumer, Herta Herzog's studies of gratifications obtained from daytime radio serials, and the development by Robert K. Merton and his associates of the "focused interview" method. These efforts did not appear as part of an ongoing program of interpretive media studies, nor did they involve a critique of the dominant models of mass communication research. A critical assessment

of media effects research, coupled with a proposal for a processual and contextually grounded approach to how audiences interpret a dynamic media environment, finally did appear in Blumer's (1969) essay "Suggestions for the Study of Mass-Media Effects" (pp. 183-194, originally published in 1959).

    3. Anderson's remark in a 1980 paper still resonates: "We have approached questions of why to the exclusion of what and how. We have attempted to describe the causes and consequences of televiewing without an adequate understanding of what it is and how it gets done. This imbalance has littered our field with hypotheses of little utility" (Anderson, 1980, p. 2).

■ References

Allor, M. (1988). Relocating the site of the audience. *Critical Studies in Mass Communication, 5,* 217-233.

Anderson, J. A. (1980, November). *An agenda for the social sciences and the study of mass communication.* Paper presented at the annual meeting of the Speech Communication Association, New York.

Anderson, J. A. (1987). *Communication research: Issues and methods.* New York: McGraw-Hill.

Anderson, J. A., & Goodall, H. L., Jr. (1994). Probing the body ethnographic: From an anatomy of inquiry to a poetics of expression. In F. L. Casmir (Ed.), *Building communication theories: A socio/cultural approach* (pp. 87-129). Hillsdale, NJ: Lawrence Erlbaum.

Anderson, J. A., & Meyer, T. P. (1988). Mediated communication: A social action perspective. Newbury Park, CA: Sage.

Becker, H. S. (1958). Problems of inference and proof in participant observation. *American Sociological Review, 23,* 652-660.

Berger, P. L., & Luckmann, T. (1967). *The social construction of reality.* Garden City, NY: Doubleday.

Bernstein, A. (1993, August 16). Show time in the Rush Room. *U.S. News & World Report,* p. 36.

Blumer, H. (1969). *Symbolic interactionism: Perspective and method.* Berkeley: University of California Press.

Bryce, J. (1987). Family time and television use. In T. R. Lindlof (Ed.), *Natural audiences* (pp. 121-138). Norwood, NJ: Ablex.

Correll, S. (1995). The ethnography of an electronic bar: The Lesbian Cafe. *Journal of Contemporary Ethnography, 24,* 270-298.

DeGrane, L. (1991). *Tuned in: Television in American life.* Urbana: University of Illinois Press.

Delli Carpini, M. X., & Williams, B. A. (1994). Methods, metaphors, and media research: The uses of television in political conversation. *Communication Research, 21,* 782-812.

Drotner, K. (1995). Ethnographic enigmas: "The everyday" in recent media studies. *Cultural Studies, 9,* 341-357.

Eastman, S. T., & Land, A. M. (1995). *The best of both worlds: Sports fans find good seats at the bar.* Unpublished manuscript, Department of Telecommunications, Indiana University.

Ellen, R. F. (1984). *Ethnographic research: A guide to general conduct.* London: Academic Press.

Fish, S. (1980). *Is there a text in this class?* Cambridge, MA: Harvard University Press.

Fiske, J. (1988). *Television culture.* London: Methuen.

Ganas, M. C. (1995). *"Queen for a Day," the Cinderella show: Broadcasting women's true stories.* Unpublished doctoral dissertation, University of Kentucky.

Geertz, C. (1973). *The interpretation of cultures.* New York: Basic Books.

Hall, S. (1980). Encoding/decoding. In S. Hall, D. Hobson, A. Lowe, & P. Willis (Eds.), *Culture, media, language* (pp. 128-138). London: Hutchinson.

Hobson, D. (1990). Women audiences and the workplace. In M. E. Brown (Ed.), *Television and women's culture* (pp. 61-72). Newbury Park, CA: Sage.

Hoijer, B. (1990). Studying viewers' reception of television programmes: Theoretical and methodological considerations. *European Journal of Communication, 5,* 29-56.

Jankowski, N. W., & Wester, F. (1991). The qualitative tradition in social science inquiry: Contributions to mass communication research. In K. B. Jensen & N. W. Jankowski (Eds.), *A handbook of qualitative methodologies for mass communication research* (pp. 44-74). New York: Routledge.

Jenkins, H., III. (1988). "Star Trek" rerun, reread, rewritten: Fan writing as textual poaching. *Critical Studies in Mass Communication, 5,* 85-107.

Jensen, K. B. (1991). When is meaning? Communication theory, pragmatism, and mass media reception. In J. A. Anderson (Ed.), *Communication yearbook 14* (pp. 3-32). Newbury Park, CA: Sage.

Jensen, K. B. (1993). The past in the future: Problems and potentials of historical reception. *Journal of Communication, 43*(4), 20-28.

Jensen, K. B., & Jankowski, N. W. (Eds.). (1991). *A handbook of qualitative methodologies for mass communication research.* New York: Routledge.

Jensen, K. B., & Rosengren, K. E. (1990). Five traditions in search of the audience. *European Journal of Communication, 5,* 207-238.

Kirschner, S. R. (1987). "Then what have I to do with thee?": On identity, fieldwork, and ethnographic knowledge. *Cultural Anthropology, 2,* 211-234.

Lemish, D. (1982). The rules of viewing television in public places. *Journal of Broadcasting, 26,* 757-781.

Lepter, J. (1996). *A root metaphor analysis of Nazarene discourse regarding media attendance.* Unpublished doctoral dissertation, University of Kentucky.

Liebes, T. (1988). Cultural differences in the retelling of television fiction. *Critical Studies in Mass Communication, 5,* 277-292.

Lindlof, T. R. (1988). Media audiences as interpretive communities. In J. A. Anderson (Ed.), *Communication yearbook 11* (pp. 81-107). Newbury Park, CA: Sage.

Lindlof, T. R. (1991). The qualitative study of media audiences. *Journal of Broadcasting & Electronic Media, 35,* 23-42.

Lindlof, T. R. (1995). *Qualitative communication research methods.* Thousand Oaks, CA: Sage.

Lindlof, T. R. (1996). *Fugitive audiences in broad daylight: Theorizing the practices of public media use.* Unpublished manuscript, College of Communication and Information Studies, University of Kentucky.

Lindlof, T. R., & Grubb-Swetnam, A. (1996). Seeking a path of greatest resistance: The self-becoming method. In D. Grodin & T. R. Lindlof (Eds.), *Constructing the self in a mediated world* (pp. 179-205). Thousand Oaks, CA: Sage.

Lull, J. (1980). The social uses of television. *Human Communication Research, 6,* 197-209.

Lull, J. (1982). A rules approach to the study of television and society. *Human Communication Research, 9,* 3-16.

Lull, J. (1988). The audience as nuisance. *Critical Studies in Mass Communication, 5,* 239-243.

Lull, J. (1990). *Inside family viewing.* New York: Routledge.

Lull, J. (1995). *Media, communication, culture.* New York: Columbia University Press.

Lunt, P., & Livingstone, S. (1996). Rethinking the focus group in media and communications research. *Journal of Communication, 5*(2), 79-98.

Machin, D., & Carrithers, M. (1996). From "interpretive communities" to "communities of improvisation." *Media Culture and Society, 18,* 343-352.

McCarthy, A. (1995). "The front row is reserved for Scotch drinkers": Early television's tavern audience. *Cinema Journal, 34*(4), 31-49.

Meyer, T. P. (1995). Integrating information technologies in the household: Using case studies to understand complex and rapidly changing processes. In D. Fortin (Ed.), *Living and working in cyberspace: New technologies at home and work.* Kingston: University of Rhode Island Press.

Meyer, T. P., & Meyer, K. A. (1994). The videocassette recorder: An historical analysis of consumer expectations and post-purchase uses and satisfaction. In R. King (Ed.), *Research in retailing: The future agenda* (pp. 75-79). Richmond, VA: Academy of Marketing Science.

Moores, S. (1994). *Interpreting audiences: The ethnography of media consumption.* Thousand Oaks, CA: Sage.

Morley, D. (1986). *Family television: Cultural power and domestic leisure.* London: Comedia.

Morley, D. (1992). *Television, audiences, and cultural studies.* New York: Routledge.

Pacanowsky, M., & Anderson, J. A. (1982). Cop talk and media use. *Journal of Broadcasting, 26,* 741-756.

Potter, W. J. (1996). *An analysis of thinking and research about qualitative methods.* Hillsdale, NJ: Lawrence Erlbaum.

Press, A. L. (1991). Working-class women in a middle-class world: The impact of television on modes of reasoning about abortion. *Critical Studies in Mass Communication, 8,* 421-441.

Radway, J. (1984). *Reading the romance.* Chapel Hill: University of North Carolina Press.

Ricoeur, P. (1977). The model of the text: Meaningful action considered as a text. In F. R. Dallmayr & T. A. McCarthy (Eds.), *Understanding and social inquiry* (pp. 316-334). Notre Dame, IN: University of Notre Dame Press.

Schaefer, R. J., & Avery, R. K. (1993). Audience conceptualizations of *Late Night With David Letterman. Journal of Broadcasting & Electronic Media, 37,* 253-274.

Schoening, G. T., & Anderson, J. A. (1995). Social action media studies: Foundational arguments and common premises. *Communication Theory, 5,* 93-116.

Schroder, K. C. (1994). Audience semiotics, interpretive communities and the "ethnographic turn" in media research. *Media, Culture & Society, 16,* 337-347.

Schutz, A. (1967). *The phenomenology of the social world.* Evanston, IL: Northwestern University Press.

Seiter, E. (in press). Power rangers at preschool: Negotiating media in child care settings. In M. Kinder (Ed.), *Children's media culture.* Durham, NC: Duke University Press.

Smith, D. H. (1972). Communication research and the idea of process. *Speech Monographs, 39,* 174-182.

Spigel, L. (1992). *Make room for TV: Television and the family ideal in postwar America.* Chicago: University of Chicago Press.

Spiggle, S. (1994). Analysis and interpretation of qualitative data in consumer research. *Journal of Consumer Research, 21,* 491-503.

Tesch, R. (1990). *Qualitative research: Analysis types and software tools.* New York: Falmer.

Traudt, P. J., & Lont, C. M. (1987). Media-logic-in-use: The family as locus of study. In T. R. Lindlof (Ed.), *Natural audiences* (pp. 139-160). Norwood, NJ: Ablex.

Traudt, P. J., Anderson, J. A., & Meyer, T. P. (1987). Phenomenology, empiricism, and media experience. *Critical Studies in Mass Communication, 4,* 302-310.

Warren, C. A. B. (1988). *Gender issues in field research.* Newbury Park, CA: Sage.

Wellman, D. (1994). Constituting ethnographic authority: The work process of field research—An ethnographic account. *Cultural Studies, 8,* 569-583.

PART III

The Integration of Quantitative and Qualitative Research Paradigms in the Study of Television

Part III, the final part of this volume, focuses on how both quantitative and qualitative methods can be used in the study of television's influence on social behavior and on how these methods, although used for different purposes, can complement one another in our search for answers. This is not to say that an investigator will feel comfortable conducting studies as both a positivist and a phenomenologist given that the philosophical underpinnings of each perspective are unique. In reality, the comfort with and merits of each perspective will be weighted differently depending on where the investigator stands relative to these ideological opposites. On the other hand, it is this very diversity of thought that will aid in the discovery process.

Carolyn A. Stroman and Kenneth E. Jones discuss the analysis of television content and how such analyses have been of interest for roughly a half decade and continue to be of interest as we enter the 21st century. What these researchers propose is that for the field to advance in its knowledge of the relevance of television content to the development of social attitudes, the complementary relationship that quantitative and qualitative paradigms can serve toward this end needs to be valued.

Kevin A. Clark focuses on the research implications raised by contemporary instructional media, specifically instructional television and computer-assisted instruction. In his chapter, he traces how the design and development of instructional technology has progressed through a series of developmental phases from behavioral, to cognitive, and now to constructivist. Each phase of this developmental process has contributed a certain body of knowledge on which the subsequent developmental phase is able to build.

The chapter by Jerome L. Singer and Dorothy G. Singer is quite unique in that these researchers provide readers with an opportunity to see how an entire research agenda evolves from a single study that began as an evaluation of a television program for preschool-age children. From each study during the evaluation process, new questions emerged that refocused the development of subsequent investigations. During the course of the evaluation, it is apparent how quantitative and qualitative methods were selected, depending on the purpose at hand.

Finally, John P. Murray ends Part III of this volume with a his chapter on the status of studying television violence as we enter the 21st century. Clearly, the findings to date from using diverse methodological paradigms support the conclusion that televised violence does influence the attitudes, values, and behaviors of the viewers. What this researcher proposes is that we still are deficient in our understanding of the "process" associated with these effects, what in our society contributes to the "prevalence" of televised violence, and what sorts of "prevention" can be introduced to counteract the harmful effects of televised violence.

7

The Analysis of Television Content

Carolyn A. Stroman ■ Kenneth E. Jones

Communication research is replete with content analyses of the print, visual, and electronic media. Many of these studies have focused on analyzing the content of television programming. In fact, content analyses of television programs began appearing as early as 1954 (Head, 1954; Smythe, 1954), and by 1975 more than 200 content analyses of television had already been conducted (Comstock, 1975). Continuing this tradition into the 1970s and 1980s, several scholars conducted in-depth, book-length analyses of the content of prime-time television programming (e.g., Cantor, 1980; Cassata & Skill, 1983; Greenberg, 1980; U.S. Commission on Civil Rights, 1977; Vande Berg & Trujillo, 1989). A perusal of major mass communication journals published in 1995 indicated that the analysis of television content still is of considerable interest to researchers.[1]

Underlying the raison d'être of most content analyses is the sometimes stated and sometimes unstated assumption that media content influences audiences' social perceptions and conceptions of "social reality." Children, in particular, are purported to learn behaviors from television content. Using the socialization function of television as a rationale, analyses of television content often have focused on the potential for portrayals of various groups (e.g., African Americans, the elderly), various behaviors (e.g., drug and alcohol usage, sexual behavior, violence), and various roles (e.g., occupational roles, sexual roles) to affect viewers' beliefs, attitudes, and behaviors. Examples of questions that have served as focal points of such analyses include the following. How realistic is the portrayal of aggressive behavior in television entertainment programming (Potter et al., 1995)? What features of organizational life are presented on prime time (Vande Berg & Trujillo, 1989)? What particular values are promoted by popular television series as effective conflict resolution standards (Chesebro, 1991)? How has the portrayal of African Americans in prime-time fiction changed since the publication of the Kerner Commission report (Stroman, Merritt, & Matabane, 1989-1990)?

There are many and varied definitions of content analysis. For example, Stacks and Hocking (1992) defined content analysis as "a research method or measurement technique that involves the systematic study of the content of communication messages" (p. 250). In placing emphasis on the word *systematic,* most definitions of content analysis implicitly refer to quantitative analysis. In this chapter, however, we focus on both quantitative and qualitative analyses of television content. After giving brief overviews of the two approaches, we examine studies in which researchers have integrated the two approaches. We conclude the chapter with a comparison of the strengths and weaknesses of the two approaches.

We do not wish to resurrect the debates about the relative merits of quantitative versus qualitative research methods; instead, we wish merely to note at this initial juncture that we view the two approaches as different yet complementary. This contrasts with the view that the two approaches are at opposite ends of the ideological spectrum.[2]

■ Quantitative Analysis of Television Content

Why do researchers conduct content analyses? Researchers may conduct content analytic studies for any one (or combination) of the following reasons discussed by various writers (Holsti, 1969; Krippendorf, 1980; Wimmer & Dominick, 1994): (a) to describe trends in communication content and patterns of communication, (b) to test hypotheses of message characteristics, (c) to compare media content to the "real world," (d) to assess the image of particular groups in society, and (e) to establish a starting point for studies of media effects. Of significance to this book and to researchers who conduct content analyses are the relationships between television content and viewers' values, behaviors, beliefs, and so forth.

In carrying out any of the purposes just noted, researchers have to confront several major methodological decision points. Among these decisions points are the determination of (a) what will be analyzed, (b) what sampling technique will be employed, (c) how the categories will be constructed, (d) how reliability will be assessed, and (e) how the issue of validity will be addressed. All of these decisions are, of course, a function of the research question employed by the researchers. The following section elaborates briefly on all of these decision points.

Content analysis of television programs begins with a statement of purpose, which may take the form of description or hypothesis testing. For example, a content analysis in which one of the present authors was involved had as its purpose (a) to document the present-day portrayal of African Americans in recurring roles on prime-time fictional television and (b) to provide more comprehensive data on the contexts or settings in which these African Americans are presented (Stroman et al., 1989-1990).

Determining the unit of analysis in content analysis of television content may be problematic. The unit of analysis varies; for example, it may be the entire television show, the character, the news story, or the air time provided a program. Additional possibilities for analysis include movies, cartoons, commercials, public service announcements, sports, and so forth.

Content analysts frequently use two or more units of analysis. For example, in an examination of sexual behaviors occurring on the major networks, Shidler and Lowry (1995) used the word or phrase as the unit of analysis when coding "verbal suggestiveness" and used a behavior (kissing) as the unit of analysis when measuring erotic touching. Gerbner and his colleagues measure violence by the violent action and the amount of time devoted to each action (Signorielli, Gerbner, & Morgan, 1995). Again, the most appropriate unit of analysis will depend on the research questions or hypotheses being tested.

Clarity regarding the unit of analysis is essential because sample selection depends largely on what constitutes the unit of analysis. After the time frame of the analysis has been determined, a sample must be selected. The objective in content analysis, as in other methodologies, is to select a sample that is representative of the population from which it is drawn; therefore, random sampling is the preferred method. However, in many instances, the content analyst selects a nonprobability sample based on his or her judgment of what would constitute a representative sample.

One of the most important aspects of any content analysis is the construction of categories that accurately describe the content of television programs. Operational definitions of the content under study must be clear. In addition, the categories must meet three criteria: They should be mutually exclusive, equivalent, and exhaustive (Budd, Thorp, & Donohew, 1967).

It is worth noting that operationalization and category development may be problematic. The ongoing discussion surrounding the measurement of television violence, one of the most analyzed variables, illustrates the difficulty (see Kunkel et al., 1995, and Signorielli et al., 1995, for a historical perspective).

As with any other methodology, reliability and validity should be major considerations in content analysis. Content analysts frequently will address the reliability of their coding categories by calculating intercoder and/or intracoder reliability tests. Recently, published television content analyses reported reliabilities ranging from .74 to .99 using Holsti's (1969) formula and .88 to 1.00 using Scott's pi.

Many researchers do not pay as much attention to constructing valid content categories as they do to constructing reliable ones. Content analysts often either fail to address the issue of validity or rely solely on face validity, the weakest form of validity. This is partially due to validity not being as easily demonstrated as reliability.

After systematically collecting the data, researchers must analyze the data. Content analysts typically will use descriptive statistical procedures to report on the presence or frequency of the variables coded into categories and will use inferential statistics to generalize from the sample to the larger population and to test for significant differences.

As the foregoing would suggest, researchers conducting content analyses of television face the same problems of measurement as do researchers using other approaches such as survey research. There are, however, some issues that are specific to content analysis. Several essays and empirical studies have wrestled with methodological problems inherent in content analytical studies. For example, researchers have examined (a) the most effective way in which to obtain a representative sample in analyzing television newscasts (Riffe, Lacy, Nagovan, & Burkum, 1996), (b) the use of statistical analysis in content analyses (Stempel, 1981), and (c) issues involved in measuring televised violence (Gunter, 1981; Kunkel et al., 1995; Lometti, 1995; Signorielli et al., 1995).

In an earlier article, we noted our discomfort with the inability of quantitative research to get at the underlying meaning of the data: "As scholars we are concerned about relationships between images as symbols imbued with dominant culture and dominant political meanings, some overt, some imbedded and not readily identified" (Stroman et al., 1989-1990, p. 53). In the next section, we discuss a methodology that attempts to get at the meaning associated with the content.

■ Qualitative Analysis of Television Content

As noted in the foregoing section, the quantification of television content works quite well with respect to describing succinct and observable elements of mediated messages. Content analysis as qualitative research, however, is significantly different. One of the keys to qualitative content analysis is the use of descriptive techniques to interpret observations in their symbolic form and to search for meaning in the content. Qualitative researchers look for the inherent meaning in content; this distinctive step enables them to offer more insightful and complete analyses.

Qualitative content analysis deals more with the latent content of the message. Qualitative content analysts arrive at meaning holistically in their contexts (Fink & Gantz, 1996). That is, "The analysis is extended to an interpretative reading of the symbolism underlying the physically presented data" (Berg, 1995, p. 176). It is this emphasis on the latent content rather than the manifest content that distinguishes qualitative content analysis from quantitative content analysis.

With qualitative data, observations are not easily reduced to numbers (Babbie, 1995). Therefore, in many cases, qualitative data emerge strictly from perceptions/observations of the researchers. For example, counting the frequency of occurrence or co-occurrence of physical events in television content becomes more dependent on the subjectivity of the operationalization of variables defined by the observer.

Hsia (1988) provided succint guidelines for conducting qualitative research; these guidelines are suggestive of the tasks that confront those conducting qualitative content analyses of television programming. These guidelines include collecting data from television programs; reducing the scope of data by selecting, focusing, simplifying, abstracting, and transforming but not quantifying the data; and searching for the pattern, trend, explanation, and causality of the phenomenon under examination (p. 289).[3]

Category development in qualitative content analysis is equally important as in the case of quantitative content analysis, for example, making the categories mutually exclusive, exhaustive, and reliable. Development of categories in qualitative content analysis can be both an inductive process and a deductive process. Some texts suggest that when developing a basis for identifying categories for content analysis, the research should begin with what has been referred to as "grounded theory" (Strauss, 1987). The theory stems from the notion that, during the process of evaluation of research data, patterns or impressions emerge. These findings might be traced back or grounded to similar impressions that the researcher developed while gathering data, primarily a process of induction. The notion that one might be able to arrive at a foundation for analysis of the development of content categories through an inductive process rather than a deductive process might be troublesome to some, especially when quantitative approaches to analysis are under consideration. Abrahamson (1983) suggested that the researcher would need to be totally immersed in the content to detect identifiable patterns that can be traced back to message producers. Categorization that results from inductive reasoning allows the researcher to "ground" those categories from the data (Berg, 1995).

Whether the approach is qualitative or quantitative, content analysts should take care in developing operational definitions of categories. The extent to which the empirical manifestations are grounded is key.

Qualitative content analysis has the benefit of affording researchers the opportunity to analyze data during the course of study. If a significant variable or construct emerges during the course of analysis, then a new course can be taken accordingly (Wimmer & Dominick, 1994).

Gray (1987) directed attention to the wide variety of techniques available to qualitative content analysts including "the structural form and organization of a news story, the sources cited (especially the differences in power), whether voices used are active or passive, camera angles, editing, pacing, and narrative style of presentation (close-up camera shots, interviews, voice-overs)" (p. 393). It is his view that such techniques produce richer and more reliable interpretations of media images and their meanings.

■ Qualitative/Quantitative Content Analyses

Although content analysis is more closely associated with quantitative research, both qualitative and quantitative techniques can be used and blended together. Furthermore, researchers can analyze both the manifest and latent content. Indeed, over the past decade, the communication field has witnessed an increase in the number of studies that combine both qualitative and quantitative methods of analysis (for content analytic examples, see Barkin & Gurevitch, 1987; Rakow & Kranich, 1991; Shah & Thornton, 1994).

In an interesting example of the integration of the two techniques, Larson's (1991) study of the sexual content of the soap opera *All My Children,* the author explicitly states that she used quantitative content analysis to determine the frequency of romantic kissing and qualitative content analysis to gather meaning from the story lines. By coding the act of kissing as either forced or unforced and by examining the degree of commitment between the kissing couple as a variable, Larson was able to argue that the "wrong messages" given on soap operas are not about the frequency of sexual interaction between unmarried consenting couples but rather about the glorification of sexual aggression.

Unlike quantitative data, qualitative data are not readily observable or immediately measurable by researchers. For example, quantitative research is driven by the fundamental principles of scientific observations. Researchers approach the data from a broad perspective rather than a narrow perspective, and the data are reduced to their most minimal terms. In the use of the scientific method to the analysis of data, an informed hypothesis emerges from a careful examination of the current status of the problem area. The hypothesis becomes the standard against which inferences about the data are made. These statements of conjecture are posed systematically, outside of the cognitive dimension of the observers, weighing only the merits of the data whose reduction, interpretation, and presentation are actualized through statistical analysis.

Shoemaker and Reese (1996) provided an elegant comparison of the two approaches to content analysis:

> Humanistic analysis tends to take content as a starting point and work backward, to understand the culture producing it; behaviorists have traditionally taken content as a starting point and worked forward, to examine the effects external to and created by the message. For the former, content is artistry, a "text" worthy of study in its own right. For the latter, it is part of a chain of cause and effect. (p. 32)

Rossman and Wilson (1991) suggested three reasons for linking the two approaches: (a) to enable confirmation or corroboration of each other via triangulation; (b) to elaborate or develop analysis, providing richer detail; and (c) to initiate new lines of thinking through attention to surprises or paradoxes, providing fresh insight (see Table 7.1 for a comparison of the two approaches). Speaking directly to content analysis, Vande Berg and Trujillo (1989) illustrated the second reason in their explanation of why they conducted both quantitative and qualitative analyses in an effort to develop a realistic picture of television's portrayal of organizational life.

Researchers who combine both approaches seek to provide greater meaning to their data (see Table 7.2 for a summary of the research integrating qualitative and quantitative research). As an example, Rakow and Kranich's (1991) study applies both quantitative and qualitative approaches to an examination of how women appear as

TABLE 7.1   A Comparison of Quantitative and Qualitative
Content Analysis Methods

Quantitative	*Qualitative*
Deductive	Inductive
Hypothesis driven	Data driven
Manifest interpretation	Latent meaning
Coded	Coded
Object centered	Process centered
Unobtrusive	Obtrusive
Standardized	Less standardized
Empirical	Abstract

television network news sources. In terms of the former, they used the *Television News Index and Abstracts* to determine the frequency of the appearance of women as sources on the CBS, NBC, and ABC evening news programs during the month of July 1986. After determining the major categories under which women appeared, the authors selected for more detailed analysis 46 stories in which women were likely to be significant to the meanings of the stories. Noting that "the frequency or infrequency of women's appearance do[es] not give a complete picture of how women are used to carry meaning in news stories" (p. 15), Rakow and Kranich classified the content of the news stories qualitatively to arrive at the conclusion that women apearing in news stories are not there to speak but rather are there to serve as signs. Chesebro's (1991) study followed a similar pattern. After examining more than 900 series and classifying them as either ironic, mimetic, leader-centered, romantic, or mythic communication systems, he provided an interpretation of their value orientation. Through the use of qualitative content analysis, he identified the values promoted by the television shows: existentialism, individualism, authority, idealism, and theology.

Barkin and Gurevitch's (1987) work provides an interesting example of using qualitative analysis to supplement quantitative analysis and to present a perspective that is not captured by the numbers. After an extensive examination of network news coverage of unemploy-

TABLE 7.2   Studies Integrating Qualitative and Quantitative
Analyses of Television Content

Study	Focus of Analysis	Topic(s) of Analysis	Integration Method[a]
Barkin & Gurevitch (1987)	National evening newscasts	Unemployment	Qualitative and quantitative techniques are used equally
Chesebro (1991)	Prime-time dramatic shows	Conflict resolution values	Quantitative method is used to embellish a primarily qualitative study
Entman (1990)	Local evening newscasts	African Americans	Quantitative method is used to embellish a primarily qualitative study
Larson (1991)	Soap operas	Sex, morality, sexual aggression	Qualitative methodology is used to help explain quantitative findings
Rakow & Kranich (1991)	National evening newscasts	Women	Qualitative methodology is used to help explain quantitative findings
Vande Berg & Trujillo (1989)	Prime-time dramatic shows	Industries, occupations, organizational actions and values	Qualitative and quantitative methods are used equally

a. This typology was suggested by Steckler, McLeroy, Goodman, Bird, and McCormick (1992).

ment, the researchers identified themes to conclude that although television news stories offer few direct explanations of unemployment, they do provide an abundance of explanatory frameworks of themes. Interpreting and drawing meaning from their findings led Barkin and Gurevitch to conclude that the story of unemployment is told in diverse, often contradictory ways. Such a finding was not apparent solely from the quantitative analysis.

Entman (1990) also illustrated how the two approaches to studying television content enhance each other. Using quantitative data pertaining to the appearance of African Americans on local television news programs in Chicago, the author attempted to demonstrate qualitatively television's role in cultural change. Blending empirical evidence with an abstract concept, he concluded that television content stimulates the production of what he termed "modern racism."

Graber (1989) posed the following question: Should social scientific studies of content focus on words and sentences isolated from context, or must they consider the context as well as the intention of message senders? Scholars who blend quantitative and qualitative analyses use their research to argue that context must be considered. For example, in a content analysis of television's sexual messages, Larson (1991) argued, "The context of an activity needs to be examined before labeling it morally unacceptable; therefore, storyline should be examined as well as demographic characteristics, such as marital status" (p. 157). Similarly, Lometti (1995) issued a call for measuring both the acts of violence and the context in which the acts occurred on television. He noted that context can include production elements such as setting and special effects as well as story elements including motive, consequences, morality, and level of graphic depiction.

Instead of viewing qualitative and quantitative methods as opposites, researchers used as exemplars in this section viewed them as complementary. Indeed, they used statistical analyses to reduce their data to meaningful proportions and used qualitative data in their studies to better understand what they were studying. As Miles and Huberman (1994) noted,

> The careful measurement, generalizable samples, and statistical tools of good quantitative studies are precious assets. When they are combined with the up-close, deep, credible understanding of complex real-world contexts that characterize good qualitative studies, we have a very powerful mix. (p. 42)

This is not to imply that the integration of the two approaches is not without problems. A central concern with the combining of the two approaches has been the question of whether findings generated by the two approaches are compatible. As mentioned earlier, there is the view that the epistemological differences beween qualitative and quantitative methods mean that the findings from each method may reflect different realities. Researchers integrating the two approaches in the study of television should recognize and acknowledge the implications of fusing the two approaches.

It also should be acknowleged that qualitative and quantitative methods both have strengths and weaknesses. However, their weaknesses, to some extent, are offset by their strengths. In the works cited in this chapter that integrated the two approaches, the strength of the quantitative portion was the use of precise, established procedures that facilitated a factual, reliable examination of television content. The qualitative segment's contribution was the generation of rich, detailed, valid data revealing features that were not identified using strictly quantitative methods. Combined, they provided a more balanced picture than either of the approaches could have accomplished alone.

■ Summary and Conclusion

Content analysis is an important measurement technique. As such, it has been used by scholars from a wide variety of disciplines. In this chapter, we have examined how content analysis has been used to study television and indicants of viewers' perceptions and behaviors.

One's approach to the study of television content can be qualitative or quantitative in orientation. Whereas quantitative research, with its use of statistical techniques, emphasizes a systematic, objective, precise way of examining social phenomena, qualitative research offers great depth of information and richness for understanding social phenomena.

Traditionally, communication researchers have used either the qualitative or quantitative paradigm. But, increasingly, the two approaches are being combined. Indeed, as the sources of messages have multiplied, scholars have argued that we need new ways of conducting content analysis (Gaunt, 1993; Kunkel et al., 1995; Lometti, 1995; Weaver, 1993).

In concert with those content analysts who have integrated the two approaches, we view qualitative and quantitative analyses as complementing each other. Although the examples we have highlighted are not free of error, and although we caution researchers who combine qualitative and quantitative analyses of television content to be aware of and reflect on what it means to combine the two approaches, we recommend that more investigators consider doing so in future research. Such a recommendation connotes our agreement with those who argue that we need "to gather all the data we can from whatever sources offer the possibility of scholarly inference and to compare and argue over the validity of those inferences" (Thomas, 1994, p. 686).

■ Notes

1. Examples of recent analyses of television content include "The Sound Bites, the Biters, and the Bitten: An Analysis of Network TV News Bias in Campaign '92" (Lowry & Shidler, 1995); "Living Room Pilgrimages: Television's Cyclical Commemoration of the Assassination Anniversary of John F. Kennedy" (Vande Berg, 1995); "Network TV Sex as a Counterprogramming Strategy During a Sweeps Period: An Analysis of Content and Ratings" (Shidler & Lowry, 1995); "How Real Is the Portrayal of Aggression in Television Entertainment Programming?" (Potter et al., 1995); and "Emotional Portrayals in Family Television Series That Are Popular Among Children" (Weiss & Wilson, 1996).

2. See Bryman (1988) for a discussion of the debate and the view that qualitative and quantitative methods are based on competing, incompatible epistemological positions.

3. Miles and Huberman's (1994) detailed handbook on qualitative analysis provides an excellent framework for conducting qualitative analysis in general. Much of the material may be applicable to qualitative content analysis. Lindlof (1987) also contains useful information.

■ References

Abrahamson, M. (1983). *Social research methods.* Englewood Cliffs, NJ: Prentice Hall.

Babbie, E. (1995). *The practice of social research* (7th ed.). Belmont, CA: Wadsworth.

Barkin, S. M., & Gurevitch, M. (1987). Out of work and on the air: Television news of unemployment. *Critical Studies in Mass Communication, 4,* 1-20.

Berg, B. L. (1995). *Qualitative research methods for the social sciences* (2nd ed.). Boston: Allyn & Bacon.

Bryman, A. (1988). *Quantity and quality in social research.* London: Unwin Hyman.

Budd, R. W., Thorp, R. K., & Donohew, L. (1967). *Content analysis of communications.* New York: Macmillan.

Cantor, M. G. (1980). *Prime-time television: Content and control.* Beverly Hills, CA: Sage.

Cassata, M., & Skill, T. (Eds.). (1983). *Life on daytime television: Tuning in American serial dramas.* Norwood, NJ: Ablex.

Chesebro, J. W. (1991). Communication, values, and popular television series: A seventeen year assessment. *Communication Quarterly, 39,* 199-219.

Comstock, G. A. (1975). *Television and human behavior.* Santa Monica, CA: RAND.

Entman, R. M. (1990). Modern racism and the images of blacks in local television news. *Critical Studies in Mass Communication, 7,* 332-345.

Fink, E. J., & Gantz, W. (1996). A content analysis of three mass communication research traditions. *Journalism and Mass Communication Quarterly, 73,* 114-134.

Gaunt, P. (Ed.). (1993). *Beyond agendas: New directions in communication research.* Westport, CT: Greenwood.

Graber, D. A. (1989). Content and meaning: What's it all about? *American Behavioral Scientist, 33,* 144-152.

Gray, H. (1987). Race relations as news: Content analysis. *American Behavioral Scientist, 30,* 381-396.

Greenberg, B. S. (1980). *Life on television: Content analyses of U.S. TV drama.* Norwood, NJ: Ablex.

Gunter, B. (1981). Measuring television violence: A review and suggestions for a new analytic perspective. *Current Psychological Reviews, 1,* 91-112.

Head, S. W. (1954). Content analysis of television drama programs. *Quarterly of Film, Radio, and Television, 9,* 175-195.

Holsti, O. R. (1969). *Content analysis for the social sciences and humanities.* Reading, MA: Addison-Wesley.

Hsia, H. J. (1988). *Mass communications research methods: A step-by-step approach.* Hillsdale, NJ: Lawrence Erlbaum.

Krippendorf, K. (1980). *Content analysis: An introduction to its methodology.* Beverly Hills, CA: Sage.

Kunkel, D., Wilson, B., Donnerstein, E., Linz, D., Smith, S., Gray, T., Blumenthal, E., & Potter, W. J. (1995). Measuring television violence: The importance of context. *Journal of Broadcasting & Electronic Media, 39,* 284-291.

Larson, S. G. (1991). Television's mixed messages: Sexual content on "All My Children." *Communication Quarterly, 39,* 156-163.

Lindlof, T. R. (Ed.). (1987). *Natural audiences: Qualitative research of media uses and effects.* Norwood, NJ: Ablex.

Lometti, G. E. (1995). The measurement of television violence. *Journal of Broadcasting and Electronic Media, 39,* 292-295.

Lowry, D. T., & Shidler, J. A. (1995). The sound bites, the biters, and the bitten: An analysis of network TV news bias in campaign '92. *Journalism and Mass Communication Quarterly, 72,* 33-44.

Miles, M. B., & Huberman, A. M. (1994). *Qualitative data analysis: An expanded sourcebook* (2nd ed.). Thousand Oaks, CA: Sage.

Potter, W. J., Vaughan, M. W., Warren, R., Howley, K., Land, A., & Hagemeyer, J. C. (1995). How real is the portrayal of aggression in television entertainment programming? *Journal of Broadcasting & Electronic Media, 39,* 496-516.

Rakow, L. F., & Kranich, K. (1991). Woman as signs in television news. *Journal of Communication, 41*(1), 8-23.

Riffe, D., Lacy, S., Nagovan, J., & Burkum, L. (1996). The effectiveness of simple and stratified random sampling in broadcast news content analysis. *Journalism Quarterly, 73,* 159-168.

Rossman, G. B., & Wilson, B. L. (1991). Numbers and words: Being "shamelessly eclectic." *Evaluation Review, 9,* 627-643.

Shah, H., & Thornton, M. C. (1994). Racial ideology in U.S. mainstream news magazine coverage of black-Latino interaction, 1980-1992. *Critical Studies in Mass Communication, 11,* 141-161.

Shidler, J. A., & Lowry, D. T. (1995). Network TV sex as a counterprogramming strategy during a sweeps period: An analysis of content and rating. *Journalism and Mass Communication Quarterly, 72,* 147-157.

Shoemaker, P. J., & Reese, S. D. (1996). *Mediating the message: Theories of influences on mass media content* (2nd ed.). New York: Longman.

Signorielli, N., Gerbner, G., & Morgan, M. (1995). Violence on television: The Cultural Indicators Project. *Journal of Broadcasting and Electronic Media, 39,* 278-283.

Smythe, D. W. (1954). Reality as presented in television. *Public Opinion Quarterly, 18,* 143-156.

Stacks, I. W., & Hocking, J. E. (1992). *Essentials of communication research.* New York: HarperCollins.

Steckler, A., McLeroy, K. R., Goodman, R. M., Bird, S. T., & McCormick, L. (1992). Toward integrating qualitative and quantitative methods: An introduction. *Health Education Quarterly, 19,* 1-8.

Stempel, G. H., III. (1981). Statistical designs for content analysis. In G. H. Stempel III & B. H. Westley (Eds.), *Research methods in mass communication* (pp. 119-131). Englewood Cliffs, NJ: Prentice Hall.

Strauss, G. (1987). *Qualitative analysis for social scientists.* New York: Cambridge University Press.

Stroman, C. A., Merritt, B. D., & Matabane, P. W. (1989-1990). Twenty years after Kerner: The portrayal of African Americans on prime-time television. *Howard Journal of Communications, 2,* 44-56.

Thomas, S. (1994). Artifactual study in the analysis of culture: A defense of content analysis in the postmodern age. *Communication Research, 21,* 683-697.

U.S. Commission on Civil Rights. (1977). *Window dressing on the set: Women and minorities on television.* Washington, DC: Author.

Vande Berg, L. R. (1995). Living room pilgrimages: Television's cyclical commemoration of the assassination anniversary of John F. Kennedy. *Communication Monographs, 62,* 47-64.

Vande Berg, L. R., & Trujillo, N. (1989). *Organizational life on television.* Norwood, NJ: Ablex.

Weaver, D. H. (1993). Communication research in the 1990s: New directions and new agendas? In P. Gaunt (Ed.), *Beyond agendas: New directions in communication research* (pp. 199-220). Westport, CT: Greenwood.

Weiss, A. J., & Wilson, B. J. (1996). Emotional portrayals in family television series that are popular among children. *Journal of Broadcasting & Electronic Media, 40,* 1-29.

Wimmer, R. D., & Dominick, J. R. (1994). *Mass media research: An introduction.* Belmont, CA: Wadsworth.

8

Intersection of Instructional Television and Computer-Assisted Instruction

Implications for Research Paradigms

Kevin A. Clark

According to Gagné (1965), "Learning is a change in human disposition or capability which can be retained and which is not simply ascribable to the process of growth" (p. 5). The change that occurs must be long lasting or permanent and must be represented in the learner's behavior. In addition, the change in the learner's behavior must be due to the learner's experience, not to a "natural" growth process. Because learning and instruction do not occur in a vacuum, there are many factors that affect learning; these factors are called conditions of learning (Gagné, Briggs, & Wager, 1992). There are two types of conditions that affect learning: internal conditions and external conditions.

Internal conditions are those qualities and capacities that the learner brings to the learning situation. Examples of internal conditions of learning are intellectual skills, selective attention, expectations, creativity, problem-solving ability, and cognitive learning style.

External conditions are those environmental (not just physical) conditions that may affect learning. Examples of external conditions of learning are feedback, gaining attention, prerequisite learning, giving objectives, presenting the stimulus, giving guidance, eliciting performance, evaluation, and enhancing retention and transfer (Gagné et al., 1992).

After getting a clear picture of learning and the conditions that affect learning, one must relate this to instruction. Gagné et al. (1992) defined instruction as a deliberately arranged set of external events or conditions designed to support internal learning processes.

Instruction can be presented using a variety of media: expository, television, radio, hands-on, and computer.

The idea of educating and training people through the use of visual technologies, such as television and computers, grew out of a need to educate and train large numbers of people in a manner that was efficient and consistent. The systemic and systematic application of strategies and techniques derived from behavior and physical science concepts and other knowledge to the solution of instructional problems is defined as instructional technology (Anglin, 1991). In the early stages of instructional technology, the technological focus was on films. The introduction of television and computers created additional modes of presenting instruction.

Many instructional models have been formulated for instructional television and computer-assisted instruction, but this chapter focuses primarily on the research paradigms used to generate these models. The following research paradigms are discussed in this chapter: behaviorism, cognition, and constructivism. The use of television and computers in presenting instruction and its impact on research paradigms are investigated. In addition, this chapter discusses the emergence of new technologies and their impact on research paradigms.

■ Instructional Television

No discussion about instructional television would be complete without first discussing its foundation in instructional films. From

1945 to 1965, extensive research was conducted on the development and implementation of instructional films and television. The first 10 years of research focused specifically on instructional films. Much of this research was stimulated by the shortage of qualified teachers combined with the need to educate a rapidly growing population that had to learn more than ever because of the explosion of human knowledge during this period (Cambre, 1987).

Instructional film research examined the effect of sound and silent motion pictures on learning or the modification of existing behavior. According to Carpenter (1971), the six basic assumptions of film research were that (a) learning is expressed in behavioral modifications; (b) motion picture films are composed of malleable characteristics that act as contingencies or causative mediators of varying degrees of strength in determining the effectiveness of films for producing definable behavioral modifications; (c) the functional relation of film characteristics to the intervening and dependent variables of learning and performance can be studied by appropriate experimental research and the analysis of the effects produced in target groups; (d) experimental research requires the designing or planning of experiments in which hypotheses are formulated, questions are stated, and specially designed experimental films are produced in different versions; (e) the experimental approach is only one approach to learning and understanding how to increase the instructional effectiveness of motion picture films (other approaches include research and development, systematic observations and experience, the use of informed judgment and assessments of experts, and the use of relevant creative talent and advanced knowledge about learning and communications generally); and (f) the quality and effectiveness factors that are built into instructional films exist operationally and are validated by adequate evidence that their characteristics actually produce the intended or expected changes in the performances of selected subjects or people.

From 1955 to 1965, research focused on instructional television. Anglin (1991) defined instructional television as television designed and produced specifically for elementary and secondary grade students with the expectation that it will help those students achieve specific learning objectives. According to Seels, Berry, Fullerton, and Horn (in press), there are two terms that come to mind when discussing the use of television as a tool for instruction: *instructional television* and *educational television*. Instructional television is transmitted by satellite to a school where it is either recorded and used when convenient or used immediately and interactively through a combination of computers and telecommunications. Educational television is intentional in its purpose to teach educational objectives through planned manipulation of technical effects and program content.

In the late 1950s and early 1960s, instructional television was promoted as a vehicle for disseminating exemplary teaching (Anglin, 1991). After this period, instructional television was promoted for its ability to bring the world to the classroom. Television was to be used as a tool to take children to different places outside of the classroom and to convey the human aspects of situations.

The majority of the early research conducted in the area of instructional television was focused in the area of relative effectiveness, where instruction via television is compared with face-to-face direct instruction. Many of the early research studies on instructional television were reviewed and analyzed by Chu and Schramm (1967). Their analyses revealed that children learn efficiently from instructional television under the right conditions. In addition to examining learner effectiveness, Chu and Schramm also examined research related to the efficient use of television in instruction. According to research, television was most effective when it was used in a situation that was most advantageous for the use of one-way communication.

Much of the research reviewed by Chu and Schramm (1967) can be divided into five categories: physical variations, pedagogical variations, viewing conditions, two-way communication, and student response.

Research on physical variations showed that attributes such as magnification of objects on the screen, variation of production techniques, attention-gaining cues that are not related to learned content, and the use of color had no positive effect on learning of concepts via television. However, the research did find significant results in the use of subjective angle presentation. The research on pedagogical variations revealed that the use of animation, humor, dramatic presentations, and embedded questions did not have a significant effect on the use of instructional television. Research studies did show significant results in the use of subtitles and repeated showings of the instruction to students via television (Chu & Schramm, 1967). Research on viewing conditions found that students will learn more effectively when they are placed in motivated conditions and that this effectiveness is not dependent on the size of the viewing group. Research involving two-way communication showed that students learn more when they can be given immediate knowledge of their instructional response. In addition, research on student response revealed that task-appropriate practice improves learning from instructional television (Chu & Schramm, 1967).

Instructional Television Research Implications

The theoretical foundation of instructional television is rooted in behaviorist psychology. The basic tenets of the behaviorist are objectivism, environmentalism, and reinforcement (Cooper, 1993). Objectivism is where the key to analyzing human behavior lies in the observation of external events. Environmentalism is where the environment is the significant factor in determining human behavior. Reinforcement represents the phase in which the learner receives feedback related to his or her actions. The view of feedback as reinforcement was derived from Skinnerian behaviorism (Clark, 1994). A behavior or response is strengthened when it is followed by a pleasant response. According to the law of effect, a behavior followed by a pleasant response makes it more likely that the behavior will be repeated. The law of effect is the basis for operant conditioning. In operant conditioning, a behavior or response is followed by an "action" that reinforces behavior. Operant psychologists in the 1960s supported and popularized the notion of feedback as a reinforcement, arguing that learning tasks should be analyzed and broken down into small enough steps so that the probability of a successful response would be ensured (Clark, 1994). The operant viewpoint is based in the response-strengthening theory, which provides a foundation for much of the research dealing with knowledge of results feedback (Roper, 1977).

Behaviorists consider the potential for behavioral change to be heavily influenced by the current behavior of the learner and the way in which that behavior either competes with or enhances the development of new behaviors. The first technology-based instructional programs were task based and developed stimulus-response chains of behavior that were shaped toward a desired terminal or final behavior. Experimental research concluded that although feedback is an effective tool, the quality of feedback is dependent on the quality of the information it imparts to the learner (Clark, 1994).

Reinforcement and the concepts that are associated with reinforcement include stimulus control, chaining, shaping, competing, enhancing repertoires, and interpersonal and intrapersonal behaviors. Knowledge of results feedback as reinforcement gave way to a more complex notion that, although learning increases the likelihood of the emergence of target behaviors, the primary reinforcers are considered to be learner generated (intrinsic) and that external feedback (extrinsic) is most effective as either correctional or motivational feedback. Feedback as reinforcement has been subjected to some criticism as research has emerged demonstrating that, under certain circumstances, delayed feedback is more effective than immediate feedback. Students spend more time studying feedback if it is delayed and if it is provided immediately after difficult material has been presented. Student control of feedback can lead to students not interacting with the material if they can obtain the feedback without such interacting. Using the behavioral paradigm, instructional television is centered around the idea that independent variables affect dependent variables, that is, learning outcomes in the form of knowledge or skill acquisition. The presentation of educational material will have little impact on learning without feedback that is appropriate and relevant to the learner's response (Clark, 1994). Kulhavy (1977) indicated that providing feedback following incorrect answers is likely to be more valuable to a learner than giving feedback after correct answers. He contended that, with correct responses, there is the probability for repetition. Conversely, giving the learner feedback after incorrect answers serves to remove the wrong answers and to replace them with the correct answers (Kulhavy, 1977). According to Kulhavy, feedback has its greatest impact when the learner is confident about his or her response and is told that it is incorrect. Given this situation, the learner will spend substantially more time reviewing the response to determine where the error occurred (Kulhavy, 1977).

In the late 1970s, instructional television research was characterized by a merging of interest in both developmental aspects of learning and cognitive processing of information (Seels et al., in press). Two events prompted this shift in the emphasis of research: the initial success of *Sesame Street* and *Children's Television Workshop* and the increased criticism of television and its alleged negative effects by a number of popular writers (Mielke, 1990). Cognitive effects focused on features such as pacing, audio cues, camera effects, animation, and editing techniques.

The cognitive research paradigm recognizes an interaction between external stimuli and internal processes that support learning. Cognitive processing is studied as an outcome of experimental studies where learner characteristics are examined as independent variables. Research began to investigate the effects of elements of an instructional message that entails the way in which different modes of information presentation are processed by the learner and how these processing capabilities are developed (Jonassen, 1988). The cognitive paradigm does not assume that instructional power exists only in media.

Typical studies compared the relative achievement of groups that received similar subject matter from different media. Because of new media, studies began to examine the effectiveness of the new media versus the old media. Media comparison studies tended to reveal no significant effects. Meta-analyses of media comparison studies provided evidence that any reported differences in performance were due to confounding in the study treatments (Carpenter, 1971), the confound being the method of instruction. The research suggests that any gains in learning achieved with the use of new instructional media may be associated not with the media itself but rather with the method of instruction (Anglin, 1991).

Realizing the limitation of media comparison studies, research began to examine the attributes of media and their influence on the way in which information is processed. The promise of the media attributes approach to conducting research is based on three expectations: (a) that the attributes are an integral part of media and would provide a connection between instructional uses of media and learning, (b) that attributes would provide for the cultivation of cognitive skills for learners who needed them, and (c) that identified attributes would provide unique independent variables for instructional theories that specified causal relationships between attribute modeling and learning. Media are best conceptualized as a means of delivering instruction as opposed to being a direct influence on the learning process (Cambre, 1987).

A significant amount of research has been done on attitudes toward media. Researchers believe that attitudes, beliefs, and values influence motivation to learn. Motivation typically is measured by one's willingness to engage in a task or to invest effort in a task he or she has selected to perform. Motivation is a necessary component of learning. Although our expectation of a positive relationship between attitude and learning is generally demonstrated via the research, there are a significant number of studies in which negative attitudes result in more learning (Anglin, 1991).

The paradigm shift from behaviorist to cognitive psychology spurred research on mental processing and formal features. The focus of future research was to determine necessary conditions for learning such that the unique aspects of instruction were delivered by a medium that models the cognitive process (Cooper, 1993).

■ Computer-Assisted Instruction

Computer-assisted instruction is defined as any instance in which instructional content or activities are delivered via computer (Hannafin & Peck, 1988). According to Hannafin and Peck (1988), the following are characteristics of effective computer-assisted instruction: specifies instructional objectives, matches learner characteristics, maximizes interaction, adapts to the needs of individual students, maintains student interest, approaches the learner positively, provides a variety of feedback, fits the instructional environment, evaluates performance appropriately, uses computers' resources wisely, is based on principles of instructional design, and has been evaluated thoroughly.

Computer-assisted instruction can be divided into four categories: (a) drill and practice, (b) tutorial, (c) games, and (d) simulation. Drill and practice provides the learner with practice and feedback on a topic taught previously. A tutorial teaches new information to the learner. Games are used to teach new information or concepts and also are used to reinforce previously learned concepts. Simulations model complex concepts or events by allowing the learner to experience the results of good and bad decisions without risky or expensive consequences. Effective computer-assisted instruction also was revealed through research that was conducted in the areas of screen design, learner control, and feedback.

Research on screen design has identified five functional areas. First, a screen should have orienting information. Second, the screen should display directions for the learner in a consistent location. Third, the program should echo or display the student's responses. Fourth, a display area for informative error messages should be provided. Fifth, the options available to the student should be displayed in a consistent area. Much of the research on computer-assisted instruction screen design has paralleled the research on printed materials. An area that received less research attention is screen density. Screen density refers to the number of words, sentences, or ideas presented in a single frame. Research suggests that different perspectives be used when evaluating screens with realistic content because of the need to process the information so that it can be recalled or applied at a later time (Anglin, 1991).

Another area of computer-assisted instructional research is learner control. Even though the ability to implement learner control is one of the advantages of computer-assisted instruction, research suggests that learner control options may not always be a feasible method for individualizing instruction (Anglin, 1991). If the learner lacks the knowledge and motivation to make appropriate decisions regarding conditions such as pacing, sequencing, learning aids, and amount of practice, then learner control will not prove to be a valuable feature. Although there were no significant effects on achievement, research suggests that learner control was used by students in adapting the density variations to their reading levels. Less skilled readers were more likely to select the high-density version, whereas more skilled readers were more likely to choose the low-density version. These findings suggest that learner control is not a unitary construct; rather, it is a collection of strategies that function in different ways depending on what is being controlled (Ross & Morrison, 1989).

Feedback also is an important aspect of computer-assisted instructional research. Computer-assisted instruction, as a means of effective teaching and learning, has many unique capabilities. One of the unique capabilities of computers is that they are able to provide users with immediate feedback; the problem is that very rarely is this capability used to its fullest potential. With the growing use of computers in the classroom, it is incumbent on researchers to identify the elements of computer-assisted instruction that are most effective for improving the performance of the learner. It is believed that the design of current instructional software fails to accommodate major individual differences in learning styles (Nishikawa, 1988). Learning styles may vary based on the type of information presented to the student or on the way in which the instruction is presented.

Feedback promotes learning during instruction by providing the learner with information about his or her performance. A learning activity accompanied by feedback can help the learner maintain or adapt cognitive operations according to how new information about the learner's performance matches his or her expectations about performance (Clark, 1994).

Feedback given immediately after the learner makes a response is called immediate feedback. Delayed feedback is described as feedback given after time has elapsed. The amount of time that elapses can range from a few seconds to a number of days. Results suggest that immediate feedback is more effective than delayed feedback, and most forms of feedback yield better results than does no feedback (Kulik & Kulik, 1988).

Computer-Assisted Instruction Research Implications

The beginnings of computer-assisted instruction were in programmed instruction. Programmed instruction was behaviorally based and was characterized as having three stages: (a) analysis, (b) design, and (c) evaluation. Behavioral psychology is based on the premise that learning results from the pairing of responses with stimuli (Steinberg, 1991).

The four principles guiding the design of computer-assisted instruction that derive from behavioral learning theory are (a) contiguity, (b) repetition, (c) feedback and reinforcement, and (d) prompting and fading (Hannafin & Peck, 1988). Contiguity is demonstrated when the response follows the stimulus without delay. The stimulus to which the learner is to respond must be presented contiguously in time with the desired response. Repetition refers to practice that strengthens learning and improves retention. The stimulus and response must be practiced to strengthen the bond between the stimulus and the response. Feedback and reinforcement occur when the learner receives knowledge concerning the correctness of his or her response. Feedback provides the learner with knowledge of his or her results, which may be used to modify existing behavior or possibly to affect subsequent behaviors. Prompting and fading refer to the process of providing several or alternate stimuli to shape the desired response.

A negative reaction to behaviorism is that the technological developments have not been used effectively; in particular, the use of computers and interactive media has yielded few realistic educational applications (Hannafin & Peck, 1988). In addition, the application of behaviorist principles leads to a reductionist and fragmented program, which concentrates on low-level skills at the expense of complex conceptual behavior. Behaviorist attributes are found in most technology-based instructional applications in the learning of small chunks of material related to a single skill and the use of reinforcement through reward. Behavioral-based instruction seems to be most useful for clearly delineated content where the branching is constrained and learner responses are categorized as right or wrong. Although computer-assisted instruction began within the behaviorist paradigm, it soon embraced many of the theories associated with cognitive psychology.

Cognitive psychology is described as how we gain information from the world, how such information is represented and transformed as knowledge, how it is stored, and how that knowledge is used to direct our attention and behavior (Hannafin & Peck, 1988). There are three principles in cognitive psychology that are used in designing computer-assisted instruction: (a) orientation and recall, (b) intellectual skill, and (c) individualization. The orientation and recall principle involves the synthesis of prior information that must be recalled to active memory. The intellectual skill principle involves learning what is facilitated by the use of existing processes or strategies. The individualization principle suggests that learning may be more efficient when the instruction is adapted to the needs and profiles of individual learners (Hannafin & Peck, 1998).

There are two computer-assisted instruction design principles that cross the theoretical boundaries of behaviorism and cognition. Learning time and affective considerations, such as attitude, focus on the behavioral aspects of learning while also making an argument for cognitive attributes. Academic learning time focuses on the amount of time a learner spends actively engaged in profitable instructional activities and the amount of learning that will occur. The principle of affective considerations states that the attitudes of the learner in an activity are important to its success. The stimulus of a learner wanting to be successful may result in the cognitive response of the learner wanting to learn more.

Research in cognitive psychology suggests that the learner constructs understanding rather than reproduces instruction (Resnick, 1981). Information is not simply added to the knowledge the learner has previously stored in memory; the learner tries to link new knowledge to old knowledge, selecting, reorganizing, and restructuring it in the process. Instruction involves the stimulation of the learner's information processing strategies, aptitudes, and stores of relevant specific memories in relation to the information to be learned. Decoding skills also influence comprehension. Good readers can devote most of their attention to comprehension because they decode almost automatically. Readers who expend considerable effort on decoding have few resources left for understanding. Some research even suggests that slow decoding is a cause of poor comprehension (Sticht, 1984).

The research conducted in computer-assisted instruction moved from emphasizing behaviorist attributes to investigating cognitive issues. This shift was necessitated partially by the advances in computing technology. The processing power of computers enabled developers of instructional technologies to address the needs of complex cognitive development.

■ Intersection of Instructional Television and Computer-Assisted Instruction

Two of the most promising qualities of instructional television are its distributive properties and its use of realistic graphics. Although those qualities are desirable, instructional television alone does not have the ability to provide feedback to the learner or to provide the learner with the practice and repetition that make learning more effective.

On the other hand, because of the processing power of computing technology, computer-assisted instruction has the potential for a variety of feedback and processing solutions that may range from the very simple to the very complex. In addition, computers possess the power to store and retrieve information that can be used to provide practice and repetition. Even with all the power of computers, the ability to produce graphics as realistic as television images has lagged behind. Using graphics in computer-assisted instruction used to mean that they had poor screen resolution or had limitations in colors. Furthermore, a significant amount of time and work was required to produce high-quality graphics. Today, there are computers that can display realistic graphics, but usually they are at a reduced size or resolution.

In 1962, computers and television projection systems were first combined to create simulated environments for training aircraft pilots and testing new aircraft designs (Hodge, 1995). Although the early systems were very large and very expensive, they represented a significant step for instructional technology—the birth of interactive technology. The birth of interactive technology also signaled the birth of virtual reality. Interactive technology can be defined as the control of graphics, animation, and/or video by the learner or the use of high-quality audio and graphics combined in an environment where the learner is an active participant (Giardina, 1992). This control can be accomplished by the selection of new video or by making decisions that manipulate the flow of information in the teaching machine.

Interactive technology represents the technological merging of television and computers; however, more important, it facilitates the theoretical merging of instructional television and computer-assisted instruction. Interactive technology creates a new medium to convey instruction. Because technology constantly is moving forward, the visual and computing capabilities will continue to improve and, hence, expanding the research possibilities (Anglin, 1991).

■ Research Implications

There has been a progressive shift from the behavioral to the cognitive, which has been matched by a corresponding shift in the research and implementation of instructional technology supporting individualized instruction.

As behaviorist ground gave way, the need to encompass individual differences emerged and brought with it an increased complexity in the technology required. Computer-assisted instruction was forced toward the handling of the complexity of individual differences, but the technology of programmed texts and electromechanical teaching machines proved to be the limiting factor to the instructional accommodation of such individual differences (Moldstad, 1974). The emergence of interactive technology has changed the way in which learning is viewed. The way in which we view learning and acquire information is affected by the advances in technology because they can address a variety of learning styles. Interactive technology relieves the heavy reliance on visual skills by being able to introduce high-quality audio, animation, and interactivity.

Learning by listening is different from learning by reading in two ways. Listening skills develop before reading skills (Sticht, 1984), and people take cues from the speaker's intonation. The implication for computer-assisted instruction is that, for the immature reader, the most appropriate topics for computer-assisted instruction lessons might be those that depend primarily on nonverbal information. A heavy demand is placed on the student's visual skills because the standard output device for computer-assisted instructional systems is a monitor. Because the majority of the content is transmitted by text, the student's ability to read can be a major factor influencing the effectiveness of computer-assisted instruction lessons. Although cognition is firmly rooted in the framework of instructional technology, a constructivist approach is beginning to emerge.

The constructivist sees reality as determined by the experiences of the learner. The move from behaviorism to cognitivism to constructivism represents shifts in the emphasis away from an external view to an internal view. To the behaviorist, the internal processing is of no interest. To the cognitivist, the internal processing is of importance only to the extent it explains how external reality is understood. The constructivist views the mind as a builder of symbols, which are the tools used to represent the learner's reality. The constructivist views reality as personally constructed and states that personal experiences determine reality, not the other way around (Cooper, 1993). For the constructivist, learning is problem solving based on personal discovery, and the learner is intrinsically motivated. The learner needs a responsive environment in which consideration has been given to the learner's individual style as an active, self-regulating, reflective learner. Changing the learning environment to incorporate a constructivist view adds complexity. Interactive technology can be used to absorb that complexity as other forms of managing complexity become overloaded. The technology on the desktop is not the major hardware issue of importance in supporting the implementation of a constructivist approach, although the hardware must be powerful enough to support large and complex software.

The development of interactive technology also is undergoing a shift in emphasis. New approaches, such as object-oriented analysis and design, allow for easier development. The building process, especially in areas such as user interface, has been semi-automated. There is a much stronger emphasis on applications that allow exploration such as database management systems, microworlds, and expert systems. In these applications, the learner can interactively store and retrieve information, explore reality through simulations, and create his or her own environment.

■ Conclusion

Designed instruction has moved through a series of developmental phases since its reliance on the early behaviorist research. The move from instructional theory emphasis on the environmental to emphasis on the internal has been accompanied by similar changes in three technologies: (a) instructional design methodology, (b) the physical technology with which the instruction is implemented, and (c) the programming mechanisms used to develop the instructional technology conveying the subject content. A relationship exists between instructional theory and its dependent technologies.

The design and development of instructional technology tools must continue to use techniques and strategies that are appropriate and state of the art. According to Peck and Dorricott (1994), there are 10 reasons to use technology in instruction. First, because learners develop at different rates, technology can individualize instruction. Second, on-line tools and resources will help the learner become proficient at accessing, evaluating, and communicating information. Third, technology can foster an increase in the quantity and quality of the learner's thinking and writing skills. Fourth, the learner can solve complex problems by independently organizing, interpreting, developing, and evaluating solutions and strategies. Fifth, the advent of technology-based art forms (e.g., video production, digital photography, computer-based animation) has great appeal and encourages artistic expression among a variety of populations. Sixth, technology allows the learner to reach the world outside of his or her physical location. Seventh, technology can provide opportunities for the learner to create meaningful work through publication, postings, and other media outlets. Eighth, the learner will have access to high-level and high-interest educational materials. Ninth, the learner must feel comfortable with the tools of the information age. Last, technology can be used to make instruction more productive and efficient.

The implementation of instructional technology, grounded in theory, is limited by the available technology paradigms. The newest technology paradigm is interactive technology, the intersection of the visual capabilities of television and the processing capabilities of computers. The emergence of this technological paradigm must be used to improve current instructional strategies and to create new instructional models.

■ References

Anglin, G. J. (1991). *Instructional technology: Past, present, and future.* Englewood, CO: Libraries Unlimited.

Cambre, M. A. (1987). *A reappraisal of instructional television.* Syracuse, NY: Syracuse University Press. (ERIC No. ED296720)

Carpenter, C. R. (1971). Instructional film research: Brief review. *British Journal of Educational Technology, 3,* 229-246.

Chu, G., & Schramm, W. (1967). *Learning from television: What the research says.* Stanford, CA: Institute for Communications Research.

Clark, K. A. (1994). *The effect of different types of computer-assisted feedback on learner achievement and learner response confidence.* Doctoral dissertation, Pennsylvania State University.

Cooper, P. A. (1993). Paradigm shifts in designed instruction: From behaviorism to cognitivism to constructivism. *Educational Technology, 33,* 12-18.

Gagné, R. M. (1965). *The conditions of learning.* New York: Holt, Rinehart & Winston.

Gagné, R. M., Briggs, L. J., & Wager, W. W. (1992). *The principles of instructional design.* Fort Worth, TX: Harcourt Brace Jovanovich.

Giardina, M. (1992). *Interactive multimedia learning environments: Human factors and technical considerations on design issues.* New York: Springer-Verlag.

Hannafin, M. J., & Peck, K. L. (1988). *The design, development and evaluation of instructional software.* New York: Macmillan.

Hodge, W. W. (1995). *Interactive television: A comprehensive guide for multimedia technologies.* New York: McGraw-Hill.

Jonassen, D. H. (1988). *Instructional designs for microcomputer courseware.* Hillsdale, NJ: Lawrence Erlbaum.

Kulhavy, R. W. (1977). Feedback in written instruction. *Review of Educational Research, 47,* 211-232.

Kulik, J. A., & Kulik, C. (1988). Timing of feedback and verbal learning. *Review of Educational Research, 58,* 79-97.

Mielke, K. (Ed.). (1990). Children's learning from television: Research and development at the Children's Television Workshop. *Educational Technology Research and Development, 38*(4), 7-16.

Moldstad, J. A. (1974). *Computer assisted instruction: Current approaches and trends.* Bloomington: Indiana University Press.

Nishikawa, S. (1988, February). *Effects of feedback strategies in computer-assisted instruction and the influence of locus of control on the performance of junior high students.* Paper presented at the 10th annual proceedings of the Association for Educational Communications and Technology, New Orleans, LA.

Peck, K. L., & Dorricott, D. (1994). Why use technology? *Educational Leadership, 51,* 11-14.

Resnick, L. B. (1981). Instructional psychology. *Annual Review of Psychology, 32,* 659-704.

Roper, W. J. (1977). Feedback in computer-assisted instruction. *Programmed Learning and Educational Technology, 14,* 43-49.

Ross, S. M., & Morrison, G. R. (1989). In search of a happy medium in instructional technology research: Issues concerning external validity, media replications, and learner control. *Educational Technology Research and Development, 37*(1), 19-33.

Seels, B., Berry, L., Fullerton, K., & Horn, L. J. (in press). Research on learning from television. In D. Jonassen (Ed.), *Handbook for research on educational technology communications and technology.* New York: Macmillan.

Steinberg, E. R. (1991). *Computer-assisted instruction: A synthesis of theory, practice, and technology.* Hillsdale, NJ: Lawrence Erlbaum.

Sticht, T. G. (1984). Listening and reading. In P. D. Pearson (Ed.), *Handbook of reading research* (pp. 293-317). New York: Longman.

9

Barney & Friends as Entertainment and Education

Evaluating the Quality and Effectiveness of a Television Series for Preschool Children

Jerome L. Singer ■ Dorothy G. Singer

In 1993, the Connecticut Public Broadcasting Station aired a new series aimed at preschool children called *Barney & Friends*. Within months after the show spread to national Public Broadcasting System (PBS) exposure, it had moved to the leadership in terms of viewers of all children's programming. This quick success in ratings also was associated with a truly remarkable acceleration in national attention.

AUTHORS' NOTE: Support for the research described herein came from a gift to Yale University by Connecticut Public Broadcasting, Larry Rifkin, vice president for programming. Our research assistants for this project are too numerous to mention, but we particularly acknowledge David Sells, our New Haven field coordinator, and Robert Miller, our national field coordinator. Valuable suggestions on research and educational issues came from Sheryl Leach, the creator of *Barney & Friends,* as well as Kathy Parker, Mary Ann Dudko, and Margie Larsen of the Lyric Corporation.

Such attention included mass turnouts at the occasional public appearances of Barney at charitable events. The series also evoked widespread media attention, some of it caustic and derogatory and some of it perhaps more playfully humorous as in the notices of the show by comedians such as Jay Leno. The attraction of the show for children between 2 and 7 years of age was reflected in a remarkable economic event. The parent company of the television series was a closely held family corporation with headquarters in Texas, and the income from licensed plush toys (Barney soft toys, Barney pillows, blankets, etc.) quickly put the company near the very top in terms of income for entertainment figures nationally. Indeed, Barney was listed as third in income in 1994 alongside personalities such as Oprah Winfrey, Michael Jackson, and the "regulars" who make up the list of high-earning entertainers. As the national interest in Barney surged in terms of popularity among preschoolers and their parents as well as economically within the toy industry, the Connecticut Public Broadcasting Corporation approached the authors of this chapter and the Yale University Family Television Research and Consultation Center to help with an evaluation of the quality of the program from the standpoint of its educational potential. We were fortunate, therefore, in having an opportunity to set up a series of studies that, at least in the short term, could evaluate both the educational and entertainment qualities of this continuing series. In this chapter, we describe the procedures employed to assess this series from the standpoint of a number of dimensions that may serve as suggestive models to other researchers in the future seeking to evaluate educational programming. With the increasing pressures on the networks, local stations, and cable systems for attention to the needs of the child audience, it is our hope that we can raise significant questions that should be taken into account by other television researchers.

■ Objectives

1. What are the theoretical, methodological, and practical issues involved in mounting an evaluation of a television series?

2. What are the specific components that need to be considered in an evaluation of a specific series?

3. What were the actual outcomes found in the course of 10 separate studies that sought to examine a range of issues related to *Barney & Friends*?

■ How does this type of research apply to the more general study of early childhood?

■ Can we draw any conclusions about the implications of early television viewing as a possible resource in readying children for entry into the regular school system by 6 years of age?

■ Can we draw any conclusions from our analysis of the content and child response to the *Barney* series that might be useful, not only for future researchers but also for producers of children's programming?

■ **Background: *Barney & Friends* in the Context of a Readiness-to-Learn Movement**

In 1991, the Carnegie Council for the Advancement of Teaching produced a widely read and provocative report (hereafter the Carnegie Report) summarizing a major national problem: Millions of children are beginning formal schooling at 6 or 7 years of age inadequately prepared for the necessities of effective school learning (Boyer, 1991). The preparation could be attributed to a variety of possible causes including poverty, increased fragmentation of traditional family structures, and insufficient or inadequate preschool services for the majority of children whose parents nowadays are not available as full-time caregivers. The report outlined specific areas from cognitive skill preparation to sound physical health practices that are necessary for children with optimal school readiness. Among the seven major national initiatives called for by the Carnegie Report (and by related reports from the National Center for Clinical Infant Programs and the National Governors Association) was an increased effort to involve the television industry and producers of related electronic media in providing early school preparation for preschoolers. As the author of the Carnegie Report, the late Ernest Boyer wrote that "television next to parents is the child's most influential teacher" (p. 140).

The Corporation for Public
Broadcasting Report to Congress

In the early 1990s, there began to be increasing pressure from Congress to influence the television industry to play a role in meeting national goals of educational preparation for young children. In response to a request from Congress and with its own initiative derived from the television recommendation of the Boyer Report, the Corporation for Public Broadcasting (CPB) asked the Yale University Family Television Research and Consultation Center to prepare a report on the feasibility of establishing a "ready-to-learn" service devoted exclusively to preschoolers. This extensive report (J. L. Singer & D. G. Singer, 1993b) in modified form was submitted by CPB to the Secretaries of the Senate and the House of Representatives for their consideration in February 1993. This report defined more specifically than the Carnegie Report the needs of preschool children and the demands on them as features of adequate school preparation. It focused on those components of a ready-to-learn effort that could be provided through the attractive medium of television, especially when supplemented by parental or child caregivers' use of television-related videotapes and print materials to expand the child's *active* participation. More specifically, the readiness for school entry to which television programming might contribute included the following items:

1. Providing, in an entertaining fashion, information on basic cognitive skills such as concepts of left-right and up-down; awareness of shapes, colors, and sequences; and, most important, presentation of new vocabulary

2. Fostering imagination and pretend play as a critical feature, not only of personal entertainment but also as a means of processing new information and of fostering curiosity

3. Encouraging awareness of one's own and others' emotional responses as part of the inevitably more complex social experience of being in a classroom with many other children

4. Helping children to develop constructive prosocial attitudes and actions (e.g., sharing, turn taking, self-restraint, cooperation) that can lead to effective functioning in the face of the teaching and disciplinary demands of the classroom

5. Exposing children to the varieties of culturally and physically different types of children and adults with whom they might have to interact in the school setting and fostering a sense of mutual respect for these cultural and physical differences

6. Perhaps most important, contributing to children's sense of "basic trust"—the feeling that they are cared about, that they can be trusting of adults and other children, and that they can find regularities in their world rather than constantly confronting the unexpected

In the longer form of this report to CPB, we sought in separate chapters to outline a variety of means of implementing these goals through television and related electronic media. Also included were presentations of how to obtain parental involvement and how to include caregivers, such as day care center operators, in this effort. A further chapter outlined specific ways in which producers could meet these goals in the course of considering individual television shows and possibly even series.

The Origins of the *Barney & Friends* Phenomenon

The idea of a videotape that might be entertaining for children was devised in the late 1980s by Sheryl Leach, a young mother who felt that there was insufficient material available for her child either in a video store or on television. She and her group produced several videotapes that featured a fantasy figure, a purple dinosaur, Barney. He is a presumed figment of the imagination of a group of live children and serves in various ways as a benevolent adult. A team of writers and educational advisers also was recruited and established the format of the program with educational goals specified from the outset. A total of 68 episodes of the series were produced in the period between 1993 and 1995. These came in three separate cycles of 30, 18, and 20 episodes. Our evaluation of the content was carried out separately for each of these three series of episodes. The episodes are regularly shown on PBS as part of the ready-to-learn series system that has emerged from the CPB report. *Barney & Friends* has held its leadership in ratings among children's shows during the 3 years of its regular airing on PBS. It also has received high ratings among minority group children, something not expected by many adult critics when the show

began its initial run. Despite a multicultural group of child participants, its themes and atmosphere often were labeled as "white bread."

The Need for Evaluation of the Series

Although there may well be extensive *proprietary* research studies
of children's programs, formal publicly available reports of children's
programs are actually rather limited in number. Perhaps the first show
systematically evaluated was *Mister Rogers' Neighborhood,* which
evoked a series of studies because of its ostensibly prosocial goals
(Friedrich & Stein, 1973; Friedrich-Cofer, Huston-Stein, Kipnis, Susman, & Clewett, 1979; J. Singer & D. Singer, 1976; Tower, Singer,
Singer, & Biggs, 1979). Studies of *Sesame Street* have been reported
by Ball and Bogatz (1970, 1971); Cook et al. (1975); Huston, Wright,
Rice, Kerkman, and St. Peters (1990); Zill, Davies, and Daly (1994);
and most recently by Wright and Huston (1995). The series of studies
on *Barney & Friends* described here represents an effort to address
various aspects of the show including content as evaluated by adult
developmentalists, assessments of the behavior of groups of children
while actively watching the show, assessments of the response of
toddlers, assessments of the ability of preschoolers to report and
apparently to understand the content of an ongoing show, and, finally,
studies of relatively short-term pre- and postviewing responses under
controlled conditions by children. Special attention is paid to the
significance of adult follow-up. Only the most recent *Sesame Street*
study (Wright & Huston, 1995) has provided a sufficient long-term
follow-up under controlled conditions. It should be noted, however,
that that study includes other educational television programming
along with *Sesame Street.*

In effect, we review studies that deal with, first of all, evidence that
the content of this series may be viewed as meeting some of the
ready-to-learn goals outlined earlier. In addition, our concern is
whether the program not only seems entertaining but also holds the
attention of relatively young children. We also ask whether the show
has a constructive effect, not only for a largely middle-class white
majority group of children but also for children drawn from the inner
cities who are from the lower socioeconomic or minority status groups

of our society. Evidence of longer term gains currently is not obtainable but may be obtainable for future research.

■ Adult Evaluations of the Educational Potential of the *Barney & Friends* Series

The Format and Content of a *Barney* Episode

Each of the 68 *Barney & Friends* half-hour segments contains essentially the same format and location. Following a brief introduction with a title and the song "Barney is a dinosaur from our imagination . . ." sung to the tune of *Yankee Doodle,* we see a playground outside a small suburban or rural elementary school. Almost all episodes are either inside the classroom or on the outside with only occasional shifts of scenes to flashbacks or shifts of setting when these are presented as imaginative activities. Initially, Barney is a stuffed toy purple dinosaur portrayed during the opening section in real size. Shortly into the segment, a need for Barney's help arises in connection with some momentary crisis or planned event. All or some of the children cry "We need Barney!" and, presumably by their imagining him, the small toy (with a sound effect "ping") becomes a nearly 7-foot *Tyrannosaurus rex,* albeit one without any teeth and rather chubby in the midsection. The cast of characters regularly includes Barney, who prances around, claps hands, and speaks "proper English" in a deep male voice with much chortling and "ho ho" laughter. The cast regularly includes four to six children between 5 and 12 years of age. The cast of "real" children is constant except that, because of natural growth processes, new characters have replaced some of the older children in the second and third series. All children speak "proper English" but represent varied ethnic groups. Usually, one or two in each episode are European American and the other characters include children of African American, Hispanic American, and Asian backgrounds. They do not vary much in their standard English speech patterns, but from time to time across the 68 episodes they demonstrate their cultural background differences. Each episode essentially tells a rather simple story built around a central theme with perhaps a few subthemes. The main theme usually is something reflective of identifying colors and shapes, counting, learning new vocabulary, physical health and safety, or using one's imagination. Two other fantasy characters appear: a dinosaur representing a 3-year-old girl child, Baby Bop, who talks in a voice designed to reflect "baby talk," and a taller dinosaur, B. J., who behaves like an 8- or 9-year-old "Little League boy." Baby Bop's character is designed to be somewhat helpless, needy, and self-centered. B. J. is designed to be more assertive and impulsive.

A plot usually involves some adventure such as the discovery of a map leading to a buried treasure somewhere in the schoolyard, the classroom, or the area around them. Sometimes the plot involves overcoming a series of obstacles or putting on a carnival. Barney's role throughout is as an expeditor, an explainer, and frequently a teacher. The episodes are completely lacking in any physically aggressive behavior, and only occasionally is a plot advanced through a verbal dispute between some children. The children's talk is characterized by considerable politeness, and there is much turn taking and lining up for participation in certain activities. Every few minutes, there is a lead-in to a song whose lyrics elaborate on or emphasize a particular issue under discussion earlier. The songs themselves are a mixture of original melodies and words and of folk songs such as *Old MacDonald* or *This Old Man* to which new words have been added appropriate to the particular plots. Each episode ends with the whole cast looking out at the audience and singing "I love you, you love me, we're a happy family. . . ." Just after this moment, Barney appears to say a few sentences summarizing the main points of the particular episode as if he were talking to the parents as well as the children. At the end, he returns to his original small plush toy form.

For an adult, viewing episodes of *Barney & Friends* for the first time without a child present may be disconcerting. The show seems "hokey" and too "goody-good," and the dinosaur costumes appear primitive. The children on the show, although engaging and sprightly, also are, in a sense, too "squeaky clean." Some of these characteristics undoubtedly have led people in the entertainment industry to mock the show, and, indeed, even children in elementary school find it too sweet. After all, 9- and 10-year-olds are beginning to develop a capacity for criticality and cynicism. Anything that smells of the nursery for them is to be abhorred. That is probably why the *I Love You* song that closes *Barney* has been turned, perhaps by the older siblings of preschoolers, into a song like "I hate you, you hate me, we'll get a gun and shoot Barney. . . ." This intense adult or teenage distaste for the show, manifested in a few instances of attacks on individuals dressed in Barney outfits (perhaps to entertain at birthday parties or at sales promotions in malls), merits further discussion, to which we will return.

The issue in evaluating a series such as *Barney & Friends* is to adopt the perspective of preschool or early school-age children to whom the show is directed. That it is an entertaining show for such children is clear from the ratings and from the vast demand for licensed Barney products that followed the show's appearance on television. Our concern was whether one could demonstrate that the show had educational features beyond the apparent ability to entertain and hold the attention of young children. Are there elements in the show that can prepare children for the beginnings of school? The very setting of each segment in a schoolroom or schoolyard environment obviously was an important conception in this regard. It was designed to familiarize children with a school atmosphere and, just by the surroundings alone, to introduce youngsters to the various features of "formal" education with papers and books. The developers of the *Barney* series seemed to be on the right track whether or not they knew anything of the Carnegie foundation data.

Research Design

Our first step in this study was to establish specific variables that could be assessed from each of the 68 *Barney & Friends* episodes. We began this investigation by looking at the first 30 episodes of the "100" series. Subsequently, as the "200" and "300" series were produced and aired, we repeated this procedure so that we could make comparisons across series and obtain an overall perspective on the teaching potential of the *Barney* show. The variables we chose were designed to reflect the types of cognitive, physical health, emotional, and social attitudinal features that, if provided to a child by a caregiver, would increase the likelihood that the child would (a) look forward to school as a positive experience; (b) experience a sense of personal security and trust that might reinforce abilities to confront the school experience; (c) demonstrate cognitive preparation for the effort of learning reading, writing, and arithmetic skills; and (d) manifest the emotional enthusiasm, curiosity, self-restraint, emotional awareness, and cooperative social attitudes necessary in a classroom learning setting.

Research evidence clearly suggests the value for the child of early exposure to adults who not only are consistent and loving but also provide a physically safe and healthy environment. A critical feature of this process is communicating regularly with the child, labeling and explaining the environment, and helping the child to form cognitive schemas (Desmond, Singer, & Singer, 1990; D. Singer & J. Singer, 1990). Such mediation also should include fostering the child's capacity for *imagination*. The abilities to pretend, to think in a narrative fashion, and to entertain *possibilities* may be critical features of cognitive and emotional development (Bruner, 1986; D. Singer & J. Singer, 1990). It is evident from the very structure of the *Barney & Friends* show that it regularly addresses two of the features just cited: the emphasis on the classroom and the emphasis on loving and trusting. The focus on mutual trust, respect, and love (repeated regularly in the closing song) may seem overly saccharine for some cynical adults but clearly is much needed by children.

For our purposes, an evaluation required a more precise quantitative documentation of the other components of a ready-to-learn atmosphere. Our procedure was, therefore, to draw up a specific list of variables that might be identified in each episode and that would mirror the types of *mediation* that might be offered by a confident parent or other child caregiver. We assembled a team of child development trained raters, who independently scored each episode for these variables. Because of the critical role of adult mediation in effective teaching, we not only emphasized *exposure* of child viewers to a color, shape, or concept but also required some evidence that Barney or one of the show's children (or occasionally a guest) actually pointed to, labeled, or explained the relevant material much as a mediating parent would.

Table 9.1 provides a list of the variables scored for their occurrence by our team of raters as they watched each half-hour episode of the *Barney & Friends* series. Large rating sheets were provided to the individual judges. They scored the occurrence of mediated instances of each of these variables for each of the characters in an episode. We

TABLE 9.1   Specific Variables Rated by Observer Team

1. Cognitive
   a. New vocabulary
   b. Alphabet
   c. Numbers
   d. Imagination
   e. Colors
   f. Shapes
   g. Concepts
   h. Sorting
   i. Sequencing
   j. Science, nature
   k. Achievement
   l. Riddles, metaphors

2. Emotional awareness
   a. Joy, approval
   b. Surprise, excitement
   c. Interest, curiosity
   d. Empathy, sympathy
   e. Anger
   f. Shame, shyness
   g. Disgust
   h. Jealousy, envy
   i. Fear, tension
   j. Crying, sadness
   k. Pain

3. Social/constructive attitudinal
   a. Sharing
   b. Turn taking
   c. Cooperation
   d. Self-restraint, control
   e. Interpersonal skills
   f. Helping, teaching
   g. Disciplining

4. Physical
   a. Fine motor skills
   b. Large motor skills
   c. Eye/hand coordination
   d. Nutrition, health
   e. Handicaps
   f. Injury
   g. Personal grooming

5. Music and entertainment
   a. Song related to instructional incident
   b. Song and dance combined
   c. Dancing alone
   d. Singing alone
   e. Musical instruments
   f. Games

6. Multicultural exposure
   a. Language
   b. Custom
   c. Food
   d. Song
   e. Dancing
   f. Name of country
   g. Discussion of country
   h. Reference to ethnic group
   i. Ethnic guest

could tell at the end whether particular children, Barney, or the younger dinosaurs were playing special roles in this episode or more generally as mediators.

The raters were provided with separate spreadsheets for each of the six dimensions displayed. On the cognitive spreadsheet, to the left would be a list of all of the specific components of the cognitive area, and across the top would be the listing of characters who mediated these characteristics in the particular episode. The raters had ample room on a scoring sheet to make tick marks for each mediated occurrence of defining a new word, demonstrating counting, exemplifying imagination, demonstrating colors, explaining some new concept, pointing out sequences of events, and the like. Essentially the same procedure was used for each of the separate variables. For example, in the case of emotional awareness, examples of the emotion alone without some follow-up or additional explanation would not be sufficient to lead to a score. In the case of the social/constructive attitudes, again, not only was it necessary to have some of the events occur, but some reference to them would have to be made verbally or through nonverbal follow-up by one or several characters. In the case of music, because this is such a critical component with perhaps as many as six to eight songs per episode, the relevance of the music or dancing episode to the main theme of the episode or to the theme just discussed could be scored. In some instances, the music is simply carried out for pure entertainment purposes, and that in itself was not scored. In the case of multicultural exposure, although the show's children themselves are of varied cultural or ethnic backgrounds, this in itself was not scored. Instead, we sought examples of references to the backgrounds or, in a few instances, the appearances of guests on the episodes (e.g., a storyteller who tells stories of Africa, an episode in which dances and music of different countries are demonstrated).

Rating Procedures

For purposes of this chapter, we are combining the findings for the three separate ratings of the 100, 200, and 300 series. Because our original intent was to provide feedback to the producers of the series on the general educational elements of the overall series and of individual episodes, readers can refer to reports available from Connecticut Public Television (D. Singer, J. Singer, & Sells, 1995; J. Singer & D. Singer, 1993a, 1994). The first two series were largely completed by the time our reports were available, but the educational director of the series undoubtedly made use of this material in guiding the third series. Nevertheless, the consistency of scores for the various dimensions across the three series is remarkable. We also had the opportunity to provide feedback to the producers about the strengths and weaknesses of particular episodes and also, on the basis of our cumulative data, to suggest possible areas to be covered in future episodes because of limited or absent coverage in the episodes thus far produced. As will be seen shortly, we also used these ratings from the 100 and 200 series to identify the top 10 educationally rich episodes, which could then be employed in our experimental studies with children. Following some trial procedures in which we used senior child development researchers just to give us a "feel" for the likelihood of effective response and agreement, we then identified graduate students or senior undergraduates who had been trained in developmental psychology and, more specifically, in the theoretical issues relating to mediated learning by young children. We averaged five raters for each of the three studies with an equal balance of men and women wherever possible. These raters had very little previous exposure to the *Barney & Friends* series.

A series of training sessions took place with the team using sample videotapes not actually employed in the study. Following trial tests of rater agreement that proved satisfactory, the group began watching the particular series of the 30, 18, or 20 tapes. They watched each episode from beginning to end, scoring occurrences of each variable as indicated earlier. The raters could ask for tapes to be stopped and rerun if they felt they had missed something, and this was regularly done because our goal was not reaction to the pace of the show but rather a clear identification of specific instances of mediated teaching.

Every effort was made to ensure the independence of the ratings. Periodic checks on rater agreement were made by the principal investigators to ensure that none of the reviewers was an "outlier," that is, a person who shows scoring patterns grossly different from the rest of the group. There did not appear to be any outliers in the group. Qualitative comments on the strengths and weaknesses in presentation and performance of particular episodes were gathered after formal ratings. To establish reliability for raters, we randomly selected 10 episodes from each of the series to examine rater scores variable by variable. We found agreement to be quite high across all five raters for these 10 episodes. Our reliabilities were generally between .80 and .90. Scores that appear in the tables that follow reflect the averages across all five raters for each variable.

TABLE 9.2   Rank Order of *Barney & Friends* Episodes by
Total Potential Teaching Elements ("300" series)

Rank	Episode Number	Episode Name	Score
1	314	It's Raining, It's Pouring	178.00
2	320	Up We Go	154.25
3	307	Twice Is Nice!	150.00
4	319	Hats Off to B. J.	148.25
5	302	If the Shoe Fits	146.25
6	312	Gone Fishing!	134.75
7	316	Who's Who on the Choo-Choo?	130.50
8	318	Ship Ahoy!	119.60
9	305	Shopping for a Surprise	113.75
10	315	Camera Safari	108.25
11	313	At Home With Animals	101.50
12	301	Shawn and the Beanstalk	100.00
13	310	Classical Cleanup	98.75
14	317	Are We There Yet?	91.60
15	304	I Can Be a Firefighter!	91.25
16	311	Our Furry Feathered Fishy Friends	83.25
17	308	On the Move	80.00
18	303	Room for Everyone	74.25
19	309	A Welcome Home	70.00
20	306	Any Way You Slice It	64.40
		Mean = 111.93	

Results of the Ratings

A sample set of results, in this case for the 20 episodes of the 300 series, indicates results variable by variable for each specific episode watched and with averages of the variables across the episodes and across the series (see Table 9.2). As one can observe from the table, the series demonstrates an average of nearly 112 instances of mediated demonstrations of the component variables per episode. Certain episodes, such as "It's Raining, It's Pouring," show an extremely high level of teaching elements with great strength in the cognitive, emotional, and social components as well as the multicultural one. Only a few episodes demonstrate fewer than 100 instances of mediated teaching. This average compares closely with the averages obtained for the 100 and 200 series, with the 100 series showing a total of 111 teaching instances and the 200 series averaging nearly 118. The difference between the series is that the 100 and 200 series are quite low in multicultural demonstrations. It is very likely that the higher rate and greater show-by-show manifestations of multicultural teaching in the 300 series reflect input from our scorings for the earlier series.

The quantitative scoring of the potential teaching elements of each episode provides us with an opportunity to examine not only the variations between series but also the strengths or limitations of particular episodes variable by variable. The data suggest that for particular teaching purposes, one might focus on a particular series of episodes if one wanted to emphasize the social aspects of civility that are constantly present in a *Barney & Friends* episode. Or, one could, for cognitive teaching purposes, choose another set. For example, it happens that "If the Shoe Fits" and "It's Raining, It's Pouring" are laden with cognitive instances. "Twice Is Nice!" and "I Can Be a Firefighter!" are good episodes to use for demonstrating issues of physical safety, health, and/or nature. Another use of the scoring approach is to examine, for a particular series or across the whole *Barney* series, which subcomponents of each separate variable are particularly emphasized. Thus, examining results for the 300 series, the variable subcomponent receiving the highest score as observed is *helpfulness* as expressed through advising and teaching others (a social component with 238.5 instances across the series). *Courtesy* also is a prominent feature of this dimension. Demonstrations of positive emotions, specifically *affection,* rank second in frequency. For the cognitive area, the introduction of new words with their definitions or demonstrations is present 203 times in the series. In the physical health and safety area, demonstrations of exercise and *large motor skills* appear 162 times. The multicultural awareness demonstrations of other *languages* (e.g., Swahili, Spanish) is most prominent, occurring 23 times.

Because our raters also provided qualitative reports, it was interesting to compare these with the quantitative ratings. In general, there was moderate agreement between the quantitative scores and our developmentalists' qualitative judgments, which are based more on balance and entertainment value for the list presented in Table 9.2. "It's Raining, It's Pouring," "Up We Go," and "If the Shoe Fits," all of which had very high quantitative scores, also appear among the top 10 on qualitative bases. Other episodes, such as "Classical Cleanup" and "A Welcome Home," are rated high qualitatively, especially because of their social, musical, and general entertainment possibilities, even though they did not rank as highly in quantitative scores.

This use of both quantitative and qualitative scoring with adult raters focusing on the combined teaching and entertainment potential of the episodes makes it possible to provide producers or writers with concrete suggestions about particular episodes or about future episodes. Thus, for example, in this particular series, one episode had high quantitative ratings but evoked considerable criticism because of the extremely rapid speech of one of the guests who was introducing words from a foreign language. The *Barney & Friends* series contains within it rich opportunities for children to acquire cognitive, emotional, and social skills. The high emphasis on civility, helping, and sharing is very much to be commended at a time when there is great concern about excessive brashness and impetuousness or tentativeness in children entering the school system, as documented by the Carnegie Report.

■ Children's Retention of Content After Watching a *Barney & Friends* Episode

Objectives of This Study

Having demonstrated that adult scoring of the mediated instances in a *Barney & Friends* episode indicates a high level of teaching potential, we still are left with the question of what children make of the show. In this next study, our intent was to test the hypothesis that those *Barney* episodes that reflected the highest levels of teaching potential as rated by our adult panel also would show evidence of more comprehension by children, better retention of vocabulary, and perhaps greater ability by the children to describe what they have seen in a narrative form. Our general plan called for developing a set of follow-up questions and then training interviewers to question each child immediately after a *Barney* episode viewing. It should be stressed

TABLE 9.3   *Barney & Friends* Episodes Used in the
Comprehension Study

Episode Number	Title	Adult-Rated Mediated Teaching Elements	
		Total	Cognitive
125	A World of Music	159	17.00
204	Red, Blue, and Circles Too	149	47.67
216	The Alphabet Zoo	147	44.00
107	The Treasure of Rainbow Beard	141	50.60
129	Hola Mexico	140	10.00
212	My Favorite Things	129	19.00
124	A Carnival of Numbers	127	32.60
218	A Very Special Delivery	123	14.00
121	Hi Neighbor!	120	27.80
211	The Exercise Circus	117	17.50

that our interviewers were not familiar with the ratings that each
Barney episode had obtained from the panel of developmentalists. We
sought in this study to ascertain whether particular *Barney* episodes
differed systematically in evoking various reactions from the children
specifically relating to retention of content and use of vocabulary
related to the episode just watched.

Procedure

A first step in this study was to identify those episodes that might
be considered richest in potential teaching elements. At the time of
this study, we already had completed ratings for the 100 and 200
series. When examining the quantitative scoring, we found that 5 episodes from each of the series fell into the top 10 on adult ratings. These
subsequently were used not only in this study but also in all the
experimental studies. Table 9.3 presents the episode number and title
and the adult-mediated teaching elements for each in order as well as
the specific cognitive elements that, for the purposes of this study, are
most relevant.

All the children saw the same episodes over a 2-week period, although order of presentation was varied to avoid biases based on presentation sequence. We obtained entry to three day care centers by first contacting their directors. Subsequent to the consent of preschool directors, all parents received descriptions of the project and signed informed consents. In addition, formal statements of agreement for participation from the directors of the schools were obtained. Anonymity was ensured for all children, and only code numbers were employed in our records. All procedures for this study and for all the studies described subsequently were in accordance with the requirements of Yale University's Human Investigations Committee, which reviewed and approved the project.

Initially, we received parental consent forms for 49 children, each of whom was enrolled full-time in one of the three day care sites. The ethnicity and socioeconomic status (SES) of the participants were mainly white and middle class, respectively. The children came from apparently stable or intact family environments. Of the 49 children, 13 had to be dropped, however, because of extensive absenteeism through sickness, family moves, or, in a few cases, extreme shyness that precluded satisfactory interviewing of these children. The quantitative analysis showed that this loss from the sample was not systematically related to ethnic background, gender, or SES. The total for this study came to 36 children. Of these, 18 were male and 18 were female, and the average age was 48.22 months with a standard deviation of 7.42. In effect, then, we were dealing with 3- and 4-year-old children, who are the heaviest viewers of the *Barney & Friends* series on television. The children watched one episode of *Barney* daily in their day care centers for 10 days over a 2-week period. Immediately following each presentation of the *Barney* episodes, a group of interviewers specially trained for this purpose (undergraduates and graduate students from various colleges) asked a series of questions of each child. Examples of the questions were as follows:

"Tell me what happened on the *Barney* show today."

"Tell me what the children did on the *Barney* show today."

"What did you see?"

"What did everybody do?"

"What did Barney do?"

Complete information on the questioning and various features of organizing the data is available from our report to Connecticut Public Broadcasting (J. Singer, D. Singer, Sells, & Rosen, 1995).

The interviews lasted roughly 10 minutes per child. To control for any temporal interviewing effects, no more than three interviews were conducted by any one interviewer, thus limiting the elapsed time from the completion of an episode to the start of an interview to no more than 20 minutes following the *Barney & Friends* viewing. Generally, we found that we could conduct interviews well within a 10-minute postviewing period. All interviews were audiotaped. As in all our studies, we observed the children as they watched each daily half-hour *Barney* episode. We had established a scoring system to observe the responses to the show. Because viewing was in groups, it was not feasible to score each individual child, but we did make individual tick marks and then totaled these into group responses. Each *Barney* showing was observed by one of our field staff members (a total of 50 observations of groups of children watching *Barney* at their preschool). We were careful to observe responses to music, cognitive reactions shown by the children, indications of concentrated attention on the show, and emotional reactions by the children. If children repeated words from the episode or provided other evidence of cognitive responses as they watched, then these were marked. Laughing and enjoyment/excitement were scored as positive affective responses, whereas anger, apparent distress, and tendencies to distract other children from watching were scored as signs of negative emotionality.

A major problem in dealing with 3- and 4-year-olds is their limited verbalization ability. The interviewers were unfamiliar to them, although the interviewers had had some occasions to meet with the children prior to the actual study. Nevertheless, we sought in the types of questions just mentioned to see whether we could identify primarily main content ideas and produce a type of comprehension or content score. For example, from the interviews, we looked for any words or actions that were directly and *accurately* related to the content of a given episode. An example would be the comment, "They all had a party with lots of candy that came out of a toy animal," relating directly to the piñata seen in the episode titled "Hola Mexico." It should be stressed that all scorings of videotapes were carried out by "blind" raters who had not actually conducted the interviews. We did, however, resolve occasional ambiguities by consulting the interviewers.

Results

We created quantitative scores for each variable of relevance to the comprehension phase of this study by scoring each clearly expressed accurate content feature of an episode produced by a child interview. We also scored each use of a new vocabulary word related to the episode. We could identify words not ordinarily a part of a preschooler's vocabulary and specifically traceable to the *Barney & Friends* episode just viewed. We also scored for number of references to each character in an episode (e.g., Barney, Baby Bop, Min, Derek, Tosha). We also rated evidence that the child produced a full-fledged narrative account of an episode. Keep in mind that because some children mentioned nothing at all for a given episode in response to our questions, our average scores often were low.

Despite our hopes, we found that there were so few references by children to "pretending" or "make-believe" for an episode (despite the frequent references to such activity in the *Barney & Friends* show) that our average scores were too low to be useful for further analysis. When we considered the percentage of children who could give at least one accurate statement about program content, we found an adequate range of responses for content comprehension, vocabulary, and identification of characters. The average across the 10 episodes indicates that nearly two thirds of the children could report accurately on what they had seen. About 55% of the children also managed to mention some characters. Sometimes, children did demonstrate evidence of new words in their vocabularies relating to a specific episode. Certain episodes, such as "The Treasure of Rainbow Beard," "A Carnival of Numbers," and "Hi Neighbor!," were most likely to have higher percentages of children specifically using the episodes' vocabularies. What stood out from these analyses was the episode-by-episode variation and children's ability to reflect what they had seen. A statistical analysis indicated that variation across episodes was especially striking for content comprehension, vocabulary, the use of motion verbs, character references, imagination references, and references to a foreign language. This analysis suggests that such young children's ability to account verbally for what they had seen was very much a function of the special characteristics of a particular *Barney* episode.

Of special importance for the present chapter is the question of whether the presumed teaching characteristics of the *Barney & Friends*

TABLE 9.4   Comparison of Adult Ratings of Teaching
Content With Children's Content Comprehension
and Vocabulary for Each Episode

Episode Number	Title	Adult Rating of Cognitive Content	Children's Comprehension of Content (N = 31)	Children's Use of Vocabulary (N = 31)
107	The Treasure of Rainbow Beard	50.60	1.10	1.45
204	Red, Blue, and Circles Too	47.70	0.97	0.31
216	The Alphabet Zoo	44.00	0.97	0.11
124	A Carnival of Numbers	32.60	0.75	0.50
121	Hi Neighbor!	27.80	0.90	0.47
212	My Favorite Things	19.00	0.71	0.20
211	The Exercise Circus	17.50	0.63	0.33
125	A World of Music	17.00	0.63	0.44
218	A Very Special Delivery	14.00	0.67	0.12
129	Hola Mexico	10.00	0.68	0.36

episodes, as rated by adults, were related to children's subsequent comprehension or vocabulary acquisition. In Table 9.4, we present a comparison of adult ratings of teaching content with the children's accurate reports of program content and with their use of vocabulary.

Examination of the table presents a dramatic demonstration that those programs rated highest in cognitive content by the adults also are likely to evoke greater comprehension of content by the children and greater use of vocabulary from the program by the children. The correlation between the adult-rated cognitive scores for the 10 episodes (based on ratings carried out more than a year before this study) and the average accurate content comprehension score obtained by the 31 children who were able to respond in all of the 10 posttests is an impressive $r = .93$ ($p < .001$). We find here a striking validation for the meaningfulness of using an adult panel to estimate mediated teaching in the *Barney & Friends* episodes. It is evident that our pooled estimate of the didactic value of each episode in the area of cognitive skills (e.g., vocabulary, counting, numbers, shapes) is a striking predictor of what 3- and 4-year-olds will retain and verbalize from an episode just viewed. For our specific 10 episodes in this study, "The Treasure of Rainbow Beard," with the highest score in the cognitive area, evokes the highest average accurate content report, followed closely by "Red, Blue, and Circles Too" and "The Alphabet Zoo."

When we look at some of the items included in the cognitive area, a similar finding emerges for children's use of new vocabulary words from each episode. The correlation, although lower ($r = .47$), is substantial. It must be stressed that this particular study focused primarily on children's cognitive responses. We cannot evaluate whether programs with high adult rating scores for emphasis on socially constructive behavior or on physical health and safety would evoke responses because we had no way of observing such actual behavior in this study. As might be expected, age was the only demographic variable that was linked to children's ability to report accurately on what they had just seen. Age was significantly, if very modestly, correlated with vocabulary. Multiple regression analyses designed to predict content comprehension from an array of demographic variables indicated that only age and the adult scoring of cognitive teaching elements for the episodes combined to predict children's content comprehension scores. The statistical analyses indicated that a cluster analysis of scores obtained by multiplying the number of children by the number of episodes each child viewed indicated that content comprehension was the dominant feature of a single cluster of variables that emerged. It correlated significantly and positively with the number of characters recalled per episode, the use of specific new vocabulary terms specific to an episode, the use of transitive verbs such as those used in episodes, references to songs in the episodes, and the ability to form accounts into narrative structure. Because content comprehension also is significantly and positively associated with the number of cognitive teaching elements provided by the adults, we again have reason to believe that the adult ratings are tapping into the significant learning potential of an episode.

Because we could not observe the attentiveness that children manifest in the home when watching a *Barney & Friends* episode, we took advantage of the opportunity to watch the children in their day care centers as they observed a *Barney* episode once a day for 10 days in a 2-week period. The question that often arises is whether young children can sustain viewing of a program as relatively slowly paced without the intercuts and dramatic shifts that characterize most programming for children. The evidence was very clear from this study. We found periods of concentrated group attention throughout more than 60% of the time in the half-hour episodes. Ratings by observers indicated many signs of open enjoyment, smiling, and laughing about 70% of the time as the children watched the episodes. We also found groups of children actually repeating words, phrases, and/or numbers on numerous occasions during their viewing. Singing along with some of the songs was common for a great many children during the musical episodes. Although our data do not allow us to coordinate specific children's behaviors while watching *Barney* to their comprehension, we did find suggestions in our observers' reports that children who showed high levels of attention did appear to gain in vocabulary use.

Implications

Two major outcomes have emerged from this first-ever study. First, we can assert that in this middle-class, largely European American sample of viewers, the children did appear to be able to verbalize accurately the main content of the episodes they had just witnessed. Although they rarely could provide more than three major themes, they were able to demonstrate (with their limited verbalization skills and in interviews with relative strangers) reasonable retention of plot content, correct use of at least one or two episode-related vocabulary words, and some indications of transitive verbs. They were somewhat less able to provide and organize the narratives of the episodes they had seen, at least in the face of an interviewer's question. Clearly, the children are not simply mindlessly viewing the *Barney & Friends* episodes or watching mainly in relation to the liveliness of the music.

Second, we obtained a high correlation between the number of cognitive teaching elements in a given *Barney & Friends* episode, as rated by our adult panels, and the children's ability to provide accurate accounts and to use the vocabulary of an episode they had just witnessed. This finding makes it clear that our technique of having each television show rated by an adult panel may be of value generally for the children's educational television medium. It also points out the great importance for children's grasp of what they have seen when the videotape plot incorporates carefully presented teaching elements related to words, counting, and shapes. We believe this study strongly affirms the fact that a carefully designed educational show such as *Barney* can be entertaining as well. The children watched attentively and laughed and enjoyed what they watched, but they also showed that they could retain useful material from each episode.

■ Can Children Learn From Watching *Barney & Friends?* The Middle Socioeconomic Class Study

Objectives and Research Design

Following up on the Carnegie Report's call for a significant role for television in school readiness for children, we sought to determine whether there might be a place in day care settings for exposure of children to the *Barney & Friends* series as a useful addition to a readiness-to-learn curriculum. A considerable percentage of American children 3 to 4 years of age are now in day care or nursery school. We thought it appropriate to test the teaching potential of the series in such a setting, making use of the day care providers or teachers as participants in the process. The research literature on parental mediation as well as the studies carried out on *Sesame Street* and *Mister Rogers' Neighborhood* have pointed up the importance of parents or teachers following up on simple viewing for children with various types of reinforcement through games or discussion. We, therefore, designed this study so that we could evaluate the effect on learning of (a) exposure of the children to *Barney* episodes alone and (b) exposure to the series episodes when viewing was followed by specially prepared half-hour lesson plans taught by the day care center caregivers. We had anecdotal evidence that preschoolers do pick up new material from simply watching at home (e.g., a 3-year-old who told us that she had learned from the *Barney* show that a "bunch of stars together" was a "constellation"). Nevertheless, there was good reason to believe that adult mediation often is critical for long-term effective learning (D. Singer & J. Singer, 1990; J. Singer & D. Singer, 1993a). One of our goals, then, was to develop lesson plans that could become resources for day care center teachers or parents seeking to build on the effects of sheer *Barney* exposure.

Our procedure involved choosing the 10 episodes from the 30 *Barney & Friends* episodes in the 100 series (the only ones that had aired when we began the study) that ranked highest in potential teaching features. We then exposed preschoolers to one of four conditions in their nursery schools or day care centers:

1. *Experimental Group A:* Viewing of the 10 *Barney & Friends* episodes over a 2-week period, but with viewing followed by a teacher "lesson" or set of exercises augmenting the material included in the episode

2. *Experimental Group B:* Viewing of the same 10 *Barney* episodes within a 2-week period with no teacher follow-up

3. *Control Group A:* A special group to control for *Barney*-related attention (the group was taught the *Barney* lesson plans prepared for Group A but with no exposure to the *Barney* episodes themselves in the classroom)

4. *Control Group B:* No exposure to *Barney* (these children simply followed the usual day care center routine)

Before the implementation of the experiment, all children were tested on a series of cognitive, emotional, social, health, nature, and multicultural awareness variables. Following the approximately 2 weeks of experimental conditions, all were retested to see whether there were any changes in knowledge on these measures. While the children were watching their daily *Barney & Friends* episodes, five in each of 2 weeks, we had assistants who observed the children as they viewed these episodes and who made notes on attention and affective reactions or motor responses. Our assistants also observed the teachers during the follow-up sessions to determine whether they had grasped the details of the lesson plans and were following them up appropriately. In summary, we sought to answer, at least to some extent, the following questions:

1. Do children exposed to 10 episodes of *Barney & Friends* in their preschools show gains in cognitive, affective, and social skills, at least as reflected in their knowledge of such issues (given that behavioral follow-ups were not practical)?

2. To what extent are gains greater when exposure is supplemented by adult teaching of material in the episodes?

3. In what areas of skills are gains evident, or are they apparent across the board for all of the readiness-to-learn variables we have identified?

4. Are gender or social class differences significant influences on children's learning after exposures to *Barney*?

5. To the extent that we were able to obtain records of home *Barney* viewing, does such prior experience play a role in the children's reactions to classroom *Barney* showings?

6. How do children react in the day care centers while actually watching the episodes? Are there great individual or group fluctuations of attention? Do the children seem directly responsive and interact with material being presented on the show? Are there special reactions to the music?

7. How do teachers in the day care centers respond to the children's watching of the show and to their subsequent behavior?

Procedure

Selection of *Barney & Friends* Episodes

Our first step was to identify the 10 episodes from all 30 of the first (100) series of aired *Barney* episodes that quantitatively demonstrated the best mix across the board of the major variables we would be examining: Cognitive Emotional Awareness, Social Attitudinal, Physical-Health/Safety, and Multicultural Awareness dimensions.

Although we chose the "richest" of the episodes (in part as a way of serving the schools that had agreed to participate), the differences in scores between these and the other 20 episodes are actually relatively slight given that the average number of teaching elements per show is more than 100.

Developing Lesson Plans

To provide teachers with suggested exercises that could supplement particular themes emphasized in each of the 10 episodes, we reviewed each episode in detail. Our intention was not to dictate a specific set of steps for teachers to follow but rather to identify categories within each *Barney & Friends* show that could serve as the basis for a follow-up game or exercise. Examples of such activities were provided. It was made clear to teachers, however, that they could use their own judgment and knowledge of the school's curriculum to supplement the material in *Barney* for the half hour of teaching immediately following each viewing. For example, one teacher, in following up the "Dr. Barney" episode, weighed and measured each child, pretended to listen to his or her heart with a toy stethoscope, and then gave each a "health certificate" she had prepared in advance.

The form of each lesson plan consisted of (a) a synopsis of the *Barney & Friends* episode, (b) objectives derived from the main themes of the episode (e.g., counting, number recognition, vocabulary), (c) new words to learn, (d) materials needed for each activity during the lesson, (e) questions and discussion ideas for the children about what they had seen, (f) descriptions of some specific activities (e.g., counting various objects, making musical instruments), and (g) books that could be read to the children after the *Barney* viewing.

Individual consent forms were obtained from parents for all children, and the general outline of the study was presented in a form that would preclude potential biasing effects. At the end of the study, each school received a small donation (although this had not been promised) and each child participant received a booklet titled *Barney's Hats*.

The preschools were located in New Haven, Connecticut, and its immediate suburbs. Because of the time constraints and limited number of observers and testers, our samples for this study and the preschools were drawn largely from a middle SES level where scores on a 4-point scale were $M = 1.97$ $(SD = 1.21)$.

Only children whose parents returned signed consent forms participated in the study in one of the four conditions. Arrangements were made with the schools to provide alternative activities for those children whose parents did not consent to participation. Fortunately, there were extremely few such instances. The data of children from foreign backgrounds whose English precluded effective testing were excluded from the statistical analyses, although they participated fully in the experiment. We had to conform to the wishes of the different school directors or teachers. Because of natural changes in teaching, there was a total of 120 participants with somewhat uneven numbers among our groups. Schools were somewhat more reluctant to engage in the teaching alone control condition (without *Barney & Friends* viewing), and so that group is not as well represented. There was a

very nearly equal balance of boys and girls with no significant differences in age, SES, the age of parents, or the number of older siblings
across all four groups. We also inquired about home television viewing
of *Barney*. About half of the children had watched the show at least
to some extent. There were no differences based on parents' reports
and children's comments in prior exposure to the show by experimental conditions. Our sample of children was predominantly composed
of white children of European descent. There were a few African
American, Asian American (Chinese or Indian), and Hispanic American children, who also were equally distributed across groups. In
general, the groups were, therefore, quite well balanced on the independent variables of relevance.

Measures

Our primary objective for this study was to determine whether
exposure of the children would lead to gains in the particular cognitive
or attitudinal skills we had identified earlier from our adult-rating
studies. We prepared a simple questionnaire designed to be appropriate for children between about 36 and 50 months of age, who made
up the great bulk of our sample. A group of primarily Yale undergraduate and graduate students were trained in administration of the tests
during practice sessions. Common definitions and suggestions about
establishing rapport with such young children were presented. Methods for nonleading question probes were provided. To avoid systematic bias effects, the testers generally were unaware of the children's
experimental or control group status, and different testers conducted
pre- and postexperiment interviews with the children.

The first phase of the testing was designed to establish rapport and
to obtain basic information on the children's favorite games and toys,
Barney & Friends exposure, and other television watching. The interview then moved into simple questions about numbers and counting,
identifying shapes and colors, common neighborhood activities or
locations (e.g., "Where do we borrow books?"), and identification of
occupations (e.g., "mail carrier"). A set of pictures of people expressing emotions sought to test children's ability to identify facial expressions. A series of questions about nature and ecology followed (e.g.,

"How do we keep our streets clean?," "What do we do with empty bottles, cans, or newspapers?"). Questions about good manners and civility then followed. The next group of questions involved basic issues of health and safety. Some very simple multicultural references came next (e.g., "Do you know the names of any languages besides English?"). Finally, a 10-item vocabulary test of words such as *map* and *campfire* was administered. These words were well above the level of 3- and 4-year-olds, but they had been defined on the *Barney* episodes to which some of the children were going to be exposed.

These questions were repeated about 3 to 4 weeks after the children had participated in one of the four experimental conditions. In effect, this test tapped into the readiness-to-learn areas that the *Barney & Friends* series addresses. What could not be known in advance was how well or poorly such young children would perform. A few items simply were too easy from the start and, thus, had no room for improvement. Others were too difficult to measure; for example, emotion identification, however well represented in the *Barney* series, turned out to be too difficult to measure accurately by the facial expressions we exposed to the children without context. All our questions were based on material that had been shown in a teaching fashion (e.g., identifying, modeling, labeling) in some of the 10 episodes. Some also had been touched on in the lesson plans. But the question remained: Would the children show any gains in these tests after exposure to the various conditions?

What Changes Occurred After *Barney & Friends* Viewing?

Following is a list of the specific 13 items for which we obtained quantitative measurements reflecting the variables under study:

A. Counting skills
   1. Free counting from 1 to as high as the child could count
   2. Counting the number of "shells" presented
   3. Matching written numbers to arrays of objects

B. Cognitive identification
   4. Shapes
   5. Colors

C. Vocabulary
   6. Defining words

D. Emotionality
   7. Identifying the emotions associated with the facial expressions

E. Social attitudes and civility
   8. Knowledge of neighborhood
   9. Identifying occupations
   10. Awareness of good manners

F. Nature and health
   11. Nature factors
   12. Health factors

G. Multicultural awareness
   13. Other languages and countries

We began our review of the results by first determining whether the children changed from pre- to postexperimental testing. The children were very young and had been unreliable in their responses to comprehension of the questions. These factors made it likely that the children may have, as a whole, shown no change or even gotten worse in their responses following the 3- to 4-week interval between pre- and posttesting.

If we consider the direction of changes before and after the study conditions, it is clear that the small Control Group A ($n = 11$), which received the lesson plans without the television viewing, showed a significant improvement on only 1 of the 13 measures. For Control Group B, which received no lessons or exposure to *Barney & Friends*, the children showed either no change or worse performance on the follow-up test for 5 of the 13 measures. By contrast, the *Barney* viewing plus teacher follow-up group showed significant gains on 8 of the 13 posttests. The children exposed only to *Barney* viewing without the lessons showed appreciable improvement on 6 of the 13 measures. The *Barney* plus teaching group showed some improvement on all 13 measures, although some changes were not statistically significant.

Clearly, the children who saw the *Barney & Friends* television episodes and had teacher follow-up consistently performed better on posttests. The group of children who saw *Barney* only followed

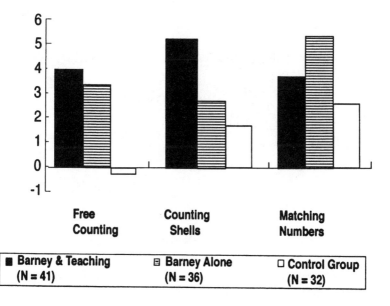

Figure 9.1. Normalized Pre- and Postchange Scores for Counting Skills by Experimental Groups

somewhat behind. These findings are statistically reliable by simple nonparametric tests. The *Barney* plus teaching group surpassed the control group in improvement scores on 10 of the 13 measures, as did the *Barney* viewing alone group.

We can now turn to some of the specific patterns of differences.[1] In counting skills, if we examine free counting, counting shells, and matching numbers, then it is clear from Figure 9.1 that the children exposed to *Barney & Friends* plus teaching made strong gains compared with the control group on each of the measures and that the *Barney* viewing alone group was superior on all three as well. For the next set of cognitive variables, identifying colors and shapes, the *Barney* plus teaching group was clearly superior on both conditions; the *Barney* viewing alone group was superior only on identifying colors. For the very critical measure of vocabulary, we found that the *Barney* plus teaching group made strong gains and was clearly superior to the control group, which actually was worse on the second try (see

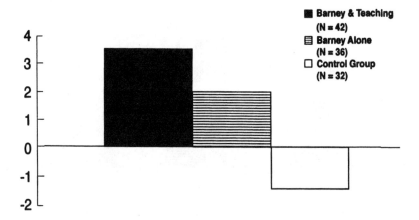

Vocabulary

Figure 9.2. Normalized Pre- and Postchange Scores for Vocabulary by Experimental Groups

Figure 9.2). The *Barney* viewing alone group was somewhat less strongly superior to the control group.

In the area of emotionality, our results were not supportive. This was the only variable on which an effect of this type occurred.

Of great importance is the issue of social attitudes and civility. In knowledge of the neighborhood, there was a clear superiority for both *Barney & Friends* plus teaching and *Barney* viewing alone. Identifying occupations did not show any effect for either of the *Barney*-exposed groups. Of considerable importance to our vantage point was the awareness of good manners or civility items. There were very strong effects for both *Barney* viewing conditions, as is typical, the strongest for the *Barney* plus teaching condition, followed by the *Barney* viewing alone condition (see Figure 9.3). Both were statistically reliable, showing gains much greater than those of the control group. In the area of nature, we did not find strong results for *Barney* plus teaching, although *Barney* viewing alone was definitely superior to the control group. In the area of awareness of health factors, both *Barney* viewing conditions were clearly superior to the control group. Finally, with respect to multicultural awareness, although both *Barney* viewing

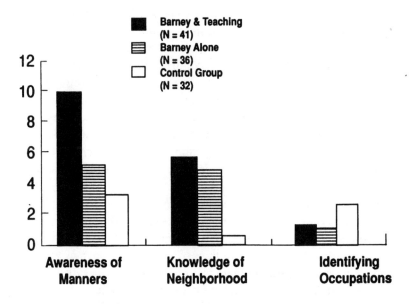

Figure 9.3. Normalized Pre- and Postchange Scores for Social Knowledge and Civility by Experimental Groups

groups were superior to the control group, the results were not very striking. This result is, we believe, in part a consequence of the fact that there was very little multicultural content in this first series of *Barney* episodes.

Figure 9.2 shows what we found to be the relatively typical pattern emerging from this study. It displays the gains in vocabulary made by the various groups. *Barney & Friends* plus teaching is a consistent leader on almost all the variables, followed by *Barney* viewing alone and then by the control condition with almost no change or an occasional loss.

What seems to emerge from our data is that exposure to 10 *Barney & Friends* episodes led children to increase their scores on cognitive variables such as counting and vocabulary, two fundamental school readiness skills, and on some important social awareness and civility measures. There also is some evidence of greater appreciation of issues of physical health. Although the teaching follow-up on the lessons generally led to better performance than did just viewing *Barney* alone, the sheer exposure to the televised episodes seems to be critical given that receiving lessons about the content without television exposure was essentially unsuccessful for that group of children. Considering all of the variability that such young children manifest, the consistency of the findings of a benefit from viewing *Barney* in the group setting of a preschool is impressive. We can surmise that home viewing alone or viewing with a mediating parent might yield even stronger benefits.

We followed up these results with various correlational analyses, factor analyses, and multiple regression analyses. We created independent variables based on demographics and on prior exposure at home to the *Barney & Friends* series.

The older children generally scored higher on most tests, as would be expected. They showed a trend toward seeming to gain more from the *Barney & Friends* plus teaching condition. As expected, girls generally performed better than boys on a few tasks, such as vocabulary and counting skills, but there was no general gender effect on the experimental outcome. Parental age occasionally was linked to higher initial scores on some of the variables for the children, but it proved to be irrelevant to the effects of the *Barney* classroom exposure. No effect of reported home viewing emerged.

We also were concerned with the way in which this large group of children responded as they watched *Barney & Friends* episodes. Here, of course, we are dealing only with children in those two conditions that saw *Barney* in the classroom. We obtained 65 observational reports from our team of the behavior of the children as they were watching *Barney*. In 53 of the 65 instances, we found descriptions of children clapping along with songs or swaying or dancing to music. We found 40 or more described instances of children mimicking on-screen physical, verbal, or musical activity or of children keeping time with their hands or feet, singing along to the opening theme, or showing enthusiastic comments and/or verbalized opinions. There were 24 observations in which children actively repeated words, phrases, or colors and 27 observations in which children were reported as laughing aloud at humorous skits or smiling broadly. Some degree of group inattentiveness was observed only 11 times during the 65 periods, and these most often were during the brief summaries when Barney comes out apparently to talk to the parents. Instances of negative affect were extremely rare.

A review of these observations makes it clear that there was a highly positive response to the viewing of the *Barney & Friends* episodes in the preschool setting. Based on many years of observing children watching a variety of shows, it was our opinion that preschool children showed, on the whole, a much more positive response to this series than to any other children's series we had studied directly. The level of continued attentiveness to the *Barney* episodes was much higher than we had seen previously. The children not only were "wide-eyed," as our observers reported, but also actively reacted to the show by singing along, even dancing as a group for certain episodes, and they clearly seemed to be following the "plot lines." Open imitation of material from time to time may lay the basis for effective learning. We know that an active rehearsal process helps in encoding and retaining new words and concepts. There were, of course, some variations from school to school. In one setting, children were seated in rows of chairs in theater fashion before a central wall-mounted television set. In others, they sat on the floor before a mobile set or on cushions in a casual fashion around the set. The more formally seated group surprisingly was *most* responsive to the viewing. The entire group of children rose from their seats and engaged in a rock and roll dance to one musical number about good manners. The overall enthusiasm of the children reflects the remarkable potency of the series' mix of music and dance. At the same time, it is clear from the observations that there also was a considerable response to the child characters beside Barney. Their names were called out frequently as they appeared.

The general positive feeling that characterized the children's responses to the show seems to these investigators to reflect a national phenomenon, a type of yearning of preschoolers for the good feeling and security offered by Barney and his child friends. To see as many as 10 or 12 child viewers holding hands, singing the *I Love You* song and embracing each other at the end of a viewing without adult coaxing (as has occurred in the dozens of observations), is a powerful message to us all.

We also questioned teachers at some length about their responses to the lesson plans and received reactions from 17 teachers or directors. It must be stressed that the teachers did not know all the details of the design, the specific items, or, of course, the scores of any of the children on the items. The teachers' comments were well summarized in one report: "*Barney* is a good show for children. It promotes love, friendship, kindness, and self-esteem and encourages children's use of their imagination. Each videotape has a central theme and is not a rapidly changing series of unrelated ideas."

Teachers made many favorable remarks about individual episodes, with "Carnival of Numbers," "Oh What a Day," and "Hola Mexico" singled out. They did feel that there ought to be more adult guests and more focused multicultural emphasis in this series. They were especially appreciative of the child characters and their behavior in episodes such as "Oh What a Day." Teachers reported that this episode actually evoked much follow-up discussion by the children about emotions during the school day.

■ A National Study of Poor and Minority Children's Responses to *Barney & Friends*

Objectives and Design

As mentioned earlier, the *Barney & Friends* show has been criticized from time to time in popular media as being too much oriented toward a white, middle-class audience. A study was designed, in part, to extend our sampling of children from the largely white, middle-class sample we had employed to test the learning possibilities of the *Barney* show. In the study that follows, we sought to broaden the range to day care centers that reflected a largely inner city or rural population of either minority children or poor white children. Accordingly, the study was conducted in five regions of the United States. We again chose New Haven but in this case focused on inner-city day care centers. We also included Atlanta, Georgia, where the inner-city population was largely African American; Columbus, Ohio, where there were inner-city whites from poor backgrounds, generally representing families from Appalachia; Tucson, Arizona, where the inner-city population consisted of a mixture of Hispanic American and some poor white and African American children (we also included children from day care centers on two Native American reservations in the Tucson area); and Los Angeles, where there were inner-city schools that included African American, Hispanic American, and some poor white children. In addition to geographic and cultural diversity in this study, by obtaining equal numbers of participants in each city, we could, in effect, replicate our New Haven findings five times over and accumulate a sizable number of participants.

National ratings indicate that the *Barney & Friends* television series is the most heavily viewed preschool show among inner-city minorities. The question of whether they can benefit from viewing in the format we had used in the first New Haven study was still open. We also redesigned the study slightly, taking account of some of our experience in carrying out the work with the middle-class sample.

The design of this study involved assigning children randomly in each day care center to one of three conditions: a *Barney & Friends* viewing plus teaching group (Group E_1), a *Barney* viewing only group (Group E_2), and a control group (Group C) that simply followed the normal preschool routine with the children being unaware of the exposure to *Barney* that other children received. Once again, we focused on a sample of 3- and 4-year-olds. Our experience from the earlier experiment had suggested that there was no evidence that the simple attention from the teachers coupled with teaching the same lesson plans without *Barney* viewing had an impact to compare with the combination of *Barney* viewing and teaching lessons or to *Barney* viewing alone, and so we eliminated this condition. Practical considerations of organizing the study in what turned out to be 25 different day care centers also played a role in our eliminating the teaching-only lesson plan condition.

Coordinators identified by professors at major universities in the five cities were brought together at Yale University. There, we and our television center staff provided several days of intensive training on the structure of the project, the types of children and preschool settings needed, the specific measures to be used to evaluate children's performance before and after the study, the training steps for testers and for teachers of the *Barney & Friends* lesson plans, and the collection and management of the data. Each of the five field coordinators, together with the local university faculty members and our national field coordinator, then identified appropriate settings. They also arranged, through these settings, for obtaining informed consent from parents to allow specific child participation. It also was necessary at each setting to select testers (generally psychology students with early childhood experience) and to train them for the specific measurement procedures to be used pre- and postviewing or for the control children. The coordinators also were trained in explaining the lesson plans to those teachers involved in that phase of the study, observing the teachers' use of the lesson plans, and observing the responses of the children who were actually watching the *Barney* episodes. Each participating school was visited personally by the authors and by our national field coordinator.

Approximately 2 weeks of pretesting of the children in each school was followed by 2 weeks of daily exposure to the half-hour *Barney & Friends* segments (for Groups E_1 and E_2). For Group E_1, the children were, as in the earlier study, exposed to a teacher going through a relevant *Barney* lesson plan after each segment. Our field staff in each city also observed the children's responses to each *Barney* viewing and recorded reactions on special scoring sheets. Coordinators also subsequently collected reports from the participating day care center staff members on their reactions to the *Barney* project and their observations of the children's responses. It should again be stressed that efforts were made to ensure that the testers were not themselves familiar with the particular condition in which a child had participated.

All the data from each city were then forwarded to Yale for scoring and data entry. This was a further check to avoid bias given that the scorers and raters of the interview and testing material at Yale had no knowledge of a child's group status (J. Singer & D. Singer, 1995).

The Participants

As indicated through the connections of the field coordinators in each city, it was possible to identify 25 preschools that were chiefly composed of children from poor or lower middle-class family backgrounds with a good mix of the minority groups available in the five cities. The original total of 530 children for whom we obtained parental permission to participate eventually was reduced by 56 because families moved or because children were removed from those schools, were absent during much of the experiment, or were, for some other reason, unavailable for pre- and posttesting. This loss of 10% of the sample is not uncommon in large field studies. Our

TABLE 9.5 Participants by Site, Gender, Ethnicity, and Condition

	Los Angeles	Tucson	Columbus	Atlanta	New Haven	Total
Number of subjects	85	107	94	81	107	474
Gender						
Boys	43	61	50	38	55	247
Girls	42	46	44	43	52	227
Ethnicity/race						
Caucasian	36	13	61	2	62	174
African American	30	4	32	78	34	178
Asian American	1	0	1	1	2	5
Hispanic	17	36	0	0	8	61
Native American	0	54	0	0	0	54
Other	1	0	0	0	1	2
Experimental condition						
Group E_1: *Barney plus teaching*	31	34	31	26	36	158
Group E_2: *Barney viewing alone*	25	34	33	33	36	161
Group C: *Control*	29	39	30	22	35	155

analyses showed that the children who could not participate were not systematically reflective of a particular ethnic or racial background or gender or came from a particular school. Our final sample consisted of 474 children. Table 9.5 provides a breakdown of city, gender, racial or ethnic status, and experimental condition.

As in previous studies, we followed the requirements of Yale's Human Investigations Committee, which had reviewed and approved the project. In addition to ensuring anonymity for all children, we were requested by many of the school directors to avoid any comparisons school by school, city by city, or across ethnic or racial minority groups. Thus, in reporting our data, we focus on a comparison of the experimental groups and do not attempt any further breakdowns. Although we had given no notice in arranging for the schools' participation, at the conclusion of the study, each school received a small monetary donation. A booklet, *Watch Play and Learn* (which teachers could use for further lesson plans about the *Barney* series), was given to each director. In addition, each child in each school (including those in the control group) received a *Barney & Friends* gift at the conclusion of the study.

Procedure

Selection of *Barney & Friends* Episodes

Because by this time the 200 series had been videotaped and was in the process of being aired and also had been scored by our team of developmentalists, we decided to mix the best of the 100 series with the new 200 series to produce 10 tapes for viewing by the children over a 2-week period. As it turned out, 5 tapes from each of the series emerged in the top 10 based on our ratings, and these were, therefore, employed in the series. New lesson plans had to be written for them.

Evaluating the Children's Skills and Knowledge

The critical data for this study are the test scores of the children before and after the exposures to *Barney & Friends*. We did change some of the questions based on our experience in the earlier study so that, for example, much more attention was given to trying to clarify the children's awareness of emotional experiences.

It is important to stress that, in training the testers at each of the cities, we conducted trial demonstrations to minimize leading questions, hinted answers, or tendencies to embarrass children for wrong answers. Methods of how to draw out shy children, how to follow up on vague answers, and how to give children every opportunity to demonstrate knowledge and skill were provided. The importance of fully recording children's responses or actions for each of the questions was stressed.

The number of specific items was increased to a total of 18. Based on the earlier study, we were especially curious to see whether the pattern would emerge of the greatest gains for the *Barney & Friends* viewing plus teaching condition (Group E_1) followed by *Barney* viewing alone (Group E_2) with only minimal gains evident for the control children (Group C), who simply followed the regular school routine.

Results

How Well Matched Were Our Groups?

The first question we needed to address was the degree to which random assignment of the children in each condition yielded comparable baseline findings. In this respect, we were quite fortunate, for no significant differences emerged either on demographic measures or on scores for the 18 critical variables tested quantitatively. For example, in simple counting ability, the average score for Group E_1 was 13.0, for Group E_2 was 13.1, and for Group C was 12.9. For ability to identify animals in the zoo, the average numbers correct in this particular question were 3.5, 3.6, and 3.8, respectively. In the extremely important area of vocabulary (i.e., knowledge of tested words that were drawn from *Barney & Friends* episodes prior to the onset of the experiment), Group E_1 scored 2.0, Group E_2 scored 1.8, and Group C scored 2.0. Our baseline data were almost identical for all three conditions of the study.

How Did Children Compare Subsequent to *Barney & Friends* Exposure on the Measures of the Study?

Data on 17 of the 18 questions showed that children from the *Barney & Friends* plus teaching condition made greater average increases than did the children in the control group. This result was highly statistically significant by a simple nonparametric test. For the group that saw *Barney* alone without teaching, there was only a modest advantage over the control group in this question-by-question comparison.

We also totaled the change scores for all 18 questions to get a single summary change score (Figure 9.4). This summary score indicates that *Barney & Friends* plus teaching showed an average overall gain of 9.6 points, whereas the control group gained 5.0 points just by following the school routine. The greater gain by Group E_1 is statistically reliable ($p = .001$). Children in the *Barney* viewing alone group gained 4.7 points and were not statistically different from those in the control group.

In effect, these data indicate that the *Barney & Friends* plus teaching children showed 92% greater improvement in performance than the

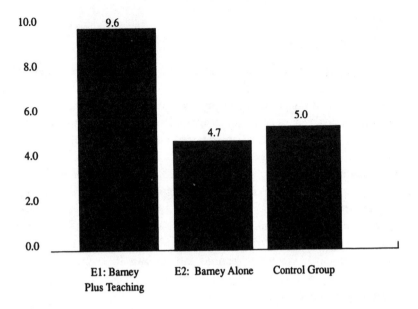

Figure 9.4. Total Change Scores From Pre to Post by Experimental Condition

children who simply followed the usual preschool routines in the 25 participating day care centers. The gains for the children who watched the *Barney* videotapes without teacher supplementation were less impressive, however. This is a striking difference from what we found in our earlier study on middle-class children. The general trend of the data is, on the whole, supportive of our early results in suggesting that classroom exposure to *Barney* can lead to improved performance with children from a broad national sample but with the special feature that some form of teacher follow-up of the lessons seems critical.

The questions, when further analyzed statistically, seem to cluster roughly into two groups: those items especially linked to verbal skills and those more related to performance/social skills. When we created separate statistical factor scores for each of the clusters, our results again pointed in each case to much greater gains for the *Barney & Friends* plus teaching condition in both verbal and performance/social domains. Of special importance are the gains made in the vocabulary test (see Figure 9.2). For this larger, more socially diverse sample, the children in the *Barney* plus teaching condition gained about twice as much as the control group with the *Barney* viewing alone condition intermediate, above the control group. This graphic pattern is very similar to the ones found for most variables in the earlier study.

The data we have presented so far reflect the averages across the full sample of 474 children from five different cities. One way of establishing reliability or potential replicability of the findings is to break down the sample and to determine whether comparable results emerge for the subcomponents of the total sample (Thompson, 1994). Results, city by city, showed findings comparable to the overall pattern already described. Two of the five cities yielded especially clear, statistically reliable results, whereas the findings in the three other cities showed essentially the same pattern of outcome, although there was some greater variability in the statistical significance of the findings.

One major disappointment in these data is the failure of the children in all the *Barney & Friends* viewing conditions to show strong gains in measures of knowledge of manners or civility. Such gains had been one of the clearest results of our earlier study with the middle-class children. In reviewing our results and the research process to try to explain the specific failure of replication, we reexamined our videotapes and lesson plans. It turned out that in combining videotapes from the 100 and 200 series, we had excluded a specific 100 series tape that had been featured in the middle-class study. This was "Splash Party," an episode that particularly emphasized good manners and courtesy. By simply using our quantitative overall scores as a basis for combining the two series, we neglected to examine the very high level of emphasis on good manners and courtesy in the "Splash Party" segment. By not including that episode, we may have weakened the impact of the series for this group of children. It may well be that despite the good manners that all the children in the program displayed in every episode, *reinforcement by adults* is crucial for the conveyance of such behavior patterns to children. Previous studies we had conducted indicated the importance of such adult mediations of television content by teachers or parents if, indeed, children are to internalize such concepts relating to civility (D. Singer & J. Singer, 1983).

In summary, children from predominantly poor and culturally diverse backgrounds exposed in their day care centers to 10 episodes of the *Barney & Friends* television series with the teaching follow-up by adult caregivers showed consistent score increases on readiness-to-learn questions when compared with children who were simply following the regular school routine. Children who watched the same *Barney* episodes without teacher follow-up showed some gains compared with controls, but such results were not as impressive as those observed in our earlier study with children from middle-class backgrounds.

Patterns of data were consistent across a variety of verbal and performance or social skills measures. The clearest results were apparent for the vocabulary test, which, as it so happens, is generally the best single measure of school readiness and achievement. The pattern shows twice as high gains in vocabulary for the *Barney & Friends* viewing plus teacher supplementation, followed by some gain for viewing alone and only slight gain for the controls, a finding comparable to that in our earlier study (see Figure 9.2).

What Factors Best Predict the Improvements Shown by Children in This Study?

To determine whether other factors beside the *Barney & Friends* viewing played any role in gains made by the children, we conducted hierarchical multiple regression analyses to estimate what combinations of variables best predicted the changes from pre- to posttesting in the children. Variables incorporated into these analyses included, in addition to age and gender, parental status, SES, degree to which the children had watched *Barney* at home before the experiment, and frequency of attendance for the *Barney* viewings (because some children missed a few episodes due to sickness). From this analysis, it is clear that neither the ages of the children nor their genders significantly influenced the gains. There was a trend for greater gains to be made by children from the lower or poorer social class backgrounds even within this generally lower SES group. Of greater importance was the children's parental status. Children from *two-parent* families in general made more gains from pre- to posttesting. Greater previous viewing of the *Barney* series did not affect the gains. The major predictor of improvements on total score shown by the children was the classroom exposure to the *Barney* videotapes, especially the *Barney* plus teaching condition. Sheer number of tapes viewed within the two experimental conditions did not make a difference, but almost all of the children saw at least eight episodes. Our analyses further support the major impact of the *Barney* plus teaching experience for these children.

Watching Children as They Watch *Barney & Friends*

Of the 319 children in our study who watched up to 10 episodes of *Barney & Friends* in their preschool settings, it was possible to have observers scoring every observation in all 25 schools. In many of these schools, Groups E_1 and E_2 watched together and then went to separate areas of the school so that the E_1 children could be exposed to the lesson plans. Thus, we ended with a total of 250 separate observation reports on children as they viewed the *Barney* episodes.

Our scoring sheets were comparable to those for our other studies. What emerged was a clear similarity between the data for these inner-city, poor children and the findings for the middle-class children. We found comparable rates of prolonged attention, positive emotionality, enthusiasm, and active cognitive processing such as repeating phrases, words, or numbers. Despite our anticipation of more disruptive or restless behavior and negative emotion, differences between those children and the other groups were slight. They scored higher in restlessness, but only minimally.

We personally took the opportunity to attend schools and to watch the *Barney & Friends* observations of children in a number of the different schools from the five cities around the country. The 3- and 4-year-old children seemed much more alike than different despite great variations in the quality, organization, and location of the day care centers in which they were observed. We watched the Native American children on the two Indian reservations included in our study, and it was impressive to note the way in which they responded so positively to the *Barney* episodes and were clearly able to follow and react to the rather traditional suburban middle-class "look" of the episodes. With respect to reactions of the children to individual episodes, it was possible quantitatively from our analyses to show significant variability in the domains of attention, cognitive response, and positive emotionality across episodes. Thus, episodes such as "A Carnival of Numbers" and "The Alphabet Zoo" evoked especially strong responses in the cognitive area, whereas "My Favorite Things," "Hola Mexico," and "Hi Neighbor!" elicited especially high positive emotional responses from the child viewers. We found that the children's reactions to the different episodes roughly mirrored the adult panels' ratings of the relative cognitive, emotional, and musical teaching emphases of the episodes.

Teachers' Responses

It was apparent that the physical characteristics and the organization of the premises for the schools did not vary greatly. As many as five of the schools had especially large and attractive physical settings, but none of the others seemed excessively cramped for space or appeared in any way messy, unsafe, or physically unappealing. All were attractively decorated with children's artwork, child-oriented pictures or cartoons, cultural artifacts, or mottos or diagrams about good health or safety. In this respect, we were much impressed with the leadership shown by the directors of the centers.

Much more variable were the relative professionalism, curricular skills, and enthusiasm of the teachers. Some showed considerable creativity, energy, and psychological sensitivity and demonstrated a good deal of ongoing verbal interaction with the children. This was especially evident for those few teachers who were somewhat better educated and had advanced early childhood training backgrounds. Most of the teachers were extremely well meaning, careful, and attentive, but they did not manifest great verbal skills. A few seemed little more than responsible but inarticulate baby-sitters. Our experiences in visiting these schools led us to the belief that national efforts to enhance readiness-to-learn skills through day care center interventions, with or without television materials, would depend heavily on how much our society is willing to invest in more extensive early childhood worker training. Without a serious effort to enhance the professionalism of the field, the educational goals of day care training may be put in jeopardy.

Our observers made diagrams of the ways in which teachers approached the lesson plans. At the beginning of the 10 *Barney & Friends* episodes, most followed the suggested guidelines quite closely. Apparently as the teachers became more used to the procedure of employing lesson plans, they showed somewhat greater variation (and, one might even add, creativity) in their application of these lesson plans in the teaching follow-up for *Barney*. What the teachers added to what we saw in our observational reports was the *persistence* of the reactions in free play. They also reported spontaneous follow-up of sharing, cooperation, and "cleanup" singing as well as a reported reduction of overt aggression and of violent play themes.

In summary, the data from this much larger study essentially replicate the findings from the middle-class sample of children with respect to showing gains for those children exposed to *Barney & Friends* with follow-up for about a half hour on the key content areas by the teachers. In this sense, the viewing of a carefully developed program that combines entertainment and education can be of considerable value in the curriculum of a day care center as part of the effort to meet readiness-to-learn goals. Such material can be valuable for children who come to day care settings from a range of socioeconomic backgrounds or ethnic groups. The possibility of supplementing school viewing by home viewing opportunities with follow-up by parents or other home caregivers is strongly suggested. A follow-up or adult mediation seems to be especially critical for children from poorer backgrounds.

■ **The Educational Limits of *Barney & Friends*:**
The Kindergarten Study

Another approach to evaluating the *Barney & Friends* series' educational potential is to consider what might be called the upper limits of the educational potential of the program. Therefore, we conducted a study with 74 children who were attending a kindergarten in a small industrial city in the New Haven region. These children were generally from lower-middle-class, blue-collar backgrounds. The study was an exact replication of the study done in New Haven with the middle-class sample of children. We used the same four conditions as in that study, again employing the teaching of the lesson plans without exposure of *Barney* for one group of children in kindergarten. It soon became apparent that the kindergarten children were already scoring so high on the pretests as to create what might be called a ceiling effect. In other words, the type of material we had developed that we thought could be taught through the *Barney* episodes was already largely available to children who were by now nearly 5½ years of age. Their scores did not show the degree of variability that would permit evaluations across the four groups for sufficient improvement from pre- to posttest. The observational scores indicated that the children responded to the show as wholesome entertainment and indeed demonstrated some positive modeling opportunities while viewing and immediately afterward. The children, however, had to some degree grown up with *Barney* and, more so than in the other studies we conducted, were initially more familiar with the material and found it somewhat less novel and intriguing.

The observational behavior of the 5½-year-olds in this study indicated considerable similarity to the behavior of the 3- and 4-year-olds while they were watching with the exception of somewhat more restlessness and suggestions of boredom in the older children. There still was evidence that, like the preschoolers, they had some difficulties in differentiating fantasy figures from the children in the series, and they did not seem to have a sense of how Barney goes from being a stuffed toy at the outset to becoming the giant dinosaur that he represents throughout most of an episode. This is where a recommendation to the producers of the show can be useful in the planning of future episodes so that more attention can be given to explaining real, pretend, or fantasy/reality elements.

Data on child viewing indicate that the *Barney & Friends* series is indeed viewed by a significant number of children 5 to 7 years of age. The program may, therefore, continue to be entertaining, and it may well also convey useful educational material that we were not able to tap from the tests we had developed or to enhance by the lesson plans we had developed. It is, nevertheless, our judgment from the extensive observations we made of the large range of children in our various studies that, somewhere in the 6th year of life, children are moving beyond what the *Barney* series can offer educationally. That it remains an entertaining show even for this age group is clear, however.

■ A Study of Toddlers Watching *Barney & Friends*

Why Study Toddlers?

In general, we do not recommend to parents that children below 2 years of age watch television or videos. In these preverbal first years of life, it is crucial that they bond visually, orally, and tactilely with the "real" caregivers in their environment and that they develop the critical face-to-face interactive communication skills that are the foundations of language development. According to statistics from the *Barney & Friends* fan club, in 1995 more than 220,000 parents signed up their 2-year-olds, and this number comprised 27% of the total fan club membership. Given the reality of such early television viewing of the *Barney* series, our objective in the following study was to examine how 2-year-olds responded to the episodes. We asked whether a half-hour *Barney* episode could hold the attention of toddlers watching in their preschool or day care setting. We also wanted to observe the degree to which toddlers showed attentiveness, interest, and appropriate reactivity comparable to that which we observed in hundreds of 3- to 5-year-olds we had studied. We also were intrigued to determine whether regular watching over a short period might yield evidence of later socially appropriate or constructive spontaneous behavior of the viewers, even though, at this age, they are just about walking and are largely nonverbal. To the extent that the *Barney* series does emphasize the relatively carefully paced communication pattern, we thought that perhaps certain civilities of behavior (e.g., politeness, nonaggression) also might be manifested in the postviewing behavior of the children. We also were curious as to whether the emphasis on pretend play might be reflected in some of the actions of the toddler viewers after viewing.

Some Specific Expectations

The beginning of the 3rd year of a child's life is generally characterized by a rapid acceleration of motor skills such as walking, climbing, and manipulating objects. It also is a period of escalation in comprehension and in production of speech. The security of bipedalism and of receptive and productive language that characterizes this period also is associated with a liveliness, vigor, and curiosity that often is wonderful to behold. It is the period in which children try more than they can accomplish and also learn for the first time to say "no" by gesture or word. What might we expect from a toddler's exposure to *Barney & Friends* episodes? Our earlier research showed children to increase their levels of imaginative play through exposure to *Mister Rogers' Neighborhood* (J. Singer & D. Singer, 1976; Tower et al., 1979). Very little research of that type for toddlers is available. Thus, we had little precedent for establishing formal hypotheses.

We were, first of all, curious about whether toddlers could sit quietly for an entire *Barney & Friends* episode and whether they could show an attentiveness and, to some degree, indicate appropriate reactions to what they were watching. Such reactions would be apparent in laughing or smiling as related to what happened on the television monitor, singing along as best they could to the musical sequences, clapping, dancing, and imitating gestures or, in a very limited way, spoken words. By using the observation coding sheets, teams of trained observers watched the children every day over the 10 viewings to ascertain reaction patterns. On completion of the episodes, we had observer teams, previously trained, record what the children did on their own in spontaneous activities. Carrying on interviews or tests with the children seemed largely impractical because they were relatively nonverbal at that age. Instead, we looked specifically for evidence of imaginative play (as primitive as such activities may be for such an age), signs of cooperation with peers or adults, and indications of overt aggressive behavior or negative emotions such as anger, sadness, or distress. It was important for us to have a control group also observed by teams unaware whether the children had seen *Barney* in school earlier. A comparison of the ratings of the play of the control children could serve as an indication of a possible impact of *Barney* viewing on the behavior of the experimental group toddlers who had watched the episodes. Our general expectations were that those toddlers exposed to *Barney* would prove to show at least some greater evidence of imagination, somewhat less aggressive behavior, and perhaps more positive social and affective stances.

Research Design and Participants

We were able to obtain parental consent to show the 10 episodes of *Barney & Friends* (those employed in the national study) daily over a 2-week period to a group of 11 toddlers whose average age was 27.7 months. The control group also consisted of 11 toddlers whose average age was 27.3 months. By various means, we arranged for separation of the children so that we could observe the toddlers' free play activities. The control group had not seen *Barney* just before free play, whereas the experimental group had seen the episode. Groups were equally matched in gender and demographic characteristics. We also obtained reports from the parents about the level of children's language abilities, their favorite toys and activities, and the extent of their television viewing. Scoring procedures while viewing were essentially carried out in much the manner that has been described in the previous studies. Scoring of behavior focused on variables that have been studied extensively in some of our earlier observational research with children (see J. Singer & D. Singer, 1981). These included the variables such as imaginativeness of play, persistence, and aggression. Videotaped samples of children's play from other studies were employed in training the observers who rated these variables. A number of training sessions were carried out until we could obtain a high concordance of staff ratings for the behaviors presented on tape. Observations of each toddler participant in the experimental group were conducted simultaneously by two observers for a 10-minute period at two points in time within each of the phases of the study. Similarly, observations of each toddler participant in the control group were conducted simultaneously by two observers at two points in time within both the pre- and postviewing phases of the study.

It was important to determine that our observers showed independent agreement in their ratings. For imagination, we found an average of $r = .91$ on the scores, for persistence an average of $r = .96$, and for aggression an average of $r = .76$.

Results for Toddlers Watching *Barney & Friends*

For this sample of 11 lower middle-class children, scores for attentiveness were only slightly lower (an average of 10.3 instances per episode) than those we had found for our 3- and 4-year-olds. The toddlers showed comparable ratings to our reports for the national study in terms of positive emotionality. More negative affective instances were recorded—approximately five per episode, which was higher than the number found for the older children we had been studying but not really very different. Scores for music also were quite similar to those of the older children.

Another way of breaking down the responses of the children was to look at their reactions to specific episodes of the 10 that were presented. Of the 10 episodes, 3 could be identified as having evoked strongly positive responses. None of the episodes could be identified as having evoked a strong negative reaction from the toddlers. In general, the toddlers showed a surprising level of positive responsiveness, attention, and even cognitive reactivity to the *Barney & Friends* episodes. The strong response to a particular episode, "Red, Blue, and Circles Too," reflected a prominence of Baby Bop in that episode. Baby Bop's behavior is intended to resemble that of a toddler, and it evoked a strong reaction from the viewing children. In another episode, "Hi Neighbor!", Derek, one of the cast, wears a false mustache that causes him to sneeze while he pretends to be an Italian chef. This evoked considerable laughter, as well as imitation of the sneezing, from the preschoolers. The "Red, Blue, and Circles Too" episode of Baby Bop playing a mischievous role evoked considerable laughter from the children. A scene in which Barney exclaims "peekaboo" while looking through Baby Bop's hula hoop also evoked a considerable response. As expected, the greatest distractibility shown by the toddlers came in episodes where either there was generally a more disconnected pattern to the goings-on or they became stimulated by lively music and movement but at the same time could not follow the language being used (as in the case of the "Hola Mexico" episode).

How Did the Toddlers Behave After Viewing
Barney & Friends in Comparison With the Control Children?

Although the numbers in this study were too small to permit highly refined analyses of the quantitative observational data in the 10-minute periods observed after the *Barney & Friends* viewings, the general thrust of the results was very clear. The children in the experimental group showed more signs of imaginative play than did those in the control group. They also were rated lower in aggressive behavior than were the children in the control group. When we combined variables such as persistence and cooperation, all exemplifying socially appropriate behaviors, we found more evidence of such responses in the children who had just watched the *Barney* episodes than in the control group children, who had not seen them. Because these schools had a strongly constructive curriculum in general, we did not find any difference in positive emotionality between the control and experimental children.

In summary, exposure to the *Barney & Friends* episodes for the 11 toddlers in this study yielded indications that the children who watched *Barney* may have benefited in areas of showing somewhat greater inclination to symbolic play, showing less anger or aggressive behavior, and showing some indications of more socially appropriate actions. If we keep in mind that the best results from our earlier research with the 3- and 4-year-old samples emerged when the *Barney* viewings were extended through follow-up lessons by the teacher, any findings by 2-year-olds based *only* on *Barney* viewing are impressive.

Correlates of Toddlers' Behavior and Variables of Gender, Age, and Home Viewing of Television

Some of our most interesting results in the study came when we considered the background variables linked to the overt behavior of the toddlers combining both experimental and control groups. Although there were no differences for the genders, we did, of course, find major results for age. Even within the limited range of ages in this 2-year-old sample, it turned out that age correlated significantly with imaginative play ($r = .41$, $p = .05$), persistence ($r = .52$, $p = .01$), interaction with peers ($r = .75$, $p < .001$), and cooperation with peers ($r = .43$, $p < .05$). Older 2-year-olds also were reported as watching more television ($r = .43$). In general, our data captured the very rapid growth of changes that characterized this age group even within the limited range around our mean of 27 months.

One of the strongest associations that emerged was a negative correlation between television viewing by the children (with or without parent coviewing) and imaginative play. Thus, hours of television viewing by children was correlated with imaginative play as reported by the observers ($r = -.43$, $p = .05$). This result, to the best of our knowledge, has never been reported previously with so young a group. It does conform to our earlier findings with older preschoolers (D. Singer & J. Singer, 1980; J. Singer & D. Singer, 1981). We have found that early heavy television viewing may preempt children's opportunity to develop and to practice skills in pretending through natural floor play. Because for the toddlers in this study imaginative play and television viewing both were positively correlated with age, we partialed age out from the correlation. This yielded an even stronger finding of a partial correlation of $r = -.53$ ($p = .01$) between television viewing and the signs of imaginative play reported by the observers for our 22 children.

Heavier television viewing (with or without parents) was positively associated with more aggressive behavior in the toddlers as reported by the observers and also was strongly correlated with more displays of anger by the children during play ($r = .58, p < .0005$). In addition, we found that children who showed more negative emotions also were reported as watching more television at home. However, home viewing of *Barney & Friends* was not associated with any of these negative behavioral trends, nor was the indication from parents' reports that *Barney* was their children's favorite show. The only other striking result that was obtained was a strongly positive relationship between favorite home viewing of *Mister Rogers' Neighborhood* and a number of positive outcomes, most notably imaginative play ($r = .58$, $p < .005$) and cooperation with peers ($r = .33, p = .12$)—again, a result confirming our earlier studies on this particular show with older preschoolers. Of special interest, and in confirmation of our earlier research (D. Singer & J. Singer, 1990), was a finding hitherto not reported for toddlers. Children who played more imaginatively also were reported by observers as showing more positive emotionality such as smiling, laughing, or excitement ($r = .63, p < .001$).

Because of their lack of linguistic expressiveness, toddlers are a difficult group to study, especially in relation to their capacity to respond to particular types of video exposure. Our data provided good evidence that children whose average age was 27 months could show relatively frequent periods of concentrated attention while watching the half-hour episodes of *Barney & Friends*. They also showed reasonable evidence of grasping certain cognitive details from the episodes through their actions, and they were quite responsive to the music, particularly the tunes that are generally sung by parents or caregivers for toddlers. They showed numerous signs of enjoyment throughout the series. Our small number of participants precluded very strong findings for the more experimental phase of this study. The results in general confirmed our expectations that although toddlers are just at the beginning of engaging in pretend play, the *Barney* series' emphasis on pretending might stimulate some acceleration of this ability in toddlers. The data supported these expectations. Those children who were exposed to the series did manifest higher levels of make-believe play than did the control group. We also were fortunate enough to observe actual processes of imaginative transformation following a *Barney* episode, as demonstrated by one of our experimental group participants. A little girl first sat herself squarely at the front of a large box-like wooden bus in the playroom and, subsequently, declared that everyone in the area should "climb aboard." She then took the steering wheel front of the bus and began manipulating it in driver-like fashion as other children joined her on the bus. Moments later, she announced it was about to rain and so burst into a rendition of "Rain, rain, go away . . ." as she removed the steering wheel from the bus and propped it above her head as if it was an umbrella shielding her person from the elements. She then placed the umbrella back into the wooden structure and yelled again, "All aboard!" It is significant to note that only minutes later, after singing a number of the usual day care center songs, she finished with *I Love You,* the well-known closing song from the *Barney* show. She soon was joined by the rest of the children as if they all were participating in the closing to an actual episode of *Barney.*

Although we cannot recommend that toddlers watch much television, it is clear that viewing just a small amount of the *Barney* show in a day care setting may indeed be associated with some acceleration in developing imaginative play skills. Such viewing also may serve in furthering more constructive behaviors and in reducing or minimizing aggressive behaviors. We also suggest the importance of careful restriction and monitoring of children's home viewing. This study brought out, for the first time, evidence that heavier home viewing by such young children with or without parents is associated with signs of more aggressive or angry behavior by children in free play in day care centers. At the same time, the demonstration that watching *Barney & Friends* or that home viewing of *Mister Rogers' Neighborhood* both are associated with more constructive behavior by the children in day care centers suggests that selective and limited television viewing may not be harmful and may actually be of some help in steering children in a more constructive direction.

■ Acquiring Verb Meanings and Forms From
  Watching *Barney and Friends*: The Language Study

The final study of this series was carried out as a collaboration between Letitia Naigles, a Yale psycholinguist, and her laboratory group working with our own staff. Because this study is reported in technical detail elsewhere (Naigles et al., 1995), we offer only a brief description of the method and results.

Can Children Learn Verb Meanings and
Verb Forms From Watching *Barney & Friends*?

One of the issues that has emerged in the very few studies that have been conducted of children's learning through watching television has been the question of whether they can acquire subtleties of verb structure and usage from the television medium. In the few studies available on learning words and language functions from watching television, it has been found that when children watch programming in which the words are presented with careful demonstrations, slowness of pace, and the melodic types of vocal emphasis that adults use when talking to children, gains in noun vocabulary are possible (Rice, 1983; Rice, Huston, Truglio, & Wright, 1990). One might think that clear presentation of certain types of actions or movements on television would have an impact on the learning of verb forms, but this has not been demonstrated from regular television programming (Naigles & Kako, 1993). In this study, therefore, we sought to determine whether children between 3 and 5 years of age could increase their understandings of verbs after exposure (without adult mediation) to 10 episodes of *Barney & Friends* in their day care centers.

We chose two types of acquisition of verb meanings and grammatical structure: the ability of the children to discriminate mental state verbs (specifically *think, guess,* and *know*) and the grammatical usages of the transitive verbs *come* and *go*. The mental state verbs differ in degrees of certainty, and there is research evidence that somewhere between 4 and 5 years of age, children are able to understand that saying "I know the toy isn't in that box" indicates a clear certainty, whereas "I think it is" or "I guess it is" both have strong elements of uncertainty. Similarly, in the case of intransitive verbs, children gradually learn that *come* and *go* cannot take an object in the same way that *bring* and *take* can (e.g., "I bring the toy tiger here," "I take the toy elephant and put it on the toy Noah's Ark").

We sought to determine whether, with exposure to the *Barney & Friends* series, where words are presented with relative clarity and where a teaching focus is emphasized as we have already discussed, children would learn more clearly the subtler distinctions among the mental state verbs. They would also come to realize that one could not say "I come the toy tiger to the ark" or "I go the toy elephant . . ." even though prior sentences have used the *frame* correctly (e.g., "I bring the tiger . . . ," "I take the elephant . . .").

Procedure

We studied 50 children whose average age was 48.5 months (SD = 7.4, range = 36-66). Using the same format as in our earlier studies, an experimental group watched the *Barney & Friends* show daily for 10 episodes with no teacher mediation. The children were pretested by established game procedures to demonstrate whether they could discriminate among *think, guess,* and *know* as well as whether they could use the verbs *come* and *go* correctly even after an adult presented them incorrectly as transitive verbs (e.g., "I come the elephant out of the ark").

The posttests were carried out following the 10 days of viewing *Barney & Friends,* and then the control group had the opportunity to observe the 10 episodes of *Barney.* Posttesting was again carried out for the former experimental group and the new group that had observed *Barney* at the end of the 10 viewings. Thus, we were able to observe effects over time.

Results

Findings can be summarized briefly. The children seemed in general to improve their ability to use intransitive verbs correctly after exposure to the *Barney & Friends* episodes. They demonstrated that they could recognize the special sentence structure limits of words such as *come* and *go* after having watched *Barney* episodes in which such words were used correctly.

More surprising, however, were the results for the mental state verbs. Although evidence that children in the control group by 4 years of age were beginning to learn the distinctions among *think, guess,* and *know,* those children exposed to *Barney & Friends* actually demonstrated a *blurring* of this distinction. This led us to a detailed examination, episode by episode, of the actual ways in which the three mental state verbs were used in *Barney.* It turned out that the correct distinction was not made by the children or by Barney on the show. The detailed content analysis suggested that the cast's usage of the three words took on a natural colloquial form rather than a precise semantic form. Our child participants were in effect led away from the formal usage toward a more colloquial or socially natural style.

The method we employed in this study of actually counting the ways in which verb forms were used by the various speakers, although tedious, nevertheless demonstrates another way in which program content can be evaluated in future studies. Such program content does indeed influence what children retain and, later on, how they use language.

■ Some Conclusions From Our Studies of *Barney & Friends*

Methodological Implications

Our studies have suggested the importance of detailed content analyses and judgments by adults with special training in agreed-on definitions. The significance of learning potential on an array of variables ranges from cognitive to multicultural awareness. Of special importance, we believe, is producers' emphasis on social attitudes, courtesy, and civility. This is particularly important because much of the adult programming viewed by children in the evening hours is characterized by attempts at "realism" that are likely to reinforce tendencies for not only "bad language" but also impulsivity, abruptness, and, of course, anger and aggression.

In addition to detailed content analyses, we have shown that actual word counts of particular words or concepts may be related to the type of learning shown by the children, especially in the area of language. We also have pointed to the importance of careful observations of how children watch programming. It may be possible in future studies to relate specific patterns of viewing to acquisition, retention, and later usage of words and concepts presented in the programming. The importance of experimental intervention is necessary if we attempt to suggest causal statements. A report by Wright and Huston (1995) sought to evaluate longer term effects on some of the same types of variables we have reported here based on home viewing of preschoolers. Their data indicate that viewers of *Sesame Street* and other public broadcasting educationally focused series can yield increases in verbal skills. In their longitudinal study, they found, as we reported in our own research, that the strongest effects usually came with the younger children. Wright and Huston also called attention to the fact that watching educational television may not be sufficient and that, as our studies indicate, day care teachers' or adult caregivers' follow-up is critical even though some learning can also be seen simply by watching.

Implications for Children's Television Programming

The results of our studies—the earlier ones with the *Mister Rogers' Neighborhood* show and this series with *Barney & Friends*—and the recent report by Wright and Huston (1995) highlight a major message to well-meaning children's programmers. Television programming can play a significant role in providing children with opportunities for acquiring school readiness skills. The use of real people as well as fantasy characters in the episodes is extremely important in this process. The children in the *Barney* show not only demonstrate courteous and friendly behavior to each other but also explain and demonstrate words, counting, and other concepts for the viewing preschoolers. Producers' beliefs that they must rely on cartoons and animation is not supported by our data and especially not by the findings of Wright and Huston. *Sesame Street, Mr. Rogers' Neighborhood,* and *Barney & Friends* all make use of fantasy settings from time to time but refer to them as imagination and make-believe rather than blending them casually with real people. *Barney* has demonstrated that there can be lively stories, colorful settings or costumes, music, and even some degree of tension and drama while at the same time words, procedures, and attitudes are clearly mediated or explained at a pace children can grasp. Perhaps we need a new type of aesthetic in video cinematography. It might be called the art of making beautiful and intriguing pictures geared to the cognitive level of the viewing audience.

A critical feature in producing educational programming is to recognize that it must be supplemented by adult follow-up in some form. Lesson plans, curricular guides, games, and other materials that can be used following the children's viewing may help parents and teachers of preschoolers to enhance the impact of the shows. As part of the *Barney & Friends* series of studies, we carried out a demonstration workshop for operators of home day care, that is, individuals who take up to five children into their own homes as a form of early child monitoring. Home day care operators are much more likely than nursery schools to use television (J. Singer & D. Singer, 1993b). Demonstrating to them how they could use programs such as *Mister Rogers' Neighborhood, Sesame Street,* and *Barney & Friends* came as a revelation to the large group that attended (D. Singer & J. Singer, 1995). We would argue that if television is to play a role in the ready-to-learn movement, much greater effort must be made to involve those individuals with limited child training and formal education who do take children into their homes. Producers must be ready to provide materials for home day care operators as well as parents.

■ A Final Word About the *Barney & Friends* Series

Perhaps a sociologist will examine in greater detail why the *Barney & Friends* program, once aired on public television, became a national phenomenon. Passing through stores, we could hear children from all socioeconomic backgrounds and ethnic groups talking about Barney and pointing to representations of Barney or to the various soft toy products reflecting Barney. We could hear children as they walked along singing the much-repeated introductory or closing songs from *Barney.* We have come to believe that the continuous references to love, good feeling, courtesy, and the "sweetness and light" demonstrated by Barney and the characters on the show have touched a deep vein of need in preschool children and even toddlers. We can attest from our observations to the ways in which Barney and his delightful cast have fostered a sense of "secure attachment" in their child audience. In view of so many fragmented families and children out of necessity raised in varying types of day care arrangements, the stability and direct expression of love from this show seems highly desirable. From some nursery schools in affluent neighborhoods to inner-city Head Start programs or day care settings on Native American reservations, children all have watched the series eagerly and have sung together the *I Love You* song at the end. Is there a lesson for all of us in this vast outpouring of affection by child viewers?

■ Note

1. The *Barney* lessons alone without television exposure group demonstrated, for our purposes, that combined teacher attention plus lessons had minimal impact. Because of the much smaller *n* for this group, we do not include it in further discussion or in the figures.

■ References

Ball, S., & Bogatz, G. A. (1970). *The first year of Sesame Street: An evaluation*. Princeton, NJ: Educational Testing Service.

Ball, S., & Bogatz, G. A. (1971). *The second year of Sesame Street: A continuing evaluation*. Princeton, NJ: Educational Testing Service.

Boyer, E. (1991). *Readiness to learn: A mandate for the nation*. Princeton, NJ: Carnegie Council for the Advancement of Teaching.

Bruner, J. (1986). *Actual minds, possible worlds*. Cambridge, MA: Harvard University Press.

Cook, T. D., Appleton, H., Conner, R. F., Shaffer, A., Tamkin, G., & Weber, S. J. (1975). *"Sesame Street" revisited*. New York: Russell Sage.

Desmond, R., Singer, J. L., & Singer, D. G. (1990). Family mediation: Parental communication patterns and the influences of television on children. In J. Bryant (Ed.), *Television and the American family* (pp. 293-309). Hillsdale, NJ: Lawrence Erlbaum.

Friedrich, L., & Stein, A. H. (1973). Aggressive and prosocial television programs and the natural behavior of preschool children. *Monographs of the Society for Research in Child Development, 38*(4, Serial No. 151).

Friedrich-Cofer, L., Huston-Stein, A., Kipnis, D., Susman, E., & Clewett, A. (1979). Environmental enhancement of prosocial play and self-regulation in a natural setting. *Developmental Psychology, 13*, 637-646.

Huston, A. C., Wright, J. C., Rice, M. L., Kerkman, D., & St. Peters, M. (1990). The development of television viewing patterns in early childhood: A longitudinal investigation. *Developmental Psychology, 26*, 409-420.

Naigles, L., & Kako, E. (1993). First contact: Biases in verb learning with and without syntactic information. *Child Development, 64,* 1665-1687.

Naigles, L. R., Singer, J. L., Singer, D. G., Jean-Louis, B., Sells, D., & Rosen, C. (1995). Barney and Friends *as education and entertainment—The language study: Barney says, "come, go, think, know."* Hartford: Connecticut Public Broadcasting.

Rice, M. L. (1983). The role of television in language acquisition. *Developmental Review, 3,* 211-224.

Rice, M. L., Huston, A. C., Truglio, R., & Wright, J. C. (1990). Words from "Sesame Street": Learning vocabulary while viewing. *Developmental Psychology, 26,* 421-428.

Singer, D. G., & Singer, J. L. (1980). Television viewing and aggressive behavior in preschool children: A field study. *Annals of the New York Academy of Sciences, 347,* 289-303.

Singer, D. G., & Singer, J. L. (1983). Learning how to be intelligent consumers of television. In M. Howe (Ed.), *Learning for television: Psychological and educational research* (pp. 203-222). New York: Academic Press.

Singer, D. G., & Singer, J. L. (1990). *The house of make-believe: Children's play and the developing imagination.* Cambridge, MA: Harvard University Press.

Singer, D. G., & Singer, J. L. (1995). *Readying children for school through brief exposure to television segments from* Barney and Friends, Mister Rogers' Neighborhood, *and* Sesame Street: *A report on workshops for day care teachers and family home care providers.* Hartford: Connecticut Public Broadcasting.

Singer, D. G., Singer, J. L., & Sells, D. (1995). Barney and Friends *as education and entertainment: Content analysis of series "300."* Hartford: Connecticut Public Broadcasting.

Singer, J. L., & Singer, D. G. (1976). Fostering creativity in children: Can TV stimulate imaginative play? *Journal of Communication, 26,* 74-80.

Singer, J. L., & Singer, D. G. (1981). *Television, imagination, and aggression: A study of preschoolers.* Hillsdale, NJ: Lawrence Erlbaum.

Singer, J. L., & Singer, D. G. (1993a). Barney and Friends *as education and entertainment: Phase 1, Study 1.* New Haven, CT: Yale University Family Television Research and Consultation Center.

Singer, J. L., & Singer, D. G. (1993b). *A role for television in the enhancement of children's readiness to learn: In preparation for a report to the Congress of the United States.* New Haven, CT: Yale University Family Television Research and Consultation Center.

Singer, J. L., & Singer, D. G. (1994). Barney and Friends *as education and entertainment: Phase 2—Can children learn through preschool exposure to* Barney and Friends? New Haven, CT: Yale University Family Television Research and Consultation Center. (Report available from Connecticut Public Television, Hartford)

Singer, J. L., & Singer, D. G. (1995). Barney and Friends *as education and entertainment: Phase 3—A national study: Can children learn through preschool exposure to* Barney and friends? New Haven, CT: Yale University Family Television Research and Consultation Center. (Report available from Connecticut Public Television, Hartford)

Singer, J. L., Singer, D. G., Sells, D. J., & Rosen, C. S. (1995). Barney and Friends *as education and entertainment: The comprehensive study—Preschoolers' cognitive responses immediately after viewing a* Barney *episode.* New Haven, CT: Yale University Family Television Research and Consultation Center.

Thompson, B. (1994). The pivotal role of replication in psychological research: Empirically evaluating the replicability of sample results. *Journal of Personality, 62,* 157-176.

Tower, R. B., Singer, J. L., Singer, D. G., & Biggs, A. (1979). Differential effects of television programming on preschoolers' cognition, imagination, and social play. *American Journal of Orthopsychology, 49,* 265-281.

Wright, J. C., & Huston, A. C. (1995). *Effects of educational TV viewing of lower income preschoolers on academic skills, school readiness, and social adjustment: One to three years later—A report to the Children's Television Workshop.* Lawrence: University of Kansas, Center for Research on the Influences of Television on Children.

Zill, N., Davies, E., & Daly, M. (1994). *Viewing of* Sesame Street *by preschool children in the United States and its relationship to school readiness.* Rockville, MD: Westat, Inc.

10

Studying Television Violence:
A Research Agenda
for the 21st Century

John P. Murray

Television broadcasting in the United States began on May 2, 1941, when the Federal Communications Commission (FCC) issued the first license for a commercial television station (W2XBS, NBC, Channel 1), which was to commence its licensed broadcasting on July 1 from the Empire State Building in New York City. However, the public was introduced to this new concept of television several years earlier, on April 30, 1939, when President Franklin D. Roosevelt participated in a 3½-hour program on WNBT (NBC) opening the 1939 World's Fair in New York. Apparently, social scientists were not in the audience, or they were not paying attention to this new phenomenon, because research on the impact of television did not begin until almost two decades later.

Despite this delay in the scientific study of television, one of the first topics of interest to researchers and public policy specialists was the issue of *television violence*. The signal events for this 40-year program

AUTHOR'S NOTE: Preparation of this chapter was supported by a fellowship from the Mind Science Foundation, San Antonio, Texas.

of research were the public hearings in the U.S. House of Representatives in 1952 and in the Senate in 1954 (U.S. Congress, 1952, 1955). These early expressions of concern about the issue of television violence included testimony by a psychologist, Eleanor Maccoby of Stanford University, and a sociologist, Paul Lazarsfeld of Columbia University (Lazarsfeld, 1955; Maccoby, 1954). These two distinguished social scientists noted that there was very little research on the specific issue of the impact of television violence but felt that we could draw some inferences from the research that had accumulated on the influence of films (e.g., Charters, 1933; Cressey & Thrasher, 1933).

This chapter is a review of the approaches and outcomes in television violence research over the past half century in an effort to identify opportunities to expand our knowledge in this area during the coming century. One might hope that we have addressed these issues in sufficient detail over the past 40 years to allow us to "declare victory" and move on to other topics concerning the impact of television. But, alas, much remains to be discovered about the process of effects and ways in which to mitigate the influence of television violence. For example, we have moved from the early investigations that included surveys of children's viewing patterns to more detailed studies of the impact of television violence in laboratory-based investigations and in more natural settings using typical television programming.

However, it should not be assumed that there is a linear progression in the development of research strategies from A to Z and that Z is "better" than A. Rather, there are unique circumstances and specialized research questions for which a particular research strategy is best, and there are periods in history in which some strategies are dominant because the societal questions being asked are best answered by a particular genre of research. So, although this review begins at a particular point in history (i.e., the 1950s), the description of various research paradigms will double back time and again.

■ Identifying the Concern: Early Studies

To begin at the beginning with an "early theorist" on the harmful influence of media, Plato observed in *The Republic,* "And shall we just carelessly allow children to hear any casual tales which may be devised by casual persons, and so receive into their minds ideas often the very opposite of those we shall think they ought to have when they are grown up?" (Plato, 374 B.C./1943, p. 73). Indeed, both Plato and Aristotle warned that we should be concerned about the ways in which a society chooses to amuse itself; Aristotle was concerned about the effects of observing violence in cockfighting and bearbaiting, but the issues are similar to media violence. So, too, a more recent social commentator, Neil Postman, echoed these concerns about violence in popular media in his book, *Amusing Ourselves to Death* (Postman, 1985). The persistence of these concerns about violence and popular culture is testimony to the serious nature of media violence and the "stakes" that society recognizes it has in this issue.

The early studies of television's influence began almost simultaneously in England and the United States in the mid-1950s. In England, a group of researchers at the London School of Economics and Political Science under the direction of Hilde T. Himmelweit, a reader in social psychology, began the first study of children's television viewing patterns while television was still relatively new (only 3 million television sets had been installed in the 15 million households in England). This study was proposed by the audience research department of the British Broadcasting Corporation (BBC) but was conducted by independent researchers and funded by a private foundation, the Nuffield Foundation. The research, which began in 1955, was published in a 1958 report, *Television and the Child: An Empirical Study of the Effect of Television on the Young* (Himmelweit, Oppenheim, & Vince, 1958).

In the United States, a similar survey of children's television viewing was undertaken by a research group at Stanford University under the direction of Wilbur Schramm, a professor of communication. This study, which began in 1958, was published in a 1961 report, *Television in the Lives of Our Children* (Schramm, Lyle, & Parker, 1961). The project began with a pilot study in San Francisco (with funding from the Ford Foundation) and was later expanded (with funding from the National Educational Television and Radio Center) to communities in Colorado and Canada that had differing levels of television access. In the main plan for this study, the researchers would contrast the patterns of daily life of children in four Colorado communities with differing levels of television exposure from "theoretically none" (Durango) to multiple choices (various areas near Denver). However, research never quite works according to plan; as one of the research directors of this landmark study, Jack Lyle, described the situation,

> Wilbur [Schramm] turned to Colorado for his field study locale. With the help of the TV station's staff [KERA, Denver Public Schools television station], he identified four towns which it was anticipated would provide a range of TV available, from none to a choice of stations. Even at this date, 1959, however, this proved extremely difficult. One of the four towns was, indeed, outside of any off-air signal area, but there was a primitive cable service operating in town that had a small, yet significant, subscriber base. It was anticipated, however, that TV exposure level could still be controlled by comparing kids from homes with and without cable. . . . Wilbur's grand plan proved flawed as soon as he walked into the classroom in Durango, the no off-air-TV town. When he asked how many kids had watched the TV the day before, every hand was raised—and it turned out that this was not just the result of watching with a friend next door whose family had cable. Good researcher that he was, Wilbur investigated. The coaxial line used by the cable company was insufficiently shielded. The leak was so strong that if the cable came down the street, almost anyone could pick up at least a fuzzy signal and since there was no converter box, they had no difficulty with channel selection. (J. Lyle, personal communication, October 22, 1996)

Undaunted, the researchers added some comparison towns in Canada, one in the suburbs of Vancouver, British Columbia (where viewers received signals from both Vancouver and Seattle, Washington), and the second 400 miles north for a true "no-TV" town. The result of this reengineering was the development of a major benchmark study of children and television in the United States and Canada.

These two early studies set the stage for later efforts by establishing the basic paradigm of correlational research based on surveys of viewing habits and self-reports, or teacher/parent reports, of children's behavior. Both studies found that the time spent with television displaces time spent with other (older) media. Also, both studies found that there were differences between the television viewers and the control subjects (those who did not have access to television) in various domains. For example, Himmelweit et al. (1958) noted,

We have found a number of instances where viewers and controls differed in their outlook, differences which did not exist before television came on the scene. There was a small but consistent influence of television on the way children thought generally about jobs, job values, success, and social surroundings. (pp. 17-18)

With regard to aggression, these correlational studies were less specific, as Himmelweit and her colleagues noted,

We did not find that the viewers were any more aggressive or maladjusted than the controls; television is unlikely to cause aggressive behaviour, although it could precipitate it in those few children who are emotionally disturbed. On the other hand, there was little support for the view that programmes of violence are beneficial; we found that they aroused aggression as often as they discharged it. (p. 20)

In the case of the Schramm et al. (1961) study, their conclusions about television violence included the observation that those Canadian and American children who had high exposure to television and low exposure to print were more aggressive than those with the reverse pattern. Thus, the early correlational studies or surveys identified some areas of concern about television violence and set the stage for more focused investigations. Finally, it should be noted that these 1950s studies of viewers and nonviewers took place when television was new in the United States and England. Later studies—in the 1970s—would revisit these issues and this research strategy when television was being introduced into isolated communities in Australia (Murray & Kippax, 1977, 1978, 1979) and Canada (MacBeth, 1996; Williams, 1986).

Moving beyond these 1950s surveys, there was another set of studies that emerged in the early 1960s—not surveys or correlational studies but rather experimental studies that were addressed to cause-and-effect relationships in the television violence/aggressive behavior equation. These initial experiments were conducted by two prolific researchers who were studying two distinctly different age groups: Albert Bandura, at Stanford University, conducted studies with pre-school-age children, and Leonard Berkowitz, at the University of Wisconsin, worked with college-age youths. In both instances, the studies were experimental in design, which meant that subjects were randomly assigned to various viewing experiences, and, therefore, the results of this manipulated viewing could be used to address the issue of causal relationships between viewing and behavior.

The early Bandura studies, such as "Transmission of Aggression Through Imitation of Aggressive Models" (Bandura, Ross, & Ross, 1961) and "Imitation of Film-Mediated Aggressive Models" (Bandura, Ross, & Ross, 1963), were set within a social learning paradigm and were designed to identify the processes by which children learn by observing and imitating the behavior of others. In this context, therefore, the studies used stimulus films (videotape was not generally available) back projected on a simulated television screen, and the behavior of the children was observed and recorded in a playroom setting immediately following the viewing period. Despite the structured nature of these studies, Bandura's research was central to the debate about the influence of media violence, and his popular article, "What TV Violence Can Do to Your Child" (published in *Look* magazine [Bandura, 1963]), ignited a firestorm of social concern.

The works of Berkowitz, such as "Effects of Film Violence on Inhibitions Against Subsequent Aggression" (Berkowitz & Rawlings, 1963) and "Film Violence and the Cue Properties of Available Targets" (Berkowitz & Geen, 1966), studied the simulated aggressive behavior of youths and young adults following the viewing of segments of violent films, for example, a Kirk Douglas boxing film, *The Champion*. The demonstration of increased willingness to use aggression against others following viewing further fueled the debate about the influence of media violence.

These early surveys of Himmelweit and Schramm and their colleagues, as well as the experiments of Bandura and Berkowitz and their colleagues, set the stage—in the late 1950s and early 1960s—for serious discussions of television violence and established the broad paradigms that have been employed in this field through the 1990s. Naturally, there have been many modifications and refinements in the later studies, but these researchers and their students helped to shape the debate over the second half of the 20th century. However, although we learned much from the early studies, we have much more to learn in subsequent research.

■ **Setting the Agenda: Public Reviews and Commentary**

As the 1960s progressed, concern in the United States about violence in the streets and the assassinations of President John F. Kennedy, Martin Luther King, Jr., and Robert Kennedy stimulated continuing interest in media violence. In response, several major government commissions and scientific and professional review committees were established, from the late 1960s through the 1990s, to summarize the research evidence and public policy issues regarding the role of television violence in salving or savaging young viewers.

The five principal commissions and review panels—the National Commission on the Causes and Prevention of Violence, the Surgeon General's Scientific Advisory Committee on Television and Social Behavior, the National Institute of Mental Health Television and Behavior Project, the Group for the Advancement of Psychiatry Child and Television Drama Review, and the American Psychological Association Task Force on Television and Society—have been central to setting the agenda for research and public discussion.

Violence Commission

The formal expressions of concern progressed from the 1950s congressional hearings on television and juvenile delinquency to the establishment of the National Commission on the Causes and Prevention of Violence by President Lyndon Johnson (Executive Order 11412) on June 10, 1968, and its extension by President Richard Nixon (Executive Order 11469) on May 23, 1969.

The "Eisenhower Commission" (so-called because it was chaired by Milton Eisenhower, a distinguished university president and the brother of former President Dwight Eisenhower) concluded its review and issued a final report in December 1969. One of the 15 reports (Volume 9) was devoted to the topic of *Mass Media and Violence* (Baker & Ball, 1969). In this report, the commission staff members provided summaries of research issues and appended the reports of commissioned reviews of the literature or special studies undertaken for the program.

Among the special studies for the Eisenhower Commission were surveys of public opinion about—and experience with—violence conducted by Louis Harris and Associates. In addition, the report included a study of the content of television programming conducted by George Gerbner and his colleagues at the Annenberg School of Communication at the University of Pennsylvania.

This approach by the commission added a new set of research techniques and a new frame of reference for the discussions of television violence. For example, the Louis Harris and Associates (1969) poll found that there was a similarity between those who held norms that approved of the use of violence (the "approvers") and those who had firsthand experience with real-life violence as either victims, assailants, or observers (the "violents"). So, too, the analysis of television content found that 81% of the programs studied in 1967 and 1968 (prime time and Saturday morning) contained some form of violence (Gerbner, 1970). Indeed, in the case of "content analysis" and interpretation, the commission initiated a line of research on television that was to prove central to all future discussions of this topic. This research tradition is manifested in more recent, although modified, approaches to content analysis conducted for the cable television industry (Mediascope, 1996; National Television Violence Study, 1997) and broadcast network television (UCLA Center for Communication Policy, 1995).

Surgeon General's Study

On June 3, 1969, while the Eisenhower Commission was developing its final report, the secretary of the Department of Health, Education, and Welfare, Robert Finch, announced the establishment of the Surgeon General's Scientific Advisory Committee on Television and Social Behavior with a mission to

> study the effects of television on social behavior, with its focus on the effects of televised violence on the behavior, attitudes, development, and mental health of children; the study is to be confined to scientific findings and the committee will make no policy recommendations. (Surgeon General's Scientific Advisory Committee on Television and Social Behavior, 1972, p. 139)

This new committee resulted from testimony by Surgeon General William Stewart on March 12, 1969, before the U.S. Senate Subcommittee on Communications. In his testimony, Stewart noted that the task of assessing television violence

> cannot be accomplished by narrowly focused studies, since the violence a child sees on television is randomly interwoven into the total skein of television fare. . . . It is essential to recognize that, with such a complex phenomenon, all the answers will not be forthcoming within the next few weeks or the next few months. The panel's findings and recommendations should be an important step in increasing our understanding of our social environment and of ourselves. (Surgeon General's Scientific Advisory Committee on Television and Social Behavior, 1972, p. 139)

One of the major accomplishments of the surgeon general's study was the ability to keep faith with Stewart's views by commissioning almost 60 studies by more than 80 researchers throughout the United States and several other countries. The end result was a concentrated study of television violence by researchers drawn from multiple disciplines (e.g., psychology, education, sociology, communications, psychiatry, anthropology, political science), using diverse methodological approaches (e.g., surveys, content analysis, laboratory experiments, field studies, cultural contrasts), and studying viewers in diverse ages and stages of development. This was not only the first time such a focused study was undertaken but also the first time these diverse studies would be reviewed by a panel of 12 social scientists and clinicians who had expertise in research, mental health and education practice, and the communications industry.

The committee members were drawn from both academic and professional settings because the surgeon general felt that approach worked in the earlier studies of smoking and health. The 12 members and their affiliations were as follows: Ira H. Cisin, George Washington University; Thomas E. Coffin, National Broadcasting Company; Irving L. Janis, Yale University; Joseph T. Klapper, Columbia Broadcasting System; Harold Mendelsohn, University of Denver; Eveline Omwake, Connecticut College; Charles A. Pinderhughes, Boston University; Ithiel de Sola Pool, Massachusetts Institute of Technology; Alberta E. Siegel, Stanford University; Anthony F. C. Wallace, University of Pennsylvania; Andrew S. Watson, University of Michigan; and Gerhart D. Wiebe, Boston University. The committee was chaired by Eli A. Rubinstein, deputy director of the National Institute of Mental Health (NIMH), who was vice chairman and representative of the surgeon general. In addition, the secretary of Health, Education, and Welfare appointed a direct representative, Richard A. Moore, a former general manager of a Los Angeles television station.

This committee structure was innovative but not without considerable controversy. In particular, concerns were expressed that there were too many committee members with ties to the television industry who might influence the interpretation of research findings and committee recommendations (see Cater & Strickland, 1975). In the end, the committee members, under strenuous urging by Rubinstein, unanimously agreed to a committee report that, although cautious, did conclude that viewing television violence can lead to increases in children's aggressive behavior (Murray, 1973; Rubinstein, 1974).

One of the unexpected outcomes of the surgeon general's study was the expansion of support for studies of the impact of television. For example, bibliographies of research and commentary on the topic of television and behavior chronicled a marked increase in publications on this topic from 285 in 1971 (Atkin, Murray, & Nayman, 1971), to about 1,200 in 1975 (Comstock & Fisher, 1975), to almost 3,000 in 1980 (Murray, 1980). There was some slowing of the growth in publications in the 1980s (Wartella & Reeves, 1984) but the cumulative impact of the surgeon general's study could be felt into the 1990s (Huston et al., 1992). Much of the strength and diversity of research on television violence, as well as the establishment of a research agenda, is directly attributable to the impetus of the Surgeon General's Scientific Advisory Committee on Television and Social Behavior.

National Institute of Mental Health Study

In 1982, the NIMH published a 10-year follow-up of the 1972 surgeon general's study. That two-volume report (NIMH, 1982; Pearl, Bouthilet, & Lazar, 1982), collectively titled *Television and Behavior: Ten Years of Scientific Progress and Implications for the Eighties,* provided a reminder of the breadth and depth of knowledge that has accumulated on the issue of television violence, although the NIMH report was not focused solely on violence. However, with regard to television violence, the NIMH (1982) staff and consultants concluded,

After 10 more years of research, the consensus among most of the research community is that violence on television does lead to aggressive behavior by children and teenagers who watch the programs. This conclusion is based on laboratory experiments and on field studies. Not all children become aggressive, of course, but the correlations between violence and aggression are positive. In magnitude, television violence is as strongly correlated with aggressive behavior as any other behavioral variable that has been measured. The research question has moved from asking whether or not there is an effect to seeking explanations for the effect. (p. 6)

The release of the NIMH report caused some concern in the television industry (Wurtzel & Lometti, 1983), but it was generally supported by knowledgeable researchers. For example, in a survey conducted shortly after the release of the NIMH report (Murray, 1984), the majority of the 109 psychologists, sociologists, and communications researchers strongly agreed with the NIMH conclusions. Moreover, an earlier study of 468 communications professionals found strong support for the proposition that television violence is causally related to aggressive behavior in children (Bybee, Robinson, & Turow, 1982).

Group for the Advancement of Psychiatry Report

The Group for the Advancement of Psychiatry (GAP) is an organization established in 1946 to foster innovation and interdisciplinary reviews of issues in mental health and human relations. In 1982, the Committee on Social Issues of GAP, chaired by Roy W. Menninger, undertook a review of the role that television plays in the socialization of young children. This report, *The Child and Television Drama: The Psychosocial Impact of Cumulative Viewing,* provided an overview of the research and professional insights that have accumulated from the Eisenhower Commission through the surgeon general's study and the NIMH report. In the concluding section of its report, the GAP committee elaborated a series of recommendations for parents, mental health professionals, public policymakers, and the television industry.

One of the recommendations to the television industry was particularly relevant to the issue of violence and the portrayal of conflict:

> Television dramas ought to reconfirm the reality that human behavior is complex, that motivations are many, and that the personal and social problems to be solved have many answers. In this vein, drama should not portray human conflict as responsive to simple solutions, simple choices, snap decisions, or violence. Drama should reinforce the fact that no human being is free from anxiety, immune to conflict, or likely to live happily ever after. (GAP, 1982, p. 118)

Many of the GAP report recommendations urged a more collaborative spirit in the search for solutions to this historic concern about media violence and violence in society. The GAP report helped to move professional discussions from research findings to the development of practical guidelines for positive mental health practices in programming, a theme that has been revisited in later reports from the Institute for Mental Health Initiatives (Livingstone, 1994) and the OKTV Foundation (1995).

American Psychological Association Report

In 1986, the American Psychological Association (APA) impaneled a Task Force on Television and Society to review the research and professional concerns about the impact of television on children and adults. One specific charge was the following:

> Review and integrate existing research on the positive and negative effects of television advertising and programming on particular segments of the United States population, specifically women, children, minorities, and the elderly. Emphasize research since the 1982 report from the National Institute of Mental Health, which updated the 1972 Report of the Surgeon General's Scientific Advisory Committee on Television and Social Behavior.

The nine psychologists assigned to this committee undertook reviews of relevant research, conducted interviews with television industry and public policy professionals, and discussed concerns with representatives of government regulatory agencies and public interest organizations. The final report, titled *Big World, Small Screen: The Role of Television in American Society* (Huston et al., 1992), included the following observation about television violence:

> American television has been violent for many years. Over the past 20 years, the rate of violence on prime time evening television has remained at about 5 to 6 incidents per hour, whereas the rate on children's Saturday morning programs is typically 20 to 25 acts per hour. There is clear evidence that television violence can cause aggressive behavior and can cultivate values favoring the use of aggression to resolve conflicts. (p. 136)

The report ends with a plea to the television industry and government to rethink and renew our commitment to enhancing children's television, noting, "Our failure to realize the potential benefits of the medium is perhaps more significant than our inability to control some of its harmful effects" (p. 145). The report speculates that if we were to devote efforts using television to stimulate children's minds, stretch their horizons, and teach them about the world, we might find that this educational and entertaining programming would displace some of the violence that children experience.

■ **Exploring the Issue: Paradigms**
   for Studying Television Violence

Over the past half century, about 1,000 reports have been published on the issue of television violence. Of course, only a small percentage of these thousands of pages represent original studies or research reports, but there is an extensive body of research on the impact of television violence.

Throughout this history of concern, there have been diverse questions raised about the extent of television violence and the nature and scope of its impact. Social scientists have employed three broad strategies to answer questions about prevalence, correlation, and causation. Questions about the prevalence of television violence have been addressed by *content analysis* of selected broadcast periods. Questions about the correlation between television violence viewing and aggressive behavior have been addressed by *surveys* of viewing patterns in relation to viewers' attitudes or overt behavior. Questions about causation of aggressive behavior by television violence viewing have been addressed by *experiments* conducted in either laboratory or field settings. These three approaches, and the exemplary studies outlined in the following sections, provide an overview of the major findings and concerns about television violence.

Prevalence

One of the earliest studies of television content was the work of Gerbner and his colleagues. These analyses began in conjunction with the National Commission on the Causes and Prevention of Violence (Gerbner, 1970) and the Surgeon General's Scientific Advisory Committee on Television and Social Behavior (Gerbner, 1972), and they have continued annually through the 1990s (e.g., Gerbner, Gross, Morgan, & Signorielli, 1994).

In the typical study, Gerbner and his colleagues would videotape all evening, prime-time television programming and all Saturday morning television programs broadcast or cablecast during 1 week following the advent of the new television season in the fall of each year. The analysis of these programs included an extensive coding of the frequency and nature of violence portrayed. Violence was not the only issue addressed in Gerbner's "Cultural Indicators" program, but violence was important because it was a "definer of power" in the sense that those who were the victims of violence usually were portrayed as powerless. Thus, Gerbner's analyses extended beyond mere body counts and described the social structure of violence. In this regard, these studies often found that those who committed violence frequently were white males in their 20s or 30s, whereas those who were the victims of this violence often were female, nonwhite, elderly, or foreign born.

With regard to the prevalence of violence, Gerbner (1972) found that 8 out of every 10 plays broadcast during the survey period in 1969 contained some form of violence. Similar studies conducted each year have documented consistently high levels of violence. Figure 10.1 displays the annual reports on the percentages of programs containing violence on the three major networks (ABC, CBS, and NBC) from 1973 to 1995 and the newer FOX network from 1993 to 1995. It can be seen that the average for the three major networks is about 70% of

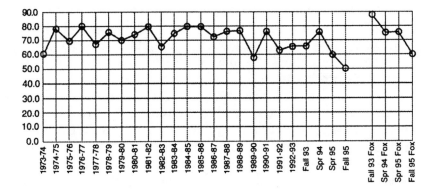

Figure 10.1. Trends in the Level of Violence on Four U.S. Television Networks, 1973-1995
SOURCE: G. Gerbner (personal communication, January 12, 1997).

all programs, with peaks at 80% and several drops to around 60% or even 50%. These drops or "valleys of violence" usually correspond to years in which there was significant public "outcry" about media violence (e.g., 1973-1974 following the 1972 release of the surgeon general's report on the harmful effects of television violence, 1982-1983 following public concern about the bloody 1981-1982 season that saw an all-time peak in the number of violent acts on children's Saturday morning television [about 31 acts per hour], drops in 1990 and 1995 following congressional hearings on the Children's Television Act and continuing congressional and FCC hearings concerning the V-chip and educational programming); even the very violent FOX network dropped from 90% to 60% from 1993 to 1995. Nevertheless, over almost a quarter century of yearly monitoring of television violence levels, this analysis has found the average level of violence in *prime time* holding at about 5 violent acts per hour, whereas *children's* weekend morning programming has averaged around 25 violent acts per hour.

Other studies designed to assess the prevalence of television violence have found even more worrisome levels of mayhem. In 1992, the Center for Media and Public Affairs (Lichter & Amundson, 1992) monitored 1 day (6 a.m. to midnight) of television fare available on broadcast and cable channels in Washington, D.C. This analysis recorded 1,846 violent scenes during this one 18-hour period on an April day in 1992. Moreover, a follow-up study in 1994 found 2,605 violent scenes in a similar 18-hour day, a 41% increase from 1992 to 1994 (Lichter & Amundson, 1994).

Continuing studies of the prevalence of television violence have included more qualitative approaches to this issue. The UCLA Center for Communication Policy (1995), in a study funded by the commercial television networks, concluded, "The world of television, from broadcast networks, to syndication, to cable, to home videos, is not as violent as we had feared and not as wholesome as we might have hoped. There is room for substantial improvement" (p. 151). At the same time, another study (Mediascope, 1996), funded by the National Cable Television Association, found evidence of fairly extensive levels of violence on both broadcast and cable television based on an analysis of a 20-week composite involving 2,693 programs on 23 channels. The Mediascope (1996) results showed that the percentage of programs containing violence on the *broadcast network stations* was 44%, whereas the figure for *independent broadcast stations* was 55%, for *basic cable stations* was 59%, for *premium cable subscription channels* was 85%, and for public television was only 18%. And, once again, this most recent study reconfirmed that there were ethnic and gender differences in television violence; the typical perpetrator of violence was adult (76%), male (78%), and Caucasian (76%). Also, the context of the violence included the observation that 90% of movies contained violence and that 67% of the violence in children's programs was set in a humorous context; indeed, only 5% of the violence in children's programming portrayed any long-term negative consequences of the violent acts.

Clearly, the studies of *prevalence* of television violence, indexed by content analysis of programming, demonstrate pervasive and persistent levels of violence in television entertainment. The various studies have used somewhat different approaches to sampling: 1 week, prime time and Saturday morning (Gerbner & Gross, 1976); one 18-hour day (Lichter & Amundson, 1992, 1994); and a composite 20-week period (Mediascope, 1996). Nevertheless, the overall conclusions from these diverse studies are similar in demonstrating extensive violence in television programming. The next step in assessing televi-

sion violence is to move from studies of prevalence to studies of impact by demonstrating a relationship between viewing violence and
aggression.

Correlation

The demonstration of a relationship between viewing and aggressive behavior is a logical precursor to studies of the causal role that
television violence may play in promoting aggressive behavior. However, as discussed in the earlier section on the history of concern about
television violence, the correlational or survey studies assessing real-
world *relationships* developed almost simultaneously with experiments designed to assess the causal influences of viewing violence.
Nevertheless, it is important to keep the correlation versus causation
approaches separate because they represent different paradigms with
different logical interpretations and implications. In these correlational studies, the issue of causation is not relevant; rather, the
emphasis is on the co-occurrence of viewing and aggression.

The early surveys of the impact of television on children, conducted
by Himmelweit et al. (1958) and Schramm et al. (1961) and discussed
in an earlier section, addressed some of these concerns about violence.
However, later research was more focused in studying the correlations
between television violence viewing and aggression.

In typical correlational studies such as those conducted for the
surgeon general's research program (Dominick & Greenberg, 1972;
McLeod, Atkin, & Chaffee, 1972a, 1972b; Robinson & Bachman,
1972), the researchers found consistent patterns of significant correlations between the number of hours of television viewed or the
frequency of viewing violent programs and various measures of aggressive attitudes or behavior. In a later study, Atkin, Greenberg,
Korzenny, and McDermott (1979) found that heavy television violence viewers were more likely to choose physical and verbal aggressive responses to solve hypothetical interpersonal conflict situations;
fully 45% of the heavy violence viewers chose physical/verbal aggressive responses versus 21% of the low violence viewers who did so.
Similarly, a more recent study in this genre (Walker & Morley, 1991)
found that adolescents who reported enjoying television violence were

more likely to hold attitudes and values favorable to behaving aggressively in conflict situations.

A somewhat different set of correlational studies was designed to assess subtle shifts in attitudes and behavior that might be observed only in large samples of the population. Two studies in this genre, conducted by David Phillips at the University of California, San Diego, assessed the effect of television on adult fatalities (Phillips, 1982, 1983). In one study, Phillips used national death certificate records compiled by the U.S. Centers for Disease Control to evaluate the impact of televised suicides portrayed in soap operas on the incidence of suicide in the U.S. population. He found that whenever a major suicide (i.e., that of a main character) occurred in a soap opera in the 1960s, there was a significant increase in the national incidence of suicide by women (a major audience for soap operas in those days) within 3 days of the telecast. Similarly, a second study found that the telecast or cablecast of a major boxing event was related to a significant increase in death by homicide for men (a major audience) who were similar in age and ethnicity to the loser of the boxing match. Phillips (1983) suggested that television portrayals can stimulate subtle changes in attitudes that might make a particular behavior or course of action, such as suicide, seem more acceptable to viewers because it is portrayed as acceptable for the television performers.

In a similar vein, another large database, the Cultural Indicators Project, has been used to explore the relationship between television portrayals and viewers' conception of the world. In a series of studies that began in 1974, Gerbner and his colleagues (1994) have tracked public perceptions of society in relation to the respondents' extent of television viewing. Of relevance to the violence issue, these researchers have identified differences in the risk-of-victimization perceptions, described as the "mean world syndrome" effect, of light versus heavy viewers. The heavy viewers (usually 5 or more hours per day) are much more fearful of the world around them than are the light viewers (about 3 or fewer hours per day). When questioned about their perceptions of risk, heavy viewers are much more likely to overestimate (i.e., greater than the Federal Bureau of Investigation crime reports for their locale would suggest) the chance that they will be victims of crimes in the ensuing 6 months, have taken greater precautions by changing the security of their homes or restricting their travels at night, and are generally more fearful of the world. As Gerbner et al. (1994) noted,

> We have found that long-term exposure to television, in which frequent violence is virtually inescapable, tends to cultivate the image of a relatively mean and dangerous world . . . in which greater protection is needed, most people "cannot be trusted," and most people are "just looking out for themselves." (p. 30)

This cultivation analysis, conducted over the past 30 years, has evolved into a new concept of evaluating the accuracy of portrayals of various social groups—the "Fairness Index"—that will be applied to an entire season of programming in a forthcoming report for the Screen Actors Guild (G. Gerbner, personal communication, January 12, 1997).

Studies such as these clearly demonstrate that violence viewing and aggressive behavior are related, but they do not address the issue of cause and effect. Yet, there are some special correlational studies in which "intimations of causation" can be derived from the fact that these studies were conducted over several time periods. There have been three major "panel" studies: one study funded by CBS (Belson, 1978), another funded by NBC (Milavsky, Kessler, Stipp, & Rubens, 1982), and the third funded by the surgeon general's committee and the NIMH (Huesmann & Eron, 1986; Huesmann, Eron, Lefkowitz, & Walder, 1984; Lefkowitz, Eron, Walder, & Huesmann, 1972).

The CBS study (Belson, 1978) was conducted in England with 1,565 youths comprising a representative sample of 13- to 17-year-old males living in London. The boys were interviewed on several occasions concerning the extent of their exposure to a selection of violent television programs broadcast during the period 1959 through 1971. The level and type of violence in these programs were rated by members of the BBC viewing panel. Thus, it was possible to obtain, for each boy, a measure of both the magnitude and type of exposure to televised violence (e.g., realistic, fictional). Furthermore, each boy's level of violent behavior was determined by his report of how often he had been involved in any of 53 categories of violence over the previous 6 months. The degree of seriousness of the acts reported by the boys ranged from only slightly violent aggravation, such as taunting, to more serious and very violent behavior such as "I tried to force a girl to have sexual intercourse with me," "I bashed a boy's head against a wall," "I burned a boy on the chest with a cigarette while my mates held him down," and "I threatened to kill my father." Approximately 50% of the 1,565 boys were not involved in any violent acts during the 6 month period. However, of those who were involved in violence, 188 (12%) were involved in 10 or more acts during the 6-month period. When Belson compared the behavior of boys who had higher exposure to televised violence with that of boys who had lower exposure (and had been matched on a wide variety of possible contributing factors), he found that the high-violence viewers were more involved in serious interpersonal violence.

The NBC study (Milavsky et al., 1982) was conducted over a 3-year period from May 1970 to December 1973 in two cities, Fort Worth, Texas, and Minneapolis, Minnesota. Interviews were conducted with samples of 2nd- to 6th-grade boys and girls and a special sample of teenage boys. In the elementary school sample, the information on television viewing and the aggression measures was collected in six time periods over the 3 years. The aggression measures consisted of peer ratings of aggressive behavior based on the work of Eron and his colleagues (Eron, Walder, & Lefkowitz, 1971). In the teenage sample, there were only five waves of interviews over the 3 years, and the aggression measures were self-report rather than peer-reported aggression. In summarizing the results of this study, the authors concluded, "On the basis of the analyses we carried out to test for such a causal connection, there is no evidence that television exposure has a consistently significant effect on subsequent aggressive behavior in the [elementary school] sample of boys" (Milavsky et al., 1982, p. 482). Similar null findings were reported for the elementary school girls and the teenage boys. However, reanalysis of these data by Kenny (1984) and Cook, Kendzierski, and Thomas (1983) concluded that there are small but clear causal effects in the NBC data and that these effects become stronger when analyzed over longer time periods through successive waves of interviews.

Finally, one of the longest panel studies, 22 years, is the work of Leonard Eron and his colleagues (Eron, 1963, 1982; Huesmann & Eron, 1986; Huesman et al., 1984; Lefkowitz et al., 1972). In the initial studies, conducted for the surgeon general's investigation of television violence (Lefkowitz et al., 1972), the researchers were able to document the long-term effects of violence viewing by studying children over a 10-year period from 8 to 18 years of age. At these two time periods, the youngsters were interviewed about their program preferences and information was collected from peer ratings of aggressive behavior. The violence levels of their preferred television programs and measures of aggression across these two time periods suggested the possibility that early television violence viewing was one factor in producing later aggressive behavior. In particular, the findings for 211 boys followed in this longitudinal study demonstrated that television violence at age 8 was significantly related to aggression at age 8 ($r = .21$), and the 8-year-old violent television preferences were significantly related to aggression at age 18 ($r = .31$), but television violence preferences at age 18 were not related to aggressive behavior at the earlier (age 8) time period ($r = .01$). When other possible variables, such as parenting practices and discipline styles, were controlled (e.g., partial correlation), it still was clear that early media violence could be part of the cause of later aggressive behavior. Furthermore, in a follow-up study, when these young men were 30 years of age (Huesmann et al., 1984), the authors found a significant correlation ($r = .41$) between television violence levels at age 8 and serious interpersonal criminal behavior (e.g., assault, murder, child abuse, spouse abuse, rape) at age 30.

Thus, it seems clear that a correlation between television violence and aggression can be established from diverse studies. In addition, some special cases of longitudinal correlational studies (described as cross-lagged/panel studies) can lead to *intimations of causation*. However, the issue of causation is best assessed in experimental designs that allow for random assignment of subjects to various treatment conditions or, in the case of field studies, take advantage of naturally occurring variations in television viewing experiences.

Causation

The potential role of television violence in the causation of aggressive behavior was, as noted earlier, among the first topics investigated by social scientists. The studies by Bandura (e.g., Bandura et al., 1961, 1963) and Berkowitz (e.g., Berkowitz & Rawlings, 1963) set the stage for later experimental studies in which causal influences of television violence could be assessed by randomly assigning subjects to various viewing conditions. These later studies employed both the structured, laboratory-based settings and more naturalistic settings in schools and communities.

One of the earlier studies in this genre (Liebert & Baron, 1972) assessed the effects of viewing segments of a violent television program, *The Untouchables,* on the aggressive behavior of 5- to 9-year-old boys and girls. In this study, the children viewed either *The Untouchables* or a neutral, but active, track race. Following viewing, each child was placed in a playroom setting in which he or she could help or hurt another child who was ostensibly playing a game in another room. The subject could help the other child by pressing a button that would make the game easier to play and allow the other child to win more points. Similarly, the child could hurt the other child by pressing a button that would make the game very difficult to play and, hence, force the other child to lose points. The results indicated that youngsters who had viewed the violent program manifested a greater willingness to hurt the other child than did youngsters who had watched the neutral program. Moreover, an elaboration of this study by Paul Ekman and colleagues included the recording of the facial expressions of these children while they were watching the television violence (Ekman et al., 1972). In this instance, the children whose facial expressions indicated interest or pleasure while watching television violence were more willing to hurt the other child than were youngsters whose facial expressions indicated disinterest or displeasure while watching television violence. Thus, this set of studies identified some potential moderating variables in the violence-viewing/aggressive-behavior equation.

Other early experiments by researchers using physiological measures of arousal (e.g., galvanic skin response [GSR], heart rate, respiration changes) while watching violent cartoons (Cline, Croft, & Courrier, 1973; Osborn & Endsley, 1971) found that children are emotionally responsive to even animated violence. So, too, other studies found that exposure to even one violent cartoon leads to increased aggression in the structured playroom settings (Ellis & Sekyra, 1972; Hapkiewitz & Roden, 1971; Lovaas, 1961; Mussen & Rutherford, 1961; Ross, 1972). Furthermore, studies by Drabman and his colleagues (Drabman & Thomas, 1974; Thomas, Horton, Lippincott, &

Drabman, 1977) showed that children who view violent television programs become desensitized to violence and are more willing to tolerate aggressive behavior in others. Moreover, later studies with emotionally disturbed children (Gadow & Sprafkin, 1993; Grimes, Vernberg, & Cathers, 1997) found that these youngsters may be more vulnerable to the influence of television violence. For example, Grimes et al. (in press) found that 8- to 12-year-olds who were diagnosed as having either attention deficit hyperactivity disorder, oppositional defiant disorder, or conduct disorder manifested less emotional concern for victims and were more willing to accept violence as justified than were a matched group of children who did not have these disorders.

All of the aforementioned studies were conducted in fairly structured laboratory or playroom settings in which the displays of aggression, emotional arousal, or desensitization were relatively contiguous to the viewing of television violence. Questions remain about what might happen in more naturalistic settings or field studies of violence viewing and aggressive behavior. One early study that assessed these issues was the work of Aletha Huston (Stein), now at the University of Texas, and her colleagues (Friedrich & Stein, 1973; Stein & Friedrich, 1972) in which they assessed the impact of viewing aggressive versus prosocial television programs on the behavior of preschoolers in their normal child care settings. In this study, the preschoolers were assigned to view a diet of either *Batman* and *Superman* cartoons, *Mister Rogers' Neighborhood,* or neutral programming that contained neither aggressive nor prosocial material (i.e., special travel stories for preschoolers). The diet consisted of 12 half-hour episodes that were viewed for a half hour per day, 3 days per week, for 4 weeks. The researchers observed the children in the classroom and on the playground for 3 weeks prior to the start of the viewing period to establish a baseline for the amount of aggression or prosocial behavior and continued to observe the children during the 4 weeks of viewing and for an additional 2 weeks. The results were that children who initially were more aggressive and had viewed the diet of *Batman* and *Superman* cartoons were more active in the classroom and on the playground, played more roughly with toys, and got into more aggressive encounters. Conversely, youngsters from lower-income families who had viewed the *Mister Rogers' Neighborhood* diet increased their prosocial helping behavior. One suggestion from this early field study is that viewing aggressive program content can lead to changes in aggressive behavior, whereas the opposite also is true for prosocial programming. Moreover, these changes were demonstrated in a relatively short viewing period (12 half hours) and in the context of other viewing that took place outside of the classroom setting.

Other field studies have used restricted populations such as boys in detention centers or secure residential settings. In one such study, conducted for NBC, Feshbach and Singer (1971) presented preadolescent and adolescent males in a security facility with a diet of aggressive or nonaggressive television programs over a 6-week period and measured their daily aggressive behavior. They found that the youngsters who watched the nonaggressive programs were more aggressive than the other group. However, this study was criticized on methodological grounds relating to the selection of subjects and the assignment of viewing conditions (Liebert, Sobol, & Davidson, 1972), and a subsequent replication (Wells, 1973) failed to duplicate the findings. Moreover, a later study conducted by Berkowitz and his colleagues (Parke, Berkowitz, Leyens, West, & Sebastian, 1977), using aggressive or nonaggressive films presented to adolescent males living in minimum-security institutions, did demonstrate increases in both verbal and physical interpersonal aggression among the teens viewing the aggressive diet.

Another approach to field studies involved the assessment of the effects of naturally occurring differences in the television exposure available to children in communities with or without television or in communities with differing television content. In one set of studies (Murray & Kippax, 1977, 1978), the researchers were able to study the introduction of television in a rural community in Australia, in contrast to two similar communities that had differing experiences with television. In a second set of studies (MacBeth, 1996; Williams, 1986), the research team studied the introduction of television in a rural Canadian community, in contrast to two similar communities with differing television experience. In general, the results of both the Australian and Canadian studies converge in showing that the introduction of television has a major influence on restructuring the social lives of children in these rural communities. In this regard, both studies found that television displaces other media use and involvement in various social activities, not dissimilar to the findings of earlier studies of children in England (Himmelweit et al., 1958) or in the United States and Canada (Schramm et al., 1961). However, with regard to the effects of television violence, these newer field studies provided stronger evidence of negative influence in differing but complementary ways.

In one stage of the Australian study (Murray, 1980; Murray & Kippax, 1977, 1978), the researchers interviewed 8- to 12-year-old children about their conceptions of crime as a way of examining the global influence of the television content that varied across the three Australian towns. The initial study assessed the effects of the introduction of television in one town (the no-TV town) by contrasting the residents' behavior and attitudes with those in two similar towns with differing television experience—low-TV (2 years experience with only public television) versus high-TV (5 years experience with both public and commercial television). At the next wave of data collection (2 years later), the no-TV town had acquired television (now the new-TV town) and the other towns had 4 and 7 years experience, respectively. The authors reasoned that the high-TV town should show a more differentiated conception of crime because it was the only town with extensive exposure to action-adventure, crime-police dramas. To test this hypothesis, children were presented with a selection of several illegal activities (spying, murder, drunkenness, assault, kidnapping, bank robbery, and shoplifting). The items were presented in pairs and repeated so that each item was paired with every other item. For each pair, the children were asked to rate the similarity of these two crimes on a 5-point scale from *very much alike* to *not at all alike*. Multidimensional scaling analysis was employed to extract the children's conceptual structure of criminal activity. The results in Figure 10.2 are the plots of the multidimensional conception of crime across the three towns. It can be noted in the top two panels (a and b) that the children in the new-TV and low-TV towns produced a straightforward two-dimensional conception of the structure of crime. The two dimensions appear to be the degree of seriousness of the crime and a property versus person dimension. However, in the two bottom panels (c and d) of the figure, it can be seen that the children in the high-TV town

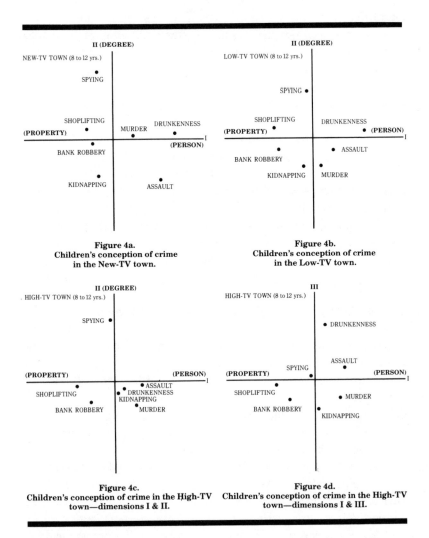

Figure 4a.
Children's conception of crime
in the New-TV town.

Figure 4b.
Children's conception of crime
in the Low-TV town.

Figure 4c.
Children's conception of crime in the High-TV
town—dimensions I & II.

Figure 4d.
Children's conception of crime in the High-TV
town—dimensions I & III.

Figure 10.2. Children's Conception of Crime in Three Australian Towns With Differing Television Programming
a. New-TV Town
b. Low-TV Town
c. High-TV Town (Dimensions I and II)
d. High-TV Town (Dimensions I and III)
SOURCE: Murray (1980).

(7 years experience with the more violent commercial television) produced a much more differentiated conception of crime consisting of three dimensions. The first two dimensions are similar to those in the other two towns, namely, seriousness and property versus person. However, the children in the high-TV town overlay these dimensions with a third dimension that may be related to the frequency with which these crimes occur in real life and on television. The possibility that this third dimension is a mélange of the real and televised worlds is suggested by the ordering of drunkenness, spying, and shoplifting. Thus, the children in the high-TV town had a much more complex conception of crime than did their peers in either the low-TV or new-TV town.

In the other community-level analysis of the impact of television, the study of children in three Canadian communities (MacBeth, 1996; Williams, 1986), the authors found that the introduction of television in a community led to increases in aggressive behavior. In this instance, the researchers compared children living in the before/after television town (Notel) with their peers in two other towns where television was well established (Unitel, receiving the government-owned commercial channel, CBC, and Multitel, receiving both CBC and three American commercial networks, ABC, CBS, and NBC). Children in all three towns were evaluated at Time 1 when Notel did not receive a television signal and again at Time 2 after Notel had television for 2 years. The results of this phase of the study demonstrated that there were no differences across the three towns at Time 1 but that at Time 2 the children from the former Notel were significantly more aggressive, both physically and verbally, than the children in the Unitel or Multitel towns. Moreover, only children in the Notel town manifested any significant increase in physical and verbal aggression from Time 1 to Time 2. The authors concluded that it is particularly striking that "the effects of television were not restricted to a subset of children. Boys and girls, children initially high and low in aggression, and those watching more or less TV were equally likely to show increased aggressive behavior [in the Notel town]" (Joy, Kimball, & Zabrack, 1986, p. 339).

In conclusion, it seems clear that laboratory experiments and field studies converge in suggesting that television violence is implicated in the production of aggressive attitudes, values, and behavior. Not all children are affected, and not all children are influenced to the same extent, but television violence can lead to increases in aggression. The questions that remain are questions about the process of effects and the nature of interventions that might mitigate the influence of televised violence on young viewers.

■ Expanding the Agenda: Whither Research?

Research conducted over the past 40 years leads to the inescapable conclusion that televised violence does affect viewers' attitudes, values, and behavior (Comstock & Paik, 1991; Hearold, 1986; Murray, 1994; Paik & Comstock, 1994). In general, there seem to be three main classes of effects: aggression, desensitization, and fearfulness.

1. *Aggression:* Viewing televised violence can lead to increases in aggressive behavior and/or changes in attitudes and values favoring the use of aggression to solve conflicts.
2. *Desensitization:* Extensive violence viewing may lead to decreased sensitivity to violence and a greater willingness to tolerate increasing levels of violence in society.
3. *Fearfulness:* Extensive exposure to television violence may produce the "mean world syndrome" in which viewers overestimate their risk of victimization.

Although the body of research on the effects of viewing television violence is extensive and fairly coherent in demonstrating systematic patterns of influence, we know surprisingly little about the processes involved in the production of these effects. So, too, we need to know more about the social factors that cause the high prevalence of television violence as well as factors that may reduce the prevalence of gratuitous violence in programming. Finally, we also require further research on efforts to intervene or remedy the harmful effects of violence viewing. Therefore, avenues for future research should include continuing analysis of the process, prevalence, and prevention of television violence.

Process

Although we know that viewing televised violence can lead to increases in aggressive behavior or fearfulness and changed attitudes and values about the role of violence in society, it would be helpful to know more about how these changes occur in viewers.

Within a social learning paradigm, we know that changes in behavior and thoughts can result from observing models in the world around us, be they parents, peers, or other role models such as those provided by mass media. The processes involved in "modeling" or imitation and vicarious learning of overt behavior were addressed in social learning theories in the 1960s (Bandura, 1962, 1965, 1969; Berkowitz, 1962, 1965), but we need to expand our understanding of the neurological processes that might govern the translation of the observed models into thoughts and actions.

As a start in this new direction, both Bandura (1994) and Berkowitz (1984) provided some theoretical foundations for the translation of communication "events" into thoughts and actions. Bandura's social-cognitive theory approach and Berkowitz's outline of a cognitive-neoassociation analysis posit a role for emotional arousal as an affective tag that may facilitate lasting influences. As Bandura (1994) noted, "People are easily aroused by the emotional expressions of others. Vicarious arousal operates mainly through an intervening self-arousal process. . . . That is, seeing others react emotionally to instigating conditions activates emotion-arousing thoughts and imagery in observers" (p. 75). With regard to aggression, we know that viewing television violence can be emotionally arousing (e.g., Cline et al., 1973; Osborn & Endsley, 1971; Zillmann, 1971, 1982), but we lack direct measures of cortical arousal or activation patterns in relation to violence viewing.

The pursuit of neurological patterns of cortical arousal in violence viewing would likely start with the amygdala because it has a well-established role (LeDoux, 1996; LeDoux & Hirst, 1986) in the control of physiological responses to emotionally arousing or threatening stimuli. Indeed, a recent National Research Council (1993) report from the Panel on the Understanding and Control of Violent Behavior concluded,

All human behavior, including aggression and violence, is the outcome of complex processes in the brain. Violent behaviors may result from relatively permanent conditions or from temporary states. . . . Biological research on aggressive and violent behavior has given particular attention to the following in recent years: . . . functioning of steroid hormones such as testosterone and glucocorticoids, especially their action on steroid receptors in the brain; . . . neurophysiological (i.e., brain wave) abnormalities, particularly in the temporal lobe of the brain; . . . [and] brain dysfunctions that interfere with language processing or cognition. (pp. 115-116)

Thus, one suggestion for further research on the impact of media violence is to assess some of the neurological correlates of viewing televised violence. In particular, the use of videotape violent scenes can serve as the ideal paradigm for assessing individual differences in responses to violence in society. However, before exploring individual differences, we need to conduct normative studies of neurological activation patterns related to violence. Figure 10.3 is a diagram of the brain sections of interest, and Figure 10.4 is a magnetic resonance image (MRI) of a human brain section containing the amygdala.

It is very likely that the amygdala will be involved in processing violence, but the projections to the cortex are not clear. However, developing hypotheses about violence viewing and brain activation would need to start with research on physiological arousal (e.g., Osborn & Endsley, 1971; Zillmann, 1982; Zillmann & Bryant, 1994) and link this to cortical arousal. In this regard, the works of Ekman and Davidson (Davidson, Ekman, Saron, Senulis, & Friesen, 1990; Ekman & Davidson, 1993; Ekman, Davidson, & Friesen, 1990) using electroencephalogram (EEG) recordings while subjects viewed a gruesome film (a leg amputation) indicate asymmetries in activation patterns in the anterior regions of the left and right hemispheres. In particular, positive affect (indexed by facial expression) has been found to be associated with left-sided anterior activation, whereas negative affect is associated with right-sided activation (Davidson & Tomarken, 1989).

One study, being conducted at the Research Imaging Center of the University of Texas Health Science Center in San Antonio (Murray, 1997), will address questions about violence viewing and arousal using

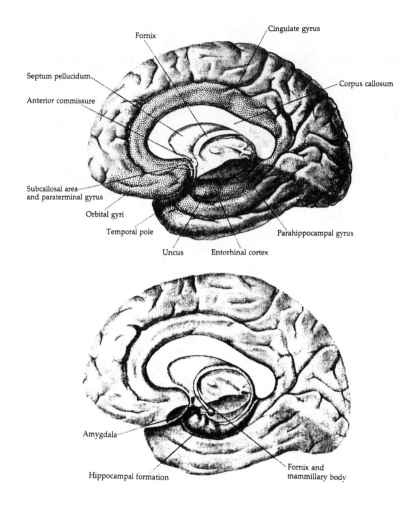

Figure 10.3. Location of the Amygdala and Surrounding Cortical Areas
SOURCE: Martin (1989).

measures of physiological arousal (e.g., galvanic skin response [GSR] heart rate) and social emotional responses (e.g., facial expressions of emotion) with neuroimaging techniques (e.g., functional MRI [fMRI] and event-related potential [ERP]) to track the emotional and neuro-

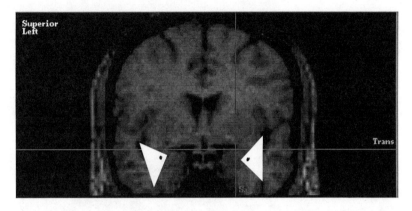

Figure 10.4. Magnetic Resonance Imaging Scan Showing Location of the Amygdala in the Human Brain
SOURCE: Research Imaging Center (1997, BrainMap database). Used with permission.

logical processes involved in viewing televised violence. The question being explored in the San Antonio study is whether 8- to 12-year-old children will display similar asymmetries in ERP recordings while watching televised violence or humor and whether fMRI activation patterns will be differentiated in ways that are consistent with facial expression and physiological measures of emotional arousal.

Whether brain mapping (Toga & Mazziotta, 1996) and other neuropsychological approaches prove to be fruitful remains to be seen, but it is one avenue for building bridges between social learning theory concepts and the manifestation of aggressive behavior. Furthermore, such research might serve as a paradigm for more focused studies of individual differences in violence and aggression.

Prevalence

A second direction for future research is a continuation of studies of the prevalence of violence in television programming. There is a long history of content analysis of television programming dating from the late 1960s (e.g., Gerbner, 1970) through the 1990s (e.g., Gerbner et al., 1994; Mediascope, 1996), and the results have been fairly consistent in demonstrating high levels of violence in televised entertainment and reality programs. However, it would be important to know more about the "social forces" that determine "outbreaks" of violence in entertainment media. What are the cultural and economic issues that support or encourage high levels of violence? We have seen, in Figure 10.1, that there have been "valleys of violence" at several points in the 22 years of monitoring television violence that appear to be related to public outcry about high levels of media violence. However, what can we learn about the economic and social conditions that may be associated with the peaks or "mountains of violence" at various periods such as the early 1980s?

The continuation of prevalence studies will provide a tracking mechanism for monitoring changes in the media environment, and it can inform broadcasters, public policymakers, and researchers about the effectiveness of various interventions such as ratings systems and electronic screening devices. However, the most important reason for the continuation of prevalence studies is to assess the fairness of the representation of our culture in society's most pervasive communicator of culture (Berry, 1980, 1988, 1993). Thus, it is important to ask questions about not only the *quantity* of television violence but also the *quality* of violence—the ways in which both victims and perpetrators are portrayed in violent programming. As G. Gerbner (personal communication, January 12, 1997) noted,

> The important question to ask is "Who is doing what to whom?" because violence is essentially a demonstration of power. It shows who can get away with what against whom; who are the most likely winners and losers, perpetrators, and victims. Violence-laden television tends to create an unfair "pecking order" with women, children, older people, and minorities at the bottom.

In this regard, Gerbner proposed the recasting of his long-established Violence Index (cf. Gerbner et al., 1994) into a Fairness Index that would assess the extent to which media portrayals provide a "fair demographic representation" of various social groups in proportion to their representation in the actual population (G. Gerbner, personal communication, January 12, 1997). As one example, he is conducting an analysis, for the Screen Actors Guild, of the fairness of representation in 1995-1996 prime-time television drama and of representation in the 1994-1995 commercially most successful films. These forms of prevalence studies provide insights into the culture of television violence and the ways in which one might fashion intervention programs to prevent harmful effects.

Prevention

The final area for much-needed research is the task of developing and assessing intervention strategies that will prevent or mitigate the influences of media violence. This prevention issue is a topic of intense recent interest (e.g., American Psychological Association, 1993; Eron, Gentry, & Schlegel, 1994; National Research Council, 1993; Prothrow-Stith, 1991) but remains the most difficult area for research and development.

There are several organizations that have developed discussion and instruction materials for use in schools and community organizations (e.g., Center for Media Literacy, 1995; Huesmann et al., 1996; Kunkel & Murray, 1991; Levin & Gerzon, 1996; Mediascope, 1993; Mind Science Foundation, 1997; Murray & Lonnborg, 1995), but there needs to be a more integrated approach to program development and a systematic evaluation of the effectiveness of these interventions. All of these programs are designed to raise awareness, in children or adults, of the ways in which television violence influences viewers, and all attempt to teach "critical viewing" skills. At present, the most elaborate of the critical viewing skills material is the video and discussion kit *Beyond Blame: Challenging Violence in the Media—A Multimedia Literacy Program for Community Empowerment,* developed by the Center for Media Literacy (1995). With regard to intervention in schools, the violence prevention program that has received the most extensive evaluation is the work of Eron and Huesmann and their colleagues (Eron, 1982; Huesmann et al., 1996). This program, known as the Metropolitan Area Child Study, is a school- and family-based intervention designed to prevent and understand the development of aggressive behavior. The ongoing evaluation involves 16 Chicago-area schools involved in one of three levels of intervention (classroom management, peer relationships, or family/parenting skills) or as control schools. The evaluation of this intervention with high-risk youngsters is still in process, but this is an ideal program for testing effective prevention strategies. Nevertheless, it remains for a new generation of researchers and clinicians to establish and evaluate new paradigms for effective intervention and prevention.

Continuing Needs

The future holds the promise of a greater collaboration between the television industry, government, and professional and community organizations devoted to the task of reducing violence in media and society.

History in the late 1970s provides examples of effective voluntary industry responses to concern about television violence through the development of alternative educational and entertaining programming such as *Fat Albert and the Cosby Kids* (e.g., Columbia Broadcasting System [CBS], 1977) and *Schoolhouse Rock* (ABC) as well as the extensive programming of public television (Children's Television Workshop, 1990; Palmer, 1988).

Finally, the collaborative efforts of Congress and the FCC (Hundt, 1994, 1996) in the passage of the Children's Television Act of 1990 and regulations concerning the establishment of electronic screening devices (e.g., the V-chip) ensure continuing emphasis on the need to address the levels of violence in television programming. So, too, the institution of ratings systems (e.g., Federman, 1996; OKTV Foundation, 1995; Wilson, Linz, & Randall, 1990) and the development of guidelines for the portrayal of violence (Livingstone, 1994) suggest that both parents and the television industry will have clearer views of the nature of television violence. As we move into the next century, process, prevalence, and prevention will serve as the central organizing themes for studies of television violence.

■ References

American Psychological Association. (1993). *Violence and youth: Psychology's response*, Vol. 1: *Summary report of the American Psychological Association Commission on Violence and Youth*. Washington, DC: Author.

Atkin, C. K., Greenberg, B. S., Korzenny, F., & McDermott, S. (1979). Selective exposure to televised violence. *Journal of Broadcasting, 23*(1), 5-13.

Atkin, C. K., Murray, J. P., & Nayman, O. B. (1971). *Television and social behavior: An annotated bibliography of research focusing on television's impact on children.* Washington, DC: U.S. Public Health Service.

Baker, R. K., & Ball, S. J. (1969). *Mass media and violence: A staff report to the National Commission on the Causes and Prevention of Violence.* Washington, DC: Government Printing Office.

Bandura, A. (1962). Social learning through imitation. In M. R. Jones (Ed.), *Nebraska symposium on motivation* (pp. 211-274). Lincoln: University of Nebraska Press.

Bandura, A. (1963, October 22). What TV violence can do to your child. *Look,* pp. 46-52.

Bandura, A. (1965). Vicarious processes: A case of no-trial learning. In L. Berkowitz (Ed.), *Advances in experimental social psychology* (Vol. 2, pp. 1-55). New York: Academic Press.

Bandura, A. (1969). Social-learning theory of identificatory processes. In D. A. Goslin (Ed.), *Handbook of socialization theory and research* (pp. 213-262). Chicago: Rand McNally.

Bandura, A. (1994). Social cognitive theory of mass communication. In J. Bryant & D. Zillmann (Eds.), *Media effects: Advances in theory and research* (pp. 61-90). Hillsdale, NJ: Lawrence Erlbaum.

Bandura, A., Ross, D., & Ross, S. H. (1961). Transmission of aggression through imitation of aggressive models. *Journal of Abnormal and Social Psychology, 63,* 575-582.

Bandura, A., Ross, D., & Ross, S. H. (1963). Imitation of film-mediated aggressive models. *Journal of Abnormal and Social Psychology, 66,* 3-11.

Belson, W. (1978). *Television violence and the adolescent boy.* Farnborough, UK: Saxon House, Teakfield Limited.

Berkowitz, L. (1962). *Aggression: A social psychological analysis.* New York: McGraw-Hill.

Berkowitz, L. (1965). Some aspects of observed aggression. *Journal of Personality and Social Psychology, 2,* 359-365.

Berkowitz, L. (1984). Some effects of thoughts on anti- and prosocial influences of media events: A cognitive-neoassociation analysis. *Psychological Bulletin, 95,* 410-427.

Berkowitz, L., & Geen, R. G. (1966). Film violence and the cue properties of available targets. *Journal of Personality and Social Psychology, 3,* 525-530.

Berkowitz, L., & Rawlings, E. (1963). Effects of film violence on inhibitions against subsequent aggression. *Journal of Abnormal and Social Psychology, 66,* 405-412.

Berry, G. L. (1980). Children, television, and social class roles: The medium as an unplanned educational curriculum. In E. L. Palmer & A. Dorr (Eds.), *Children and the faces of television: Teaching, violence, selling* (pp. 71-81). New York: Academic Press.

Berry, G. L. (1988). Multicultural role portrayals on television as a social psychological issue. In S. Oskamp (Ed.), *Applied Social Psychology Annual,* Vol. 8: *Television as a social issue* (pp. 118-129). Newbury Park, CA: Sage.

Berry, G. L. (1993). Introduction: Television as a worldwide cultural tapestry. In G. L. Berry & J. K. Asamen (Eds.), *Children and television: Images in a changing sociocultural world* (pp. 1-4). Newbury Park, CA: Sage.

Bybee, C., Robinson, J. D., & Turow, J. (1982, Summer). Determinants of parental guidance in children's viewing for a special subgroup, mass media scholars. *Journal of Broadcasting, 26,* 302-307.

Cater, D., & Strickland, S. (1975). *TV violence and the child: The evolution and fate of the surgeon general's report.* New York: Russell Sage.

Center for Media Literacy. (1995). *Beyond blame: Challenging violence in the media—A multi-media literacy program for community empowerment.* Los Angeles: Author. (4727 Wilshire Boulevard, Suite 403, Los Angeles, CA 90010)

Charters, W. W. (1933). *Motion pictures and youth: A summary.* New York: Macmillan.

Children's Television Workshop. (1990). *Sesame Street research: A 20th anniversary symposium.* New York: Author.

Cline, V. B., Croft, R. G., & Courrier, S. (1973). Desensitization of children to television violence. *Journal of Personality and Social Psychology, 27,* 360-365.

Columbia Broadcasting System. (1977). *Learning while they laugh.* New York: CBS Office of Social Research.

Comstock, G., & Fisher, M. (1975). *Television and human behavior: A guide to the pertinent scientific literature.* Santa Monica, CA: RAND.

Comstock, G., & Paik, H. (1991). *Television and the American child.* San Diego: Academic Press.

Cook, T. D., Kendzierski, D. A., & Thomas, S. A. (1983). The implicit assumptions of television research: An analysis of the 1982 NIMH report on "Television and Behavior." *Public Opinion Quarterly, 47,* 161-201.

Cressey, P. G., & Thrasher, F. M. (1933). *Boys, movies, and city streets.* New York: Macmillan.

Davidson, R. J., Ekman, P., Saron, C., Senulis, J., & Friesen, W. V. (1990). Emotional expression and brain physiology I: Approach/withdrawal and cerebral asymmetry. *Journal of Personality and Social Psychology, 58,* 330-341.

Davidson, R. J., & Tomarken, A. J. (1989). Laterality and emotion: An electrophysiological approach. In F. Boller & J. Grafman (Eds.), *Handbook of neuropsychology* (pp. 419-441). Amsterdam: Elsevier.

Dominick, J. R., & Greenberg, B. S. (1972). Attitudes toward violence: The interaction of television exposure, family attitudes, and social class. In G. A. Comstock & E. A. Rubinstein (Eds.), *Television and social behavior,* Vol. 3: *Television and adolescent aggressiveness* (pp. 314-335). Washington, DC: Government Printing Office.

Drabman, R. S., & Thomas, M. H. (1974). Does media violence increase children's toleration of real-life aggression? *Developmental Psychology, 10,* 418-421.

Ekman, P., & Davidson, R. J. (1993). Voluntary smiling changes regional brain activity. *Psychological Science, 4,* 342-345.

Ekman, P., Davidson, R. J., & Friesen, W. V. (1990). The Duchenne smile: Emotional expression and brain physiology II. *Journal of Personality and Social Psychology, 58,* 342-353.

Ekman, P., Liebert, R. M., Friesen, W., Harrison, R., Zlatchin, C., Malmstrom, E. V., & Baron, R. A. (1972). Facial expressions of emotion as predictors of subsequent aggression. In G. A. Comstock, E. A. Rubinstein, & J. P. Murray (Eds.), *Television and social behavior,* Vol. 5: *Television's effects: Further explorations* (pp. 22-58). Washington, DC: Government Printing Office.

Ellis, G. T., & Sekyra, F. (1972). The effect of aggressive cartoons on behavior of first grade children. *Journal of Psychology, 81,* 37-43.

Eron, L. (1963). Relationship of TV viewing habits and aggressive behavior in children. *Journal of Abnormal and Social Psychology, 67,* 193-196.

Eron, L. (1982). Parent child interaction, television violence and aggression of children. *American Psychologist, 27,* 197-211.

Eron, L. D., Gentry, J. H., & Schlegel, P. (Eds.). (1994). *Reason to hope: A psychosocial perspective on violence and youth.* Washington, DC: American Psychological Association.

Eron, L. D., Walder, L. O., & Lefkowitz, M. M. (1971). *Learning of aggression in children.* Boston: Little, Brown.

Federman, J. (1996). *Media ratings: Design, use, and consequences.* Studio City, CA: Mediascope.

Feshbach, S., & Singer, R. D. (1971). *Television and aggression: An experimental field study.* San Francisco: Jossey-Bass.

Friedrich, L. K., & Stein, A. H. (1973). Aggressive and prosocial television programs and the natural behavior of preschool children. *Monographs of the Society for Research in Child Development, 38*(4, Serial No. 151).

Gadow, K. D., & Sprafkin, J. (1993). Television violence and children with emotional and behavioral disorders. *Journal of Emotional and Behavioral Disorders, 1*(1), 54-63.

Gerbner, G. (1970). Cultural indicators: The case of violence in television drama. *Annals of the American Academy of Political and Social Science, 388,* 69-81.

Gerbner, G. (1972). Violence in television drama: Trends and symbolic functions. In G. A. Comstock & E. A. Rubinstein (Eds.), *Television and social behavior,* Vol. 1: *Media content and control* (pp. 28-187). Washington, DC: Government Printing Office.

Gerbner, G., & Gross, L. (1976). Living with television: The violence profile. *Journal of Communication, 26,* 173-199.

Gerbner, G., Gross, L., Morgan, M., & Signorielli, N. (1994). Growing up with television: The cultivation perspective. In J. Bryant & D. Zillmann (Eds.), *Media effects: Advances in theory and research* (pp. 17-41). Hillsdale, NJ: Lawrence Erlbaum.

Grimes, T., Vernberg, E., & Cathers, T. (1997). Emotionally disturbed children's reactions to violent media segments. *Journal of Health Communication, 2,* 157-168.

Group for the Advancement of Psychiatry. (1982). *The child and television drama: The psychosocial impact of cumulative viewing.* New York: Mental Health Materials Center.

Hapkiewitz, W. G., & Roden, A. H. (1971). The effect of aggressive cartoons on children's interpersonal play. *Child Development, 42,* 1583-1585.

Hearold, S. (1986). A synthesis of 1043 effects of television on social behavior. In G. Comstock (Ed.), *Public communication and behavior* (Vol. 1, pp. 65-133). New York: Academic Press.

Himmelweit, H. T., Oppenheim, A. N., & Vince, P. (1958). *Television and the child: An empirical study of the effects of television on the young.* London: Oxford University Press.

Huesmann, L. R., & Eron, L. D. (Eds.). (1986). *Television and the aggressive child: A cross-national comparison.* Hillsdale, NJ: Lawrence Erlbaum.

Huesmann, L. R., Eron, L. D., Lefkowitz, M. M., & Walder, L. O. (1984). Stability of aggression over time and generations. *Developmental Psychology, 20,* 1120-1134.

Huesmann, L. R., Maxwell, C. D., Eron, L., Dahlberg, L. L., Guerra, N. G., Tolan, P. H., Van Acker, R., & Henry, D. (1996). Evaluating a cognitive/ecological program for the prevention of aggression among urban children. *Journal of Preventive Medicine, 12*(5), 120-128.

Hundt, R. (1994, August). *A role for psychologists in the communications revolution.* Address presented at the annual meeting of the American Psychological Association, Los Angeles. (Available on Internet: www.fcc.gov/speeches/hundt/spreh425.txt)

Hundt, R. (1996, October). *Making tomorrow a better day for our children.* Address presented at the annual meeting of the American Academy of Pediatrics, Boston. (Available on Internet: www.fcc.gov/speeches/hundt/spreh648.txt)

Huston, A. C., Donnerstein, E., Fairchild, H., Feshbach, N. D., Katz, P. A., Murray, J. P., Rubinstein, E. A., Wilcox, B., & Zuckerman, D. (1992). *Big world, small screen: The role of television in American society.* Lincoln: University of Nebraska Press.

Joy, L. A., Kimball, M., & Zabrack, M. L. (1986). Television exposure and children's aggressive behavior. In T. M. Williams (Ed.), *The impact of television: A natural experiment involving three towns* (pp. 303-360). New York: Academic Press.

Kenny, D. A. (1984). The NBC study and television violence. *Journal of Communication, 34*(1), 176-182.

Kunkel, D., & Murray, J. P. (1991). Television, children, and social policy: Issues and resources for child advocates. *Journal of Clinical Child Psychology, 20*(1), 88-93.

Lazarsfeld, P. F. (1955). Why is so little known about the effects of television and what can be done? *Public Opinion Quarterly, 19,* 243-251.

LeDoux, J. (1996). *The emotional brain: The mysterious underpinnings of emotional life.* New York: Simon & Schuster.

LeDoux, J. E., & Hirst, W. (Eds.). (1986). *Mind and brain: Dialogues in cognitive neuroscience.* New York: Cambridge University Press.

Lefkowitz, M., Eron, L., Walder, L., & Huesmann, L. R. (1972). Television violence and child aggression: A follow-up study. In G. A. Comstock & E. A. Rubinstein (Eds.), *Television and social behavior,* Vol. 3: *Television and adolescent aggressiveness* (pp. 35-135). Washington, DC: Government Printing Office.

Levin, D., & Gerzon, C. (1996). *Help children see through violence in the media.* Boston: Wheelock College.

Lichter, R. S., & Amundson, D. (1992). *A day of television violence.* Washington, DC: Center for Media and Public Affairs.

Lichter, R. S., & Amundson, D. (1994). *A day of TV violence: 1992 vs. 1994.* Washington, DC: Center for Media and Public Affairs.

Liebert, R. M., & Baron, R. A. (1972). Short term effects of television aggression on children's aggressive behavior. In J. P. Murray, E. A. Rubinstein, & G. A. Comstock (Eds.), *Television and social behavior,* Vol. 2: *Television and social learning* (pp. 181-201). Washington, DC: Government Printing Office.

Liebert, R. M., Sobol, M. D., & Davidson, E. S. (1972). Catharsis of aggression among institutionalized boys: Fact or artifact? In G. A. Comstock, E. A. Rubinstein, & J. P. Murray (Eds.), *Television and social behavior,* Vol. 5: *Television's effects—Further explorations* (pp. 351-358). Washington, DC: Government Printing Office.

Livingstone, J. B. (1994). *The violence framework: Guidelines for understanding, reporting, and portraying violence.* Washington, DC: Institute for Mental Health Initiatives.

Louis Harris and Associates. (1969). The American public looks at violence: 1968. In R. K. Baker & S. J. Ball (Eds.), *Mass media and violence: A staff report to the National Commission on the Causes and Prevention of Violence* (pp. 503-517). Washington, DC: Government Printing Office.

Lovaas, O. I. (1961). Effect of exposure to symbolic aggression on aggressive behavior. *Child Development, 32,* 37-44.

MacBeth, T. M. (1996). *Tuning in to young viewers: Social science perspectives on television.* Thousand Oaks, CA: Sage.

Maccoby, E. E. (1954). Why do children watch television? *Public Opinion Quarterly, 18,* 239-244.

Martin, J. H. (1989). *Neuroanatomy: Text and atlas.* New York: Elsevier.

McLeod, J. M., Atkin, C. K., & Chaffee, S. H. (1972a). Adolescents, parents, and television use: Adolescent self-report measures from Maryland and Wisconsin samples. In G. A. Comstock & E. A. Rubinstein (Eds.), *Television and social behavior,* Vol. 3: *Television and adolescent aggressiveness* (pp. 173-238). Washington, DC: Government Printing Office.

McLeod, J. M., Atkin, C. K., & Chaffee, S. H. (1972b). Adolescents, parents, and television use: Self-report and other measures from the Wisconsin sample. In G. A. Comstock & E. A. Rubinstein (Eds.), *Television and social behavior,* Vol. 3: *Television and adolescent aggressiveness* (pp. 238-313). Washington, DC: Government Printing Office.

Mediascope. (1993). *The kids are watching: A 13-minute video for teachers, parents, and community organizations.* Studio City, CA: Author. (12711 Ventura Boulevard, Studio City, CA 91604)

Mediascope. (1996). *National television violence study: Executive summary, 1994-95.* Thousand Oaks, CA: Sage.

Milavsky, J. R., Kessler, R. C., Stipp, H. H., & Rubens, W. S. (1982). *Television and aggression: A panel study.* New York: Academic Press.

Mind Science Foundation. (1997). *Minding media: Helping children use TV wisely.* San Antonio, TX: Author.

Murray, J. P. (1973). Television and violence: Implications of the surgeon general's research program. *American Psychologist, 28,* 472-478.

Murray, J. P. (1980). *Television and youth: 25 years of research and controversy.* Boys Town, NE: Boys Town Center for the Study of Youth Development.

Murray, J. P. (1984, Fall). Results of an informal poll of knowledgeable persons concerning the impact of television violence. *Newsletter of the American Psychological Association, Division of Child, Youth, and Family Services,* pp. 2-3.

Murray, J. P. (1994). The impact of televised violence. *Hofstra Law Review, 22,* 809-825.

Murray, J. P. (1997). *Neuroimaging and TV violence viewing: A research proposal.* San Antonio: University of Texas Health Science Center at San Antonio, Research Imaging Center.

Murray, J. P., & Kippax, S. (1977). Television diffusion and social behavior in three communities: A field experiment. *Australian Journal of Psychology, 29*(1), 31-43.

Murray, J. P., & Kippax, S. (1978). Children's social behavior in three towns with differing television experience. *Journal of Communication, 28,* 19-29.

Murray, J. P., & Kippax, S. (1979). From the early window to the late night show: International trends in the study of television's impact on children and adults. In L. Berkowitz (Ed.), *Advances in experimental social psychology* (Vol. 12, pp. 253-320). New York: Academic Press.

Murray, J. P., & Lonnborg, B. (1995). *Children and television: Using TV sensibly.* Manhattan: Kansas State University, Cooperative Extension Service.

Mussen, P., & Rutherford, E. (1961). Effects of aggressive cartoons on children's aggressive play. *Journal of Abnormal and Social Psychology, 62,* 461-464.

National Institute of Mental Health. (1982). *Television and behavior: Ten years of scientific progress and implications for the eighties,* Vol. 1: *Summary report.* Washington, DC: Government Printing Office.

National Research Council. (1993). *Understanding and preventing violence.* Washington, DC: National Academy Press.

National Television Violence Study. (1997). (Vol. 2, March). Thousand Oaks, CA: Sage.

OKTV Foundation. (1995). *Comments of the OKTV Foundation: Submission to the Federal Communications Commission inquiry on policies and rules concerning children's television programming* (FCC 95-143, MM Docket No. 93-48). Cambridge, MA: Author.

Osborn, D. K., & Endsley, R. C. (1971). Emotional reactions of young children to TV violence. *Child Development, 42,* 321-331.

Paik, H., & Comstock, G. (1994). The effects of television violence on antisocial behavior: A meta-analysis. *Communication Research, 21,* 516-546.

Palmer, E. L. (1988). *Television and America's children: A crisis of neglect.* New York: Oxford University Press.

Parke, R. D., Berkowitz, L., Leyens, J. P., West, S., & Sebastian, R. J. (1977). Some effects of violent and nonviolent movies on the behavior of juvenile delinquents. In L. Berkowitz (Ed.), *Advances in experimental psychology* (Vol. 10, pp. 135-172). New York: Academic Press.

Pearl, D., Bouthilet, L., & Lazar, J. (Eds.). (1982). *Television and behavior: Ten years of scientific progress and implications for the eighties,* Vol. 2: *Technical reviews.* Washington, DC: Government Printing Office.

Phillips, D. P. (1982). The impact of fictional television stories on U.S. adult fatalities: New evidence on the effect of the mass media on violence. *American Journal of Sociology, 87,* 1340-1359.

Phillips, D. P. (1983). The impact of mass media violence on U.S. homicides. *American Sociological Review, 48,* 560-568.

Plato. (374 B.C./1943). *The Republic, Book II.* In B. Jowett (Trans.), *The works of Plato translated into English with analyses and introductions.* New York: Tudor.

Postman, N. (1985). *Amusing ourselves to death: Public discourse in the age of show business.* New York: Penguin.

Prothrow-Stith, D. (1991). *Deadly consequences.* New York: HarperCollins.

Research Imaging Center. (1997). *MRI of human brain showing position of the amygdala.* San Antonio: University of Texas Health Science Center at San Antonio, BrainMap database.

Robinson, J. P., & Bachman, J. G. (1972). Television viewing habits and aggression. In G. A. Comstock & E. A. Rubinstein (Eds.), *Television and social behavior,* Vol. 3: *Television and adolescent aggressiveness* (pp. 372-381). Washington, DC: Government Printing Office.

Ross, L. B. (1972). *The effect of aggressive cartoons on the group play of children.* Unpublished doctoral dissertation, Miami University.

Rubinstein, E. A. (1974). The TV violence report: What's next? *Journal of Communication, 24,* 80-88.

Schramm, W., Lyle, J., & Parker, E. B. (1961). *Television in the lives of our children.* Stanford, CA: Stanford University Press.

Stein, A. H., & Friedrich, L. K. (1972). Television content and young children's behavior. In J. P. Murray, E. A. Rubinstein, & G. A. Comstock (Eds.), *Television and social behavior,* Vol. 2: *Television and social learning* (pp. 202-317). Washington, DC: Government Printing Office.

Surgeon General's Scientific Advisory Committee on Television and Social Behavior. (1972). *Television and growing up: The impact of televised violence.* Washington, DC: Government Printing Office.

Thomas, M. H., Horton, R. W., Lippincott, E. C., & Drabman, R. S. (1977). Desensitization to portrayals of real life aggression as a function of television violence. *Journal of Personality and Social Psychology, 35,* 450-458.

Toga, A. W., & Mazziotta, J. C. (1996). *Brain mapping: The methods.* New York: Academic Press.

UCLA Center for Communication Policy. (1995). *The UCLA television violence monitoring report.* Los Angeles: Author.

U.S. Congress, House Committee on Interstate and Foreign Commerce. (1952). *Investigation of radio and television programs, hearings and reports, 82nd Congress, 2nd session, June 3-December 5, 1952.* Washington, DC: Government Printing Office.

U.S. Congress, Senate Committee of the Judiciary, Subcommittee to Investigate Juvenile Delinquency. (1955). *Juvenile delinquency (television programs), hearings, 83rd Congress, 2nd session, June 5-October 20, 1954.* Washington, DC: Government Printing Office.

Walker, K. B., & Morley, D. D. (1991). Attitudes and parental factors as intervening variables in the television violence-aggression relation. *Communication Research, 8*(2), 41-47.

Wartella, E., & Reeves, B. (1984). Trends in research on children's television. In J. P. Murray & G. Salomon (Eds.), *The future of children's television: Results of the Markle Foundation/Boys Town conference* (pp. 23-35). Boys Town, NE: Boys Town Center for the Study of Youth Development.

Wells, W. D. (1973). *Television and aggression: Replication of an experimental field study.* Unpublished manuscript, Graduate School of Business, University of Chicago.

Williams, T. M. (Ed.). (1986). *The impact of television: A natural experiment in three communities.* New York: Academic Press.

Wilson, B. J., Linz, D., & Randall, B. (1990). Applying social science research to film ratings: A shift from offensive to harmful effects. *Journal of Broadcasting and Electronic Media, 34,* 443-468.

Wurtzel, A., & Lometti, G. (1983). *A research perspective on television and violence.* New York: ABC Social Research Unit.

Zillmann, D. (1971). Excitation transfer in communication-mediated aggressive behavior. *Journal of Experimental Social Psychology, 7,* 419-434.

Zillmann, D. (1982). Television viewing and arousal. In D. Pearl, L. Bouthilet, & J. Lazar (Eds.), *Television and behavior: Ten years of scientific progress and implications for the eighties,* Vol. 2: *Technical reviews* (pp. 53-67). Washington, DC: Government Printing Office.

Zillmann, D., & Bryant, J. (1994). Entertainment as media effect. In J. Bryant & D. Zillmann (Eds.), *Media effects: Advances in theory and research* (pp. 437-461). Hillsdale, NJ: Lawrence Erlbaum.

Epilogue

Research Paradigms, Television, and Social Behavior: A Scientist's Contribution to Initiating Social Change

Joy Keiko Asamen

After a half century's worth of social science research, we have proposed some answers to how television influences our behavior and attitudes while at the same time raising new challenges for social scientists to pursue. Even when answers have been proposed, there still are the philosophical differences as to how best to study the influences of television on human behavior.

Social science tends to dichotomize research as falling into one of two major theoretical perspectives: positivist or phenomenological. The former has its roots in the natural and physical sciences and seeks specific causes or facts that explain human behavior. These deductive studies are quantitative and tend to occur within a more constrained context so as to enhance the certainty that the identified cause or fact is valid. The latter perspective is inductive and qualitative in nature with its emphasis on why people behave in the manner they do or on how one makes sense of his or her world; the social context in which the investigation is conducted obviously has high salience. Given the different objectives these two camps of studies set forth to achieve, it is not surprising that different methodologies are needed to seek the answers that are being sought.

Diversity of method affords us the opportunity to achieve new levels of understanding for what we have learned to accept as convention. I am convinced of the important contribution of each camp toward enhancing our understanding of how this ubiquitous medium affects our lives. By virtue of the underlying philosophies that drive the research paradigms, we would logically be achieving diverse outcomes that I believe complement rather than contradict one another. Only by approaching the concerns raised about the influence of television (and other electronic media) on social behavior as positivists and phenomenologists can we expect to achieve answers that will be empirically substantiated and meaningful to society.

Through studying the influence of television over the years, we have begun to come up with answers for some of our research questions. We appear to know who is influenced by television—children and adults from all parts of the world. We appear to know something about what influences viewers—for instance, the effect of "program-length commercials" or violence in children's programming. We also know what is influenced by television—for example, attitudes toward specific groups in society, such as persons of color or the physically challenged, or a child's capacity to engage in imaginative play.

On the other hand, we still are faced with a number of challenges regarding television's influence on the development of attitudes, values, and behaviors in its viewers. For instance, for each generalization that investigators identify, there are exceptions. Why are some viewers exceptions to the "rule"? Why can some children view a steady diet of violent television programming and not act out aggressively? Furthermore, what is the mechanism that explains how television influences the formation of attitudes and values as well as the display of behaviors in viewers? Given the complexity of these issues, it is evident that only through the collaborative effort of scientists from diverse perspectives, the positivists and the phenomenologists, can answers unfold that are both scientifically valid and contextually relevant.

■ Social Scientists as Agents of Change

Social scientists involved in television research have played an integral role in the formation of communication policy in our nation. For example, in the area of children's television programming, we have been able to establish how children's attitudes, values, and behaviors may be influenced by the programming they view, be it violent or, for example, inaccurate portrayals of various groups. Varied research paradigms have been used to establish this relationship, strengthening the validity of this finding. It is through the work of social scientists coming from diverse methodological viewpoints that policymakers eventually drafted the Children's Television Act, which was approved by the U.S. Congress in 1990. Similarly, it is the work of social scientists that has fueled the national concern regarding violent television programming and the introduction of the V-chip.

Given the global presence of television, the influence this medium has on the attitudes and values of persons from all stages and walks of life, and the potential for this medium to encourage both prosocial and antisocial behavior, social scientists have a responsibility to continue seeking answers as to the influence of this medium on its viewers. Once a social scientist engages in television research, whether he or she intends to or not, the scientist also becomes an agent of change. A scientist cannot study the influence of television and expect that what is found will be overlooked by the policymakers who have been put on alert by their constituencies. If, in fact, social policy develops out of what social scientists uncover, then a scientist must thoughtfully consider the full range of methodologies available in planning the investigation. As responsible scientists, we assess our strengths and limitations and practice our trade in a manner that does not compromise its scientific integrity. Some of us are inclined toward being more positivist, whereas others are phenomenological in our research practices. Given the different intent of these two camps of research, it is important to respect and actively encourage that studies continue to be conducted from both perspectives. As we enter into a new century, this appears to be the only route to uncovering the answers we seek in studying this complex medium.

Index

DATE D

NOV 18 1998

HIGHSMITH #45115